Rod Taylor

AN AUSSIE IN HOLLYWOOD

STEPHEN VAGG

Published in the USA by:
BearManor Media
P O Box 71426
Albany, Georgia 31708
www.bearmanormedia.com

978-1-59393-511-5

Printed in the United States of America.
Book design by Brian Pearce | Red Jacket Press

TABLE OF CONTENTS

EARLY LIFE (1930 – 1948)..11

AUSTRALIAN ACTOR (1949–1951)..................................19

AUSTRALIAN FILMS (1951 – 54).....................................29

AMERICA (1955 – 59)..45

BECOMING A STAR (1959 – 1961)..................................63

CONSOLIDATION OF STARDOM (1962 – 64).....................83

AT MGM (1963 – 65)...93

RIDING THE TIGER (1965 – 1966)..................................105

THE HOLLYWOOD PEAK (1966–68)...............................123

STAR DECLINE (1968–70)...135

STARDOM SUNSET (1971–73).......................................167

INTERNATIONAL FILMS AND TV (1974 – 76)..................181

TELEVISION (1976 – 1980)...191

THE '80S (1980 – 88)..205

NOSTALGIA STAR (1988 ONWARDS)............................219

CONCLUSION..237

CREDITS...253

ACKNOWLEDGMENTS...259

REFERENCES...263

INDEX...289

"*The most important thing in my life to me is my work. I couldn't live without it. And I don't do it just for money. I love it. It is an honourable art. I am proud to be an actor. I pray and try every day to be a better actor. I have no use for incompetents who come into my profession for what they call the glamour. Without employment he respects and a goal, a man is a rotting shell. I would miss meals, sleep in alleys, walk to the office of every manager in town every day in my bare feet if I had to maintain myself in my line of work.*"

ROD TAYLOR (1961)

"Russell Crowe touched with Baryshnikov"

FEW MOTION PICTURES WERE MORE ANTICIPATED BY THE Australian public of 1963 than *The VIPs*. The film seemed to have everything going for it: a lavish budget and glossy MGM production values; gorgeous color photography and costumes from Givenchy and Pierre Cardin; and an acting line-up that included Orson Welles, Louis Jourdan and Margaret Rutherford. Most of all, the lead roles were played by arguably the most famous couple in the world at the time, Richard Burton and Elizabeth Taylor, fresh from their adulterous affair on the set of *Cleopatra* (1963).

Australian exhibitors had an extra reason for confidence in *The VIPs*' local performance, however: the presence in the cast of the Australian actor Rod Taylor. And what's more, Rod Taylor was coming home to promote the film

Anticipation for the visit ran high — movie stars were a rare enough sight in Australia at the time; movie stars who had grown up in Sydney were extraordinary. But there he was, flying home to promote a genuine all-star blockbuster in which he played a major role: our Rod, the boy from the suburbs who had gone to Hollywood, taken on the Yanks at their own game on their own turf in one of the toughest industries there is — and won.

In recent years, stories of Australians who have "conquered" Hollywood have become increasingly frequent; so frequent, in fact, that they now seem almost commonplace. Australians can be found on studio A-lists for actors, directors, editors, designers, composers and screenwriters. In 2002 Baz Luhrmann pointed out that a film could be cast solely with Australians yet still feature the world's top stars. This was not the case, however, in 1963, when Rod Taylor was the biggest antipodean success story in Hollywood.

Until the arrival of Mel Gibson, Rod Taylor ranked behind only Errol Flynn and perhaps Peter Finch as the best-known Australian movie star in the world. Other Australian actors had enjoyed international popularity during and before that time, such as Cecil Kellaway, Judith Anderson, Ron Randell, Louise Lovely,

Snowy Baker, Shirley Ann Richards and Jocelyn Howarth — but they were character actors, support players, or B-picture leads. Rod Taylor was the real thing, a genuine above-the-title star of big-budget studio films and television series, born and raised in Australia.

When Rod landed at Sydney's Mascot Airport on September 4, 1963, the actor was at the height of his fame. Only a year before he had starred in *The Birds* (1963), which was currently in release around the country and already a big hit; his recent television series, *Hong Kong* (1960-61), had been hugely popular in Australia; an earlier film, *The Time Machine* (1960), was already on its way to classic status. Added to this was the number of high-profile support roles Rod had played recently, including *Giant* (1956), *Raintree County* (1957), *Separate Tables* (1958) and *Ask Any Girl* (1959). Now, Rod was featured alongside the most celebrated pair in the world in *The VIPs*; what's more, he would actually be playing an Australian on screen.

Rod strode into the terminal to be met by swarms of fans and press. His arrival was front-page news around the country: "Star Back as VIP," blared the *Sun-Herald*; "Rod's Pot of Gold: £600,000 Movie Offers," gasped the *Sun*. Journalists asked him about working with the Burtons, Alfred Hitchcock and Montgomery Clift; he spoke of contracts to make eleven movies at an astonishing US$75,000 a film; he joked about his off-screen romances with Frances Nuyen and Anita Ekberg. Photos were taken of Rod kissing his parents, waving to fans and hugging his wife, stunning former model Mary Hilem — whom he had married only months before, at a ceremony attended by Jane Fonda and John Wayne, no less.

Rod was delighted by the reception, but trod warily. He knew that Australia was the land of knocking the tall poppy and locals would like nothing more than to think the returning actor had grown a big head (which he had, but there was no need for anyone to know that just yet). So Rod cranked up his Aussie accent, asked repeatedly for a cold beer and encouraged Mary to play with a toy koala; he asked after old friends, made self-deprecating comments about his love life and image as a tough guy and apologized for the broad Australian accent he used in *The VIPs*. Australia was still the best country in the world, the Barrier Reef was beautiful and Sydney sophisticated; we should make more films here — in fact, he had some projects in mind.

Rod then visited his parents' home in Lidcombe, the unpretentious Sydney suburb he had grown up in. Crowds of media and onlookers followed: "Golly, cars arrived, people arrived," remembers Meryl Wheeler, his childhood neighbor. "We had a brick front fence and people not only sat on our fence, they stomped on our flowers."

But Rod embraced the reception, staying out the front, signing autographs and chatting to fans. The public lapped it up; it seemed that despite the fame, the money and the ex-model wife, Hollywood had not changed him. He was still the same simple boy he'd been when he left Sydney nine years ago. Australia would always be his home. He was still "our Rod."

The Sydney premiere of *The VIPs* was held at the State Theatre on September 5, a black-tie charity event on behalf of the Royal New South Wales Institute for Deaf and Blind Children. Two thousand fans lined the pavement; floodlights erected by the army and navy lit up the sky; a highland pipe band and troupe of uniformed drum majorettes performed a march down the street in front of the theatre as a prelude to Rod's arrival.

Rod was driven to the theatre in a limousine and walked inside through a guard of honor formed by the drum majorettes. The theatre was packed with 1,313 business and community leaders and assorted special guests, including Rod's parents, the Governor of New South Wales, and Cabinet Minister (and later high court judge), Sir Garfield Barwick. During the film's interval, Rod appeared on stage to thank the spectators for their support.

The next day, Rod and Mary flew to Melbourne for another charity premiere. He was greeted by similar crowds and another guard of honor, this time of hospital nurses. The public response was overwhelming: at a time when there were just over ten million people in Australia, an estimated quarter of a million of them saw *The VIPs* in its first six days of release.

"After a reception like that I feel it is my duty to return to Australia regularly," enthused Rod. "I hope to come back for a visit every two or three years."

This hope was never fulfilled: Rod did not return to Australia until five years later, then not for another seven after that. During that period, his career declined and he became increasingly forgotten on his native soil — something that has only accelerated with the passage of time.

Mention Rod Taylor's name to most Australians today and you generally draw a blank expression; even movie buffs need to be prompted by mentioning *The Time Machine* or *The Birds*. He is far less known as an Australian movie star than, say, Errol Flynn or Peter Finch (even, some might argue, George Lazenby). In the late 1990s, Rod had the second lead in an AU$10-million film, *Welcome to Woop Woop* (1998), but his face was left off posters in favor of the younger Jonathan Schaech and Susie Porter. Rod has gone from being one of the most famous Australians in the world to somewhat unknown in his own country.

How big a star was Rod Taylor? The best description is perhaps provided by writer Peter Yeldham, who dubbed him "A2 category." Rod never quite made the top rank of fame enjoyed by contemporaries such as Paul Newman or Rock Hudson (for example, he was never included in any of the lists compiled by film exhibitors of the top ten most popular stars). He was never a "prestige" star, either, in the way Peter Finch was and Cate Blanchett is today — that is, a performer who is not necessarily a major box-office draw but who is a critical favorite. Yet, he definitely was a star.

During Rod's peak years of fame — running roughly from *The Time Machine* in 1960 until *The Deadly Trackers* in 1973 — he co-starred twice with the top box-office attraction in the US (Doris Day); was entrusted with two studio "franchises" (*The Liquidator*, *Darker Than Amber*); produced his own films (*Chuka*) and ensured a picture was green-lit merely by his presence in the cast (*The Hell with Heroes*). He worked with directors such as Alfred Hitchcock, John Ford and Michelangelo Antonioni; producers like Walt Disney, Ray Stark and Joe E Levine; and screenwriters such as Gore Vidal, Terence Rattigan and Sam Shepard. His co-stars included Elizabeth Taylor, Richard Burton, Jane Fonda, Julie Christie, Maggie Smith, Montgomery Clift and John Wayne. His love life and bank balance were discussed in fan magazines, his opinions on art, politics and women sought by newspapers; he even presented an Oscar. He starred in two films which became undoubted classics (*The Time Machine*, *The Birds*) and provided the voice for a third (*One Hundred and One Dalmatians*), as well as appearing in a handful of others that have remained perennial favorites on television and video.

Rod's popularity declined in the late 1960s after a number of his movies under-performed at the box office. He developed a problem with alcohol, seemed to become more interested in maintaining his star image than in being an actor and suffered from the economic shakeups that affected the entire film industry. Nonetheless, he remained a star until the late 1980s, playing the lead in numerous TV series, telemovies and European features. By the standards of most actors, he has enjoyed an accomplished and triumphant career.

Rod never had the individuality of the truly great superstars like Errol Flynn or Humphrey Bogart. However, he compensated by being more versatile — a genuinely talented actor, he was comfortable in a variety of genres (especially actioners, dramas and comedies) and could play all sorts of roles.

Rod's best-known character might best be described as a "sexy, intellectual, heterosexual, man's man" — that is, someone able to hold his place in a white-collar environment, but who is also capable of physical activities (particularly fighting), is appealing to women and gets along with other men. For instance, in *The Time Machine*, he plays a scientist who beats up creatures of the future, romances Yvette Mimieux and has a strong friendship with Alan Young; in *Young Cassidy*, a playwright who digs ditches, brawls with the British, romances Maggie Smith and boozes around Dublin with his mates.

This persona reflected aspects of the real-life Rod Taylor, who liked a drink and a fight, but also trained at art school and would sketch and paint for relaxation; who was married three times and had an active love life, but also enjoyed carousing into the small hours with stuntmen. Rod painted, sculpted, drank, womanized, fought and acted — an unusual combination for an Australian man, even today. An early girlfriend, Beryl Eager, perhaps summed Rod up best when she described him as a "Russell Crowe touched with Baryshnikov."

Rod Taylor also had special importance for his homeland. As the leading Hollywood-based Australian star for over twenty years, he was a significant ambassador for his native country, helping fix its image in the eyes of the world. Although Rod rarely played Australian characters (for reasons I will explore), he was always known as an Australian actor. In addition, regardless of the nationalities he played, the essence of his characters — rough, tough men who worked with their hands, attractive to women but more comfortable among men — was often in line with the "typical" Australian of myth. This image of Australia, while it certainly had its flaws, was in the main a positive, attractive one — after all, Rod was a handsome, charismatic actor who usually played heroes in films aimed at large audiences.

Rod also helped develop the sort of rugged acting style and screen persona that later Australian-based talent, such as Mel Gibson and Russell Crowe, would demonstrate. Errol Flynn had already starred in many action movies, it is true, but he generally played the classic romantic hero. Rod Taylor's image was tougher and more no-nonsense; more contemporary and recognizably Australian. It is easy to see the lineage from Rod to later Aussie stars such as Mel Gibson, Russell Crowe, Heath Ledger, and so on. While he often described himself as a "phoney American," he was a very Australian one. That is what has prompted me to write this book.

FOR THE READER'S INFORMATION, I SHOULD POINT OUT THAT Rod Taylor has not participated with this project, aside from providing me with some phone numbers back in 2000. This has meant I have made speculations at certain points throughout the book as to his motives (mostly his career decisions and creative impulses); I have tried to put all these in some sort of context so that a reader may draw alternative conclusions if they wish. Despite this, however, after working on this book for a number of years, my admiration for Rod has not diminished; I believe as much now as I did when I started that his career is worth serious study and appreciation.

CHAPTER 1

"Whenever the opportunity arose he'd put on a pose."

EARLY LIFE (1930–1948)

RODNEY STURT TAYLOR WAS BORN IN SYDNEY, AUSTRALIA, ON January 11, 1930. The "Sturt" was in honor of Rod's great-great-grandfather, the British army officer and explorer Sir Charles Sturt (1795–1869). Sturt was one of history's less colorful explorers, mainly because his missions tended to be well-executed and successful: he made three major expeditions to the Australian interior during the nineteenth century; the second (in 1829–30) was particularly important as it traced two of the country's most important rivers, the Murray and Murrumbidgee, to their sources and prompted Britain to establish the colony of South Australia.

Charles Sturt lived in South Australia for a while and many of his family settled there, including his sister, Eliza. It became a family tradition to use "Sturt" as a middle name: Eliza's daughter was named Sarah Sturt Milton, and Sarah's grandson was Bill Sturt Taylor — Rod's father.

Bill was born in 1903, in the small town of Two Wells, just outside South Australia's capital city of Adelaide. Both his parents died when he was a young man and he moved to Sydney, where he settled in the inner-city suburb of Darlinghurst; the 1928 electoral roll lists his occupation as "commercial artist."

On July 28, 1928, Bill married Mona Thompson, at St. John's Church, Darlinghurst. Mona was a 26 year-old English migrant, the daughter of a works manager from Hull; she listed her occupation on their wedding certificate as "business proprietress."

"My parents' relationship was one of those mad Dickensian things," Rod claimed later. Bill was a knockabout man fond of a drink; Rod described him as a "tough son of a bitch." Not for nothing was his nickname "Squizzy," after "Squizzy" Taylor, a notorious Melbourne gangster. In contrast, the English-born Mona was a refined, beautifully spoken lady who gave the impression of being highly educated. Bill's natural habitats were the pub and the construction site; Mona's the garden and living room.

"If you were to pick a pair you never would have picked Squizzy to marry Mrs. Taylor," says Max Walker, a childhood friend of Rod's. "Squizzy was a rough-and-ready bloke, he liked a beer. Mrs. Taylor was very academic."

Les Wilson, another childhood friend, remembers the couple as "very odd… He was a real knockabout; he'd be at the pub. Mrs. Taylor was aloof about it. I don't think they got on a hundred percent together."

Yet, both had an artistic streak: Bill had a talent for drawing and worked as a commercial artist and Mona became a writer who was fond of the Ouija board. Despite their differences, the two would stay married for over fifty years, until Bill's death in 1983.

The year Rod was born, Bill and Mona were living in the seaside suburb of Bondi, but they soon moved out to the suburbs: the 1931 electoral roll lists them residing at 40 Mary St., Lidcombe, about fifteen kilometres west from the center of Sydney. The Taylors stayed there until 1934, after which they moved to a nearby house at 18 Swete St. Bill and Mona would remain at that address for the rest of Bill's life and it is where Rod lived until he moved out of home in his late teens.

Lidcombe is probably best known to non-residents for being the site of the junction for railway lines which stretch from the city out to Liverpool and Par-ramatta. A program of celebrations for Lidcombe's Gala Week of 1933 described the neighborhood as "the great gateway through which the steam horse moves south and west," where "freights, richly laden with the fruits of the earth and the great secondary industries from the golden west and south pass daily through her portals."

When the Taylors moved there, Lidcombe was largely a self-contained and working-class area, where most of the local men were employed in factories, abat-toirs and on the railways. The suburb was not urbanized, though; in fact, it was better described as "rural suburbia," full of paddocks and gullies, and many houses had enough room to maintain vegetable gardens and farm animals in their back-yards — something which helped shield residents from the full impact of the Great Depression. The Taylors' house at Swete Street was large enough for them to keep chickens, a vegetable garden and a sheep that doubled as a lawn mower; Rod, who was an only child, also had a succession of pet dogs for company.

Bill found it difficult to obtain work as a commercial artist, so he turned his hand to a variety of odd jobs around the neighborhood, including sign writing and drafting. As the economic climate improved, he worked on construction sites, mainly as a rigger (assembling and installing rigging gear such as cables, ropes and pulleys) and dogman (directing the movement of loads handled by cranes). It was a tough, dangerous job — dogmen often had to go up in the air with their loads several times a day — but Bill was skilled at it and prospered, eventually working his way up to running his own crew.

To help bring in extra money, Mona turned to writing. She says her first story was inspired after watching toddler Rod walk toward a kiosk in Parramatta Park, having his "first adventure in the world... I decided then to be Rod's eyes and write of this adventure." By the early 1960s, Mona estimated she had written over 100 short stories for a number of publications, including *The Australian Women's Weekly*, as well as having several novels and poems published.

Next door to the Taylors lived the Wheeler family, whose daughter Meryl became Rod's first girlfriend at the ripe old age of ten. Meryl remembers the Taylors as a polite family who kept to themselves. "Mona used to make her own clothes. Most of her clothes were green and grey. She used to make Rod's... He always looked nice, he was always clean, he was always tidy. Always wore shoes and socks. Back in those days, the boys used to be barefoot, some of them because they couldn't afford shoes, some of them by choice. She was strict in that sense, I should say, because he always looked nice. She always looked nice. I don't think I ever saw her dishevelled. Her hair was always in place. Bill was a bit of a knockabout... I don't remember them having visitors. She was never one to — I suppose these days we'd call them bad mixers. She always came across as a little bit aloof."

Although the Taylors were not a particularly religious family (their nominal creed was Church of England and Bill was a freemason for a time), Mona was interested in the spiritual world and enjoyed the odd séance.

Meryl Wheeler: "She used to tell the kids that she used to talk to the fairies. She had this nice little area in their backyard where she had this large Verona chair and she used to spend a lot of time out there. I think she used to meditate a lot."

While Mona generally kept to herself, Bill was more social, spending a considerable amount of his free time at the pub. This was the era of the "six o'clock swill" in Australia, when men would go to bars after work and drink as much as they could before the taps were turned off at six p.m.; Meryl Wheeler estimates Bill would come home "tipsy" around "nine times out of ten."

A taste for alcohol was something Rod inherited from this father; Mona rarely drank — banned alcohol from the house, in fact, partly because Bill's drinking caused conflict between them. "I do know at one stage there'd been times when there'd been a bit of an uproar in the house," recalls Meryl, "and Mona would go out for a walk."

Bill's job sometimes took him away from home and he worked for a period in the steelworks at Port Kembla, a port south of Sydney. Anthony Emerson, another childhood acquaintance of Rod's, remembers Bill as "a shadowy figure" around this period "because he was travelling a lot... a boozing feller."

Bill's absences served to push Mona and her only child closer together. "She doted on him quite a bit," recalls Max Walker. "I think she had quite an influence on him, actually."

"She was the force behind him to get the way he did," says Les Wilson.

"His mother made him very self-reliant," claims Anthony Emerson. "He went off and did things on his own, not as part of a team."

"We were tolerant with him, we tried to guide him, we never stood in his way," wrote Mona of her son. "I suppose we gave him complete freedom."

From the mid-1930s until 1941, Rod attended Lidcombe Primary School, where he thrived academically and creatively; according to *This Is Your Life*, he was dux of the school on two occasions. "He was a pretty clever feller, one of the brightest in the class," confirms Anthony Emerson.

Around this time, Rod started spending his evenings at a gymnasium run by a local engineer, Dick Wilson. Rod and his friends would work out on the equipment, wrestle and generally develop their fitness. Wilson's son, Les, recalls the young Rod as being a gifted athlete and show-off, "the most natural actor you ever knew."

"He had a swagger," says Bob Duff, who also went to the gym. "You know how he kind of swaggers? That's what he was like as a boy."

"He was very sure of himself," verifies Wilson. "He would go on and do things. You'd pick that from the first moment you met the bloke."

"He was always an actor," remembers Max Walker. "Even when we played cowboys and Indians, he was the most dramatic at dying and stuff."

However, at this stage, Rod never indicated he wanted to act; his passion was drawing and art. Cliff Allen, another friend from the gym, recollects: "I thought he was going to be a commercial artist. He never mentioned acting to us. Painting and black-and-white pencil work was his main interest at that stage. He might have even done sketches that went with the stories his mother did."

Rod left Lidcombe Primary in 1941. Male students in the area tended to go on to local secondary schools, but Rod's excellent academic results enabled him to attend Parramatta High School, then a selective school requiring a special entrance exam and IQ test for admission.

One of Rod's best friends at Parramatta High was Ken Mathers, later a leading Sydney journalist. Mathers remembers the future actor having a highly competitive nature throughout his school days, one of his favorite tricks being to stand on tiptoes and try to appear taller than someone else if he wanted to win an argument or score a point in conversation.

"He was very well developed, very proud of his body," says Mathers. "Good-looking kid. He was aware of it. He was an actor even then. Whenever the opportunity arose he'd put on a pose."

Despite Rod's academic success at Lidcombe Primary, he began to slack off at high school, spending most of his spare time at the gym or mucking around on the sports oval. He tended to stay away from team sports like cricket or rugby, concentrating on individual ones such as gymnastics, swimming and hurdling — even then Rod showed a tendency to go his own way. Those sports Rod did play, he excelled at: he not only held the under 15 years shot-put record at Parramatta High, at the 1944 school swimming carnival he was the overall champion of the under 15 years division, winning the 110 yards and 220 yards freestyle and the 55 yards breaststroke and backstroke.

Parramatta High was one of the few co-educational schools in Australia in the 1940s. But although Rod later became a ladies' man, Mathers claims his friend's dealings with female students were fairly G-rated: "Girls sat in the same classroom we did but did tend to stick pretty much to themselves... I can't remember that he got up to anything."

Mathers does remember Rod expressing some interest in acting while at school, impersonating stars such as Errol Flynn after watching them at the movies on Saturday afternoons.

"He could take people off, he could mimic very well," says Mathers. "He'd pretend he was the Hunchback of Notre Dame. He'd come at you, dragging one leg on the ground, grab hold of you and wrestle you to the ground. He was full of fun."

High school students at this time generally completed their intermediary certificate at the end of three years' study, after which they had the option of staying on for two more years. Rod decided against this and left school in December 1944. Too young for the army, he did not enter the workforce or go on to a trade school, as many of his schoolmates might have done. Instead, with his parents' encouragement, he elected to study art at East Sydney Technical College in the inner-city suburb of Darlinghurst.

IN THE LATE 1940S, EAST SYDNEY TECH (AS IT WAS INFORMALLY known) was one of the leading art schools in Australia. Certainly when Rod studied there it housed an amazing collection of talent; the teaching staff included such noteworthy artists as Douglas Dundas, Lyndon Dadswell and Frank Medworth, while several of the students went on to become significant players in Australia's post-war art world, including Margaret Olley, David Boyd, Guy Warren, Tony Tuckson, Warren Stewart, Lindsay Churchland, Tom Bass and Stan de Teliga. The main reason for this was the massive increase in enrollment that followed the end of World War II, when large numbers of returned servicemen began attending under the Commonwealth Reconstruction Training Scheme; the school was even forced to open a second campus at Strathfield, although Rod appears to have spent all his time at Darlinghurst.

Tom Bass recalls Rod as being "a rather dynamic young man who looked as though he was going somewhere" while at East Sydney Tech. Margaret Olley, who went on to become one of Australia's finest artists, remembers him from a ceramics class they attended taught by Lyndon Dadswell. "Some woman had done a pottery of a rabbit and put it in the fire," she says. "He did pellets and put them next to the rabbit, so to make it seem like the rabbit had done a 'poop.'"

Rod was certainly not short on confidence during this time. In his first year at school, he approached teacher Dorothy Thornhill, looking for modelling work in one of her life drawing classes. Initially, Thornhill was unimpressed, as Rod looked "an awkward sort of youth." However, since she had a vacancy for the following week, she decided to give him a try. He turned up, stripped — and promptly dispelled all Thornhill's earlier fears. "He was magnificent — he posed like a Greek god," she said.

Former student Pam Waugh (née Cashel) says Rod soon earned a name at the school as a lady-killer. "There was the reputation that he was doing over these women in the igloos in the art school. One was Skippy and the other was called Flippy and they were friends. We were so virginal in the '40s that this sort of gossip would make our eyes water."

An early girlfriend of Rod's was Kate Coolahan (née Castle), who later migrated to New Zealand and became one of that country's top artists. She recalls Rod being an artistic youth interested in acting, music and reading. "He was broad in his basics like I was so we were able to talk instead of sitting there going, 'Ooh ah think think.' There were some quite amazing intellectual conversations that not many of the boys participated in but Rod did.

"He had better clothes than most of them; he was always well groomed, he had fantastic manners. He always was well turned up. He was physically well developed, muscular. I remember that he had a fondness for his mother which endeared him to me when there were so many of them who hated their mothers."

Kate says Rod eventually broke up with her and moved on to another student. "He was the first love, you might say," she says. "You never quite let go of that. Those sort of things hurt but didn't last."

The other woman was another student, Beryl Eager, who remembers her first impressions of Rod: "Good looking, physically graceful. 'A Greek god' was a term someone used to describe him. He was outgoing, self-assured — Russell Crowe with a touch of Baryshnikov. He had talent, drew fluently and well. In another sphere could have been a ballet dancer, too… Humorous, energetic, gregarious… A typical young Aussie male, but with a creative, poetic side to his nature."

While at art school, Rod started spending his weekends at Mona Vale Surf Club on Sydney's far northern beaches. He received free accommodation at the club bunkhouse overnight in exchange for working as a lifesaver during the day: watching swimmers between the flags, rowing surfboats, practicing rescues and so on.

"He liked to stomp around in his costume and show off to the girls," laughs Ken Mathers, who joined the club with him.

Rod later claimed he "learnt about life" at Mona Vale, particularly from the "hoodlums and oafs" he associated with there. Surf clubs were a bit rougher and rowdier then than they are now, with many of their members working-class types from the inner-city keen to get away for the weekend. (They also included a number of actors, giving Rod his first sustained exposure to members of that profession.) The young art student enjoyed the comradeship and physicality of club life enormously, mucking around with the blokes at night and playing in the surf during the day. He eventually worked his way up to being a junior captain of the club, putting his art skills to use by helping design the Mona Vale Surf Club badge.

Rod's other main athletic pursuit around this time was boxing, at which he became extremely proficient; he also did a little rowing. Australia was a sports mad country in the late 1940s, both in terms of participation and spectatorship, and these activities were fairly typical of young Australian men. They also meant Rod was developing certain skills — hand-eye co-ordination, an ability to throw a punch — that would become useful later on in Hollywood, particularly in action roles.

Most students at East Sydney Tech studied for five years, but Rod attended for only three. Ken Mathers believes Rod was expelled "for throwing clay or something." No admission records exist from this period, but Rod confirmed he was expelled in a 1973 interview. He does not appear to have been too distressed by this, claiming he never felt he fitted in at art school.

"I didn't wear my hair the right length," he said. "I was also too muscular and in too vulgar a way. Whereas I should have been more the pale aesthetic type, I was a ruddy and boisterous bloke."

"We were serious and I don't think he was," agrees Margaret Olley. "He was more into making mischief."

Despite this, Rod nonetheless tried earning a living as an artist for a time. He appears to have done some casual work for Martin Boyd Pottery in the northern suburb of Ryde, helping make such domestic items as ash trays, beer mugs and biscuit barrels. He also began working part-time at Mark Foys, a leading department store in the city, painting and drawing backdrops for their display windows; colleague Mervyn James remembers he "could paint a ballet scene or illustrate a winter scene, with swaying trees, with equal skill."

Rod's most serious attempt at turning art into a career came when he went into a pottery business with some friends. The pottery itself was actually owned by Jean Roche, an entrepreneur who offered it to a couple, David Boyd (of the celebrated Boyd art family) and Hermia Lloyd-Davies, on the basis that they would be paid a living wage, after which any remaining profits would be divided up between them. David and Hermia invited Rod and his girlfriend Beryl Eager, whom they knew from East Sydney Tech, to join the partnership on the same terms.

The four of them took a flat in an old terrace house overlooking Woollahra's Trumper Park; Hermia described it in her biography as being "infested with rats, mice and cockroaches from the old council rubbish dump." Rod, Hermia and Beryl painted while David operated the kiln. The designs varied from adaptations of ancient or medieval classical themes to purely modern ones; Beryl recalls Rod would concentrate on ballet subjects, while she and Hermia specialized in Shakespearian characters and the occasional Aboriginal skeletal fish or kangaroo. The partnership sold their work to various shops and wholesale merchants and they soon averaged an income of £5 a week.

As Rod explained at the time, "Ninety-nine percent of our customers are women. They like to be able to order, say, a dinner set, then come to the converted garage… where we work and watch us make it. Then they can change its shape as we go along and have it whatever size they like. Sometimes, if they are very fascinated, we let them throw a little clay themselves, decorate it as they like and they take it home as a souvenir."

The budding artists were all young, in love and making a living out of something they had a passion for. John Vader evokes the time romantically in his biography of David and Hermia: "Business quietly thrived in a pleasant environment, though no fortunes were made. Whenever work slackened, the potters would slip over the road for a beer at the pub or, to be inspired to greater effort, contemplate the sign hanging on their wall: Paris or Bust!"

The *Sydney Morning Herald* published an article on the four in August 1949, by which time the partnership was 12 months old. They said they planned to start a pottery business in London and then study ceramics in Europe, before returning to Australia.

The enterprise was not destined to last, however. Five pounds a week was enough for everyone to live on in the short term, but profits were minimal and Jean Roche was not receiving any dividends for the use of his building and equipment. In addition, Rod's enthusiasm for the business of art was fading.

"I got tired with the painting world," he reflected later. "I got off because I knew I could paint well. I'd have to go to bed with some rich broad to get an exhibition put on in Sydney."

When Hermia became pregnant with her first child, the friends decided to dissolve the partnership. She and David moved to Melbourne, then to England, eventually becoming two of Australia's leading potters. Beryl moved to England as well, where her career flourished; on her return to Australia she became an editor for *Vogue* magazine. Rod turned to a new passion — acting.

CHAPTER 2

"I thought, 'I bet I could do that.'"

AUSTRALIAN ACTOR (1949–1951)

ROD ALWAYS CLAIMED THE PERSON MOST RESPONSIBLE FOR igniting his interest in acting was Sir Laurence Olivier. In 1948, Olivier and his wife Vivien Leigh toured Australia and New Zealand with the Old Vic Company; the expedition was done at the behest of the British government, anxious to increase the Mother Country's prestige in the region following World War II. The Oliviers were probably the most glamorous couple in the world at the time and their trip was an overwhelming critical and popular triumph; eventually they performed to audiences of more than 300,000. For anyone even slightly interested in acting, the visit must have been a galvanising experience.

Rod said what he heard on Sydney radio at the time gave him confidence he could make it as an actor. "I used to listen to these awful Australian soap operas on the radio. I thought, 'I bet I could do that.'"

Georgie Sterling, an actor who became one of Rod's closest friends, always thought Rod was attracted to the performing arts because of its social dimension. "It wasn't a solitary activity the same as doing his woodwork or his art was. He liked the idea of working with other people and getting to know other people. And having an experience, something to bounce off in dialogue."

Bill and Mona were not happy about Rod's new career choice, however, and pressured their son to stick with art. Rod says, "They put up quite a struggle over that — but lost."

It was an unusual battle, especially for Sydney suburbia circa 1949: while there is a long, noble tradition of parents trying to talk their children out of going into acting in favor of something more stable, they normally push for a more secure alternative than art. However, one should keep in mind that Bill was once an artist himself and at the time commercial art was, unlike acting, at least a recognized trade you could study at a proper tech school.

Rod began taking acting lessons at the Independent Theatre School of Dramatic Art in North Sydney. The school offered training in such areas as diction, voice production, deportment, character work, mime and make-up; there was no rigid schedule, but classes were graduated so that a student could pass through "elementary" classes to "medium" ones.

But studying acting was one thing. Actually making a career out of it meant finding paid jobs and in post-war Australia there were only three places to do that: legitimate theatre, variety or radio. Rod did not have the skills for the variety circuit and there was only a limited amount of paid theatre work available. However, radio was flourishing and it was there Rod got his start.

THE YEARS FROM 1945 TO 1955 ARE KNOWN IN BROADCASTING today as the "Golden Age" of Australian radio drama. Although radio had been a feature of Australian life since the 1930s, local drama only became really established during World War II, when restrictions were placed on the importation of overseas programs. When peace came, government quotas ensured broadcasting would continue to be dominated by local shows and the industry thrived until the introduction of television in 1956.

The type of drama heard on radio was similar to that later found on television — namely, a mixture of daily serials, weekly series and one-off specials. The range of genres produced was correspondingly varied: comedies, Westerns, adaptations of books/movies/plays, crime thrillers, romances, and so on.

Steady demand ensured a prosperous industry: at the height of the boom, there was enough demand for product to support ten commercial production houses in Sydney alone, not to mention the government-owned ABC. Almost every leading Australian actor from this period worked in radio at some point: Peter Finch, Chips Rafferty, Roy Rene, John McCallum, Guy Doleman, Ron Randell, Muriel Steinbeck, Michael Pate, Charles Tingwell, Ruth Cracknell, Ray Barrett, June Salter, John Meillon, Lloyd Berrell, etc. (Several of Australia's leading post-war writers also learned their trade in the medium, including Sumner Locke Elliot, Peter Yeldham, Max Afford and Morris West.)

"There was so much work and so much variety," remembers Margaret Christensen, a leading actor at the time. "If an actor wasn't recording eight hours a day and doing one of the big shows on the weekend like *Caltex* he was considered to be out of work."

Actors might typically record up to five 15-minute episodes of a show before lunch, running from studio to studio around town. If they worked in the afternoon as well for five days in a row they could earn up to £100 per week; Brian Wright, another actor from this period, recalls that figure being "the benchmark... there was a lot of work, but there were a hell of a lot of actors around to take it."

Rod wanted to free up his days in order to audition, so he began working nights, scrubbing floors at buildings in the city. He did the rounds of the various production houses and it was not long until his first break.

Georgie Sterling: "The ABC used to have a book in the foyer where people who thought they ought to be in radio could put their name down and once every three months or so, depending on how many people had applied, they used to hold auditions and they would have a producer, actors, directors and couple of other odds and sods who would listen to these people. They'd choose what they wanted to do for their audition, whether it was Shakespeare or whatever. Anyhow, as soon as there were sufficient names on the books, they would hold these auditions and people sat in judgement on them and said, 'Yes, you pass, no, you don't.' Rod's name was down and he passed."

Among the people Rod impressed early on in his career was Neil Hutchinson, the director of drama at the ABC. Hutchinson first met Rod while producing a show of poetry readings by under-20s; he says Rod was training at the Independent at the time but "hesitating as to whether he should become a potter or an actor." Hutchinson persuaded the young man to choose acting. "I thought he was absolutely first-rate," he recalls. "Almost immediately."

Another key initial contact for Rod was Queenie Ashton, an actor who also ran a performing artists' agency with her husband, John Cover. Ashton says she first heard Rod while he was rehearsing a show at the ABC and immediately knew she had "discovered magic." She and Cover signed Rod to their books and he was away — in the words of radio historian Richard Lane, "As soon as he got work he was never out of it."

As a general rule of thumb, it is easier for men to break into acting than women, mainly because comparatively fewer of them want to do it and there are more roles available for them to play. Rod had the extra advantages of being talented, good looking and masculine (even though it was radio, those things always help), with a great facility for hard work and mimicry, particularly accents.

It was an ideal time for him to be starting out, too. *The Listener In*, a trade paper for the radio industry, ran an article in May 1950 on the shortage of decent male actors in Sydney — mostly on account of large numbers of them having recently left to seek work overseas (for example, John MacCallum, Ron Randell and Peter Finch). Rod slotted right into the gap and soon earned a strong reputation for himself around the traps.

Richard Lane: "What impressed people about Rod in those days was his earnest approach to acting, his wish to make it more than a job, to bring a fresh dimension to his work… He was a very pleasant and likeable young man, quietly-mannered at that time, very good looking and well-built, having quite an effect on the young women in the profession."

Actor David Nettheim remembers that Rod seemed to "turn up out of nowhere" at the time. "He was obviously fairly inexperienced as an actor but naturally a good actor. Very good appearance. He was quite a stunning-looking guy. He sort of created quite a frisson of attention as soon as he appeared on the scene, he was clearly going somewhere. He had a presence, a sort of natural talent."

"He was very nice, he was very charming," confirms Babs Mayhew, another actor. "I don't think anyone could meet Rod and not like him."

Colleague Dinah Shearing concurs: "He was an extraordinary radio actor, especially in the American stuff. He had a natural sort of charm and it came across. And a good voice, of course. He could adapt. He had a very good ear for certain accents, particularly American."

In June 1950, *ABC Weekly* published a small article on the emerging star, which stated: "The profession gets, so I hear tell, very incensed over many incompetent people trying to get in [to acting] — but many of them are only too willing to encourage someone like Rod. Incidentally, he's the lad for the elegant suit and the white stiff collar and he keeps his hair cut, what's more."

In the same month, Philip Lewis, the Sydney correspondent for *The Listener In*, praised Rod as "another of those new young 'uns of whom you'll be radio hearing plenty." Indeed they would.

Rod later estimated he did about twenty different shows a week on radio, "hopping from studio to studio playing every imaginable character in soap operas and stuff." Examples of his earliest work include the children's serial *Captain Singleton*, an adaptation of Daphne du Maurier's *Frenchman's Creek* and the submarine drama *Morning Departure*. His performance in *Nancy's Boy* prompted *The Listener In*'s drama critic to give the actor one of his first good reviews, declaring that "Rodney Taylor suggested well the weakness of the pacifist youth."

Listener In had not made a mistake in referring Rod as "Rodney" — for that was his stage name. Australian actors at this time were heavily influenced by British styles of performance and "Rodney" sounded more British than "Rod." It did not stop there: taped interviews from the early 1950s reveal that when Rod was in actor mode he spoke in cultured, smooth-sounding tones that attempted to hide any Australian inflections. In addition to this, Rod began to take on a more sophisticated, worldly, British appearance: growing a pencil moustache, dressing in an "elegant suit and the white stiff collar" and brylcreaming his hair.

This was entirely typical behavior for Australian actors during the "cultural cringe" of the 1950s. Australian theatre, films, literature and radio were all generally deemed to be inferior to those of other cultures, particularly Britain and America. In particular, to quote writer Alan Ashbolt, "the Australian accent was regarded as a crippling handicap and most actors laboured to rid themselves of it."

However, actors still had to exist in a very ocker, masculine society, causing them to lead something of a schizophrenic existence. John Bell describes it in his autobiography: "When I started acting I was told quite firmly by a senior actor, 'Listen, son, you have two voices, one for the stage and one for the pub and don't ever mix them up or you'll get clobbered for it.' This meant that whenever you stepped on stage (or acted on radio) you deliberately affected rounded vowels and a 'posh' phoney English accent. That's what acting was. And as soon as you stepped off stage, you switched to broad Australian in case anyone thought you were 'up yourself' or a 'poofter.'"

So, in the early 1950s, Rod Taylor's two identities began to emerge: the tough, beer-drinking "Rod" of the pub and the smooth, plum-voiced "Rodney" of the microphone. He handled the transition with apparent ease; after all, not only did he have an ear for accents, he already had experience of living in two worlds from growing up in a household that comprised his rugged, working-class Australian father and refined English mother, and from his late teen years when he would muck around at surf clubs on weekends while attending art school during the week.

However, things were harder than they seemed for the young Rod. Acting can be a terrifying experience and actors — even talented, handsome ones with the confidence of youth — can be notoriously insecure about their abilities, especially in a society that did not particularly venerate their profession. There was always someone taller, more talented or better looking; Rod later admitted it was "very lonely and very scary" for him when starting out.

Many actors of Rod's generation combated that fear by drinking. Alcohol was an inherent part of the Australian radio industry of the 1950s; most of the production houses were located in or near the city, enabling large groups of thespians to meet and socialize at the pub during lunch time, or whenever else they were not working. The Long Bar at the Hotel Australia was a particular favorite, with actors taking over their own corner during the day. (Male actors, that is — if women wanted to drink they had to go to a separate bar.)

"In those days the boys were boys and they all went off to the pub together while the girls went to drink coffee," recalls actor Barbara Brunton. "A producer would drink with a certain group and they'd be the people he'd cast."

Rod had acquired a taste for alcohol during his surf club days and soon earned a reputation as someone who enjoyed a drink. Again, this was entirely typical behavior for a male actor of the time, although Rod did seem to become a bit more boisterous under the influence than most.

"I believe the fist fights and stuff were very legion," remembers Dinah Shearing. "Every actor seemed to drink an awful amount and he was one of the lads."

"He was one of the boys, one of the mob," recollects Brian Wright. "There was nothing pansy about Rod."

Drinking initially seems to have had a positive effect on Rod's career, enabling him to build up his social contacts and self-confidence and better unleash his expressive side. "I think when you have a few drinks you communicate better," Rod once argued. "You reach out for people; you want to know more about them."

"In those days most of the actors boozed a lot, even when working," reflects Shearing. "But it made for a very uninhibited sort of performing."

"He hit the ale a bit, he loved his grog, but he was pretty reliable," recalls Wright. "There were some you wouldn't book at 5 p.m. Not him."

"He didn't get really drunk," says Charles Tingwell. "It was just noticeable that there was a difference in efficiency between working at 9 a.m. and after lunch."

The danger with social drinking, especially when it happens daily, is that it can turn problematic. Several Australian actors of Rod's generation would suffer severe difficulties with alcohol in their later life, such as John Meillon, Ray Barrett and Grant Taylor — and Rod himself. But that was a number of years away yet.

Far more useful than alcohol to the development of Rod's acting was the training he received from the husband-and-wife team of Georgie Sterling and John Saul. Indeed, in artistic terms, this was probably the most important education Rod was ever given.

For over a decade, John Saul had been acknowledged as one of the leading radio actors in Australia, best known for his role as Dave in the long-running comedy series, *Dad and Dave*. By the 1950s Saul was concentrating more on directing, earning a tremendous reputation within the industry; Charles Tingwell calls him the greatest director he worked with, while Brian Wright dubbed him "inspirational."

"Charming fellow, highly intelligent and very intense," said Wright. "Very good-looking, with eyes that could hold you, mesmerise you. Close to a Method actor in a way. Encouraged you to find the character within yourself."

Saul's wife, the actor Georgie Sterling, first met Rod when he was cast as her boyfriend on *Blue Hills*, the phenomenally popular serial about life in a small Australian country town. Sterling recalls being immediately struck by Rod's talent. "His attitude was different from other actors, who were all very old fashioned, but at that time it was not old fashioned, they were all, you know, terribly high wide and handsome. And now you would say, 'Oh dear, dear, dear — stop acting will you and get on with it.' But in those days, of course, they were all old stage people where everything was big and everything was broad and you had to be heard in the last row of the circle or the gallery or whatever and, of course, they were way over the top."

Sterling went home and told Saul she had found a new actor. They listened to Rod's performance on air that night and Sterling says her husband was greatly impressed, particularly by the young man's "self-contained quality which came from inside." The two decided to become Rod's mentors. Sterling: "We got in touch with him and said, 'You know we're impressed with your talent, that you have something that the other people don't have. Now if you want to get on in this business, you've got to start learning from the bottom up about what this business is about. It's no use listening to these old people because they're old stage people.'

"We said, 'We're tough in what we're going to do with you and if you don't choose to carry out what we suggest, forget it — we're not going to go any further because we're not going to waste our time on somebody who's just had an idea that they'd like to be an actor and it was all very easy, which it isn't.' So he said, yes, he would follow our plans and do as we said. So we said, 'Right.'

"So we started out with him in giving him what books he should read, what he should find out about English stage and radio and American stage and radio. In fact, he should know what the business is about — the modern business, not going back to these old actors who were, as I say, from the stage and all what we could call four-twelve, way over the top.

"Anyhow, we gave him books to read and suggested books and suggested actors he should look at. First and foremost, Marlon Brando… Montgomery Clift… Rod Steiger was one… Henry Fonda… All those people who came up in the business all at the one time and who were in the new era, so to speak, of new movies, television, which was just starting.

"So he put his mind to it and he did very well. He really studied very hard. We broadened his literature, suggested what books he should read, that he should get to know the old classics, he should know Dickens, Shakespeare, he should know all the up-and-coming and modern authors.

"We said, 'You must cover the whole field of visual entertainment, which includes television and the stage. Now you must find out and know the history and progress of stage in America and England, England particularly because of your background. You are not an American but you must know the history of American stage and television and film. In other words, it's no use knowing one little section of the art field and ignoring the rest. All of it is tied in together, one depends on the other, it's not just an isolated area over there that you say, 'Yes, I'll do that and I don't want to know about the other.'

"Anyhow, he studied very, very hard, he really worked very hard. And his work was improving all the time."

Although Saul and Sterling ran an actual acting school as a sideline, Sterling says neither she nor her husband took payment for the lessons they gave Rod, which took place at their house at Newport on Sydney's northern beaches. "We'd just sit around and talk. Principally over dinner and a bottle of wine. It wasn't a formal thing saying, 'Now we'll have lesson one,' it was whatever developed out of the conversation and we'd take it from there. Made it much broader in the long run of the area we covered."

Sometimes the three of them would be joined by other actors, such as Charles Tingwell and Ken Wayne. "We'd talk from seven at night to seven in the morning," recalls Tingwell. "Every possible acting theory would be discussed. It was incredible."

According to Tingwell, John Saul's primary mantra was there was no such thing as good and bad acting, only "truthful and untruthful acting." More specifically, Saul was an enthusiastic advocate of the acting theories of Konstantin Stanislavski, developed in Russia in the early 20th century. Stanislavski aimed for a more realistic mode of performing, where actors were encouraged to analyze their motivations and use their own personality and emotions when they played a character.

"He [Stanislavski] was the first person who tried to put down how you should approach character, how you should find out what makes them tick," says Sterling. "Because without that you can't portray, the words don't always tell you what the character is. You've really got to start to know and psychoanalyze the person so that you really get inside this person and take 'you' out. You hang yourself on the hook over there to be picked up later."

Stanislavski's Russian colleague, Richard Boleslavsky, moved to New York in the 1920s and began teaching Stanislavski's techniques there. Among his students were Lee Strasberg and Harold Clurman, who later used the theories in their work at the Group Theatre and the Actors Studio — where they subsequently evolved into the "Method," a system where actors learned to feel and express the emotional subtexts of scripts. Film academic Richard Maltby summarizes it as thus: "The Method constructs a character in terms of her or his unconscious and/or inescapable psychological make-up. Although in principle the Method could be used to express any psychological state, in practice it was used especially to express disturbance, repression, anguish, etc., partly in line with a belief that such feelings, vaguely conceptualizable as the Id and its repression, are more 'authentic' than stability and open expression."

By the early 1950s, the Method had become the most influential new acting technique in America, with a number of the country's most exciting new performers being associated with it, including Marlon Brando, Montgomery Clift, and James Dean. Since many of these were film stars, Australians could see examples of the Method in action relatively early.

To most Australian actors, the Method (and Stanislavski) was an exotic way of working. Its emphasis on the internal (i.e. emotion, analysis) marked a significant break with traditional British acting techniques, which tended to stress the external: diction, voice production, deportment and so on — all things Rod might have studied at the Independent.

But the post-war era was a time of change and experimentation in all walks of Australian life — in particular, a lessening of ties with Britain, politically, economically and culturally. Many actors were swept up in this, gradually breaking away from the British style of performing and taking inspiration from other countries (for instance, Peter Finch was a great admirer of French actors); Sydneysiders such as Rod were particularly receptive to American ideas and styles.

"There was a trend in those days," remembers Dinah Shearing. "Melbourne male actors did a lot of Shakespeare and turn-of-the-century plays — Wilde, Shaw. The Sydney actors seemed to do better in contemporary stuff. The contrast was extraordinary. Melbourne was cerebral and academic; Sydney was more from the hip."

Although the Method wasn't formally introduced to Australia until the late 1950s, when Hayes Gordon started teaching it at the Ensemble Theatre, its influence (or, more accurately, Stanislavski's influence) was already being felt at the beginning of the decade. Sterling says that Rod was particularly inspired by the work of Marlon Brando.

"The scene that really affected him most was the scene in the motorcar in *On the Waterfront* (1954) where Brando talks about his life, about being somebody. He watched that a million times. I said, 'You can't copy this man, you are yourself, but what you can learn from him is to be truthful to the character you are playing, know it, know it as well as you know yourself. And don't act. Just let it come from inside of the character. Read the character, know the character, know his life, know what's made him tick.' So he analyzed all these things and took it to heart and his work was improving enormously and he was starting to get work."

An early example of Rod's pursuit of naturalism in a performance can be found in Jacqueline Kent's history of Australian radio, *Out of the Bakelite Box.* She quotes radio producer Gordon Grimsdale on the time Rod was cast in a show about diamond mining in South Africa: "[Rod] had to run across the desert, so the effects were ploughing through a sand box. Then he had to come to running water, represented by a small glass tank. He was supposed to kneel down in that, scoop up a handful of gravel and discover that it contained diamonds. This all had to run for about two-and-a-half minutes; the only actor involved was Rod, puffing and panting and talking to himself the whole time. He decided to do all the effects himself so it would sound realistic.

"Off we went. So he ran up and down in the sand box, stumbling… all over the place. He got into the tank, which had about two inches of water in it, and jumped up and down in that, getting his feet all wet. It was all OK until he got down to drink water out of the tank. There he was, scooping up what was supposed to be a handful of gravel, muttering, 'Diamonds, diamonds' and trying to spit the old cigarette butts out of his mouth at the same time. It was too much, even for him!"

It would be a mistake, though, to classify Rod Taylor as a Method actor — or even a Stanislavski disciple. Firstly, the British influence on him was far too overpowering (its grip on Australian performance culture would not really be loosened until the 1960s). Secondly, Rod had some reservations with the showier, cult-like, "look-at-me" aspects of the Method.

"When you start defending the acting and making with the heroics, it becomes phoney," he once declared. "I don't believe in self-indulgence at the expense of the audience."

Rather than being a Brando clone, Rod was perhaps closer to another actor he greatly admired, Henry Fonda, a performer who once summarized his acting "credo" as to "disguise acting… not to let acting show." Fonda believed that no matter how skilled or hard-working an actor, if the audience became "aware of the wheels going around, that robs it of the illusion."

"When you put up a building you don't want to show the girders," Rod agreed. "And if Method shows then it's not good acting."

Rod's acting technique thus drew inspiration from a variety of sources: take a bit of the Method, add a dash of training from the Independent Theatre, throw in some Stanislavski, mix in Henry Fonda and Brando, add dollops of Saul and Sterling, heat it up with a lot of Rod Taylor himself (the pubs, the physicality, the art), add some seasoning through (it must be admitted) alcohol and — hey presto! — you have your own style.

Rod: "Cézanne said there is nothing between you and the canvas but God. Anything you think is sponsored by your own emotional or visual capacity, that you can put onto canvas, is your technique. There is no 'standard' technique. It's what YOU feel… and that can be fun."

This attitude, radical at the time, has since become commonplace in Australian acting schools. For instance, John Clark, one-time director of NIDA (1969–2004), the best-known acting school in the country, claims that he tried to instil into his students the idea that there was "no right way or wrong way of acting," but that each actor should "evolve an approach that is right for them." Rod Taylor would have heartily agreed.

CHAPTER 3

"He was magical."

AUSTRALIAN FILMS (1951–54)

BY ANY STANDARD, ROD'S FIRST YEAR OF ACTING HAD BEEN extremely successful. Without contacts and with limited experience he had not only broken into a notoriously competitive industry, he was able to support himself financially through his craft and was receiving private tutelage from the leading director of the day. In November 1950, *The Listener In* dubbed Rod "that clever radiator who's getting places both on and off mike." The news only got better when Rod was cast in his first film role.

NINETEEN FIFTY-ONE MARKED THE 50TH ANNIVERSARY OF THE Commonwealth of Australia and the federal government was throwing a jubilee to celebrate. There were to be festivals, parades, carnivals, military tattoos and art exhibitions, with a budget of £350,000 set aside to pay for it all.

A showpiece of the festivities was a re-enactment of Sir Charles Sturt's 1829-30 expedition down the Murrumbidgee and Murray Rivers. The six-week trip would follow the exact same route as Sturt and his crew, using a combination of personnel from the ABC and the armed forces. A historian later described it as "the greatest historical enactment ever made in Australia" and "the biggest broadcasting event that the ABC had ever staged."

Two actors were chosen to play Sturt and his second in command, George McLeay: Grant Taylor, star of *40,000 Horsemen* (1940) (and no relation to Rod, although a similarly macho type of actor) and Charles Tingwell. Students from Duntroon, the officer-training school for the Australian army, were recruited to play the rest of Sturt's crew.

Tingwell was then offered a support role in *Kangaroo* (1952), a Hollywood movie shot in South Australia and Rod stepped in to replace him. Despite Rod's familial connection with Sturt, it is more likely his rowing experience that got him the role — he and the seven others would have to row 1,000 miles of the journey in a whaleboat, just as Sturt and company had 120 years previously.

Unlike their predecessors, however, Rod and his fellow crew members at least knew where they were going. In addition, they would have a support team accompanying them, consisting of photographers, cooks, technicians, drivers and journalists, not to mention a quiz-show host who would make nightly broadcasts on the expedition from camp. There was also a film crew from the Australian National Film Board, who were producing both a newsreel on the re-enactment and a documentary about the original expedition.

Rod and his fellow explorers left Sydney on December 30, 1950. They traveled overland by coach to the inland town of Maude, whereupon they changed into costume and set sail in the whaleboat down the Murrumbidgee River. Whenever the expedition passed through a town, the procedure was usually the same: the crew were met by local dignitaries and a crowd of townsfolk; Grant Taylor (as Sturt) would relay the greetings of the Governor of New South Wales, say a few words and present the mayor of the town with a scroll; then there was some celebratory activity. People would get into the spirit of the occasion by dressing themselves in 19th-century costumes and most places the expedition stayed in declared a public holiday; this apparently led to one member of the film crew putting in for special rates of pay for every day!

Navigating the Murrumbidgee was slightly tricky, but once the boat was on the Murray the crew had regular support from the land party, who usually met them at the end of the day's row. For any stretches where access to the river was difficult, a small support group traveled amphibiously and leapfrogged the whaleboat between moorings. One of the crew members, Pat Trost, says this led to the occasional accusation that they were cheating. "There was a cartoon in the newspaper with an outboard motor and we're going — 'Quick, bring it in, the town's coming up,'" he laughs. "We didn't have an outboard motor. No room!"

Trost remembers both Rod and Grant Taylor "tended to put on a few airs at the start" of the trip. "They were Sturt and McLeay, we were convicts, sort of thing." But the two actors eventually fitted in and everyone ended up getting along well. Trost says Rod, in particular, was a "natural mixer ... tough as anything, never missed a beat on the oars."

Roy Pugh, another member of the crew, recalls Rod as being a "great fellow," a "very tough, very fit and very determined man," who "would have done well anywhere a man of strong character was required. He was a man's man."

Shooting the newsreel proved relatively easy, but filming the documentary on the original expedition was tricky, as any signs of modern life (e.g. telephone poles) had to be avoided. The rigid trip schedule did not help things either; only a few days were available for filming and when they came around the actors and crew tended to be tired. Re-staging a tense encounter between Sturt and some local Aboriginal warriors proved especially difficult, as few real Aboriginal people lived in the region in 1951 (another long-term consequence of Sturt's explorations); at one point, the unit had to cast white townspeople daubed with streaks of paint and put in loincloths. It sufficed at the time, but when the crew returned to Sydney they had to shoot some additional scenes to fill in gaps.

The expedition arrived in Goolwa, South Australia, on February 11, 1951, where they were greeted by thousands of people on land and a small flotilla of boats on the water. Rod and his fellow rowers were driven to Adelaide, where they rode the whaleboat on a horse-drawn wagon through the city streets, welcomed by the South Australian premier and an estimated 50,000 people. Grant and Rod then headed a procession through the city on horseback; when Rod had to climb on his horse, he vaulted clean over his saddle, falling flat on his back in front of the massed crowd.

Inland with Sturt, the 20-minute documentary of the original expedition, was released to some cinemas later that year. It is beautifully shot, but has minimal dialogue, relying mostly on Grant Taylor's voice-over as Sturt; Rod does little acting apart from rowing and jumping into the water in one scene. Reviewing the film, *ABC Weekly* complained that "All the little, intimate details of crew personalities and incident had to be sacrificed because there was no time to dwell on them and these are the very things that would have lifted the film to a more engrossing level."

Nonetheless, the actual trip itself had been a wonderful triumph: seen by an estimated 300,000 people in total, it provided Rod with his biggest audience to date and gave him a taste for acting in front of the camera.

ROD RETURNED HOME TO FIND HIMSELF STILL IN HIGH DEMAND for radio jobs. Eric Johns, a director who had moved to Sydney that year to work for the ABC drama department, became a fan of the actor and cast him in a number of roles. So, too, did Gordon Grimsdale, who was based at production house ARC. Working with leading directors such as these, not to mention Hutchinson and Saul, greatly assisted Rod's improvement as an actor, and he slowly, but surely, became one of the best in the country.

Although serials and drama series were Rod's bread and butter at the time, he also featured in book and play adaptations. In 1951 alone Rod performed in versions of *Point of Departure*, *Winterset*, *Madame Bovary* and *Abe Lincoln in Illinois* (in which Rod played the title role!). The majority of these shows were local versions of overseas stories, meaning Rod mostly played Americans and Englishmen. He began to show a definite aptitude for American material, especially in tough crime/mystery series like *Contraband*, *Night Beat*, *I Hate Crime* and *Man Trap*.

However, Rod did play some Australian characters: a regular part on the long-running serial *Blue Hills*, a shearer in *A Place Where You Whisper* (from a script by D'Arcy Niland) and a POW in *Time Was My Enemy*; he also starred in adaptations of two classic Australian novels, *The Sundowners* and *The Ridge and the River*.

Amidst all this professional activity, things were also busy in Rod's personal life. By the early 1950s, Rod had developed into a handsome, well-built young man, very confident in his relations with the opposite sex; as actor Barbara Brunton put it, "He was very much a man about town." Post-war Australia tended to be a conservative place sexually, but the acting and art worlds within which Rod moved inclined toward the more broad-minded end of the spectrum and he took full advantage of it, enjoying a number of flings with willing women, including fellow actors June Salter and Margot Lee.

So it was perhaps a surprise when Rod decided to get married at the age of 22. Marie "Peggy" Williams was the daughter of an Armidale grazier and one of the leading models in Sydney at the time. She and Rod wed on April 19, 1952, at St. John's Church, Darlinghurst — the same venue where Rod's parents had married over 20 years before. Actor Guy Doleman served as best man.

The glamorous young couple moved into a flat in Elizabeth Bay. However, the relationship was destined not to last long. "Their marriage was never very satisfactory," says Neil Hutchinson. "They fought like wildcats."

"Their disagreements were very major," remembers Frances Nightingale, a friend of Peggy's. "He was very charming, very good looking, intelligent and very nice; and so was Peggy. They should have made a perfect couple. Maybe he was more cerebral than Peggy."

"He treated her very badly," recalls Dinah Shearing. "I remember one night at dinner whenever she spoke it was, 'Shut up, Peg.' You know, 'Get us another coffee.' He was very much a chauvinist in those days."

Rod blamed the marriage's eventual failure on a combination of his and Peggy's youth and her reluctance to give up her modeling career. He argued that, "Marriage takes complete co-operation at all times and when you get two egos each fighting an outside war there's bound to be trouble."

By the time Rod made *King of Coral Sea*, midway through 1953, the couple had already separated and their divorce became official on April 7, 1955. Peggy's subsequent life was marked by tragedy. She remarried in 1955, to a manufacturer, Ian Suttie, and they had two children together; one of her sons, MacGregor, died of leukaemia in 1969 — a disease from which her second husband subsequently died as well. Peggy started to drink heavily and gradually became a severe alcoholic.

"She would phone and be a nuisance," remembers one friend of Peggy's. "So everyone stopped taking her phone calls. We all felt bad about it, but at the time…"

IN ADDITION TO HIS RADIO WORK, ROD TRIED STAGE ACTING. Most theatre in early 1950s Sydney came from one of either two sources: JC Williamsons Ltd, the operators who had a near-monopoly on commercial theatre in Australia; or "little" theatre, professionally managed companies which engaged actors on an amateur basis. Since JC Williamsons toured their productions around the country, no actor could afford to sign with them without risking missing out on radio work. The upside of this was that the standard of acting in little theatre was quite high: anyone putting on a play, even if they had no money for salaries, could draw upon a pool of top radio actors wanting to flex their stage muscles for a couple of weeks. During the 1950s these were increasing in number, too: television was on its way and actors wanted to prepare for it with theatre work.

Rod worked for three different little theatres during his career — the Independent, the John Alden Company and the Mercury Theatre. The Independent was the best known of these, running for over 40 years out of its base in North Sydney (both Peter Finch and Sumner Locke Elliot started their careers there). Rod appeared in two productions for them in 1950: Shakespeare's *Julius Caesar* and Arthur Laurents' *The Home of the Brave*. Co-starring in both was Charles Tingwell, who recalls Rod being very inexperienced, but he learnt fast: "You could see him tuning up for the theatre," says Tingwell.

The following year he worked for the John Alden Company, a short-lived troupe which aimed to operate along the lines of the Old Vic in England. Rod appeared in their production of George Bernard Shaw's *Misalliance*, which was praised by the *Sydney Morning Herald* as "the most exuberantly skilful and sharp-pointed comedy seen in Sydney for many years," in which Rod was "exemplary."

Rod's most significant theatrical association, however, was with the Mercury Theatre, for whom he appeared in five shows over the space of 15 months. The driving force behind the Mercury was Sydney John Kay, a German Jew who had been touring Australia with a band when World War II broke out and he was interned; after his release he decided to stay on in Sydney and worked in local radio and theatre. Kay originally established the Mercury after the war in collaboration with Peter Finch and others; their most famous production was the 1948 lunchtime presentation of Moliere's *Imaginary Invalid* on the shop floor of O'Brien's Glass Factory, which was seen by Laurence Olivier and Vivien Leigh and led to Olivier inviting Finch to London. Finch's departure saw the Mercury go into hibernation until Kay decided to revive it in the early 1950s with the goal of creating a full-time professional theatre along the lines of European municipal theatre. Based at St. James Hall in the city, the Mercury would mount several productions simultaneously, with sometimes a different play on each night of the week.

Rod's first appearance for the Mercury was in the leading roles in a double bill of Shakespeare's *Comedy of Errors* and Plautus' *Twins*. His reviews were mixed: *ABC Weekly* gave him "honours… for emerging with so few bruises from what is a most gruelling test," whereas the *Daily Mirror* was more cautious, stating Rod would "doubtless settle down better into the part and give it a little more sang-froid as time goes on." The *Sydney Morning Herald* thought Rod was "well equipped to extract all the primary juices of comedy," but did not seem to be "able to find the grace and easy playfulness of manner and speech" to prevent the "raucous shouts and spluttering exhibitions of outrage" from becoming "tedious."

Rod then played a Norwegian priest in John Masefield's melodrama *The Witch*, where his co-stars included Barbara Brunton and future Sydney newsreader Roger Climpson. Brunton remembers Rod gave a "robust" performance, but thought he had "some distance to go in the art of stage acting." She also said he could be a little irritating during rehearsals because he didn't know his lines. "When he came to rehearsal he'd act as if he was infuriated about his own inability to memorize. I remember him punching a wall as if in frustration… It was as if he was upset and showing it was beyond his control. He hit the wall so hard it damaged his knuckles. Of course, he did learn them in the end and the play was fine."

Following that, Rod played an Italian vineyard worker in Sidney Howard's *They Knew What They Wanted*. The *ABC Weekly* described his work as "splendid," but the *Sydney Morning Herald* thought the role exposed the limitations of Rod's "craftsmanship rather ruthlessly; with persistent repetition of a few stock expressions, he was not able to bring any tension to the part."

However, Rod's final appearance for the Mercury was considerably better received: portraying a lecherous French Canadian uncle in a bright adaptation of Sam Taylor's family comedy *The Happy Time*. From all accounts, this was Rod's one theatre production that was an unqualified success: "A fine, flourishing performance" (*The Bulletin*); "many a good laugh… Rodney Taylor [was]… immensely amusing" (*ABC Weekly*).

Also in the cast was Owen Weingott, an actor who had worked with Rod on *Misalliance,* but since been touring around the country.

"When I first worked with him [Rod] he was a beginner," said Weingott. "When I got back a year later something had happened. He'd become in one year a top-flight actor. It was almost miraculous. He had drive, a personality — I really can't describe it. It was extraordinary. From a rank beginner to a really consummate performer. He was terrific in *Happy Time*. It was beautiful work, really good."

The Happy Time was Rod's last performance for the Mercury — indeed, his last ever appearance on stage — but this never seems to have caused him much regret. Rod's heart would belong to radio and cinema, rather than theatre. And speaking of which, he was about to embark on his first proper movie role.

IN THE 1950S, AUSTRALIA HAD HARDLY ANY MOVIE INDUSTRY TO speak of. Although some of the earliest feature-length movies in the world had been Australian, local filmmakers faced a constant battle against Hollywood competition, foreign control of distribution and exhibition, a small domestic audience and government apathy. The industry had gone into serious decline in the 1920s and the advent of World War II, with its drain on facilities and manpower, caused it to be all but wiped out — a situation that would not really change until the late 1960s. There were occasional eruptions of activity throughout that time, though — among the most notable being the films of Lee Robinson and Chips Rafferty.

The laconic, gangly Rafferty was an actor, a familiar face to Australian filmgoers since *40,000 Horsemen* (1940), who had leapt to international fame in *The Overlanders* (1946). Although most of his subsequent pictures were less admired, he remained popular and for two decades was the closest thing Australia had to a resident film star. By the 1950s, Rafferty had become frustrated at the slump in the industry and teamed up with Lee Robinson, a radio scriptwriter and documentary filmmaker, with a view to producing movies together; Robinson would direct and write, while Rafferty would star.

Starting with *The Phantom Stockman* (1953), Rafferty and Robinson went on to make six features over the next decade, mostly action/adventure tales aimed predominantly at the international B-picture market, using exotic Australian scenery as a backdrop. *King of the Coral Sea* was their second production; chiefly shot on location on Thursday Island in far north Australia, it starred Rafferty as the manager of a pearling company who becomes involved in a murder and people-smuggling. Charles Tingwell was cast as the juvenile lead, the playboy owner of the company who romances Rafferty's daughter (Ilma Adey). Rod Taylor was given the major support role of Jack Janiero, Rafferty's American offsider.

Robinson had worked with Rod in radio on the adventure program *Chips: Story of Outback* and subsequently cast him in the title role of *The Boxer*, a pilot for a show that did not go to series. The two men also knew each other socially: both belonged to the Journalists Club and Peggy was friends with Jeanette Elphick (the star of *The Phantom Stockman,* who later had a brief Hollywood career under the name "Victoria Shaw"). Robinson says Rod was "a first-class fellow. Very physical — he boxed a lot, but was artistic."

Robinson claims he wrote the role of Jake Janiero in *King of the Coral Sea* specifically with Rod in mind. However, Charles Tingwell told me that Ken Wayne, another tough-guy actor of the time, always thought *he* was originally meant to play Rod's part. What happened? "After a few beers he [Ken Wayne] said, 'He [Rod] got in under me,'" laughs Tingwell.

Regardless of exactly how Rod got the role, the character of Jack Janiero was perfect for him: a tough, humorous outdoorsman, not without sophistication. He was also an American, a decision Robinson admitted he made with one eye on the international market — although it was not totally unrealistic to have an American in this location in the 1950s, as many American servicemen stayed on in the Pacific after the war. There was no question of an actual American actor being cast in the part. "The film had a budget of $50,000 (£25,000) and to fly an American actor out would have cost that alone," says Robinson. Rod's salary was £40 a week.

Rod flew out from Sydney to Thursday Island for filming in July 1953. Most of his scenes were with Chips Rafferty who, being 6'5," tended to tower over his co-stars — and Rod was only 5'7". No matter: Robinson told Margaret Ansara that Rod would pack his shoes full of paper in order to build himself up a couple of inches against Rafferty. "Oh, he was smart, Rod," chuckled Robinson.

Making *King of the Coral Sea* was an invigorating experience for Rod: not only was he acting in a real movie, shot on a beautiful location, he was doing it with friends in a role especially written for him. Even better, he was allowed considerable creative input behind the scenes — rewriting portions of the script, having input into story conferences, even directing some sequences. This sounds bizarre, especially when you consider what control-freaks directors can be, but Lee Robinson was aware of his own inexperience, particularly when it came to drama, and was happy to let his friends take over at times.

"As far as performance was concerned, Rod had more guidance from Chips and Bud," admits Robinson.

"We all had a go at directing — Chips, me, Rod," confirms Tingwell. "Every-one used to do so much together it was hard to work out who was responsible for what."

Robinson says when it was time for Rod to leave the unit he "cried and pleaded" to stay. "He wanted to be the underwater grip or anything; he was so in love with it all."

The final cost of *King of the Coral Sea* was £23,862 and Robinson says he got this back easily. "We took about £34,000 out of England," he said. "And we made about £26,000 here. So again that tripled its costs in about three months." When the film showed in Sydney, touring American singer Johnnie Ray tried to catch a screening but was unable to find a spare seat and had to watch from the stairs.

Rod's personal notices were excellent, from Australian critics at least: *The Listener In* claimed he gave the best performance in the film and the *Sunday Telegraph* praised his acting as "excellent," although "I can't say the same for his American accent." *Film Weekly* thought that Rod "takes the acting Oscar" despite "a possible false note in his accent... he has a screen magnetism — that screen-stealing appeal we so rarely see in Australian production."

Today, *King of the Coral Sea* stands up as a passable adventure tale whose main attraction is its location photography (unfortunately the budget could not accommodate color). Despite an intriguing scenario, the story lacks excitement and Robinson's inexperience handling drama is evident — but it is agreeable enough, with a genuine exotic flavor and an attractive lead couple in Charles Tingwell and Ilma Adey. Rod is very comfortable as the macho, two-fisted Jack

Janiero, although his part is not really necessary in the story: everything Janiero does could have easily been done by Rafferty's or Tingwell's characters. But the role was crucial to Rod's career — not only was it his first feature, it essentially established the on-screen persona he would later embrace in Hollywood.

The screen image of the Australian male at the time was best personified through the characters played by Robert Mitchum in *The Sundowners* (1960) and Rafferty in his films — the laconic bushman, most comfortable in a fight, a pub or wide-open spaces; awkward around women; a good mate; and uneasy with authority. Russell Ward's famous description of the "typical Australian" of myth in his 1958 book, *The Australian Legend*, summarizes it best: "A practical man, rough and ready in his manners and quick to decry any appearance of affectation in others. He is a great improviser, ever willing to 'have a go' at anything, but willing too to be content with a task done in a way that is 'near enough.' Though capable of great exertion in an emergency, he normally feels no impulse to work hard without good cause. He swears hard and consistently, gambles heavily and often and drinks deeply on occasion. Though he is 'the world's best confidence man,' he is usually taciturn rather than talkative, one who endures stoically rather than one who acts busily. He is a 'hard case,' sceptical about the value of religion and of intellectual and cultural pursuits generally. He believes that Jack is not only as good as his master but, at least in principle, probably a good deal better and so he is a great 'knocker' of eminent people unless, as in the case of his sporting heroes, they are distinguished by physical prowess. He is a fiercely independent person who hates officiousness and authority, especially when those qualities are embodied in military officers and policemen. Yet he is very hospitable and, above all, will stick to his mates through thick and thin, even if he thinks they may be in the wrong."

Ward based his description on Australian literature and popular culture of the 1890s, a period that helped formulate the nationalistic myths which dominated Australian culture for the 20th century. It was a restrictive myth, with no place for women and little for non-Anglo Australians, and accordingly came under a deal of criticism, even at the time. However, it was also a highly popular one, in part because it was so uniquely and recognizably Australian, and gained credence through reiteration. Popular depictions of the adventures of the diggers during the war and the peacetime achievements of lifesavers and sportspeople, only served to reinforce this myth — indeed, it lingers on today.

Rod's early Australian roles fell comfortably within the confines of Ward's description of the typical Australian: shearers, soldiers and so on. So, too, did the American character Rod played in *King of the Coral Sea*: Jake Janiero was practical, rough and ready, capable of great exertion in an emergency, looked as though he would drink and swear hard and consistently (had the censors let him), hospitable and, above all, would stick to his mates through thick and thin.

There were some important differences, though: Janiero was a genuine hard worker, not one satisfied with "near enough"; he was talkative rather than taciturn and acted busily rather than stoically. In brief, he might be summed up as a chattier and slightly more sophisticated version of Ward's typical Australian of legend. For all that, the character still fitted into that myth more than, say, the smooth irresponsible playboy portrayed by Charles Tingwell in the same film. Rod found a way to represent Australian-ness even while playing an American. This is something he would continue to do throughout his Hollywood career.

Significantly, elements of Jake Janiero were all over an original screen treatment Rod wrote himself for a possible feature shortly after he finished on *King of the Coral Sea*. He sent this to Robinson and Rafferty, and an untitled copy exists in Robinson's papers at the National Film and Sound Archive, dated September 28, 1953.

The story concerns a retired, widowed sea captain and his two sons who live in a coastal town; they lead an idyllic macho lifestyle, making their money from fishing and spend their spare time boozing and hunting. One day a tourist party comes along, including a sexy girl. The younger son, a drinker and a little unstable, falls in love with the girl and starts stealing family funds to spend on her. The elder brother believes the girl is trouble, but is unable to resist her erotic charms and falls for her, too. The younger son becomes jealous and almost kills his elder brother in a fight. Eventually, the two siblings are reunited and they walk off into the sunset together with their father, leaving the girl on her own.

The film was never made, but it is interesting to see the sort of story that Rod was interested in: macho adventure tales, where the bonds of male friendship are strong, pastimes manly and women sexy diversions who are not to be trusted. They are themes that would frequently re-appear in the movies Rod later made in his career, especially those over which he had some degree of creative control.

Another perhaps more promising-sounding project, *The Ginger Giant*, was not made either. This was one of three screenplays Rafferty and Robinson commissioned D'Arcy Niland (*The Shiralee*) to write in the mid-1950s and was envisioned as a vehicle for Rod. The story centered around an Irish-Australian boxer from a small town who is trained by his grandmother and wins the world championship, but who faces discrimination after he marries a Chinese woman.

It is significant that even though Rod had only been acting for a few years, scripts were already being written for him. In fact, in the (admittedly not very long) pecking order of local film stardom at this time, he probably ranked below only Chips Rafferty and Charles Tingwell — not bad for someone with just a few years' experience under his belt. Another indication of how highly Rod was regarded within the industry was given when he was cast in the only other feature film made in Australia that year.

LONG JOHN SILVER (1954) WAS AN UNOFFICIAL SEQUEL TO *TREASURE Island* (1950), Disney's popular adaptation of Robert Louis Stevenson's classic tale about piracy and buried treasure. The Disney film, one of the first live-action features from the studio, had been directed by Byron Haskin and starred Robert Newton as the one-legged, scenery-chewing pirate, Long John Silver. Since Stevenson's story was in the public domain, Haskin and Newton decided to form their own company and make a sequel; they were joined by producer Joseph Kaufman and screenwriter Martin Rackin.

The four of them decided to produce the film on location overseas, preferably in a country where cheap labor and/or "frozen" American funds could be used (i.e. money earned by American companies which local regulations prevented from being repatriated). Australia was selected, partly on the suggestion of Sydney actor Michael Pate, then living in Hollywood and friendly with Rackin, partly because Haskin had enjoyed working with Australians while making *His Majesty O'Keefe* (1953) in Fiji.

The filmmakers leased a studio in Sydney and announced plans to turn *Long John Silver* into a feature film, 26-episode TV series and a series of recorded radio plays. According to *Variety*, the budget would be US$770,000, $250,000 of which came from a Hollywood studio, 20th Century-Fox; $235,000 from Louis Wolfson, a Florida theatre-owner and financier; $235,000 from the newly-formed Distributors Corporation of America (who would distribute in the US); and $50,000 from Kaufman. The deal with Fox enabled the film to be shot in CinemaScope and color.

Haskin cast several actors he had worked with on *His Majesty O'Keefe*, including Grant Taylor, Muriel Steinbeck and Guy Doleman; Taylor's son Kit was picked to play Jim Hawkins. During pre-production, Marty Rackin was listening to the radio one night and was impressed by an actor he heard on a crime drama playing the part of a Brooklyn gangster; Rackin originally thought the actor must have been an American temporarily stranded in Sydney and was surprised to find that he was in fact a local, Rod Taylor. This discovery came in handy when problems developed on the film with Guy Doleman's casting.

Doleman had been hired to play Israel Hands, a former shipmate of Silver's abandoned on Treasure Island who returns to haunt Jim Hawkins. The character was written as something of a blind Wild Man of Borneo, meaning Doleman would have to grow a beard and wear cloudy contact lenses. He wanted more money to compensate for this, but Kaufman refused. When thinking of substitutes, Martin Rackin remembered Rod: if he could play a Brooklyn gangster, why not a crazy old man? Rod had no problems with facial hair or contact lenses and was promptly awarded the role.

Shooting on *Long John Silver* took place in and around Sydney throughout the middle of 1954. Production was plagued by technical difficulties — the film was the first made in Australia to use either CinemaScope or Eastmancolor; in addition, it was being shot in a standard 1:85 ratio as well as CinemaScope, so all shipping, storage, processing and cutting jobs were duplicated. (Kaufman estimated this added $500,000 to the final budget.)

There was also constant behind-the-scenes friction between Haskin and Kaufman, with the director blaming his producer for running out of money during filming. Haskin also alleged Wolfson — who later served jail time for fraud — reneged on his commitments to provide finance. "It was a case of mortgaging the mortgages, or like building a bridge and having to mortgage the first half to build the other," Haskin claimed.

Little of this affected Rod, who enjoyed the experience of working on a large-budget Hollywood production. He threw himself into the part of Israel Hands with abandon, running over cliffs and rocks despite his impaired vision, cutting his hands and gashing an arm in the process.

The feature-film version of *Long John Silver* was released near-simultaneously in Australia, America and the UK toward the end of 1954. Local critics were generally positive: *Film Weekly* thought the Australian cast, particularly Rod, turned in "first-class performances" and the *Daily Telegraph* declared Rod was "remarkably good." The Australian press, though, as was their wont, seemed more interested in what the overseas critics thought and gave greater prominence to the negative reviews the film received in London and the US.

Long John Silver is a decent children's movie; it has a strong story with plenty of twists and turns, but lacks a little polish and suffers from stilted scenes. Rod's performance is not entirely successful — a 24-year-old actor really had no business playing a crazy old man — but he does his best; he later described his acting consisting of "scrambling around the rocks giving the worst performance you've ever seen in your life." He does, however, take part in one of the film's best scenes — stalking Jim Hawkins in a cave (although for a blind man, Israel Hands is awfully successful at chasing the child around an island).

The film's box-office returns were disappointing, both locally and overseas, and after production wound up on the television series (in which Rod did not participate), Kaufman abandoned plans to make further projects in Australia. However, Rod had now developed some genuine Hollywood contacts — something that would become useful for him unexpectedly soon.

BY 1954, ROD'S ACTING CAREER WAS FLOURISHING: HE HAD obtained strong roles in the only two feature films made in Australia over a 12-month period and was earning up to £100 a week on radio — enough money for him to buy a share in a fishing bungalow at Berowa Waters with fellow actors Nigel Lovell and John Meillon. Brian Wright describes Rod as being "right at the top of the heap in those days... probably the top leading man in Sydney at the time."

The parts kept coming: adaptations of *Crime and Punishment* and *This Happy Breed*, an on-air reprise of *The Happy Time* and the title character in *Golden Boy* (playing a young man torn between becoming a boxer or violinist — highly appropriate, considering the choices Rod had to make early in his career). He also supported — and from contemporary accounts outshone — visiting American film "star" Glenn Langan in *Operation North Star*.

In *The Dance Dress*, Rod played an orphan from the slums determined to buy a dress for the girl he loves; his co-star was Amber Mae Cecil who, according to Richard Lane, found Rod even at that stage "still oddly nervous about radio work and very serious and dedicated about it." The *Listener In* thought Rod's performance in this production "was well handled in the early stages, but there was a tendency to overplay the emotional scenes" and that he could have "toned down the hysteria a bit."

However, the same paper later gave Rod one of his best-ever reviews for his work in a war drama, *Crispin's Day*. Rod's performance was delivered in front of a live studio audience who, according to *The Listener In*'s drama critic, gave Rod "the most spontaneous ovation I have heard given to an individual actor," adding that the production "was a personal triumph for the young Sydney actor, who drew a living portrait of the flying man who hid nightmare fears behind a front of breezy and nonchalant humour. His emotional breakdown following his successful landing of the plane was a masterpiece of naturalistic acting."

From these reviews, one can deduce that Rod was more comfortable playing air-force pilots in tough war stories rather than orphans in tear-jerkers, an early indication of his career's eventual direction. He was also very much at home in his best-known role around this time — *Tarzan*.

Again, Rod stepped into a job originally earmarked for another actor — in this case Lloyd Berrell, a deep-voiced New Zealander who pulled out of the show when he decided to move overseas. Brian Wright, who wrote several *Tarzan* episodes, remembers initially being "a bit worried about the deepness" of Rod's voice, "but he worked on it."

Copies of *Tarzan* are available from the National Film and Sound Archive and it sounds as if the actors had a good time making it. Rod's dialogue as Tarzan consists of lines like "me — help," "me — kill" and the famous scream. The portrayals of black Africans are not likely to win any awards for racial sensitivity, nor the portrayal of Jane any for feminism. The series proved to be a tremendous hit, however, and made Rod quite famous: as Jacqueline Kent writes in her history of Australian radio, "Kids from Kogarah to Kununurra played Tarzan games, uttering the famous backbone-crinkling cry: 'Aaargh arga ah aaargh ah!' as they swung from trees in the backyard." Rod played the role until he left Australia, after which he was replaced with Ray Barrett, because Barrett was "the best person at sending Rod up," according to Charles Tingwell, who in turn played the role when Barrett moved overseas.

While *Tarzan* was Rod's most famous radio role, his most prestigious one was probably as legless war ace Douglas Bader in a serialized adaptation of the latter's biography, *Reach for the Sky*. This was based on a script by Morris West, who later became an internationally bestselling novelist, and from all accounts both the production and Rod's acting were unconditional triumphs.

"He did it very well," says Dinah Shearing, who played Bader's wife. "He [Bader] was a very gritty, tough little man — that sort of character appealed to Rod very much."

Another co-star was John Ewart, who recalled making the show in a conversation with Richard Lane. "The day we started Bader... well, we were all sitting around the studio first thing in the morning... reading the paper, doing the crossword... you know, the things you do while you're waiting around... and then Rod was doing the first part of a page and I became conscious of something happening and we all lifted our heads. Rod was performing. It was like a shot in the arm, everyone could feel it and you got off your butt and worked instead of coasting."

Jacqueline Kent wrote about a scene involving Bader climbing out of his bed at night, getting his crutches and going down a corridor to the bathroom with no help at all. When it was time to record, Rod did the scene using real crutches. "For several minutes, he made the others in the studio believe that he was Bader, a man on crutches that he couldn't manipulate very well, making his slow and painful way down a corridor. On air, the only sound listeners heard was clunk... tap... tap... gasp, as he almost fell and steadied himself... tap as he went on. Taylor created the whole scene and made listeners feel Bader's determination and angry effort simply by using those few sound effects."

Reach for the Sky marked a peak of Rod's acting efforts in the early 1950s, a culmination of years of study and work, resulting in a performance he had every right to be proud of: tough but vulnerable; totally truthful. The broadcast was highly regarded, *The Listener In* calling it "the event of the week in radio."

THE HARDER AN ACTOR WORKS, THE LUCKIER THEY TEND TO BE and in September 1954, Rod received the luckiest break of his career yet: winning the Rola Award. This was an annual prize given by *The Rola Show*, a half-hour program on radio station 2UE which featured local actors in original Australian dramas. Each week as the plays were broadcast, listeners would nominate an actor whose performance they considered best and these went into the running for the final prize. Rod was selected over two other semi-finalists for his performance in the dual role of a father and son in the drama *O'Sullivan's Bay*. He received £500, a role in a radio play written especially for him — and a return ticket to England.

Despite the windfall, Rod later claimed he did not intend to leave Australia for good, due to his strong ties to Sydney. "I loved the place," he said. "After all, I'd spent 24 years of my life there, never been away from home, and had what success I had had there, too."

Having said that, there was little else Rod could accomplish in Australia career-wise. He had conquered radio, had minimal stage ambitions and local feature film production did not look like increasing. So it was natural that even a mildly ambitious Australian actor would look overseas.

The majority headed to England. Peter Finch was the most famous recent export, but he was only one of many: Bill Kerr, John McCallum, Coral Browne, Thelma Scott and Ruth Cracknell, for example. Even Errol Flynn had completed a stint at Northampton Rep before going on to Hollywood.

"There was quite an Australian colony in the English theatre," says Brian Wright. "People would help each other out."

However, England was not the only option.

"America was, I suppose, the El Dorado," says Georgie Sterling. "It wasn't better, it was different from England. I mean, England is our heritage, America was not. It was a foreign country."

But it was not entirely unfamiliar. Chips Rafferty and Charles Tingwell had just been to Hollywood to make *The Desert Rats* (1953). The cast for that film also included Michael Pate, who was now settled there and doing well. So, too, were Cecil Kellaway, Shirley Ann Richards, Alan Marshall and Ron Randell, not to mention Errol Flynn, Leon Errol and Edward Ashley. Rod had extensive experience with American accents and his technique of acting — such as it was — was closer to the American style than the British.

"He felt himself to be a very rough-and-ready actor," says Brian Wright. "Action stuff — the sort of stuff he later did in Hollywood."

"If he had gone to England he would have had to do a bit of theatre," argues Dinah Shearing. "I think he was drawn to the sort of genre America put out — cops-and-robbers sort of thing."

Charles Tingwell suggested that Rod stop off in Los Angeles for a few days on the way to London and look up his *Long John Silver* contacts. After all, if things did not turn out, he could always go on to England or come back home.

In hindsight, Rod definitely left at the right time. Television was introduced to Australia in 1956; the government did not bring in quotas to ensure the production of local drama, which meant that cheap imported American TV shows flooded the screens; radio drama was almost wiped out and the small number of theatre-goers diminished even further. The late 1950s and 1960s were an extremely fallow time to be an Australian actor and almost all of Rod's actor friends — Barrett, Wayne, Tingwell, Meillon, Grant Taylor — moved overseas to work for at least some period of time.

Before Rod could leave, however, there was a slight hurdle. In order for him to be able to obtain a passport, the necessary documents had to be counter-signed by Peggy. By this stage their marriage was well and truly over and she was not keen to do her estranged husband any favors.

"It was tougher for me to get into the States than a Russian with a bomb under his coat," Rod said later. "I had to lie like a… thief to get in."

The authorities were willing to grant Rod a passport if he could show he eventually intended to return home. Rod asked Lee Robinson to provide a letter confirming that the actor was required for a film in Australia down the track. Robinson, perhaps a bit sneakily, said, "I'll go one better — let's do a contract." He drew up a formal arrangement which gave their company the right to call Rod back at any time to act in a projected film; Rod was to be paid no less than his rate on *King of the Coral Sea*, i.e. £40 per week.

(Years later, Robinson says he talked to Rod's Hollywood agent Wilt Melnick about his client possibly returning to Australia for a project. Melnick said Rod's price was $300,000 per movie. When Robinson told Melnick about the agreement, the agent could not believe it — but Robinson says he had no intention of enforcing the contract.)

Rod received his passport and on November 16, 1954, he left Sydney on a Pan American Airways flight for Los Angeles. Charles Tingwell remembers his wife Audrey went to the airport to say goodbye. "The plane taxied all the way off, then there was a fault on the plane and it taxied all the way back. There was a half-hour delay. Audrey said you should have seen Rod's face — he thought Peggy had slapped an injunction on him."

The flight went ahead and Rod was off. He would only ever return to Australia for holidays, promotional tours and the occasional film. His future lay across the Pacific.

CHAPTER 4

"A pretty smug attitude."

AMERICA (1955–59)

ROD ARRIVED IN A HOLLYWOOD THAT WAS IN THE MIDST OF AN enormous transition. Only a decade earlier, film production in the movie capital had been as neatly organized on an assembly-line business as any large industry; the major studios controlled the production, distribution and exhibition of their films and maintained large numbers of staff on a permanent payroll. They could afford it — in 1946 around 90 million people went to the movies every week in the US alone.

Since then, however, things had changed markedly: peacetime brought prosperity and an increase in things other than movie tickets that consumers could spend their leisure time on, most notably television; overseas countries, trying to help their economies recover from the war, placed import tariffs on Hollywood films and helped their own movie industries through subsidy and quotas; post-war increases in wages and taxes made the maintenance of large payrolls by studios disadvantageous; cast and crew increasingly freelanced as opposed to contracting themselves to the one employer; and there was an increase in agents and lawyers working in the industry. Further complicating things was the "Paramount decree," the 1948 Supreme Court decision which ordered that all studios should divorce their theatre operations from their film ones.

Yet, it was also a time of new opportunities: a decrease in the number of long-term contracts gave filmmakers more control over their careers; studios began offering top talent increased salaries and/or a percentage of the profits of their films; independent production companies, who now had better access to theatres for their product, began to thrive and picked up much of the creative slack from the majors; new techniques, such as 3-D, Cinerama and CinemaScope, became popular and filmmakers more adventurous in their subject matter; and studios found television could actually make them money, as a market for either their movies or shows especially produced by them for the small screen.

For all its changes, Hollywood continued to be a multi-million-dollar dream factory, a modern-day Gold Rush town where fortunes could be made and immortal fame achieved seemingly overnight. In particular, it remained a Mecca for every aspiring film star in the English-speaking world and Rod was going to face fierce competition there.

IN 1954, THERE WERE ONLY A HANDFUL OF AUSTRALIANS WORKING in Hollywood. One of the more successful ones was Michael Pate, who recalls: "I can't think of there being an Australian film community, or an Australian film tech community, not at all in those days, it just wasn't on, it was heavy going to make a good living in Hollywood and the few of us that made it there and stayed there were quite unique. Today, it's far easier. People actually seem to know where Australia is: in the days I was there they thought we all came from Austria and were amazed that we spoke English so well."

Accordingly, Rod's most valuable early contacts were not Australian expatriates, but Americans who had worked on *Long John Silver*. For instance, he was met off the plane at Los Angeles Airport by representatives from the agency MCA, who had gone there on the recommendation of Marty Rackin. Rod remembers that he "looked like a crock of garbage" by the end of the flight and he "could read their one expression at the plane: Good God! They probably had expected a cross between Brando and Rock Hudson."

Nonetheless, there were some encouraging early signs. Rackin was preparing a screenplay, *Hell on Frisco Bay* (1955), with Rod in mind; Joseph Kaufman announced he intended to sign the actor for two films, *Come Away Pearler* and *Captain Henry Morgan*; and Byron Haskin lined up a screen test for a part in *The Rose Tattoo* (1955). Kaufman also put Rod to use promoting *Long John Silver* around the country.

It was a false dawn: the Kaufman films were never made, Rod missed out on *The Rose Tattoo* and it would be several months before *Hell on Frisco Bay* went into production. Rod's first real break came when he acquired an agent — or, rather, an agent who believed in him: Wilt Melnick from the Louis Shurr Agency. Michael Pate was also a client of the firm. "They approached me and said would I have any objections to them handling Rod Taylor — they had to do that because we were both Australians and we were both within the range of each other (young character leading men, I guess you could call us in those days). So I said, 'Of course not' — I felt that he should have a good agent and I didn't feel that he and I were alike, by no means, far from it, so I thought they could just as well handle him — and I think they did a very good job for him."

Louis Shurr was not an enormous agency like MCA or William Morris, but this meant that its reps, such as Melnick, could dedicate more time to promoting their lesser-known clients. In future years, Rod would always credit Melnick for kick-starting his Hollywood career: "I got jobs in the end because I had one hell of a good agent who took over where MCA were glad to leave off," he claimed.

A skillful agent is important for any performer in Hollywood, but especially foreigners: under the law of the time, any "alien" requesting an employment permit in America had to be of distinguished merit and ability and/or not be replaceable by a US citizen. Accordingly, Melnick had to undertake a great deal of hustling to prevent Rod from being deported during his first year. "Every time I had a job I had to convince the immigration authorities that I was the only man for that job and get a special work permit," says Rod. "I couldn't just go out and get a job because I had no social security card."

Rod later claimed he spent his first months in Hollywood "on the beach fishing, not for fun. If the fish didn't bite, I didn't eat. I was an alien and couldn't work so I borrowed and fished until my seat got so thin I was sitting on sheer bone."

He rented an apartment in Crescent Heights, Hollywood, which a fan magazine later described wistfully as "a dreary little room on a side street … He began walking the pavements staring longingly into the faces of the happy and obviously rich passers-by. Lonely as a cloud and wondering what had happened to the rainbow, he began to think, nostalgically, of Australia."

The work drought did not last long. Although it probably did not seem like it to Rod at the time, it was actually an ideal moment to be a young up-and-coming actor in Los Angeles. One result of the decline of the classical Hollywood system was that only a few studios still kept a strong talent roster of emerging actors under contract (and even those were smaller than they used to be). Studios became progressively more reliant on established names and by the early 1950s there was a considerable lack of new stars — at least, new stars in the numbers Hollywood was used to. Executives were aware of this — especially with television booming — and by the middle of the decade had regained their confidence enough to take steps to remedy the situation.

The call went out to find exciting new actors with star potential: Broadway was raided, as was television, record companies and foreign film industries. Most studios launched talent-recruiting programs and the number of young players under contract began to grow: Columbia signed James Darren and Jack Lemmon; Warners contracted Tab Hunter, Natalie Wood, Paul Newman and James Dean; Fox had Robert Wagner and Jeffrey Hunter and so on. Rod just had to find a way to be noticed.

Hollywood tended to slot young male actors of 1950s into one of two categories: "The Brando Boys" or "The Breeding Boys." The former were the serious types, usually with a background in the New York stage and the Actors Studio, such as Marlon Brando, Montgomery Clift and James Dean. The latter group were the pretty boys, actors with little stage experience who were often a product of studio training programs, very good looking and rarely taken seriously by critics: Rock Hudson, Wagner, Hunter, John Derek, etc.

A self-trained radio actor from Australia, Rod did not fit into either of these groups. Although handsome, his looks were rugged rather than pretty. He had some Method-like training from John Saul, but it would have been difficult in America to pass himself off as an Actors Studio alumni. So how would he market himself? By becoming a pseudo-Englishman, "Rodney" Taylor.

If no one knew where Australia was, everyone knew England. There was still a healthy English contingent in Hollywood at the time (e.g. Michael Wilding, Stewart Granger, James Mason) and there were plenty of movies and television shows which needed English actors, costume pictures especially. Rod never denied he was from Australia or hid his Australian background, but it was going to be a lot easier for him to get jobs if he became a very English Australian rather than an archetypal Aussie. After all, this was the method usually practiced by Australian actors in Hollywood at the time (Ann Richards, Errol Flynn, Ron Randell, etc.). And despite Rod's inclination toward American material, he felt it was easier to pass himself off as a phoney Englishman in Hollywood than a phoney American.

He later explained in an interview: "Look, people walked out of *Summer of the 17th Doll* in New York because they couldn't understand the Australian idiom. It would have been useless for me to have pushed the cow cockie accent. I'd have got nowhere. To succeed myself and therefore draw attention to the true Australian image, I had to lose my accent. It was just being businesslike."

Rod's first role in a Hollywood feature was in *The Virgin Queen*, a two-million-dollar epic from 20th Century-Fox concerning the relationship between Sir Walter Raleigh (Richard Todd) and Queen Elizabeth I (Bette Davis). Director Henry Koster needed someone who could speak in a Welsh accent for the small role of a corporal who delivers a message to Todd and Rod fitted the bill. Although his performance was not particularly distinguished (he lays on the Welsh accent with a trowel), it had energy and the project was a prestigious one: Rod had his start.

Roughly half of Rod's roles in his first year in Hollywood saw him cast as an Englishman, or in roles normally played by English actors: a school teacher in a television adaptation of "The Browning Version" for the anthology drama *Lux Video Playhouse* (1950-59); the stuffy son of a respectable family in "The Black Sheep's Daughter" for *Studio 57* (1955), another anthology; a diplomat in *Giant* (1956); and a scientist in *World Without End* (1955). Just as he had done in Sydney, Rod often reinforced this English connection by using the stage name "Rodney."

The most impressive of these roles was in *Giant*, even if it was the shortest in terms of actual screen time for Rod. This film was one of the big productions made in Hollywood that year: a $5.4 million adaptation of Edna Ferber's best-selling novel about Texas oil barons from A-list director George Stevens, fresh off *Shane* (1953). The story centered around the life and times of old-style Texan rancher Bick Benedict (Rock Hudson), particularly his marriage to northerner Leslie (Elizabeth Taylor) and rivalry with his former ranch hand, Jett Rink

(James Dean). Rod played the small but crucial part of Sir David Karfey, who appears early in the film as Leslie's fiancé. Described in the script as "an agreeable, charming member of the diplomatic Washington society," Karfey loses Leslie to Bick, but turns up again later in the story to marry Leslie's sister.

An early list of casting suggestions for Karfey included Richard Stapley, Tony Dearden, Richard Lupino, John Dodsworth, Bruce Lester, Patric Knowles, Mark Dana, Scott Forbes, Richard Ney, John Sutton, George Montgomery, Gil Stuart and two other Australians in Hollywood, Edward Ashley and Michael Pate. By April 22, 1955, the part had not been cast; despite the fact filming was due to begin in mid-May. "The Black Sheep's Daughter" aired on April 26 and by the following day Rod had been signed to play the role at $500 a week for a guaranteed two weeks of work.

It was a considerable coup for someone who had been in Hollywood a mere six months. Although the part of Karfey was only small, it meant Rod got to act in a scene opposite Rock Hudson and Elizabeth Taylor under the direction of George Stevens in a picture that went on to earn ten Oscar nominations and box-office rentals of $12 million, as well as later being recognized as one of the iconic films of the 1950s.

George Stevens was the first genuinely great filmmaker Rod had worked with and the actor loved the experience. "I landed in Hollywood with a pretty smug attitude," Rod later recalled. "A talk I had once with George Stevens ... put me on the right trail. He told me to respect myself as an actor, even a bit one. And I began to see the industry in a bigger perspective and I resolved to work my head off ...

"He warned me never to be impressed by the wrong values, never to compromise if I felt I was right and to believe in what I do and be happy about it regardless of criticism. Just the thought that such a famous director would take the time to help me at that time was overwhelming. And I'll try to follow his advice until I die."

A few years later Stevens returned the compliment, claiming Rod was "an extraordinarily talented player" with "many graces of the acting art plus an inimitable flair for pure mimicry. He had a difficult part in *Giant* and made it outstanding." The director went on to predict that Rod would certainly become "a star of real distinction."

After that it was something of a come-down for the actor to go into *World Without End*. This was a science-fiction adventure for Allied Artists, a minor Hollywood studio which specialized in low-budget productions; indeed, one of the main reasons *World Without End* was green-lit in the first place was to re-use footage from an earlier Allied Artists film, *Flight to Mars* (1951), although the budget did extend to include CinemaScope and color.

The main attraction of *World Without End* from Rod's point of view was it gave him his largest role yet in a Hollywood feature: he played one of four astronauts on the first trip to Mars, who are accidentally transported 522 years into the future. The astronauts discover that Earth has become a bleak world inhabited by mutants; the remnants of the human race live underground, where the women are voluptuous and smart but the men are withered and weak.

Several critics noted this plot had similarities with a novel that would later be of importance to Rod's career, HG Wells' *The Time Machine*. Writer-director Edward Bernds later denied this — which seems odd, since both stories concern time travel, hopeless impotent humans of the future under the thumb of mutants and a girl of the future being attracted to a virile time traveler (in *World Without End* she is called "Deena"; in Wells' book, "Weena").

One scene called for Rod to do battle with a giant mechanical spider. Unfortunately, the selsyn motors that were meant to operate the spider legs did not work, meaning the actor had to provide most of the struggle. "I dove into it and wrestled with it for all I was worth," Rod told *Starlog* magazine, adding wryly that he even made "a major creative contribution" to the scene by adlibbing that he was vomiting when he came out of the cave, "because it was such a horrific experience with that bunch of rubber and felt."

There was plenty of rising talent on *World Without End* apart from Rod: a young Sam Peckinpah worked as the dialogue director, future Oscar-winning producer Walter Mirisch was an executive at Allied Artists, and the art director was noted illustrator Alberto Vargas. Despite this, however, the film turned out to be one of the more mediocre science-fiction efforts of the 1950s, hampered by sluggish pacing and poor performances. Rod's English accent is surprisingly weak, though his performance is better than that of the lead, Hugh Marlowe. And Rod certainly found the experience invaluable, claiming *World Without End* gave him the confidence to know he "could work with established Hollywood professionals and come out maybe equally as well."

WHILE ROD INITIALLY LENT TOWARD ENGLISH-TYPE ROLES during that first year in Hollywood, he also found himself portraying American characters on occasion: a gangster in *Hell on Frisco Bay* (1955), cowboys in *Top Gun* (1955) and an episode of *Cheyenne* (1955–62), a New Englander in "Killer Whale" for *Studio 57* (1955). Indeed, by the end of 1955, Rod was more likely to be found cast as a phoney American rather than a phoney Englishman — thus establishing a pattern for the rest of his career.

Top Gun was a low-budget B-western, a knock-off of *High Noon* (1951), in which Rod played the minor role of a cocky cowboy who repeatedly challenges Sterling Hayden to a shoot-out. It is an amateurish performance, with Rod clearly grappling with his accent and a tendency to overplay, although his enthusiasm is sweet to see.

He turned in a stronger effort in a movie made two months earlier, *Hell on Frisco Bay* — the script written by Martin Rackin with Rod in mind. This was an unremarkable (though enjoyable) action vehicle for Alan Ladd, who starred as a cop unjustly imprisoned for a crime he did not commit thanks to a gangster (Edward G. Robinson); Rod played one of Robinson's henchmen. As in *Giant*, Rod's role was small but showy: although his character was only on screen briefly, Ladd spent much of the story tracking him down, building up Rod's eventual appearance; he also got to do a fight scene with the star. Rod's $500 acting fee from the picture enabled him to buy his first car in LA.

Rod turned in an even better performance in "The Argonauts," an episode of the TV series *Cheyenne* made over at Warner Brothers. Like many *Cheyenne* episodes, the story was a remake of an old Warners movie — in this case, *The Treasure of the Sierra Madre* (1948), the classic John Huston-directed tale about three Americans driven mad with greed while searching for gold in the Mexican hills. Rod played the old Tim Holt role of the essentially decent man who almost succumbs to the weaker part of his nature, with series regular Clint Walker in the Walter Houston part. The episode is superbly performed, written and directed — it holds up extremely well today — and earned *Cheyenne* its best ratings since it began. Rod received his strongest reviews yet, with *Variety* declaring he delivered "the standout performance."

That sort of praise does not go unnoticed in Hollywood: in the wake of *Cheyenne*, producer Roy Huggins wanted to sign Rod to a long-term contract with Warners, with a view to starring him in a regular series. However, Rod turned him down on the grounds he "did not like TV in general and Warner Brothers in particular," according to *TV Guide*.

The decision was probably the right one. Warners was notorious for the low fees they paid their TV stars: Clint Walker, Jim Garner (*Maverick* [1957–62]) and Edd Byrnes (*77 Sunset Strip* [1958–64]) all had highly-publicized contract disputes with the studio which resulted in them leaving their shows for a time.

"He said he'd turned down contracts," recalls Charles Tingwell. "I said, 'That's very gutsy.' Very gutsy feller, was Rod."

It actually was not *that* brave, as Rod had another, better opportunity waiting for him, over at MGM.

ROD FIRST CAME TO METRO-GOLDWYN-MAYER IN LATE 1955 TO test for the lead in *Somebody Up There Likes Me* (1956), a biopic based on the true-life story of boxer Rocky Graziano, a troubled Brooklyn youth who became middleweight champion of the world. Rod had the looks and physique of a boxer and could pull off the accent.

"The test was very good," recalls director Robert Wise, who remembers Rod as "a very personable man and a great talent." However, Wise ultimately decided to cast James Dean instead; after Dean's death in a car crash, the role was taken by Paul Newman, whose performance launched him to the top flight of young Hollywood stars.

Any disappointment Rod had at missing out on the part of Graziano was partly quashed when, in September 1955, MGM offered him a seven-year contract starting at $450 a week. Rod had little hesitation in signing — this was security at last, not only financially, but against being deported home by immigration authorities. Unlike the deal offered at Warners, MGM was offering reasonable pay and their focus would be on films rather than television.

The news was reported back home in Australia with pride, *Film Weekly* boasting: "As Australian Rodney Taylor joins his celebrated namesakes at MGM (Robert and Elizabeth) winning praise for self and country, no one is more pleased than yours truly. We sang his praises in our review of Chips Rafferty's *King of the Coral Sea*, hinting he had what Hollywood wants. That was well before any announcement of a trans-Pacific deal. Our only regret: the Australian film industry couldn't keep him. He's a versatile and well-disciplined performer and that's often worth more than raw talent, no matter how brilliant."

The studio Rod had joined was perhaps the most famous of them all. Throughout the 1920s and '30s, no company epitomized Hollywood glamour more than MGM: it had the biggest budgets, the largest profits, the most lavish sets and costumes... not to mention being the home of "more stars than there were in Heaven." Their talent roster ranged from Fred Astaire and Greer Garson to Judy Garland and Spencer Tracy; they were the ones who spotted potential in Clark Gable and Greta Garbo and made idols out of unlikely candidates such as Esther Williams, Marie Dressler and Mario Lanza. MGM was the "Tiffany's" of the film industry.

By 1955, however, the studio was in decline, mostly due to a combination of management instability and a failure to adapt to the new post-war filmmaking environment. In addition, it had struggled to unearth new stars ever since the departure of the legendary Louis B. Mayer four years previously.

When Rod arrived at the studio, MGM had 14 big names under long-term contract: Glenn Ford, Grace Kelly, Stewart Granger, Eleanor Parker, Elizabeth Taylor, Howard Keel, Cyd Charisse, Ava Gardner, Pier Angeli, Leslie Caron, Debbie Reynolds, Gene Kelly, Walter Pidgeon and Robert Taylor. Of these, only three had signed post-Mayer — of which two (Parker, Ford) had achieved stardom earlier at other studios, while the third (Grace Kelly) enjoyed her greatest success outside MGM. Since star-making had once been Metro's greatest claim to fame, the lack of new names was something of an embarrassment for studio head Dore Schary. MGM went on a major talent drive and Rod was swept up in it along with such young actors as Dean Jones, Leslie Nielsen, Taina Elg, John Cassavetes, Gena Rowlands, Irene Papas and Bill Travers.

In the heyday of the classical Hollywood system, studios were often highly controlling of the actors they had under contract, even to the extent of interfering with their private lives. Schary initially tried a little old-style manipulation with Rod, requesting he change his surname on the grounds it would cause confusion with two other studio contractees, Elizabeth Taylor and Robert Taylor. Rod refused — something that could have damaged his career 20 years earlier. But this was 1955, independent-minded actors were becoming the norm rather than the exception and MGM did not press the matter. After all, they already had a particular role in mind for him.

THE CATERED AFFAIR WAS AN ADAPTATION OF A TELEVISION play by Paddy Chayefsky, then the hottest writer in Hollywood due to the success of *Marty* (1955). *Marty* had been a Chayefsky television play that was turned into an Oscar-winning hit movie, prompting an explosion of studio films adapted from the small screen. MGM, in particular, began to embrace the new medium with the passionate intensity of a convert, putting a number of big-screen versions of television plays into production.

The Catered Affair was Chayefsky's attempt at domestic comedy, centering around a working-class Bronx housewife determined to give her daughter a splendid wedding whether she likes it or not. The project must have seemed like a sure thing to MGM: like *Marty*, it was steeped in then-trendy social realism, but it was also a feel-good comedy in the vein of an earlier Metro hit, *Father of the Bride* (1950). (Throwbacks to earlier successes were a frequent hallmark of the Schary regime.)

MGM certainly gave the picture deluxe treatment, assigning one of its best producers, Sam Zimbalist, to oversee it and allocating directing duties to Richard Brooks, coming off the highly successful *Blackboard Jungle* (1954). The screenwriter was Gore Vidal, then one of the leading TV writers in the country and Oscar-winners Bette Davis and *Marty*'s Ernest Borgnine were cast as the bride's parents; the studio's most popular young star, Debbie Reynolds, was selected to play the bride and another Oscar winner, Barry Fitzgerald, was given the role as the family lodger.

The one remaining important part was that of Reynolds' manly-yet-sensitive fiancé, who watches bewildered as Bette Davis takes over his wedding. It was originally announced that this part would be played by MGM contractee Leslie Nielsen, but Rod ended up getting the role instead, presumably on the strength of his Graziano test. Rod's radio experience and talent for mimicry ensured he had little trouble speaking in Bronx-ese.

The Catered Affair was a superb way for Rod to launch his MGM career: a potent role in a major production stacked with A-list talent in front of and behind the camera. He knew it and worked very hard on his performance.

"I recall how impressed everyone was with his American accent," remembers Gore Vidal. Also pleased was Richard Brooks, who later enthused that Rod "acts the way he is," adding that, "His principal asset, as an actor and a person, is the fact that he listens well to a director and other players. His actions are all normal to the scene and honest, particularly in a role which will permit him to exploit his own personality."

There was only one problem: the resulting movie was poor and not particularly liked by critics or the public; it received no Oscar nominations and *Variety* described its box-office fate as "a mild success." Rod and Reynolds at least received some excellent personal notices, the *Los Angeles Examiner* saying they were "so genuinely touching that they make the entire production most worthwhile."

Looking at the film today, audiences were not really wrong in staying away. *The Catered Affair* has its moments but is flawed at its center: it is fun to see vanity cause wealthy, happily married Spencer Tracy to waste his money in *Father of the Bride*, but not poverty-stricken, miserable Bette Davis here. Rod plays his scenes with tenderness and sensitivity and his accent is totally convincing; indeed, everyone in the cast is excellent, except for Davis, who — to this viewer, at least — gives one of her worst, most mannered performances and totally ruins the film. Fortunately for Rod, no one at MGM blamed the movie's failure on him and his next role for the studio was in an even more important project.

RAINTREE COUNTY WAS BASED ON THE BESTSELLING NOVEL BY Ross Lockridge Jr., which tells the life story of an Indiana man, John Wickliffe Shawnessy, in a series of flashbacks occasioned by the events of a single day in 1892. The novel had been kicking around MGM since the late '40s, when the studio announced a proposed adaptation starring Lana Turner and Robert Walker — but this fell through, partly because of negative publicity arising from Lockridge's suicide in 1948. The project was re-activated in the early 1950s, with Schary thinking the novel might form the basis of another *Gone with the Wind* (1939). (Part of the story involves Shawnessy's time as a Union soldier in the Civil War and his marriage to an unstable Southern beauty.)

Schary decided to give *Raintree County* the blockbuster treatment, with the lead roles allocated to one of Hollywood's most sought-after leading men, Montgomery Clift, and MGM's brightest star, Elizabeth Taylor. The film would be shot in widescreen and released on a "road show" basis (a method used for blockbusters in the 1950s that consisted of showing them in one city at a time, with reserved seating, higher ticket prices and an intermission). The budget was penciled in at $5 million, making it the most expensive US-based film in MGM's history.

There was a first-rate supporting part available for a young male actor, that of Garwood Jones, Shawnessy's rival in love and politics. Screenwriter Millard

Kaufman described Jones as, "The antithesis of Clift's character — aggressive, outgoing, he made bad jokes, he was terribly politically ambitious. This made a terribly good character when put against Clift's character who was sensitive, decent, almost plodding. [Jones] wasn't vicious or brutal or any of that. He was an antagonist but not a stereotypical American villain."

According to Kaufman, Rod actively pursued the role. "He did a rather smart thing, a truly Hollywood sense of interaction. He read the script — I don't know where he got it, he didn't get it from me, it was around the studio. He went to Dore Schary and said he'd like to play that part. Dore gave it to him. He actually got it himself. Dore was susceptible to that sort of thing — I guess you call it filmic romance. The stand-in goes on for the star who breaks her leg, that sort of thing... [Rod] had a great gift of brass. He knew what he wanted and he got it. Became a hell of a movie actor."

Filming started in April and took place in the studio and on location in Kentucky, Mississippi, Tennessee and Indiana. Five weeks into the shoot, Montgomery Clift crashed his car into a telegraph pole on the way home from a party, causing severe damage to his face. Shooting was postponed while Clift recovered; his teeth were reconstructed and his jaw was wired, rendering the left side of his face mostly immobile. Nonetheless, he improved sufficiently to go back to work and filming resumed on July 23.

The two stars on *Raintree County* ensured production was a colorful experience: Clift constantly battled his addiction to alcohol and painkillers and was found running naked through the streets on at least two occasions; he also burnt his hand one night after falling asleep holding a cigarette. Elizabeth Taylor was conducting an affair with Mike Todd while still married to Michael Wilding and fell ill during filming, requiring her to be hospitalized for a week. Rod had a quiet time of it comparatively, apart from the occasional drinking escapade with Lee Marvin. "I was little bit shy that this was my first big movie and I was the new kid on the block," he recalls.

By the time principal photography finished in October, the budget had blown out to $6 million. This, combined with a number of recent box-office flops (including *The Catered Affair*), meant MGM would show a loss for the first time in its corporate history at the end of 1956. The studio's new president, Joe Vogel, ended up sacking both Dore Schary and *Raintree County*'s producer, David Lewis.

After a long post-production process, including several re-shoots, *Raintree County* was launched with a *Gone with the Wind*-type premiere in Louisville, Kentucky, on October 2, 1957, attended by two planeloads of stars and press. Rod would have felt that at least he was on his way. However, critical reception to the movie was generally uninspired — "begins in tedium and ends, 168 minutes later, in apathy" (*Time*) — with Rod's performance barely mentioned. During the first few weeks of release box office was poor and it seemed MGM might have a disaster on its hands.

The studio arranged for the running time to be cut by 17 minutes and abandoned the road show policy. It worked and *Raintree County* ended up showing unexpected legs at the box office: by January 1958, *Variety* could report the movie's performance was "a happy surprise… Epic's not likely to come out on top but still won't mean such a big loss as feared earlier." The film ended up earning rentals of $6 million, making it the ninth-biggest earner of 1958.

To be frank, MGM was lucky not to take a bigger loss. *Raintree County* symbolizes much of Dore Schary's MGM — to wit, an attempt to duplicate an earlier success (in this case, *Gone with the Wind*), which, despite many talented people and interesting elements, never quite gels. The story is slow and the characters, despite their promise, are not terribly involving; the effect of Clift's accident is all too apparent on screen and Elizabeth Taylor does not do the possibilities of her role full justice. For all the hefty $6 million price tag, the production values are mediocre; there is also no sense of historical sweep, atmosphere or authenticity and the photography never comes to life beyond looking picture-book pretty.

Rod's performance is an interesting one. His character operates as an effective counter-point to Clift's, but Rod perhaps then lacked the experience and/or the genuine mischievous flair to make the most of the part. Rod did not generally excel in unsympathetic roles, although one feels that a few years later he would have made a better fist of it. It's not a poor performance, but it is a run-of-the-mill one.

AFTER FINISHING *RAINTREE COUNTY,* ROD SPENT THE NEXT few months idle under his MGM contract. His regular paychecks enabled him to move into a house at Malibu Beach, which he shared with Bob Walker, a casting director who had become a close friend, and Jeff Richards, another actor under contract to the studio. An up-and-coming young performer called Charles Bronson lived with them for a period and one of their neighbors was Russ Tamblyn. "We liked to party, I can tell you that," chuckles Tamblyn.

Living on the beach enabled Rod to indulge his passion for swimming and sailing. Later on he took up archery and would go hunting for game in the wooded area around Mulholland Drive. He also tried his hand at the two main networking sports in Hollywood, tennis and golf; he was never that comfortable with the latter, but became highly adept at the former. And, of course, there were plenty of parties and women to keep him busy.

As a high-profile Australian actor in Los Angeles, Rod inevitably received numerous visitors from home passing through. Two always welcome were John Saul and Georgie Sterling, who visited in the late '50s. Indeed, on the basis of

Rod's enthusiasm for Saul's work, Bob Walker tried to get the director to move to Hollywood permanently; Saul declined, but he continued to offer support and advice for his most famous pupil until his death in 1979.

Rod was also visited during production of *Raintree County* by Charles Tingwell, stopping off in Los Angeles en route to England. He remembers Rod's girlfriend at the time was Nikki Schenck, daughter of Nicholas Schenck, the former president of MGM and still a power behind the throne. Tingwell says Rod did everything to make him and his wife feel welcome, taking them out to dinner and introducing them to people; Rod even got his old friend some work, helping Tingwell get cast in an episode of *Studio 57*. Tingwell later wrote in his memoirs that Rod was "a delight" at this stage, but felt he might already be "becoming part of the Hollywood myth, the whole star thing, a little bit."

By now, Rod wanted more than just to be just a working actor — he wanted to be a star. He said he wanted to "get up there with a couple of stars I used to dream about when I was trying to get my foot on the first rung of the ladder back in Sydney — Brando and Clift."

In the months leading up to *Raintree County*'s release, it seemed Rod's dreams might become a reality. In March 1957 the actor was listed by the Motion Picture Export Association as a youngster with "star potential," along with Anthony Perkins, Paul Newman, Joanne Woodward, Dennis Hopper, John Saxon and Leslie Nielsen. MGM were making positive noises about its star-building program and Rod was mentioned as a top contender to play the second lead in a TV series based on the film *Northwest Passage* (1940). An article on the young actor in the fan magazine *Photoplay* pictured him as a name in the making. "With some first-rate pictures behind him and poised on the brink of further successes, Rod Taylor is earnestly and happily on his way. Whatever fortune, a notoriously fickle dame, has in store for him, no one can tell, least of all Rod. One thing may be said with certainty: he'll keep on giving his career the old college try, like the good Aussie he is."

However, Rod lost out on the *Northwest Passage* (1958–59) role to another MGM contractee, Don Burnett, and his performance in *Raintree County* was not the breakthrough he had hoped for. MGM became embroiled in a series of proxy attacks from various forces hostile to the studio and it became clear they had no plans in mind for the young actor.

Even though Rod was earning a regular income whether he worked or not, he would have been concerned about remaining inactive for too long. Not for the last time in his career, he decided to take charge and had Melnick renegotiate his contract: in July 1957 it was announced that Rod's seven-year MGM deal was now a five-year non-exclusive one, enabling him to take jobs outside the studio. It gave Rod the best of both worlds: he did not have to fully abandon the safety of the MGM "nest," but he also had a greater degree of control over his own career.

FROM 1957–59 ROD WORKED MOSTLY ON TELEVISION, IN LOW-budget films or for independent producers. These years could be roughly described as Rod's "secondary lead" phase, as he specialized in playing either romantic leads for a female protagonist (*Step Down to Terror*, "The Best House in the Valley") or the best friend of the male hero ("The Great Gatsby," "The Long March").

Although Rod was a long way from the A-list at this stage, he had accumulated some money and confidence and could afford to be reasonably selective. For instance, he never guest-starred on an episode of a regular dramatic TV series, only in anthologies, which were slightly more prestigious and gave him a greater chance to shine. He even turned down offers to star in shows (one of them apparently *Maverick*), because he had his eye on becoming a film star and did not want to be tied down to a long-term television commitment. "I was offered certain things but held out in a kind of long-range determination that it was better to take good parts even if they were little ones," claimed Rod later.

There is no better example of this approach than *Separate Tables* (1958), an adaptation of Terence Rattigan's play about the lives and loves of the inhabitants of a seaside boarding house in England. Rod played a medical student living in sin with his girlfriend (Audrey Dalton), whose relationship operates as a sort of "D plot" to the main action. Although his role was only small, the film was a terrific one to be associated with: Rattigan himself worked on the script; Delbert Mann directed; the stars were Burt Lancaster (who also produced), Rita Hayworth, Deborah Kerr and David Niven; and the support line-up consisted of the cream of English acting talent — Cathleen Nesbitt, Gladys Cooper, Wendy Hiller and Felix Aylmer. (Sheridan Morley later described *Separate Tables* as "the last great stand of the Hollywood English." Rod was one of the few non-Englishmen in the cast, though as an Australian presumably he was close enough.) He received a fee of $7,000, plus the considerable prestige of being in a movie that received excellent reviews, several Oscars and a healthy box office of $2.7 million.

Of course, films like *Separate Tables* did not come along every day. But if a role was not prestigious then it could at least help establish Rod as a heartthrob. *Step Down to Terror* (1958) was a low-budget, undistinguished remake of Hitchcock's *Shadow of a Doubt* (1943), about a smooth-talking widow-killer who returns to his hometown and arouses the suspicions of his adoring niece. Rod played an investigating cop, the niece's love interest, played by Macdonald Carey in the Hitchcock version.

Rod is very much a handsome male prop in *Step Down to Terror*: he falls in love with the heroine and thinks of marrying her after only one meeting and manages to save the day at the end. Nonetheless, it was polished, accomplished work: *The Hollywood Reporter* correctly describes Rod as "an attractive personality and you're glad to see the heroine fall in love with him."

Most of Rod's television roles around this time were in a similar vein: he romanced Margaret O'Brien in "The Story of Margery Reardon" and "The Young Years," Kim Hunter in "Early to Die," Polly Bergen in "The Best House in the Valley," and Nina Foch in "Image of Fear." Still, they put food on the table, gave him experience and raised his profile. Occasionally, he even got the chance for something meatier, as proved by the performances he gave on *Playhouse 90* (1957–60), perhaps the greatest live drama show from television's "Golden Age."

Rod featured in five *Playhouse 90s*, each of them memorable, each of them offering him the chance to do something different as an actor. In "Verdict of Three," he plays a mother's boy who serves on a jury along with Angela Lansbury; in "The Great Gatsby," he is Nick Carraway, best friend of the title character (Robert Ryan); in "The Long March," he is the best friend of an easygoing officer (Jack Carson), whose methods clash with those of his superior (Sterling Hayden); in "The Raider," he portrays an idealistic board member caught up in a proxy fight; in "Misalliance," a madcap pilot.

Rod's work in all these shows is superb. In particular, his performances are the best thing about both "The Great Gatsby" and "The Long March," outshining his better-known co-stars. Interestingly, both these stories had Rod playing characters who, while technically not the leads, form the focus of the drama, with others battling over his "soul."

Playhouse 90 went to air live, which led to some stressful moments on occasion. Shirley Knight remembers one incident in particular during the making of "The Long March": "Jack Carson fell ill during the live broadcast due to some kind of medication. As a result he cut about five minutes out of a scene with Sterling Hayden. The producer, Fred Coe, came to Rod and I and asked us to add time to our scene and to keep going until the assistant director gave us a signal to stop. It was a scene where he told me that my husband had died. We added several minutes with me crying a great deal and his comforting me, etc. After the broadcast everyone came over to thank us, including Jack Carson. It seems they felt the scene had been better with the added dialogue. During the entire process of rehearsing and performing I admired Mr. Taylor. Both for his kindness to me and his professionalism as a performer."

For me, the best of Rod's *Playhouse 90s* was "The Raider," a splendid drama in which Rod plays a board member of a company (run by Frank Lovejoy) which comes under attack from a corporate pirate (Paul Douglas). Screenwriter Loring Mandel recalls "a very interesting dynamic" amongst the cast during the rehearsal period.

"Paul Douglas, who plays the raider, was not well. He was within, I guess, 6 to 8 months of dying when he did this. And I think he must have been quite sick. He had a very distended abdomen and was wearing a Hawaiian shirt at rehearsal to cover it up. He was also drinking during rehearsal; he hid a bottle of vodka in the corridor. He was losing energy quickly; after an hour or two, he would go out to the corridor, have a couple of drinks and come back re-energized.

"Frank Lovejoy was a man who was talking to his psychiatrist about the script almost daily and coming into rehearsal with a lot of questions. The first half hour of every rehearsal was [director] Frank Schaffner getting Lovejoy to the point where we could rehearse. During that time Paul Douglas was getting angrier and angrier so there was hostility between the two. Rod Taylor was very close to Paul Douglas and very anxious to defend Paul Douglas against Frank Lovejoy. There was one point at rehearsal where it almost came to blows between Lovejoy and Rod Taylor. It did result in some added tension in the play, but it was unfortunate it happened that way."

"The Raider" is television art at its very finest. Mandel's script is uncompromising and excellent, full of first-rate lines and interesting characters; it is also extremely well directed by Schaeffner (who also did "The Great Gatsby" with Rod and later went on to make *Patton* [1970]). The story is not a case of simple goodies vs. baddies, but characters who continually defy audience expectations: tough corporate raider Ford turns out to have a disastrous home life; a company spy reveals his dignity; the apparently principled chairman has rorted his company for millions. Smart, unpredictable and brilliantly acted, "The Raider" is a worthy example of the Golden Years of Television and one of the best things that Rod ever did; it is a shame it is not better known.

Rod was turning in consistently strong work and it was being noticed at the big end of town. Howard Hawks considered the actor for the role eventually played by Ricky Nelson in *Rio Bravo* (1959) and Alfred Hitchcock contemplated using him in John Gavin's part in *Psycho* (1960). In September 1959, *Variety* listed Rod as one of the rising stars in the industry, along with Carolyn Jones, Diane Baker, Joan Blackman, Dina Merrill, Luana Patten, Jill St. John, Carol Lynley, Robert Evans, Stuart Whitman, Troy Donahue and Cliff Robertson. MGM finally took notice and came through with an offer, recalling Rod for the romantic comedy *Ask Any Girl*. It was only a support part, but a significant one, as it was the first time Rod was really noticed in feature films.

ASK ANY GIRL WAS ONE OF THOSE BRIGHT COMEDIES THAT flourished in the '50s and early '60s about career girls living in New York who try to bag a husband without losing their virginity. The girl here was Shirley MacLaine, out to nab playboy Gig Young with the help of his brother (David Niven); Rod had the support role as a lecherous businessman who falsely pledges love to MacLaine in order to get her into bed.

By today's standards, *Ask Any Girl* is a very sexist movie: MacLaine gets two jobs on the basis of personal appearance and is sexually harassed at work; the majority of male characters are obsessed with sex and the majority of women fixated on getting husbands. But if you can set that aside it is a cheery, fun picture; producer Joe Pasternak was a dab hand in colorful escapist entertainment and MacLaine is extremely appealing; give the heroine a career and a sex life and you could remake the story easily today. The film earned an estimated $2 million at the box office and was even selected to play at the Berlin Film Festival — admittedly only one other American film was submitted, but Shirley MacLaine still picked up an award there for Best Actress.

Romantic comedies often provide a great platform for supporting actors to shine; Rod's role in *Ask Any Girl* was such an opportunity and the actor took it with both hands, giving a stand-out performance. Whether attempting to seduce MacLaine with wolf-ish sincerity or doing pratfalls, Rod is superb and steals the picture from underneath everyone's nose.

The critics noticed, too; although Rod had received some good reviews before, *Ask Any Girl* earned him raves: "Moves… Rod Taylor into the front rank of comedians" (*The Hollywood Reporter*); "shows a comedy talent he hasn't had much chance to display in his career to date" (*Daily Variety*); "as an actor he's worth marking; he's different" (*Los Angeles Times*); "establishes a place for himself with this performance… impresses with his flair for subtle shading and restrained humour. An asset to any picture, this splendid actor" (*Los Angeles Examiner*).

More specifically, *Ask Any Girl* put Rod's name into the minds of MGM executives looking for someone to play the lead in a new science-fiction film being made at the studio.

CHAPTER 5

"No one had ever accused Taylor of being reassuring."

BECOMING A STAR (1959–1961)

THE DEBUT NOVEL OF HG WELLS, *THE TIME MACHINE* WAS THE story of an unnamed scientist ("The Time Traveller") who, in 1895, invents a device that carries him forward in time to the year 802,701. He finds Earth has become a strange world populated by two different species, both descendants of humans: the passive, peace-loving Eloi and their predators, the cannibalistic, underground-dwelling Morlocks. The Time Traveller saves the life of one of the Eloi, a girl called Weena and befriends her. The Morlocks steal the time machine, but the Time Traveller manages to retrieve it after a series of adventures, one of which results in Weena's disappearance (and presumed death). He travels further into the future to discover that the Earth will become a dying planet inhabited by large giant crabs, before returning home to tell his tale.

In the 1950s plans for a big-screen adaptation of the novel came about through the efforts of George Pal, perhaps the leading science-fiction filmmaker of his day. The Hungarian-born Pal trained as an architect before entering the European film industry in the 1920s, working as a cartoonist, then moving to Hollywood, where he won a special Oscar in 1943 for his "Puppetoon" shorts of animated puppet figures. He started producing live-action features at Paramount, including *Destination Moon* (1950), *When Worlds Collide* (1951) and an adaptation of Wells' *War of the Worlds* (1953). The Wells estate liked what Pal had done with *War of the Worlds* and offered him the rights to any other story by the author; Pal chose *The Time Machine*, which had been one of his favorite books as a child.

The project commenced under great secrecy, with Pal ordering screenwriter David Duncan to work from home (the producer had become paranoid about other filmmakers stealing his ideas ever since *Destination Moon* had been beaten to the cinemas by a quick knock-off, *Rocketship X-M* [1951]). Pal and Duncan contemplated updating Wells' story to a contemporary setting, but eventually decided against it. They did change the Time Traveller's voyages to incorporate

World War I and World War II — Pal believed that if the story encompassed events the audience knew would happen, Wells' future predictions would seem more plausible.

Duncan's script made a number of other changes to the novel, such as giving the Time Traveller a name, "George" (Wells' middle name — and various hints were dropped in the script that the character was meant to be HG Wells himself) and a friend, Filby, whose descendants would run into the Time Traveller over the years. Duncan also toned down the book's anti-capitalist theme: in the novel, the Morlocks were originally forced to go underground as workers for the ruling class Eloi — but in the screenplay version it's stated they chose to go underground, thereby making their evolution into horrible creatures their own fault. In addition, there was a happier ending, with the Eloi rising in revolt to defeat the Morlocks and Weena surviving the final attack to be reunited with the Time Traveller.

Plans to make the film hit a major hurdle in 1955, when Paramount became disenchanted with science fiction and parted ways with George Pal. The film-maker subsequently announced he would make *The Time Machine* independently, but raising funds proved tricky. "We went to every studio and every executive we knew," he said later. "No one wanted to make it."

In the interim, Pal made a deal with MGM to produce and direct the musi-cal fantasy *tom thumb* (1958). This was released to critical and financial acclaim and MGM head of production Sol Siegel agreed to finance *The Time Machine* — provided it could be done in 29 shooting days on a budget of $800,000. This meant that if Pal wanted to use the special effects and design elements he envi-sioned, he would have to scrimp and save when it came to casting.

George, the Time Traveller, was described in David Duncan's script as "one of those men who are too clever to be believed, a man of subtle reserve, of ingenu-ity in ambush." Pal originally considered a number of middle-aged British actors for the role, including David Niven, Paul Scofield, Michael Rennie and James Mason. After all, the Time Traveller describes himself in the book as "not a young man" and middle-aged British actors were commonly found playing the lead in science-fiction/fantasy movies of the time (e.g. *The Lost World* [1960], *Journey to the Center of the Earth* [1959]). Eventually, however, Pal changed his thinking and ended up going with the younger, Australian Rod Taylor.

It was an inspired decision. Not only could Rod perform in an English accent and handle the physical requirements of the part, his youth would give the char-acter a greater sense of energy and idealism. The fact that Rod was under contract to MGM also meant he was cheap. (Apparently Pal also considered George Hamilton, another young actor then under contract to MGM.)

One would think most actors would leap at the chance to star in a feature, but Rod did not accept the role immediately. After all, science fiction was then something of a leading man ghetto, a place where stars went at the end of their careers, not the beginning (Hugh Marlowe in *World Without End*, for instance). Rod also may have been disappointed at the prospect of making his star debut as a nerdy British scientist rather than someone more rugged.

However, Pal talked Rod around. He told the actor he did not want to make a science-fiction picture but "an HG Wells picture." "There are areas you can help me and areas where I can be of help to you," said Pal, promising Rod the opportunity to collaborate closely, "rather than just coming to work and going home."

Once Rod thought about the project a bit more, he began to realize he could really make something of the role. Why couldn't, he reasoned, the Time Traveller "have been strong, romantic and athletic, as well as a brilliant scientist?" Rod always said that it was the "ballsiness" of George, as he played him, "combined with being highly intellectual, which sold the character."

Filming began on the MGM backlot on May 25, 1959. A number of months earlier, it appeared Pal's fears of a cheap knock-off were going to be realized when producer Benedict Bogeaus announced plans for his own version of *The Time Machine*, starring Joseph Cotten in the lead. However, MGM threatened legal action and no rival film was ever made.

Perhaps the most important design element in *The Time Machine* would be the time machine itself. The description of it given in Wells' book was vague, so Bill Ferrari, the art director, came up with the idea of basing the machine on a turn-of-the-century barber chair combined with a sled; he added the controls in front and a big, radar-like wheel at the back to indicate movement. The result was a memorable creation, for many the highlight of the film — although Rod later claimed he "felt god-damned silly sitting there in that antique contraption with lights going on and off... emoting like the devil and supposedly travelling like hell and you aren't even moving a bloody inch."

Cinematographer Paul Vogel worked out a lighting scheme to indicate the advance of time as the machine travels into the future. He built a seven-foot circular shutter and mounted it in front of each arc used to light the scene. These disks were divided into four segments: one was left clear (to indicate daylight scenes), one used a pink gel (to indicate dawn), one employed amber (for dusk) and one utilized blue (for night). In order to simulate the movement of the sun through the roof of the Time Traveller's greenhouse, the disks were synchronized on the shutter rotating at varying speeds. For the scene where the Time Traveller speeds up the machine so that each day becomes a mere flicker, the circular shutters were converted so they were composed only of alternating black-and-white segments. For the sequence where Rod is entombed in rock, Vogel employed blue-backed traveling mattes. The vision of the rocks melting away was achieved through a combination of real rocks and animation.

The Morlocks were played by stuntmen in rubber suits who wore green latex skin and masks fitted with electrical eyes, courtesy of makeup artist William

Tuttle. Special effects were prepared by Project Unlimited, a company owned by Wah Chang and Gene Warren Sr., who had worked for Pal on *tom thumb* and the Puppetoons. One of their tricks included the destruction of London by volcanic eruption: the lava was made out of a combination of chunks of burning cork and oatmeal that had been dyed red. The oatmeal caused a powerful stench on set at times — once it was left to ferment over the weekend, giving the crew a nasty shock when they arrived at work on Monday.

The complexity of these and other effects meant that although principal photography on *The Time Machine* finished in mid-1959, it was not released until August 1960. For most of that time, one gets the impression the film was very much made under the radar at MGM: for instance, a double-page ad in *Variety* at the beginning of 1960 promoting the studio's upcoming releases for that year did not even list the film. By June, however, Metro realized they had something special on their hands — so special, they even announced plans to make a sequel before the film had come out. Their confidence was proved justified when *The Time Machine* hit cinemas and was received with a torrent of acclaim: "Pal has done a remarkable job... with this portrayal, Taylor definitely establishes himself as one of the premium young talents on today's screen. His performance is a gem of straightforwardness, with just the proper sensitivity and animation." (*Variety*) "A deluxe edition of a literary classic... Rod Taylor has the intelligence and vigor for the man of science." (*The Hollywood Reporter*) "Rod Taylor gives an excellent performance, handling his role with just the right amount of conviction and humor" (*New York Journal-American*).

By the end of 1960, *Variety* estimated *The Time Machine* had earned $1.35 million in rentals at the box office; this put the film well down on the list of highest-grossers of the year (for instance, the little-remembered *The Gazebo* [1959] and *Toby Tyler* [1959] both made more money), but meant it was highly profitable. The movie went on to win the Oscar for Best Special Effects and has continued to delight audiences ever since.

And deservedly so, for *The Time Machine* is a true classic, a movie that improves with age. The time machine itself is a fabulous Victorian invention, backed up by imaginative special effects and photography. Support performances are strong, especially from Yvette Mimieux (as Weena), who invests her role with an ethereal quality, and the likeable Alan Young (Filby). A captivating feeling of melancholy and loss is felt throughout the film, giving it unexpected power; the sequence in London on the verge of World War III is particularly potent, as is Russell Garcia's haunting score. Direction and scripting are intelligent, even though the plot does have some unanswered questions of logic typical of those faced by most time travel films. (For instance, one cannot help but wonder what sort of world Rod's character goes off to join at the end of the film — now that he has taken away the Elois' food supply and re-introduced them to violence!)

Last, but not least, a great deal of the success of *The Time Machine* comes from the performance of Rod Taylor. He inhabits his part with energy, warmth and complete conviction, being particularly strong in his scenes with Mimieux and Young. He is totally believable both as a man of thought and a man of action — or, as Rod put it, a combination of "highly intellectual" and "ballsiness."

One of the best analyses of Rod's performance in the film — indeed, one of the best analyses of the actor ever — comes from Bill Warren in his book on science-fiction movies, *Keep Watching the Skies*: "Taylor is hardly a Victorian type and seems far too ruggedly masculine to embody the scientific tinkerer of the novel. But as George, he's surprisingly sensitive to his fellow players. We can imagine his being devoted to Alan Young far more easily that we can Young's being devoted to him. Although the film is not quite a love story — Taylor's interest in Mimieux seems rather avuncular — romanticism as an approach to life is evident in Taylor's playing. Perhaps passionate love was intended, but it isn't really there in the film — and the movie is the better for it. Taylor doesn't sweep Mimieux off her feet; he's just more *alive* than anyone else around. She's drawn to his caring the way a cat is drawn to a spot of sunlight: there's more warmth there. And despite what seems almost like an effort on Taylor's part in other films at times to suppress it, his biggest strength as an actor is precisely this warmth. Taylor is likeable, friendly and open; these qualities make his Time Traveller a memorable character. George is not just a Victorian visiting the future, he is Everyman and perhaps more period feeling would have lessened this. His performance is literally time-less."

For Rod, perhaps the most important review came from his former teacher, Georgie Sterling, who considers *The Time Machine* the best thing he ever did. "I thought he was absolutely first class in that and they keep repeating it monotonously. That really put him on the map. They still keep playing it because he really was excellent, he *was* that character. And it's not an easy play; it's not an easy character. But he tried to carry out everything that we told him and he did it very successfully, so we were very proud of that, I can tell you. We both preened ourselves and said, 'There goes our pupil.' Wonderful — it was great."

MGM announced *Return of the Time Machine* as part of its slate in 1961, with both Rod and Mimieux to reprise their roles. However, Pal was too busy making other films to lock down a script and no sequel eventuated. As the years passed and Rod's star rose, the actor became less enthusiastic about the prospect of stepping back in the time machine. In 1964 he told his fan club that he liked to vary his movies and did not agree "with doing sequels too close together." As Rod's career went into decline over the years, however, he became more amenable to the idea and by the 1970s Pal had a screenplay ready to go. Unfortunately, they were unable to finance production prior to Pal's death in 1980.

A sequel of a kind did appear in 1992 as part of a 50-minute documentary hosted by Rod on time travel in the movies, *Time Machine: The Journey Back*. The documentary features a self-contained five-minute scene that serves as an "epilogue" to the 1960 film, in which George returns to 1916 to persuade Filby to leave with him in the time machine. It is a touching scene with some solid performances, although the fact that all the action takes place in one room in continuous time means it feels slightly stagy. Nonetheless, Rod was so inspired by the experience that he, Young and director Clyde Lucas tried to get financing for a feature-length sequel; unfortunately, they were unsuccessful.

A new version of *The Time Machine* was released in 2002, starring another Australian actor, Guy Pearce, in the lead. Alan Young had a cameo in this film, which *Variety* said "devolves creatively as it advances dramatically." For most movie fans, the Rod Taylor *Time Machine* remains *the* big-screen *Time Machine*.

SINCE *THE TIME MACHINE* WAS SHOT IN MID-1959 BUT NOT released until a year later, any benefits accruing to Rod from starring in it took a while to eventuate. Twenty or even ten years earlier MGM would have consolidated his new standing by promptly casting him in a series of follow-up roles; however, the studio's productivity was at a low ebb at this stage, with their focus being on a handful of expensive blockbusters such as *Ben-Hur* (1959) and *Mutiny on the Bounty* (1962). In addition, two other handsome young male actors had come under contract to Metro, George Peppard and George Hamilton, both fresh off the prestigious *Home from the Hill* (1959) and they seemed to rank ahead of Rod in the in-house pecking order when it came to decent parts.

Rod's career was in an odd limbo. His name was mentioned in association with some projects that were never made (*Country of the Blind, Shark Bait*) as well as some eventually made with other actors (*The Pleasure of His Company* [1961] and a Broadway play, *The Gang's All Here*). Fortunately, Rod was able to keep busy on television anthology series, where he continued to turn out first-class work. Some of his roles, admittedly, required him to be little more than a handsome male prop for the female star — e.g. "Portrait of Sal" (Carolyn Jones), "Early to Die" (Kim Hunter) — but there were several parts he could really get his teeth into.

In particular, he shone as a madcap pilot in "Misalliance" for *Playhouse 90*, an adaptation of the Shaw play he had performed on stage in Sydney. Rod more than held his own in a line-up that included Robert Morley, Claire Bloom, Siobhan McKenna and Patrick Macnee — no mean feat. The show's producer, John Houseman, described the experience as being more like a stage performance than a television show because the cast "all behaved in the great tradition of British actors — they quarrelled, gossiped, back-bit and bitched incessantly, but performed brilliantly." Rod was the only member of the principal cast who was not British, but as an Australian he was presumably close enough. *Variety* praised the production as "one of the happiest farces to hit TV in a long time" in which Rod was "excellent."

Rod also gave an outstanding performance in "And When the Skies Were Open," a top-notch episode of *The Twilight Zone* (1959–64). He plays one of three astronauts who, on their return from a space flight, find themselves literally disappearing off the face of the Earth. It is a wonderful example of television, well written (by Rod Serling himself) and superbly acted, with a remarkable feeling of eeriness throughout. Marc Scott Zicree in *The Twilight Zone Companion* correctly describes Rod's work as "intelligent, appealing and powerful. His is a most difficult task, to make us believe that the impossible is happening — and he succeeds admirably."

A further triumph was "Capital Gains" for *Goodyear Theatre* (1957–60), which starred Rod as a TV writer who tries to get out of debt by forming himself into a company. Rod is likeable and enthusiastic as the writer: insecure, snappy and highly susceptible to flattery — a familiar version of the species. The episode demonstrates Rod's flair for high comedy once again and makes his later distaste for the genre all the more bewildering.

In contrast, his role in "Thunder in the Night" for *Westinghouse Desilu Playhouse* (1958–60) was nowhere near as good — in fact, it was a thankless, throwaway part (as an American agent murdered by spies), Rod's least impressive one since his first year in Hollywood. However, the show offered one major perk: it was filmed in Italy, giving Rod a free trip overseas. During his Italian stopover, Rod met Anita Ekberg, the buxom Swedish film star of *War and Peace* (1956) and *Artists and Models* (1956), who had recently relocated to Rome, where she was to make *La Dolce Vita* (1960). Anita and Rod hit it off and began a highly publicized romance which lasted on and off for the next few years.

The relationship was a passionate, volatile one; Rod described it later as like "living next to a powder keg." A story to illustrate: the two of them were at a bar one day when Ekberg threw a drink in Rod's face. Rod claimed he "didn't want to hit her" in response so he picked her up and threw her right over the bar. Rod says the starlet simply sat on the floor and laughed. "I ask you: what can you do with a dame like that?"

Another time Rod was filming in San Francisco when Ekberg drove up in a Rolls-Royce and announced she had brought her boyfriend a present. Rod looked in the back of the car and saw "the chauffeur, a little guy, cowering on the seat while a damn great monkey with a blue bottom clambered all over him." Anita had brought Rod a monkey as a gift. (He asked her to return it.)

A famous girlfriend can sometimes mean as much, if not more, to a young actor's career than a good movie. Anita Ekberg was news and Rod's romance with her greatly lifted his profile in Hollywood. All he needed now was another strong role to consolidate it.

EVER SINCE *CHEYENNE,* PRODUCERS HAD BEEN INTERESTED in getting Rod to star in a regular television series, but he had only been willing to commit to anthologies. However, by 1960, Rod had become a little frustrated at the progress of his career. As one fan magazine writer put it, after five years in Hollywood "his surge to fame never got beyond the fizzle stage." MGM management did not seem that interested in promoting him and, apart from *The Time Machine* and *Ask Any Girl,* television was where he had been doing his best work anyway.

So, Rod and Wilt Melnick decided it was worth seeing what small-screen offers were out there. According to *TV Guide,* they set terms they thought prohibitive but CBS, Revue, ABC and 20th Century-Fox all wanted Rod for pilots. One of these was *Hong Kong* over at Fox. It was the show which, combined with the eventual release of *The Time Machine,* was to make Rod Taylor a star.

Fox was making *Hong Kong* for the ABC network, then enjoying success with a number of action series set in exotic locations, such as *Hawaiian Eye* (1959–63) and *Adventures in Paradise* (1959–62). *Hong Kong* slotted firmly into that genre, centering around the adventures of Glenn Evans, an American newspaper correspondent based in the title city who encounters various murderers, femme fatales, communists, gangsters, etc., while occasionally writing stories for his paper. He is helped/hindered by his friend, the local (British) chief of police, and drinks in a bar, Tully's, run by another expatriate American.

Evans is a sophisticated character, capable of smooth-talking women and understanding the intricacies of international politics, yet still tough enough to be able to beat up bad guys. In other words, a natural for Rod Taylor, who later described Evans as: "Not the usually muscular moron who solves everything with either his fists or an uncanny flash of intuition never properly motivated. Instead, he is a professional newsman, practically a prototype of the foreign correspondents who actually work right now within the borders of the British colony. He works hard, shrewdly and mainly alone. He cultivates his contacts carefully. Some of these he respects greatly and some not at all. But he keeps his promises, violates no confidences, reveals no sources. His character and reputation are his main assets. He is not highly paid, seldom had more than adequate funds, lives simply, drinks a bit but never too much, is unmarried and is often cynical about women in general."

The show's executive producer, William Self, claims Rod was their first choice for the part. "He wasn't a big star but he was a very good actor, had a good reputation and seemed to be on the rise," says Self.

Nonetheless, Rod remained cautious about signing on. He was finally persuaded by two things: the fact that Ida Lupino was going to be one of the two permanent directors ("She is a real gem," Rod claimed) and a large salary: $3,750 per episode, plus 15% of the profits.

Rod filmed a 30-minute pilot for *Hong Kong* in March 1960. At this time, individual sponsors could still finance an entire television series and a multi-millionaire entrepreneur, Henry J. Kaiser (who also backed *Maverick*), agreed to fund the show to the tune of $9 million. Kaiser had a proviso, though: he wanted *Hong Kong* to run for an hour and air on Wednesday nights at 7:30 p.m. against *Wagon Train* (1957-65), then one of the most popular shows in the country.

Fox agreed and started preparation for the series; the studio's overall head of production, Buddy Adler, excitedly proclaimed to the press that Rod had the potential to become "as big as Gardner McKay," the star of *Adventures in Paradise*.

However, problems then arose when both the Writers and Screen Actors Guild went on strike in Hollywood over the issue of residuals. The strikes lasted for a number of months, causing productions to halt all over town, including *Hong Kong*. At a loose end and knowing he had a guaranteed year's worth of work up his sleeve, Rod accepted an offer to make a film in Italy. The result was one of the most bizarre interludes of his career.

COLOSSUS AND THE AMAZON QUEEN WAS A "PEPLUM," A MOVIE genre known in English as "sword and sandal films" — stories about scantily-clad muscular men and nubile women fighting and romancing in the ancient world. *Variety* summarized their requirements as thus: "Color and wide-screen are musts, as are battles and orgies and other exploitable material, preferably a milk bath by the heroine."

Peplums had been around since the birth of cinema, but the international success of *Hercules* (1958), starring Steve Reeves, prompted a boom in the genre: sixteen peplums were made in Italy from 1952 to 1958, 200 between 1959 and 1964. Many of these were aimed at the foreign market; by 1961, it was estimated over 60% of peplums featured an American or British star, usually bodybuilders or actors whose careers were in decline.

Colossus and the Amazon Queen starred two imports: Rod and Ed Fury, a bodybuilder who had featured in such Z-grade masterpieces as *Wild Women of Wongo* (1958).

Rod had just starred in a feature film and was about to headline a TV series, both for major studios — why the need to do something called *Colossus and the Amazon Queen*? Two words: paid holiday. Rod's affair with Anita Ekberg was still going strong and the project gave him an all-expenses-paid trip to Italy.

The film tells the story of two Trojan War veterans, the fast-talking Pirro (Rod) and the muscular Glauco (Fury), recruited to guard the cargo of a ship headed for a secret island destination. The cargo turns out to be the ship's crew (including Pirro and Glauco), who have been sold into slavery to the Amazons, a civilization where the women have the military and political power and the men worry about housework and what they are going to wear. Pirro and Glauco end up romancing two local women and help the Amazons fight off some marauding pirates.

Rod later claimed the film was originally entitled *The Flavor of a Kiss*, based on "the worst script I'd ever seen. It was a drama, but a dreadful one. So I rewrote it — as a comedy. And then I refused to play in it unless they used my script, embellished by a host of beautiful Italian girls."

It should be pointed out that Rod is not credited for the screenplay of *Colossus and the Amazon Queen* (no one is, at least not on the film available in general release) and I have been unable to find any evidence outside the above quote confirming or disproving Rod's claim to have rewritten it. However, there may be something to it — Rod had been interested in screenwriting for a number of years, as evidenced by the treatment he provided to Lee Robinson and Chips Rafferty; and while the Hollywood method of filmmaking discouraged actors rewriting scripts, in Italy Rod was a bigger fish in a smaller pond and could throw his weight around a bit more.

As for turning the film into a comedy... it is hard to believe from the finished product that *Colossus and the Amazon Queen* was ever originally envisioned as a drama — but it should be noted that there were a number of even sillier peplums made around this time played totally straight. And the movie features a number of what would emerge by the end of the decade as recognizable Rod Taylor "themes" — to wit, it is a buddy movie and has plenty of adventure and fighting. So perhaps Rod did rewrite the screenplay.

Whatever the extent of Rod's creative contribution to *Colossus*, he was quick to disclaim responsibility for it in later years. In 1986 he claimed that he had tried to "hide that fiasco ever since" he made it, joking it was like "a porno" from out of his past.

Actually, Rod has nothing much to be embarrassed about; *Colossus* is certainly cheesy and amateurish, with some shocking continuity and a central thesis that many will find annoying (i.e. that women, no matter how strong and independent, can't help liking those cute guys). But it is all good-natured; the role-reversal gags give the film a lot of funny, albeit politically incorrect, humor and the cast really embrace the spirit of it all. Rod himself is in top form as the smart-aleck Pirro; it is a shame he could not have played more parts along these lines in Hollywood, for he had a real gift for broad comedy.

THE ACTORS' STRIKE EVENTUALLY ENDED, ENABLING ROD TO begin work on *Hong Kong* in October. Although the series was going to be mostly filmed on the Fox backlot in Hollywood, it was decided to shoot some second-unit footage in the real Hong Kong for a period beforehand. Rod took the opportunity to stop off in Australia on his way over, making his first visit home since 1954.

Since *The Time Machine* had not yet been released, Rod's visit received respectable, but not tremendous publicity (e.g. articles on page ten of the paper, as opposed to page one). While in town he made some pro-Australian comments that the local media like to hear from returning expats, mostly extolling the virtues of his homeland as a possible film location: "It is gradually seeping through to the American film industry that Australia is a good place to make films — it's much less expensive than America — and I think it will become more of a centre for filmmaking in the future."

Rod even announced plans to produce a movie in Australia himself, "probably in about 18 months' time" — a joint Australian and American venture directed by George Pal about the life of Captain James Cook. Rod claimed he would put up some of the money and play the title role.

Although this sounds like a sop for local reporters, in fact there was something to it: George Pal had been interested in a Captain Cook project since the 1950s — specifically, an adaptation of Paul McGinnis' novel, *Lost Eden*, from which various scripts were written. However, no film eventuated.

Rod went to Hong Kong for five weeks of filming, then returned to Los Angeles to start the series. Although Rod was the star of *Hong Kong*, the actor refused to concede this meant he had become an actual Hollywood "star." Indeed, he seems to have considered being the star of a television show something of a second-rate achievement. "Stars went out with Clark Gable, Spencer Tracy and Jean Harlow. I know a lot of gas station attendants who have landed in television and now are being called 'stars.' Leading actors maybe, but stars they aren't. The term 'star' doesn't mean anything anymore…

"People playing a role in a series have no mystery or glamour about them. We come into living rooms every week. The audience can reach us. They know us too well. Even if a so-called TV 'star' wanted to live up to the star billing off-camera it couldn't be done. We never have enough free time to begin with and it isn't economically feasible. Viewers are too sophisticated now to put up with actors walking around the streets with a pair of leopards on a leash."

Nonetheless, Rod realized that if the series went well it could take his career to the next level. "Big names aren't built by movies anymore. I figure I can build my name the best way by keeping high standards in this TV series. My work as an actor is important to me. I'm not just interested in being a star. It's getting a chance to pick and choose and work where I want and have a creative say in production. And I'm just as interested in being a good human being as I am in being a better actor… In acting you have a duty to the public. It's very important for me to feel I'm doing something worthwhile. I think this series is the thing and it's going to get better. I promise you that."

Hong Kong premiered on September 28, 1960. Viewing the first episode, the *New York Times* thought that although the show "trifles with credibility, it looks like another audience winner."

Early ratings were not strong, though, and the series underwent severe birth pains during its first few months. The role of Glenn's British police chief friend, portrayed by Alex Davion in the pilot, was taken over by Lloyd Bochner in the regular series. The character of Fong (Harold Fong), Glenn's houseboy, was written out after a few episodes, replaced by Inspector Ling (Gerald Jann). Jack Kruschen, who played Tully, the owner of Glenn Evan's regular drinking haunt, became dissatisfied with the size of his part and left the show; Evans started drinking at a restaurant run by Ching Mei (Mai Tai Sing).

In October, Roy Huggins, who had wanted Rod for *Maverick*, took over Fox's television division. He soon made his presence felt on *Hong Kong*, sacking the producer, ordering a new set to be constructed and clashing with the star and directors. Fox executive William Self says Huggins was "a very opinionated guy, very talented, but he seemed to rub people the wrong way sometimes."

Self admits dealing with Rod was also occasionally rocky throughout production of the series. "He was a little temperamental, a little difficult and it was my job to meet with him occasionally and say, 'What's the problem?' He was the star of a show and when you're the star of a show you become indispensable in your own mind and you probably are. But he was very professional, he was on time, knew his lines, but that's par for the course… A very good actor, a reliable fellow."

During the show's run, *TV Guide* did a cover story on Rod, which played up the rugged, he-man image the actor had begun to cultivate off-screen in Hollywood:

"In all his 14 years as an actor, no one had ever accused Taylor of being reassuring. He has no great reputation for one thing and strangers are suspect in Hollywood and all other provinces. In appearance Taylor is the antithesis of Robert Horton; he is unclean-cut. His face is mashed in, something like Popeye's, with a long shovel nose and an indelicately large, jutting chin. He has a pair of shoulders like a bull's. He drinks. His Hollywood career got going on his spiritual and physical resemblance to the prize fighter Rocky Graziano.

"Fortunately for Taylor, as a proper British gentleman when he chooses to be, he has an inner temperament to match his outward ruggedness, for he certainly would have come unsprung years ago without this integrity. His outbursts of temper are notorious, brief, loud, unprintable, frequent and quickly forgotten. At 20th Century-Fox the four-letter sound of Taylor's stack blowing at some production stupidity… is as much a part of the workaday atmosphere as the carpenter's hammer and attracts about as much notice… Naturally, his independence and the unabashed indifference with which he expresses it have created a number of Hollywood enemies, about whom he could not now care less."

A different point of view was offered by one of the show's writers, William Froug, who remembers Rod as "a friendly, self-effacing gentleman. Stars like that don't turn up very often."

Rod admitted people occasionally called him a "louse" on the set of *Hong Kong*, but argued that since he had a "piece of the action" on the show, whenever anything went wrong it concerned him personally. "And I chew out anybody who doesn't do his work as adequately as I am expected to do mine."

Despite his efforts, however, ratings remained low. Reviewing a November episode, "Jumping Dragon," *Variety* complained *Hong Kong* "lacks dramatic novelty or production imagination," adding that Rod's "gifted physical and thespic endowments" was "all that distinguishes it from at least half a dozen similar TV entries currently running... Taylor, an effective performer, deserves better."

To its credit, ABC tried to make the show work, giving it a one-off trial in a different timeslot in January over sponsors' objections; it was hoped viewers who stumbled upon the show would like it enough to watch again the next week. The trial rated well but there was no positive flow-on effect: the following week's episode rated 10.7, putting *Hong Kong* among the bottom 10 prime-time programs in the country. NBC briefly expressed interest in taking the series for the 1961–62 season, attracted by the $5–8 million worth of billings Kaiser represented, but ultimately decided against it. Despite winning a Golden Globe Award for Best Television Program, *Hong Kong* was axed by April.

Viewed today, *Hong Kong* is a perfectly enjoyable, junky piece of Hollywood exotica, very much in the tradition of Charlie Chan, *Casablanca* (1942) and *Soldier of Fortune* (1953). Rod is confident and winning in the lead, the storylines were adequate, the acting strong — it is surprising the series did not connect with the public. Perhaps the timeslot was too early in the evening for an adult adventure show; possibly its British colony setting did not blend entirely satisfactorily with its American "feel" (gangsters, high body count, etc.). However, the best episodes were highly entertaining and Rod is in top form as Glenn Evans: he would never be more perfectly cast in his entire career and his enjoyment in the part is infectious.

"It's a true-to-life role Rod plays in *Hong Kong*," confirmed Rod's mother at the time. "I know he likes it. It's not a bit out of character with him."

Rod took the show's axing hard. He believed that *Hong Kong* had a fan base larger than its ratings indicated, pointing to the thousands of letters written in protest at the cancellation. Nevertheless, *Hong Kong* was a growing experience for the young actor. He says he "learned to work in different areas" of acting, "to relax where I'd been tense." In particular, he learned how to put more of himself into a part, "to channel more of Rod Taylor and less of Glenn Evans into the show." In other words, be truthful. Rod: "You have to give people a chance to get to know you, or feel as though they do, through your characterisation. That means being completely open and revealing our particular personality traits. You can't be phoney about it because the audiences quickly see through any sham. When you're the main character in a continuing series, people begin to accept you. Almost as though you were a friend."

Indeed, it was *Hong Kong*, rather than *The Time Machine*, which established the Rod Taylor screen persona that would follow over the next two decades: the virile, sophisticated he-man, rough with men, sensitive with women.

On a personal level, Rod was linked romantically with several of his *Hong Kong* co-stars throughout the series' run, including Inger Stevens, Mai Tai Sing and Frances Nuyen — plus a young Japanese-American art student who served as an extra and later became his third wife, Carol Kikumura. In addition, he struck up a close friendship with the actor Marco Lopez, who had a small role in the episode "Love, Honor and Perish" and would go on to become Rod's stand-in, general aide and friend.

On a professional level, *Hong Kong* confirmed Rod in the eyes of Hollywood as a genuine leading man. As one writer pointed out, with the series, he had "cleared with one leap the chasm that separates, in Hollywood, the actors from the stars."

"For me, the whole jazz was great," agreed Rod. "The name and the face are known everywhere. I'm being offered better movie roles than I ever was before." Rod was even offered another television series, but he turned it down. "It was another one of those routine things, just like a dozen others."

Not only did Rod's market price for a feature film rise to $75,000, his own fan club was set up during the series run — managed by Liz Ploger until 1971, it produced a regular fan magazine (*Rod-lore*) which it distributed to various chapters throughout the world. Hedda Hopper listed Rod as one of the 21 most promising youngsters of 1961 and his name was now well established in the fan magazines. This description of him in *Photoplay* is an example of the sort of prose he inspired: "A breath of spring in a stale-air town. A man who can have fun and accept his responsibilities to his industry and his new home at the same time. He is a perfectionist in everything, even at getting stoned [drunk] and making a girl feel like she's the only one. He is handsome in the way the great stars have been handsome, with defects that dissolve through sheer charm. He is considered, by many of those who professionally criticize such things, to be the best of the young actors to come out our way. And his star will rise in Hollywood as surely as the sun will set this evening."

20th Century-Fox released *Hong Kong* into syndication in late 1961. Although only 26 episodes were made, within a few months it had been sold to fourteen countries. As Rod had a share of the profits, he did extremely well out of the series financially.

And there was no place *Hong Kong* was more popular in than Rod's home country. The show became the third most popular series to air in Australia in 1961 (after *Bonanza* and *The Untouchables*), with a weekly audience of 1,838,000 — this when the country's population was 10.5 million. For Australians who watched television at the time, Rod was as well known for *Hong Kong* as anything else he did.

AROUND THIS TIME, ROD BECAME INVOLVED IN THE SECOND classic of his career — the Disney cartoon *One Hundred and One Dalmatians* (1961). The basic premise of the film is well known: Pongo, a dalmatian, not only arranges to marry to the female of his choice, Perdita, but for his master, Roger Radcliff, to wed Perdita's pretty mistress. Perdita soon produces a number of puppies, attracting the attention of the evil Cruella De Ville, who wants to make a dalmatian fur coat. Cruella abducts the puppies, forcing Pongo and his friends to ride to the rescue.

This film featured two male heroes, Pongo and Roger Radcliff. According to the film's pressbook, the filmmakers decided that, of the two, Pongo should have the deeper voice, since in the story the dog is supreme and the people are the pets, who do the bidding "of their canine bosses." Ben Wright was hired to voice Roger Radcliffe, while the deeper-voiced Rod was cast as Pongo. Rod's Australian background seems to have helped him get the role: he was close enough to being English to fit into a story set in England, yet his Australian accent would provide an extra rugged dimension to the feisty dalmatian.

One Hundred and One Dalmatians is a joyful and quite brilliant film, holding attention from start to finish. Scary, exciting and hilarious, it was the last uncontested animated classic made during Walt Disney's lifetime. The voice work is excellent, including Rod's; with his radio background it is a shame he did not do more roles of this sort in Hollywood. The movie earned $6.2 million in its first year of release and since then has reaped a cumulative box-office take of more than $200 million, making it the most financially successful project Rod was ever associated with.

Rod might have gone one better had he been more amenable when asked by producer "Cubby" Broccoli to test for James Bond. Or at least so Rod claims: Broccoli does not mention Rod as a possible Bond in his memoirs. Nonetheless, the story could be true — the producer was considering a number of actors for the role throughout 1961 before Sean Connery was cast and Glenn Evans was a perfect audition piece for Bond. Rod says he refused to test, however, because he thought the part was "beneath" him.

"That was one of the greatest mistakes of my career!" he admitted later. "Every time a new Bond picture became a smash hit, I tore out my hair."

Instead, Rod chose to play another adventurer, Elizabethan navy man Sir Francis Drake, in the swashbuckler *Seven Seas to Calais*. This was one of a number of co-productions MGM was making in Italy in the early '60s, with predominantly Italian cast and crew but some American talent. The film was not in the class of *The Time Machine*, but Rod had the starring role and it provided the rising star with another all-expenses-paid trip to Italy to see Anita Ekberg. (Not that Rod was a one-woman man at the time: on his way over, he stopped off in London to visit Frances Nuyen.)

The role of Sir Francis Drake was very different to the sort of contemporary parts Rod had played in recent years and the actor was initially uncomfortable with the idea of portraying a character who wore ruffled sleeves and lace collars. But Rod gave them a try and found he "didn't look quite such an idiot" as he expected; he decided just to forget he was wearing them.

"I remembered, too, that Drake was something of an actor himself — a ham admittedly — but nonetheless an actor," said Rod. "He was also a human being, a man who took his boots off if they pinched him and padded around palaces in stockinged feet. If a lace ruff bothered him, he simply ripped it off.

"Once into the skin of Drake, other ideas came naturally. We were at sea off Salerno, Italy, for example, when the sails of the Golden Hind were fouled up and the crew was unable to bring them down. I couldn't imagine a fine sailor like Drake just standing by watching without doing anything, so I jumped into the action and hauled on the rope with the crew. And that's the way you'll see it in the film."

The juvenile lead in *Seven Seas to Calais* was Keith Michell, another Australian actor who had made good internationally. (He, too, had an Olivier connection, having won a scholarship to study in London by auditioning for the Old Vic during its 1948 tour.) Michell enjoyed working with Rod, describing him as a "dinky-di Oz."

"He always seemed to be out on the tiles with Anita Ekberg and a Hollywoodian-type entourage," says Michell. "He certainly seemed to enjoy life to the full but it was a bit too hectic for me!

"Once he got himself beaten up, bless him, I think his stuntman buddy was involved and filming had to be delayed a couple of days. There was a press report [in Italian] in which I got the blame for hitting him! All very well but the film Mafia boys were after insurance money and this release made me legally responsible for stopping work of a film. London lawyers had to be consulted!

"I imagine it was impossible not to like Rod. He taught me a lot. How to swear profusely in Italian for a start and about the methods of getting your own way when filming in Italian chaos — which the world seemed to be doing at the time. Stories of *Cleopatra* (1963) abounded. He was good at making his presence felt by shouting! I remember him standing on the film boat in mid-sea where we had been served cold, clogged-up spaghetti yet again for lunch and with a loud oath of despair he threw it overboard. A fresh serve of spaghetti — or fish — was dispatched from ashore immediately!"

Seven Seas to Calais is a jolly swashbuckler with an enthusiastic Rod perhaps not entirely well cast as Drake, but he makes a solid fist of the role and has a compelling scene where he must hang an old friend who is guilty of mutiny. The script might have been better off concentrating on one or two events in Drake's life instead of using the greatest hits method and trying to cover everything of note. There are a number of unintentional laughs — some of the model ships, the painful "comic" Indian interlude, the performance of ingénue Hedy Vessel — but it is all rousing, with strong production values and plenty of action, plus an imposing turn by Irene Worth as Queen Elizabeth I.

Since Errol Flynn was an Australian and had played a character in *The Sea Hawk* (1940), loosely based on Sir Francis Drake, it is not surprising that reviews of *Seven Seas to Calais* often invoked Flynn's name when discussing Rod's performance. For example: "Rod Taylor adds touches of the traditional Errol Flynn movie mannerisms to the role" (*Motion Picture Herald*); "Rod Taylor emotes with the swashbuckling ardour and assurance of an embryo Errol Flynn" (*Variety*).

Errol Flynn had been the most successful Australian actor in Hollywood and in Rod's early days of stardom he occasionally encouraged comparisons with the Tasmanian: "I can't help it if I'm the devil-may-care type," he bragged once. "Australia breeds our kind. Don't forget Errol Flynn."

Common nationality aside, Rod's career would have some interesting parallels with the swashbuckler's: Bob Buckner, creator of *Hong Kong*, wrote and produced several Errol Flynn vehicles in the 1940s; Ranald MacDougall, co-writer one of Rod's best films, *Dark of the Sun*, co-wrote one of Flynn's best, *Objective, Burma!* (1945); Arthur Hiller directed an episode of *Hong Kong* only a year after directing Flynn's final dramatic performance; Jack Cardiff, Rod's most frequent director of the '60s, worked with Flynn on several occasions. In addition, both actors had reputations as drinkers and brawlers and enjoyed colorful love lives (including costly divorces). Both tried their hand at screenwriting and producing, rarely with much success; both had strong artistic sides, but were also "men's men" in their private lives, with a liking for male friendship and real-life adventure.

However, *Seven Seas to Calais* marked the only time Rod ever really entered into quintessential Flynn territory on screen. The personas of the two actors were not very similar: Flynn's image was of the classical, noble hero — Robin Hood, Captain Blood, etc. — whereas Rod's was less romantic, more contemporary. This was reflected in the backgrounds of the two actors: Flynn attended private schools, was the son of a university professor and worked on the English stage; Rod went to government schools, was the son of a construction worker and came up through commercial radio. Flynn had the greater star charisma, but Rod was a more versatile actor, enjoying greater success in non-action films. Rod was definitely the more disciplined of the two: while he had a fondness for

the ladies and the bottle, his appetites for both faded into insignificance compared with Flynn's (whose did not?). In addition, Flynn mostly played Europeans
throughout his career, whereas Rod mostly played Americans.

Rod admitted later that he was not a huge admirer of Flynn's. As he told *60
Minutes*, "I loved what he presented on screen, but his private life left something
to be desired, really. And people kind of took it for granted that I was just as
much of a reprobate as he was and that disappointed me a little. And they also
expected me to be as tall and good-looking and dashing, which I wasn't — so
that pissed me off, to have to live up to that, too."

The other leading Australian actor of Rod's heyday was Peter Finch who,
although born in England, spent the formative years of his life and career in
Australia. Finch never settled in Hollywood, however, basing himself in London
with only the occasional visit to the US. He specialized in depicting intellectual
characters: playwrights, doctors, writers and so on; while Rod also performed
similar sorts of roles, they seemed tougher than those of Finch — for instance,
while both actors portrayed famous real-life playwrights, Finch played the dil-
ettante Oscar Wilde (in *The Trials of Oscar Wilde* [1960]), while Rod took the
part of a two-fisted Sean O'Casey in *Young Cassidy*.

Finch also had a reputation as a magnificent actor, something Rod never
really enjoyed. Like Rod (and Errol Flynn, for that matter), Peter Finch rarely
played Australians during his career, even in Australia; most of his early Australian films saw him cast as Englishmen. However, when he did so, he had far
better luck than Rod in producing something memorable — for instance, *A
Town Like Alice* (1956) and *The Shiralee* (1957). Rod never found an Australian
role to quite match either.

Instead of being similar to Finch and Flynn, the Australian stars who pre-
ceded him, Rod Taylor was closer in image and persona to those who followed:
Mel Gibson, Russell Crowe, Bryan Brown, Heath Ledger, etc. It is certainly
easier to imagine Rod Taylor playing the roles played today by Mel Gibson and
Russell Crowe than it is the other two. Mel and Russell are very much following a trail Rod blazed.

Incidentally, with Finch based in England and Flynn having died in 1959,
Rod was now the leading Australian movie star in Hollywood. This was a position he was to maintain for the next 20 years.

SINCE THE DAYS OF *KING OF THE CORAL SEA*, ROD HAD BEEN
attracted to the behind-the-scenes machinations of filmmaking. By the time
of *Hong Kong* he was not slow in coming forward to offer his opinions (on set
or otherwise) about the projects he was working on. The next logical step was
forming his own production company, a method Chips Rafferty used so successfully back in Australia and which had become popular amongst Hollywood

movie stars since the late 1940s (for instance, *Hell on Frisco Bay* was made by Alan Ladd's company; *Separate Tables* by Burt Lancaster's).

During filming of *Seven Seas to Calais*, Rod announced he was forming his own company, Rodlor, to make movies and TV series. At best, Rodlor would enable Rod to initiate his own projects, secure improved roles for himself and make good movies; at worst it would be handy for tax purposes.

(Interestingly, a number of other Australian actors who made it in Hollywood showed a similar inclination to initiate their own projects. Indeed, there is a remarkably long tradition of this — Snowy Baker and Louise Lovely in the 1920s, Errol Flynn in the '40s and '50s, Chips Rafferty in the '50s, Michael Pate in the '60s and '70s, Mel Gibson and Bryan Brown from the '90s onwards. It probably stems from coming from a country where the local industry has always been small and multi-tasking is a pre-requisite to survival. In addition, actors with the guts to leave home and try to crack overseas are not the type of people content to sit in the backseat. In this, as in so much else, Rod was very Australian.)

Rodlor announced its first projects would be *Mistral* and *Latitude 35*, two original scripts from Alec Coppel, a Melbourne-born writer whose credits include *Vertigo* (1958). Rod first became friendly with Coppel during the making of *Hong Kong*, when he bought the latter's house in Beverly Hills. (This abode, a rambling two-story colonial, was later furnished by Rod himself piece by piece and it remains his home as of writing.)

The possibilities inherent in this combination of two Australian expatriates is intriguing — an early, rare example of the "gumleaf mafia" that was to emerge in Hollywood in the 1990s — but, unfortunately, nothing came of it. *Mistral* dropped off the Rod radar fairly quickly, later emerging without him as the undistinguished *Moment to Moment* (1966). For a while, *Latitude 35* seemed more hopeful: in 1962 Rod announced he was going to London to work out a co-production deal for the project and the following year he was reportedly trying to make it independently; however, no film resulted.

Although Rod still owed MGM one film a year, at this stage 20th Century-Fox seemed keener on promoting the young actor, notwithstanding *Hong Kong*'s cancellation. While Rod was in Italy, Fox's head of production, Peter Levathes, signed the actor to a long-term contract. Under this, Fox could pre-empt Rod for a film and, if he made a TV series for the company, for every year of that series he would be entitled to star in a Fox movie with budget of not less than $2 million opposite a "heavyweight" co-star.

"It's the old-fashioned thing of building a star — if I prove my worth," declared Rod. "And I think Peter Levathes as head of the studio will do it the right way."

Fox announced a series of films featuring Rod: *Big Man, Big River, The Jungle, The Enemy Within* (with Rod as Robert F Kennedy!) and *The Short Happy Life of Francis Macomber*, as well as a new TV series, *Dateline San Francisco*. Robert Blees, a producer at the studio, recalls that "Rod was a very good second-rate leading man. When I say 'second rate' that's a compliment — he'd be the first to admit he wasn't Gable or Redford but he was always very good or competent. Eight or nine on a scale of 10. I think Fox had a lot of ambition for him."

Rod filmed a pilot for *Dateline San Francisco* (essentially a rehash of *Hong Kong*, with Rod as a journalist based in the title city) and guest-starred on an episode of the studio's anthology series, *Bus Stop* (1961–62). However, none of the other projects went far beyond script stage: Fox became mired in a financial crisis due to the escalating costs of *Cleopatra* (1963), leading to a total revamp of the studio — including the firing of Rod's champion, Peter Levathes. For a moment it seemed that, yet again, Rod's career had stalled just when it was about to take off.

However, none of it mattered in the long run because a far better opportunity had come along. On January 29, 1962, Rod signed with Alfred Hitchcock to star in what would become the third classic film of his career.

CHAPTER 6

"I'm there. Made"

CONSOLIDATION OF STARDOM (1962–64)

IN 1961 ALFRED HITCHCOCK WAS AT THE PEAK OF HIS POWERS and the height of his fame. The portly Britisher had been one of the top directors in Hollywood for over 20 years; his television series, *Alfred Hitchcock Presents* (1957–62), was still rating strongly; his most recent film, *Psycho* (1960), had just earned glowing reviews and $14 million at the box office. He was admired around the globe, a legend in his own lifetime, one of the most influential filmmakers in the world. But he faced the perennial problem of even the most gifted artist — what to do next.

Hitchcock was considering a number of possible ideas when he read an article in the *Santa Cruz Sentinel* about a mysterious bird attack in California's Montrey Bay. For no apparent reason, a flock of shearwaters had caused extensive damage to the town by flying into streetlights and windows and pecking at or vomiting on residents. (Over forty years later, researchers deduced the birds may have been brain damaged by eating fish and algae poisoned with demoic acid produced by algae when it ran low on vital nutrients in seawater.)

The incident reminded Hitchcock of a novella he had optioned, Daphne du Murier's *The Birds*, about a series of unexplained bird attacks on a Cornish village. The director had enjoyed tremendous success with an earlier du Maurier work, *Rebecca* (1940), and he decided make *The Birds* his next project.

The adaptation was to be a loose one, though: Hitchcock told screenwriter Evan Hunter to forget the novella apart from the title and the notion of birds inexplicably attacking people. In response, Hunter came up with the idea of turning *The Birds* into a screwball comedy that would evolve into a thriller as the birds became violent.

Hunter's screenplay starts with spoilt heiress Melanie Daniels and lawyer Mitch Brenner meeting cute in a San Francisco bird shop. The two squabble their way through some unresolved sexual tension, which results in Melanie deciding, for a joke, to buy Mitch's sister a love bird and deliver it to Brenner's house in the Californian seaside town of Bodega Bay. Soon after Melanie's arrival, birds start going mysteriously berserk and the tale turns into one of survival.

Hunter says that when he began working on the script, Hitchcock was thinking of Grace Kelly and Cary Grant to play Melanie Daniels and Mitch Brenner respectively. But casting these actors would have been expensive (and, in Grace's case, politically difficult — she was by then Princess of Monaco) and Hitchcock was reluctant to give away any more of his film's profits than he had to. He also knew that by this stage his own name on the marquee was as much a box-office guarantee as any actor's. (Indeed, from *Psycho* onwards, Hitchcock only made one more film with an A-list star, *Torn Curtain* [1966]). After a few months, Grace Kelly became Tippi Hedren and then Cary Grant turned into Rod Taylor. "For now, we were casting platinum," wrote Hunter.

Tippi Hedren was a Hitchcock discovery, a model the director had spotted on a television commercial; she had never made a feature film before. By way of contrast, Rod had seven years in Hollywood and the lead in two features and a TV series behind him; even if he was not quite in the Cary Grant league it perhaps was a little unfair for Hunter to call him "platinum."

Rod was not the most obvious substitute in the world for Cary Grant, but Hitchcock had decided he wanted a younger, more physical type of actor to play Mitch Brenner. The part required a performer who could plausibly (a) attract Melanie Daniels at first meeting, (b) play a successful professional and (c) fight off swarms of attacking birds. Rod, whom Hitchcock had previously considered for a role in *Psycho*, had just demonstrated all these qualities in *The Time Machine* and *Hong Kong*. He would also, to put it bluntly, come cheap.

Rod received a call from Hitchcock and went to meet the director. According to Rod, Hitchcock told him "he didn't want an elegant actor, like Cary Grant. He wanted someone with balls." Rod felt he did not hit it off with the director to start off with, calling him "a strange man to talk to" with "very rigid ideas." But two days later Rod was cast.

At this time, Rod had commitments for three films with Fox and three with MGM, but doing a Hitchcock really put him in the top league. "In Hollywood, that means I'm there. Made," beamed Rod. "When that cunning old devil takes notice of you, everyone takes notice of you."

Hitchcock knew full well what playing the lead in one of his films meant for a young actor and the director wanted to make sure he enjoyed some of the benefits. He took out an option on Rod's services for four pictures over six years, the first of which was to be *The Birds*. Rod's fee for the film was $50,000 plus the right to purchase part of his character's wardrobe at a 50% discount; Marco Lopez was hired as his driver and stand-in.

Filming took place at the Universal backlot and on location in Bodega Bay. Rod got along marvelously with Tippi Hedren, offering her valuable off-screen support and rehearsing scenes together in their spare time. His relationship with Hitchcock was less serene; the director was sometimes uneasy in the presence of his handsome male stars (in the words of Hedren, "Hitchcock's great tragedy was that he always thought he was Cary Grant") and the two occasionally clashed.

In his book on the making of the film, Evan Hunter recalls a time when his wife visited the set; Rod was sitting in a chair watching rehearsals when Hitchcock turned to the actor and said, "Mr. Taylor, can't you see there's a lady on the set? I'm sure you'd like to give her your chair, wouldn't you?" Rod leapt up and offered his seat. Hunter says that "in an aside loud enough for Rod and every bird in northern California to hear," Hitchcock whispered to the writer, "Cattle, Evan. They're all cattle."

One other time, Rod was rehearsing a scene in the kitchen with Jessica Tandy, watched by a number of journalists. During rehearsal, Rod noticed that the light inside the fridge did not go on. Hitchcock announced they would try for a take and Rod turned to the cinematographer and told him to make sure the light went on when he opened the fridge. Hitchcock overheard and in front of the press announced that they would take a lunch break, "while Mr. Taylor — our technical advisor — tells us how to make our movie." Rod was furious. At the end of the day, Hitchcock sent his secretary to invite Rod to have cocktails with him and the press. Rod at first refused, then relented and visited the director in his office. As he walked into a room full of journalists, Hitchcock announced loudly, "Here is the one I love — my star."

Rod later complained that Hitchcock spent too much time setting up relationships that "went nowhere" in *The Birds*. He didn't think the characters were attractive or interesting, particularly his own — "a square, repressed idiot who would never have attracted a sophisticated woman like Tippi Hedren." Evan Hunter was also dissatisfied, complaining that Hitchcock "didn't get the kind of heat" between Rod and Tippi Hedren "that he normally got between his leading players."

Hunter is perhaps a little harsh on the Rod–Tippi chemistry which, to me at least, works beautifully. Admittedly, *The Birds* did lack some of the psychological depth of *Psycho* and *Vertigo* (1958). Even Hitchcock later admitted the personal story of *The Birds* was not consequential enough, claiming there was "no depth" to Hedren's character at all. (Note: It should be pointed out that the director made this comment after a personal and professional breach with Hedren following the filming of *Marnie* [1964].) But when all is said and done, the film was never meant to be Chekhov — it was basically a story about birds attacking people for no reason.

Another factor that should not be overlooked when discussing *The Birds'* (relative) lack of profundity is that Hitchcock had to spend the majority of his time during production overseeing the special effects. If these did not work and the birds were not menacing, the whole film would come across as a joke; Hitchcock and his team used a combination of traveling mattes, superimpositions, blue screen, model birds, trained live birds and dead birds nailed to the set.

Ray Berwick, a screenwriter who dabbled in bird training, was put in charge of the live animals. They lived in 40 studio pens and consumed 100 pounds of seed and 200 pounds of shrimp, anchovies and ground meat per day. The birds would constantly try to escape or not do what they were told and Berwick found he had to use a variety of methods to keep them under control: hamburger was smeared on the hands of actors to get the birds to attack them; air jets were used to ensure they flew in the right direction; cellophane kept them contained within a room; string was used to tie them down when they were not required to fly. Birds would often peck at and defecate on actors and wranglers (seagulls were the fiercest) and trips to the nurse to get tetanus shots were common.

Although the Humane Society kept an eye on the treatment of animals on set, no such protection was afforded to Tippi Hedren. For the climactic scene where Melanie Daniels is attacked by gulls in the Brenners' house, the actor had birds literally hurled at her by prop men, with air jets keeping them from flying directly into the lens. Some birds were actually tied to Hedren with elastic bands and in between shots she had to have her clothes torn and blood and cuts applied. Filming of this sequence went on for seven days, after which Hedren had a near-collapse brought on by nerves.

The finale of Hunter's original script involved Melanie and the Brenners escaping their house by car, only to face one more bird attack driving through the now-deserted town of Bodega Bay. During filming Hitchcock decided to drop this sequence, leaving the ending ambiguous: the characters carefully climb in the car and drive off, fully expecting an assault at any moment… but it never comes. It is a brilliant tease, neatly complementing the film's opening tease sequence where Mitch and Melanie's second meeting keeps being delayed.

After nine months of post-production, *The Birds* was released in March 1963, with a promotional campaign that emphasized Hitchcock, rather than Hedren or Rod, as the star of the film. A clever slogan was devised: "*The Birds* is coming!" In London, a "talking poster" was used to promote the movie in the West End, featuring a tape recorder that played the twittering of birds; this caused a commotion and the advertisement was eventually pulled.

Reviews were generally decent (though not glowing — Hitchcock was not yet then a critics' darling), with Rod's performance rarely given much serious appraisal: *The Hollywood Reporter* dubbed him "strong and convincing," the *New York Times* "stolid and sturdy" and so on. Box-office performance was robust, however, with the film earning rentals of $4.6 million. *The Birds* has remained a favorite with audiences ever since; when NBC screened it on television in 1968, the movie recorded ratings of 38.9 with a 59 share, making it the most-watched feature broadcast on American television in the 1960s.

The Birds is an absolute masterpiece from an artist at the top of his game. Funny, terrifying, always gripping, it has become a deserved classic, the last Hitchcock movie undeniably to claim this status. The special effects, photography and design are excellent, as are the performances (Jessica Tandy, in particular, makes a slightly creepy yet sympathetic mother). If the movie does not quite reach the heights of *Psycho*, on its simplest, purest level — a story about birds attacking humans — it is dazzling.

Being a Hitchcock work, *The Birds* has been heavily analyzed by writers over the years. Camille Paglia wrote an engrossing monograph on the film, which she saw "as a perverse ode to woman's sexual glamour, which Hitchcock shows in all its seductive phases, from brittle artifice to melting vulnerability." She extols Rod Taylor for "showing off the rugged masculinity that had already captivated my generation of girls in *The Time Machine*," but she had some troubles with his performance (or rather, his casting) — in particular as they related to his moments with Jessica Tandy. "The private interactions between mother and son should show a bit more neuroticism or at least ambivalence on Mitch's part to do justice to the film's complex psychodynamics. Taylor is all male, with a bluff Australian heartiness that doesn't quite catch the queasy-making possibilities here. It wouldn't be fair to cite Anthony Perkins' spectacular panoply of fussy, self-deprecating mannerisms in *Psycho*, since he is playing a reclusive lunatic. But the dashing Cary Grant, as another urban careerist in *North by Northwest* (1959), deftly captures a stymied son's sense of exasperation in his hilarious scenes with Jessie Royce Landis as his deflating mother."

A Cary Grant or even James Stewart might, admittedly, have brought more psychological depth to the part of Mitch Brenner in *The Birds*, but it could be argued that the flaw lies with the script rather than with Rod. For there is, admittedly, something missing when it comes to the character of Mitch; he is a potentially intriguing creation — a seemingly virile, uncomplicated man who nonetheless remains a mummy's boy — but Hitchcock and Hunter do not really explore it. (It feels as though there needs another scene or beat to "flesh out" Mitch Brenner a bit more.) However, to be fair, Hitchcock's focus in *The Birds* was on Melanie Daniels — and an overly neurotic Mitch would have perhaps thrown the film off-balance.

Rod, thus, does not have that many opportunities to act in *The Birds*, but he does have opportunities to be a movie star and he takes them: whether bantering with Tippi Hedren, fending off vicious crows, or piling his family into the car at the end. Fitting into the Hitchcock universe was not as easy as it looked, no matter how talented the actor, as Paul Newman later proved in *Torn Curtain* (1966) — but Rod makes it look easy. And even Evan Hunter would surely have conceded Rod was preferable to some of the male leads of Hitchcock's later films, such as Frederick Stafford, Jon Finch and Bruce Dern.

Rod's own view of *The Birds* has varied over the years. During the 1980s he was a little harsh on the film, claiming that Hitchcock did not have "any particular theme in mind beyond the actual storyline" and the characters were unpleasant because the director "wasn't interested in nice people." In recent times, though, Rod has looked upon the movie more favorably. In a documentary on the making of the picture, *All About the Birds* (2000), he described it as "a magnificent piece of film genius."

Evan Hunter always wanted to write a sequel to *The Birds* and pitched an idea to Universal in the 1990s: a bird attack would take place at the wedding of the daughter of Rod Taylor and Tippi Hedren, resulting in the destruction of most of the country. This story was never filmed, but it sounds a lot more interesting than the sequel which did eventuate, the straight-to-cable *The Birds II: Land's End* (1994) (in which Hedren had a cameo, but not Rod), a film so inept its director asked for his name to be removed from the credits.

WHILE *THE BIRDS* WAS IN PRODUCTION, ANITA EKBERG FLEW out from Rome to join Rod on set and newspapers confidently reported on the duo's impending nuptials. Various wedding dates were announced, but Rod kept postponing, claiming he was too busy filming. The ceremony was put back and put back until finally it was cancelled altogether. Rod and Anita broke up and she flew back to Italy.

In hindsight — actually, even at the time — it was obvious Rod was never meant to marry Anita Ekberg. Their relationship was too hot-blooded, too long distance, too crazy. "I couldn't keep up with the pace," Rod confessed later. "It was like an Errol Flynn movie every day."

"I love Anita and I hope I'll always have her friendship," he added. "I wish she would discard this caricature of herself which she shows to the world and be her real self."

(The relationship had an intriguing postscript: as often happens with couples in their early thirties who break off an engagement, both Rod and Anita would marry other people within the next twelve months.)

In the meantime, Rod could console himself with the fact that *The Birds* had turned him into one of the most sought-after young actors in Hollywood. His enhanced status within the industry was demonstrated at the 33rd Annual Academy Awards on April 9, 1962, when Rod co-presented the Oscar for Best Editing — making him the first ever Australian to present an Academy Award.

For all Rod's gratitude to *Hong Kong*, his eyes were now focused on confirming his position as a movie star. He felt "movies are more rewarding, artistically and financially" because "an actor gets time to show his wares… it's not a series of 13-week sprints."

Universal, who had released *The Birds*, signed Rod to a three-picture deal, meaning the actor now had commitments with four different movie companies. His first film under the new arrangement, for a $50,000 fee, was a contemporary air force drama, *A Gathering of Eagles*.

A Gathering of Eagles was, to all intents and purposes, a propaganda film for Strategic Air Command (SAC), the bomber arm of the US Air Force, in the vein of *Strategic Air Command* (1955) or *Twelve O'Clock High* (1949). The lead character is Colonel Jim Caldwell (Rock Hudson), a driven air force officer who is assigned to his first command; Rod plays Hollis Farr, Caldwell's easygoing vice-commander and former co-pilot. As the movie progresses, Caldwell becomes tougher and more demanding upon his men; his English wife (Mary Peach) is often left alone because of the time her husband spends on the job and begins an affair with Farr. The story climaxes when Caldwell's base undergoes a surprise inspection and responsibility falls on Farr, who nonetheless rises to the occasion and ensures the base passes.

Although Rod's role was only the second lead, he was at least supporting Hudson, at the time the second-most popular star in America. Also, his character had the greatest emotional journey in the story, developing from a slacker into responsible leader.

The production of *A Gathering of Eagles* received enthusiastic support from the real-life SAC, keen on Hollywood making a pro-military film after the publication of two books centered around the accidental dropping of atomic bombs: *Red Alert* (later filmed as *Dr. Strangelove* [1964]) and *Fail-Safe* (filmed in 1964). Filming took place mostly at Beale Air Force Base, just north of Sacramento in California, with additional filming in San Francisco, on the Universal lot in Hollywood, and at the SAC headquarters at Omaha, Nebraska.

The most complex sequence in the movie was a night-time shoot involving a conversation between Rod and Rock Hudson in the foreground of an MITO — a Minimal Interval Take Off, where a number of air force jets are launched into the sky at 15-second intervals. Throughout filming of the scene, turbulence and sound from the planes knocked over everything that was not tied down: a script supervisor fell off her stool, light reflector boards went flying across a neighboring field and the actors struggled to stay on their feet. However, Rod and Rock managed to finish their lines in one take.

Even scarier for Rod was a scene where his character plays the piano and sings (the song was "The SAC Song," written especially for the movie by noted satirist Tom Lehrer). This was the first time Rod ever had to sing on camera and, to make matters worse, director Delbert Mann wanted him to perform live instead of lip-synching to a pre-record. Cast member Richard Anderson remembers:

"He [Rod] was on the way up, doing a lot of projects. He was easy to be around, a lot of fun. Except one scene, he had to play the piano and sing. I happened to be there that day, I was working and I remember, it's like an actor watching another actor; you could tell he wasn't at all relaxed and full of fun that day. He came on set and he was nervous and he said so, as Aussies do. He was scared, bloody scared, actually. And they did a rehearsal. And he stopped for a minute or two, gathered himself, then he did it in one take. When it was over he was a relieved man. (*Laughs*) He took a couple of deep breaths."

Rod was not a born crooner, but he passed the test well enough. He would later go on to sing in both *Fate Is the Hunter* and *Young Cassidy*.

Although Rod's career was now very much on the rise, he still had some way to go to reach the standing of someone like Rock Hudson. If Rod needed any reminding of this, he got it after *A Gathering of Eagles* finished principal photography in October when Universal's studio heads became concerned about a sub-plot in the film where Peach's character has an affair with Rod's. Worried about the impact playing a cuckold would have on Hudson's he-man image, they requested some scenes be cut and re-shot, removing the Rod–Mary Peach romance and changing the whole movie, in the words of Delbert Mann, from a love triangle about "two buddies in love with the wife of one of them" to a "pressures-of-the-job-almost-breaks-up-marriage-but-not-quite story."

Universal's marketing department did what they could to hype *A Gathering of Eagles*, preparing poster art with a picture of Hudson and Mary Peach in bed together beneath a picture of the red phone — "The red phone... His mistress... Her rival." The pressbook trumpeted some of the exciting things you could see in the movie: "Such inspiring sights as an Alert, the method of getting a SAC bases' striking force into the air within 15 minutes of an alert order; an MITO (minimal interval takeoff) showing a group of half-million-pound B52s becoming airborne at 15-second intervals; a drill of Titan missiles, showing the 100-foot nuclear-warheaded ICBMs emerging from their 150-foot-deep silos to the launching pad; and an ORI, the heart-stirring Operational Readiness Inspection led by the surprise visit of a SAC inspection team to test the capability of a SAC base to respond to a potential war order."

This was done without irony.

Most critics took exception to *A Gathering of Eagle's* formulaic plot and devotion to nuclear preparedness, reflecting the changing fashions of the time. *Films and Filming* thought that it "may well be the most terrifying film you will see this year... in its bland acceptance of total war." *Newsweek* wondered what would happen if you took "Rock Hudson out and imagine Rod Steiger or Richard Widmark in the part. Without the distraction of Hudson's preternatural charm, it is appallingly clear that only a maniac can run SAC properly." An alternate point of view was provided by General Curtis Le May — who did run SAC and who many people thought *was* a maniac (he provided the inspiration for General Buck Turgidson in *Dr. Strangelove*); he praised *A Gathering of Eagles* for coming the closest any Air Force film ever came to "showing a true picture of what the military was all about."

Rod received some pleasant personal notices, *Variety* stating he "creates a colorful figure as the undesirably easy-going vice-commander who shapes up when the chips are down," and the *L.A. Herald-Examiner* enthusing he "imbues his role with a brashness, a fresh, breezy approach that makes for some of the best scenes in the picture. A good actor, he is well cast."

By the end of 1963, *A Gathering of Eagles* had earned an estimated $2 million in rentals — not bad but, compared with other Hudson vehicles of this time, a disappointment, especially considering the film's final price tag of $3,346,500. Public taste had shifted somewhat since the 1950s and audiences were less inclined to see a movie so joyously pro-nuclear.

A Gathering of Eagles comes across today as an interesting period piece. The film really should have concentrated on Rod's character learning responsibility, but far more time is spent instead on obsessive Hudson and the effect his job is having on his marriage (as if anyone cared). And while Hudson and the men of SAC clearly work hard, it is difficult to be too sympathetic considering what the work is — whether an SAC commander does a good or bad job, either way it's not going to be good news for the audience.

WHILE SHOOTING *A GATHERING OF EAGLES*, ROD ANNOUNCED his next project might be *Latitude 35, Alien Seed* or *The First Wife*. The first two movies were never made and the third was eventually filmed with Van Johnson as *Wives and Lovers* (1963). Instead, Rod went to Britain for two weeks to film "The Ordeal of Dr Shannon," an episode of the anthology series, *The DuPont Show of the Week* (1961–64). The episode was of some minor historical significance, as it was the first co-production between a regular American TV dramatic series and a production company from another country (in this case, England). Rod played a brilliant American physician who resigns his hospital post to find the right vaccine against a new and fatal influenza germ.

By this stage anthology television was increasingly unpopular as a genre and "The Ordeal of Dr Shannon," despite being an excellent episode, turned out to be Rod's last piece of work in the genre until the late 1970s. It was a great pity, because anthologies had been a fertile field for him, a place where he could stretch his dramatic muscles in between film roles. Only radio provided Rod with a greater variety of parts to play and further helped his development as an actor.

However, things were going so well at this point, Rod was probably not too concerned; indeed, he shortly started a relationship with a studio that would cause his star to rise even higher.

CHAPTER 7

"I'm helping them make money."

AT MGM (1963–65)

ALTHOUGH ROD WAS UNDER CONTRACT TO MGM THROUGHOUT the first few years of the 1960s, the studio never appeared that impressed by him, certainly not to compare with Fox or Universal. This changed in 1963 and Rod enjoyed an excellent relationship with his old alma mater for the remainder of the decade.

There were two reasons for this: Rod's casting in *The Birds* and a change in MGM's management. A series of flops (led by 1962's *Mutiny on the Bounty*) had caused the studio to record a $17.5 million loss in 1963; Sol Siegel and Joseph Vogel departed, replaced as head of production and company president by Robert Weitman and Robert O'Brien respectively. Little remembered nowadays, the O'Brien–Weitman regime not only succeeded in turning around MGM's financial performance, they oversaw the last real run of classic films made at the studio (including *Dr Zhivago* [1965], *The Dirty Dozen* [1967] and *2001: A Space Odyssey* [1968]).

O'Brien and Weitman wanted MGM to rebuild its in-house talent base by developing its own writers, actors and directors. Rod was the sort of star they liked — an emerging name with strong ties to the studio, whom they could build up. For the next few years Rod worked almost exclusively at MGM — indeed, he made more films there during the O'Brien–Weitman regime than any other male star except James Garner. Rod once went so far as to say O'Brien was like a father to him. "They're building me as a star and I'm helping them make money," he said. "It's a give-and-take relationship." The results were the peak "movie star" roles of Rod's career: *The VIPs, Sunday in New York, 36 Hours, Young Cassidy, The Liquidator, The Glass Bottom Boat,* and *Dark of the Sun.*

Rod's first film back at MGM was *The VIPs*. This was a modern-day updating of *Grand Hotel* (1932), a melodrama incorporating several stories which all took place in the one exotic setting — in this case an airport VIP lounge. The script was written by Terence Rattigan and featured a number of first-rate roles for what hopefully would be an all-star cast. Anthony "Puffin" Asquith was signed to direct.

When looking for a male lead, producer Anatole de Grunwald aimed high — Richard Burton, a modestly famous actor throughout the 1950s, who had just become an incredibly famous one following his well-publicized adulterous affair with Elizabeth Taylor on the set of the then-still-unreleased *Cleopatra*. Not only did Burton agree to star in the film, Elizabeth Taylor offered to join him — on the proviso that she receive a fee of $1 million, plus 10% of the gross. (The salaries and per diem expenses of the lead duo came to an estimated $300,000 more than those of the rest of the cast combined.) Nonetheless, de Grunwald happily agreed to pay it — he now had the most celebrated real-life couple in the world starring as on-screen lovers in their first project after *Cleopatra*.

Supporting Burton and Taylor was a distinguished line-up, including Margaret Rutherford, Elsa Martinelli, Orson Welles, Louis Jourdan, Maggie Smith, Linda Christian… and Rod Taylor. The Australian actor was employed under his old MGM contract; when first cast, he recalls thinking, "Oh my God, Liz and Richard Burton. I'll be here for two years at least."

On the positive side, however, it was clearly going to be a big film — and, what's more, one that gave Rod the chance to play an Australian onscreen for the first time in his career (Les Mangrum, a tractor manufacturer trying to save his firm from financial collapse).

In addition, most of Rod's scenes would be opposite Maggie Smith, who even then had a reputation as one of the greatest stage actors in the world. (Smith plays Rod's secretary, whose devotion ultimately gets her boss out of his financial trouble.) Rod decided to check out his co-star prior to filming and went to see her in a play. With him in the audience was David Nettheim, with whom Rod had worked on radio in Australia. "After the show the lights went up and I asked what he thought," recalls Nettheim. "He said, 'She'll devour me…'"

The VIPs was shot entirely at MGM's studios in London, where a two-level set was built to replicate an airport terminal; it was the largest interior ever constructed at Elstree and came complete with cafeteria, reception hall, shops and two lounges.

At this time, Elizabeth Taylor and Richard Burton were still married to their respective spouses, so throughout filming they resided in separate suites at the Dorchester Hotel. Rod also stayed at the Dorchester — as did (on the floor above him, no less) his ex-fiancée, Anita Ekberg, and her new husband, actor Rik Van Nutter.

Although *The VIPs* was technically an all-star movie, there was no doubt who the real stars were. Rod had been reminded of this when he told MGM he wanted a dressing room on the same floor as Taylor and Burton. The studio obliged — by giving him the tiny, cramped dressing room that remained. Charles Tingwell recalls visiting his old friend at the time: "I said, 'Mate, you were set up.' He said, 'I know.'"

The antics of the two stars ensured a lively set during the ten-week shoot: Burton was constantly agonizing over whether to permanently leave his wife for Elizabeth Taylor and took out his frustrations by snapping at Asquith and drinking heavily; Elizabeth Taylor damaged a cartilage in her knee, forcing her to spend a number of days in a wheelchair; Burton was mugged while returning home from a rugby match one afternoon and had to wear a patch on his face for several days; Elizabeth Taylor feuded with Louis Jourdan after the latter's wife wrote a bitchy magazine article about her; and schedules were constantly re-arranged to suit the requirements of the female star.

"Every day I phone the studio and ask if I'm needed," sighed Rod. "I don't know why I bother. I could save myself trouble and just call Liz and ask what she's doing. When she works I work. She's a wonderful girl. The film just revolves around her."

Compared to *Cleopatra*, though, the drama on *The VIPs* was relatively minimal: there were no massive cost over-runs, near-fatal illnesses, on-set mutinies, etc. Rod kept on his best behavior — he knew the film was a big opportunity for him and was keen to do as good a job as possible. Assistant director Peter Medak told *Vanity Fair* that the actor would work out constantly when not required on set. "Bar bells in the dressing room," says Medak. "I mean, in England at that time it was like, 'What is he doing?'"

Rod and Maggie Smith had electric chemistry in their scenes together and got along extremely well off camera; so well, in fact, they had a short-lived affair during filming. It seems an odd match, then and now: the rough, tough Australian with a history of dating Amazons such as Anita Ekberg and the sweet Englishwoman who looked as if butter would not melt in her mouth. Appearances in both cases, however, were deceptive — from all accounts, Rod could be sensitive and loving in his private moments and Smith was capable of a colorful love life.

Rod also hit it off with Orson Welles, who was acting in the movie to help fund his big-screen version of *Don Quixote*. "If you stood up to him, he just loved it," Rod laughed. Welles, in turn, told Peter Bogdanovich he thought Rod and Maggie were "wonderful" in *The VIPs*; he added that the cast were all "very fond" of Asquith, "though he wasn't in real control of that picture. How could he have been?"

Charles Tingwell was then living in London and occasionally invited Rod over to dinner during the shoot. He says Rod would drive his Rolls-Royce from his dressing room to the car park "a full 100 yards," where he would climb out and get into Tingwell's car. Despite this show of star behavior, Tingwell felt that his old friend enjoyed the chance to dine in "our modest Aussie-type household — sort of like the old days of Sydney radio."

The VIPs marked the first occasion Rod played an Australian on film. At the time, Australian characters in Hollywood movies were very uncommon and usually played by American or English actors: *Sister Kenny* (1946), *Million Dollar Mermaid* (1952), *The Great Escape* (1963), etc. This applied even for Hollywood films shot in Australia, such as *On the Beach* (1959), *Summer of the Seventeenth Doll* (1959) and *The Sundowners* (1960). The number of times Australian characters were actually played by genuine Australian actors were rare to the point of freakishness: Errol Flynn in *Desperate Journey* (1942) and *Montana* (1952); Michael Pate, Charles Tingwell and Chips Rafferty in *The Desert Rats* (1953); Cecil Kellaway in *Interrupted Melody* (1955) — and that was about it.

Nonetheless, by 1963, a general image of the Australian male had been established on international screens. It was one best personified by the characters played by Robert Mitchum in *The Sundowners* and Chips Rafferty in his films — to wit, the laconic bushman or soldier, most comfortable in a fight, a pub or the wide-open spaces, very much along the lines of Russell Ward's "typical Australian" of myth.

Rod's portrayal of Les Mangrum in *The VIPs* is noteworthy in that it offered audiences a different view of the Australian male: Mangrum was a businessman not a bushman, gregarious rather than taciturn and just as capable of flirting at the dinner table or running a company as he was of drinking a beer or punching someone out. Rod was highly conscious of the cultural significance of this, describing his character as "the first authentic picture of an Australian I've seen on the international screen" and "the first time an average Australian has been portrayed without slouch hat, broken-down horse and greasy merino." While Rod was perhaps overstating things a little (what character in *The VIPs* could really be described as "authentic"?), there is something to this claim.

Over the years, British cinema has generally been more sensitive to Australian culture than Hollywood's and it is significant that *The VIPs*, while Hollywood-financed, was shot in London and made with predominantly British creative talent. (The same factors would apply the second time Rod played an Australian, in *The High Commissioner*.) In particular, Rod claims Terence Rattigan allowed him a fair degree of input into the script, including letting Rod rewrite some of the dialogue to make it more "Australian."

One change to the script that Rattigan did not agree to, however, was the ending of the Rod–Maggie Smith story. Although Rod's character spends most of the film chasing Linda Christian, by the finale he seems to fall in love with Smith, kissing her lovingly before he gets on his flight. This was not contemplated in the original script, in which Rattigan describes the Smith character as being in her 40s "with thick-lensed spectacles and a nose that becomes unbecomingly red at moments of emotion" and where the final kiss "was intended as a humiliation," where Rod would go "for her lips and slipped up to her forehead, thus telling her and the audience… that bed just wasn't on for the poor bitch." However, MGM made Asquith shoot it a different way "and obviously they chose the shot which would go down best in Little Rock, Freetown and Manila" (Rattigan).

Elizabeth Taylor and Richard Burton were so famous at this time that any film featuring them together had a strong chance at the box office (a poster for *The VIPs* run prior to the film's release merely printed a picture of the two stars with the words "She and He"). And so it proved: by the end of 1963, *The VIPs* had earned $7.5 million in rentals; in comparison, *Cleopatra* took in $15.7 million… but that film had cost $40 million, whereas *The VIPs'* price was less than a tenth of that. MGM did not get away scot-free, though — at a shareholder meeting that year, Richard Burton's ex-wife Sybil received 5,791 votes for a seat on the board as a protest vote against the studio casting Burton and Taylor in a film together!

Critics generally dismissed *The VIPs*, particularly the efforts of Richard Burton and Elizabeth Taylor. However, by and large, they found nice things to say about Rod: "Rod Taylor is energetic, forceful and very likeable" (*Variety*); "[Rod] is engaging and winning" (*The Hollywood Reporter*); and "Rod Taylor's jumps of joy on hearing good news are a treat to see" (*Films and Filming*).

Seen today, *The VIPs* is an enjoyable, glossy piece of cinematic candy, very much in the old-style MGM tradition. Although the Burton-Taylor story is most prominent and Margaret Rutherford won an Oscar for her role, it's the other two stories which are more appealing: Orson Welles and Elsa Martinelli make an entertaining duo and Maggie Smith and Rod are touching together. To be honest, Rod's Australian accent sounds awkward at times, but he is very likeable and is particularly strong in his scenes with Smith (who, incidentally, steals the film).

The following year, MGM, Rattigan, Asquith and de Grunwald made lightning strike twice with another popular all-star multi-story film set in an exotic location: *The Yellow Rolls-Royce* (1964). Rod was originally announced as one of the cast, but had to pull out when he was offered the lead in *Young Cassidy*.

AFTER *THE VIPs*, ROD RETURNED TO AMERICA FOR THE LAUNCH of *Seven Seas to Calais* and *The Birds* before going into his next film. *Sunday in New York* was a glossy romantic sex comedy in the style of *Ask Any Girl*. The virgin here was Eileen, a young woman from a small town who visits her brother in New York after being dumped by her fiancé because of her refusal to have pre-marital sex. After finding out her brother is something of a Lothario himself, Eileen sets about seducing the first man she runs into — Mike, a journalist about to move overseas. Mistakes and misunderstandings eventuate, especially when Eileen's fiancé arrives to woo her back.

Norman Krasna's original play had premiered on Broadway in 1961, where it ran for a respectable 188 performances and helped launch the career of a young Robert Redford, who played Mike. Although the production was fairly tame even by the standards of the day, it received some notoriety when a school teacher marched her pupils out of a Washington performance in moral indignation during the first act. Film rights were sold to Seven Arts, an independent production company that had made a fortune in the 1950s re-selling old films to television before moving into production; *Sunday in New York* was part of a 20-picture deal they had with MGM.

The movie's $2 million budget did not accommodate top stars, so it was decided to cast up-and-comers: Natalie Wood and then-beau Warren Beatty were offered the lead roles but turned them down; Rod and Jane Fonda stepped in instead, with Rod playing Robert Redford's old part.

As part of his arrangement to make the film, Rod signed a multi-picture deal with Seven Arts; he now had commitments with them, Fox, MGM, Universal and Alfred Hitchcock Productions. "I have nine films lined up and enough money salted away to give me all the security I need," Rod bragged.

All these long-term contracts were part of a deliberate strategy by Rod and his advisers: while they meant the actor would receive less than he could get on the open market (he claimed this was $75,000 per picture going up to $200,000) it ensured several studios had a long-term financial stake in Rod's career and it made it financially easier for those studios to place him in projects with expensive directors, co-stars and/or source material.

"Look, I've got as big an ego as anyone, but I don't let my name stand alone on the marquee," said Rod. "It can break a picture. After all, people see me and say, 'Oh yeah, that guy. That's Rod Steiger. Or maybe it's Rod Serling.'"

Since *Sunday in New York* was mostly set indoors, the majority of filming took place on the MGM backlot in Hollywood, with one week's location work in Manhattan. Rod adored working with Jane Fonda and got into the habit of kissing her in front of the crew after each of their scenes together. Rod claimed this was platonic, a simple case of "showing my affection for somebody I like very much… If I had been doing something wrong, I would be sneaky about it."

Sunday in New York is a cheery, likeable film very comfortably set in the Hollywood-created New York of large fashionable apartments, swinging bachelors, sassy career girls and stressed-out virgins. Krasna's script is better with farce than in discussions on sex, causing the second half of the film to be stronger than the first, but all the cast are first-rate and the music score is enchanting. Rod gives a confident, relaxed comic performance and engages in some skillful verbal fencing with Fonda. However, as is common in these sort of films (*Ask Any Girl*, for example), the show is stolen by the supporting actors — in this case, Robert Culp (as Fonda's fiancé) and Jo Morrow (as Cliff Robertson's long-suffering girlfriend).

Reviews were generally positive, particularly for Rod. *Variety* described him as the pick of the cast, "a steadily rising and versatile actor who delivers a warm, flexible and appealing performance"; *The Hollywood Reporter* claimed he "emerges as a comedy leading man... [who] is very good at the light moments and backs them with an unobtrusive virility that is a special combination."

By the end of 1964 *Sunday in New York* had earned an estimated $1.8 million in rentals. The box-office pull of Rod Taylor and Jane Fonda clearly was not equal to that of Doris Day and Rock Hudson; in addition, virgin comedies were going out of fashion as the '60s' sexual revolution took root in the nation's cultural subconscious. However, the film has had a long life and frequently turns up on television; indeed, it ranks among the leading Rod Taylor "perennials."

ROD WOULD ALWAYS REMEMBER FILMING *SUNDAY IN NEW YORK* for one particular reason: he married during the shoot.

By the early 1960s Rod was well established in Hollywood fan magazines as an eligible heartthrob. Highly publicized romances with Anita Ekberg and Frances Nuyen had greatly assisted in raising his profile; a 1962 article listed Rod as one of the "hottest bachelors in town" and Australia's *Listener In-TV* proudly reported the following year that Rod "seems to have inherited some of Errol Flynn's standing as Australia's gift to gossip writers. Hardly a month passes that he isn't heralded up the aisle with a different bride-to-be."

Most of Rod's early girlfriends in America tended to be expatriates, like himself: Frances Nuyen, Inger Stevens, Anita Ekberg, Merle Oberon. This was no accident: Rod once declared that "American women are unbelievably spoiled to a point which makes them ridiculous" — although he was romantically linked with some locals, such as Nikki Schenck, Rhonda Fleming, Carol Kikumura, Tura Satana and MGM starlet Nicola Michaels.

Another thing many of Rod's early girlfriends had in common was they tended to be actresses, which perhaps explains why he never married any of them. For Rod was not exactly a big fan of career girls. "The sweet smell of success is no perfume for a woman," he once claimed. "Say it's old-fashioned, say it's corny. But, as far as I can see, a girl who wears a 'business scent' is not attractive. A woman who flaunts her career as though it were a new hat is not beautiful..."

"If you go back to the basis of human society, the woman's place is in the home," he later added for good measure. "However clever she is, it's the man who originally had to go out hunting the meat."

Mary Hilem was both an American and not an actress. She was a model, born in San Diego, California, one of four brothers and four sisters. Her father was a chemical engineer, once a member of John Philip Sousa's band; her mother died during Mary's graduation from high school in Florida, after which Mary moved to New York City and worked her way up through the modeling ranks.

Rod and Mary's courtship was a whirlwind one. They first met at a party at Kirk Douglas' house in Los Angeles; Rod visited her in New York on his way back from filming "The Ordeal of Dr Shannon" in England; Mary called on Rod in London while he was filming *The VIPs*; when Rod returned to LA, he announced their engagement.

Rod and Mary were married on June 1, 1963, at Westwood Community Methodist Church, in Los Angeles. It was a Hollywood wedding *par excellence* — a handsome movie star walking down the aisle with a beautiful model; the guest list included other movie stars (John Wayne, Robert Cummings, Jane Fonda), directors (Vincente Minnelli), studio executives (Ray Stark) and gossip columnists (Hedda Hopper, Louella Parsons). Rod's publicist acted as a page and his best man was Hollywood lawyer Greg Bautzer. Neither of Rod's or Mary's parents attended — Mary was given away by Rod's agent, Wilt Melnick.

The marriage got off to an awkward start that very day when Mary's father died of a heart attack in New York, only hours after speaking with the newly-wed couple on the telephone. Mary flew back for the funeral the following morning; Rod had to stay in Los Angeles as he was needed for filming *Sunday in New York*.

"When you go into marriage with a man like me, you've got a man who has a mistress," explained Rod. "When I'm making a movie, it's like another woman in my life."

Rod admitted the day after the ceremony he thought to himself, "Lord, what have I done?" Ultimately, he would have little more luck with his second marriage than his first, although it started happily enough, with a two-week trip to Australia to promote *The VIPs* that followed the end of production on *Sunday in New York*.

AFTER THE AUSTRALIA TRIP, ROD WENT ON TO SPAIN, WHERE he was needed for his next film, *Circus World* (1964). This was a production from the legendary Samuel L. Bronston, who, for a few years, blazed across the cinematic sky like a comet with his high-concept big-screen spectacles such as *El Cid* (1961).

Rod had agreed to act in the film for a reported fee of $125,000. It was another support part, but the lead was John Wayne, not only one of the biggest stars in the world, but a personal friend of Rod's, the two having discovered a mutual fondness for drinking and talking into the small hours. They had often discussed working together and *Circus World* seemed ideal: a tough, commercial story about the tour of an American circus through Europe in the early part of the 20th century. Wayne would play the owner of the circus, with Rod as a rodeo-riding employee who wants to set up his own operation, but falls in love with Wayne's ward (Claudia Cardinale).

When Rod arrived in Madrid, however, he discovered the project in a state of utter chaos. Director Henry Hathaway had only come on board two months earlier as a replacement for Frank Capra (who, in turn, had taken over from Nick Ray) and was struggling to co-ordinate the mammoth production; the script was being revised daily, with at least seven writers having worked on it; and Bronston in severe financial difficulties (he would soon fall bankrupt).

Rod read the most recent draft of the script and found, to his dismay, that his part had been whittled down from what he originally signed on for: his character now did little in the story except romance Claudia Cardinale. Rod was understandably annoyed. He had two hit films playing in cinemas around the world, *Sunday in New York* ready for release, the backing of a major studio — and here he was, being asked to play a handsome male prop again, just like he used to do on television in the '50s. Hathaway promised Rod he would oversee a rewrite, but the director clearly had his hands full dealing with hundreds of extras, animals, large sets, etc. The day before shooting began, Rod quit the film and flew home.

"Rod felt that after his successes in films this year he should take on a role that would increase his star rating," said Wayne. "He wasn't happy with the script and told us so. Personally, I think the film would have helped him, but I guess he just didn't feel that way."

An officer in Bronston's company added, "We could have held him to his contract, but we don't want an unwilling actor in the cast." An urgent search for a replacement came up with John Smith, star of TV's *Laramie* (1959–63). (*Circus World* went on to flop at the box office and helped finish off Bronston's career.)

Rod, perhaps feeling a little guilty about leaving his friend in the lurch, went into damage control as soon as he arrived back in Hollywood, informing the press that "everybody understands" about his decision and that there were "no hard feelings." However, he would have been concerned about any possible harm the incident might do to his career. The episode received considerable publicity (it was front page news in Australia) and Rod was not a big enough star to get away with any reputation for prima donna behavior.

Typically, he decided to take a pro-active approach and announced a swathe of future projects: another film with Jane Fonda, one with Wayne and Hathaway and a role in an adaptation of Harold Robbins' bestseller, *Where Love Has Gone* (1964). He also revealed he had purchased film rights to the World War II novel *Someone Will Conquer Them* by Australian author Elizabeth Kata (whose first book, *Bells with Drums,* was filmed as *A Patch of Blue* [1964]). Of these, only *Where Love Has Gone* was ever actually made (without Rod), but they served to give the impression the actor remained in demand and he soon received a concrete offer from 20th Century-Fox.

FATE IS THE HUNTER WAS BASED ON A NON-FICTION BOOK BY Ernest K Gann, a pilot-turned-author whose previous works included *Island in the Sky* and *The High and the Mighty*, both turned into popular movies. The film rights were snapped up by Darryl F. Zanuck, who originally intended to make the project as an independent production in collaboration with his son Richard. These plans were interrupted when the Zanucks re-took control of 20th Century-Fox in the wake of the *Cleopatra* debacle; they assigned *Fate* to producer Aaron Rosenberg and it became one of the first movies from the new-look studio.

The film version of *Fate Is the Hunter* centers around a fatal air crash which has killed 53 people. In charge of the investigation is airline executive Sam McBane, who happens to be an old army buddy of the pilot of the flight, Captain Jack Savage. Rumors emerge that Savage had been drinking before the flight, but McBane refuses to believe them and he sets out to uncover the truth.

Glenn Ford was signed to play Sam McBane for a minimum fee of $300,000 plus a percentage of the profits. It is little remembered nowadays, but Ford was a highly popular star in the 1950s, being rated the top box-office attraction in the US by exhibitors in 1958. Five years later his career was on the slide, but he was still considered a bigger name than, say, Rod Taylor, who was cast as happy-go-lucky pilot Jack Savage at a fee of $50,000.

Although Savage was a support role and not on-screen all the time, it was the best part in the film as he is the focus of the whole story. Savage is loud, womanizing and fond of a drink and flamboyant escapades — but when the chips are down, he pulls through. He is the alter-ego of the more buttoned-down, reliable McBane character and their unusual relationship is one of the things that make the film so watchable.

"I just coast," said Rod of his role. "I'm like Gene Tierney in *Laura* (1944), a personality moulded by flashbacks."

No airline or airport wanted to cooperate with the film — understandably, considering the plot — so Fox purchased and converted their own planes and constructed a huge airport terminal set on their backlot. Rod missed a few days of work due to an accident: he cut his forehead while filming a scene in the fuselage of one of the planes; then he developed a severe muscle spasm in his left rib cage and was driven to the doctor's. An electrical cardiogram revealed Rod had strained some of his muscles; however, he quickly recovered.

The final cost of *Fate Is the Hunter* was $2,578,300, meaning the film required $4.8 million in rentals to break even; in the final event, it made $2.21 million. The resulting movie is very enjoyable, an intriguing part-thriller, part-meditation on the workings of fate. The opening pre-credit sequence (the plane crash in which

Rod's character dies) is tremendous, the climax exhilarating and the film's philosophical theme — that everything happens for a reason — sets it apart from other airplane movies, as does the fact Ford's protagonist seems driven as much by guilt and feelings of inadequacy as from any desire to get to the bottom of the truth. Rod himself is likeable, again registering well in a story about male friendship.

AFTER FINISHING *FATE IS THE HUNTER*, ROD SIGNED A NEW contract with MGM for three films, replacing the final year of his original seven-year deal. Any fall-out from the *Circus World* experience was now officially nil. His first movie under the new arrangement (for which he reportedly received a $50,000 bonus) was *36 Hours*, from the producer-director team of Bill Perlberg and George Seaton (*The Song of Bernadette* [1944], *The Country Girl* [1954]).

36 Hours is set in the lead-up to D-Day. American Major Jefferson Pike (James Garner) is sent to Lisbon in order to make the Nazis wrongly think the Allied invasion of Europe will be at Calais rather than Normandy. But Pike is captured by the Nazis, who try to get him to reveal the true location of the invasion by convincing him that the war has been over for six years. This plan is the brainchild of Gerber (Rod), a German psychiatrist pressed into service as an intelligence agent by the Nazis and involves a nurse (Eva Marie Saint) masquerading as Pike's wife.

Again, Rod was playing a support part and James Garner was not a big star like Hudson or even Ford. But, again, Rod had easily the best role — two roles, if you count the American doctor he impersonates. Gerber is an intelligent, likeable man, a patriot but not a Nazi, who originally developed his pretend-the-war-is-over technique in order to treat shell-shocked soldiers and is only using it for evil purposes because he is forced to. Gerber outsmarts Pike all the way through the film and only the dopiness of the Nazis stops him from being ultimately victorious.

Most of *36 Hours'* filming took place at Yosemite National Park, which substitutes (very well) for Germany's Black Forest; it was the first time that location had been allowed to be used for a feature film. Production proceeded smoothly, apart from one occasion where Rod hurt his neck and shoulder while falling off a balcony during his death scene.

Rod brought Mary with him on location during the shoot and the two of them lived in their own cabin in the forest. It gave them a chance to iron out some kinks in their relationship, of which there were already quite a few. Rod took the blame for this, admitting he had not "been mature enough to handle the normal problems of the first year" of his marriage.

"Mary was much more mature and dedicated going into the marriage than I was," he confessed. "It was I who had to be taught."

Nonetheless, Rod also claimed that "the ideal of a completely harmonious marriage is a myth and you just might as well accept it." Ominous words, especially as Mary was just about to become pregnant with their first child.

By the end of 1965, *Variety* estimated that *36 Hours* had earned a respectable, though not sensational, $2 million in rentals. Box office may have been hurt by the fact that a number of other movies around this time also used amnesia as a story device (e.g. *Mirage* [1965], *Blindfold* [1966], *Mr. Buddwing* [1966] and *The Third Day* [1965]).

Nonetheless, *36 Hours* ranks today as one of Rod's finest films — not to mention as one of the best thrillers of the 1960s. It is an exhilarating suspense story, full of dense plotting and plenty of intelligent twists and turns. Characters are constantly thinking people will do something, then thinking it is a trap, then changing their plans (or not) so they won't think it's a trap, and so on. All the actors are first class, particularly Rod as the (extremely sympathetic) doctor; Gerber is so affable and his plan so audacious that at times you find yourself hoping the Germans will pull it off. The main drawback of *36 Hours* is length: the story feels as if it should end once Gerber dies and the Normandy invasion is no longer in jeopardy, but there is an additional sequence where James Garner and Eva Marie Saint escape to Switzerland.

Like *A Gathering of Eagles* and *Fate Is the Hunter*, this is a film where Rod plays a character whose strongest emotional bonds are with another man — namely, Pike. At times the film seems like a sort of platonic male love story, with Gerber telling Pike he came to really admire him after studying Pike's life story for months and informing Pike that "He's a hell of a guy."

Still on a roll, Rod then went into preparations for his most challenging part yet. This would be no supporting role or ensemble piece — he would be the sole star and, what's more, in a serious drama under one of the greatest directors of all time.

CHAPTER 8

"A star in the true, old-fashioned sense of the word."

RIDING THE TIGER (1965–1966)

ROD'S ACTING RARELY ACHIEVED MUCH CRITICAL ATTENTION throughout his career. While he was respected as a solid professional, he seldom received worshipful reviews and never won any sort of major acting honor apart from that 1954 Rola Prize (he seems never to have even been nominated for one). He was certainly never considered a great actor in the way that, say, Peter Finch was.

There were several reasons for this: Rod frequently appeared in critically maligned genres like romantic comedies, actioners, thrillers and science fiction; he rarely worked with directors who were critics' favorites; even in his best-known films, he tended to be overshadowed by others (Hitchcock on *The Birds*, for instance), and most of his post-'60s projects were simply too mediocre to warrant serious consideration. *Young Cassidy* is highly significant in Rod's career because it was the only time a performance of his received extensive appraisal.

Young Cassidy was based on the memoirs of one of the leading playwrights of the twentieth century, Sean O'Casey (1884–1964). O'Casey was born in Dublin to a lower-middle-class family that soon plunged into poverty on the death of his father. He became a manual laborer who taught himself to read and write, scripting three realistic plays about the slums of Dublin, all of which were performed at the Abbey Theatre in the 1920s. One of them, *The Plough and the Stars*, caused a riot during its initial run by audience members outraged at the playwright's on-stage depiction of subjects traditionally taboo in Catholic Ireland, such as sex, religion and patriotism. O'Casey's next play was rejected by the Abbey and the writer moved to England, where he lived for the remainder of his life.

Although O'Casey continued to write, his fame rests mainly on those first three plays, plus six volumes of autobiography he composed later and published under the umbrella title *Mirror in my House*. Film rights for the latter were bought by two journalists who had made a documentary on O'Casey's life,

Robert Ginna and Bob Graff; they hired playwright John Whiting to construct a screenplay.

Young Cassidy starts with "Johnny Cassidy" (O'Casey's alter ego) digging ditches in 1911 Dublin to support his penniless mother and sister. He writes in his spare time and is encouraged to join the Irish revolutionary movement by a workmate, Mick. Cassidy enjoys a sexual relationship with Daisy, a chorus girl he picks up after an anti-British demonstration, and falls in love with Nora, a young bookstore clerk who encourages his creativity. Cassidy's talents as a playwright are soon recognized by such Irish literary figures as WB Yeats and Lady Gregory, who agree to mount his plays at the Abbey Theatre, leading to a riot on the opening night of *The Plough and the Stars*. After the show, Mick tells Cassidy he feels betrayed by what his friend has written and that he never wants to see him again. Nora, who feels that Cassidy no longer needs her, also abandons him. The playwright decides to leave Ireland and the final shot has him boarding a boat to England.

Once Whiting finished an acceptable draft, Graff and Ginna set about finding a star and director. Richard Burton was offered the lead but turned it down claiming he was "not Irish enough," and scripts were sent to the directors Carol Reed and Guy Green. By early 1963 it looked as though Richard Harris was set to star, with Lindsay Anderson to direct; however, this eventually fell through — Harris later claimed he felt he couldn't handle the role — and by March Graff and Ginna were talking to Sean Connery and John Schlesinger. Connery was enthusiastic, but Schlesinger dropped out after Graff and Ginna refused to allow the script changes he wanted. The producers then started thinking of American directors instead.

The first one who came to mind was John Ford, the legendary Irish-American four-time-Oscar-winning director. Ford had made a number of Irish-set films throughout his career, including *The Informer* (1935), a version of *The Plough and the Stars* (1936) and *The Quiet Man* (1952); Ginna says that the latter was considered the sole exception to the Hollywood rule that "Irish movies don't make money." He sent Ford a copy of the script and the director called back three days later asking, "When do we start?"

The producers pitched their package to MGM, where they found an enthusiastic buyer in Robert O'Brien. The studio head was attracted by the idea of making another *Quiet Man*, or, even better, another *Tom Jones* (1963) — the bawdy English comedy which was a massive box-office hit at the time. (Ginna always suspected O'Brien's Irish ancestry was also a factor in his green-lighting the project.) The budget was around $1 million, with Ford agreeing to take a reduced fee to make the film.

Difficulties then emerged in locking down Connery, who eventually dropped out to make *Goldfinger* (1964). Peter O'Toole was offered the role, but turned it down ("He didn't want to be typecast as an Irishman," says Ginna); Richard Harris and Tom Courtney were also considered, but ultimately not considered "financeable" by MGM.

The producers held an emergency meeting with O'Brien and fellow MGM executive Maurice 'Red' Silverstein at the Claridge Hotel in London. "We were desperate," recalls Ginna. "We were going to scrap the whole production."

Ginna then remembered Rod Taylor from *The VIPs*. The actor looked as though he could play a laborer-turned-playwright; he was rugged yet romantic and MGM was familiar with his work. What's more, he was an Australian — he might have some Irish ancestry. Ginna says when he suggested him, Red Silverstein shouted out, "God, that's perfect! I could get the money back in Australia alone." O'Brien agreed, and Rod accepted the role with alacrity. It was an enormous opportunity, playing one of history's leading playwrights under one of the world's greatest directors. Hedda Hopper put it best when she declared, "Rod Taylor finally found the story and director he's been waiting for."

O'Casey never actually met Rod, but they spoke over the phone and the playwright gave his blessing to the casting. An excited Rod claimed *Young Cassidy* would be "a good Irish, *Tom Jones*-ean romp, with funny fights and sex, both of which I think were untrue although the old codger remembered it that way and he's still a strangely hep 84-year-old." He went on to describe Johnny Cassidy as "more than just a brawling, struggling playwright. He's a passionate and tender and dedicated young man in revolt. He's from every country, every city, now and always... It's the biggest role of my career, the biggest challenge and I believe I'm going to be great."

Rod was going to have to be great if he was to match the rest of the cast, which by now included Julie Christie (Daisy), Maggie Smith (Nora — "I got her in the picture," claimed Rod later), Flora Robson (Cassidy's mother), Siobhan McKenna (his sister), Edith Evans (Lady Gregory) and Michael Redgrave (Yeats). Sean O'Casey's daughter, Shivaun, had a bit part as Lady Gregory's maid.

It was an imposing line-up of *Separate Tables* standard and Rod later admitted most of his cockiness was pure bluster. "An Australian pretending to be an American going to Ireland, to play Sean O'Casey with Maggie Smith? You don't think I was scared?"

He gained confidence when he flew out to London and met with John Ford. The irascible director had initially been a little disappointed to discover Rod was not Irish, but that quickly dissolved after the two started talking and struck up a rapport.

"Ford liked him very much," says Ginna. "He was very much a John Ford kind of guy, a virile and husky Ward Bond kind of a guy."

Ginna remembers in particular the time he, Rod and Ford went to have tea with Edith Evans at her apartment in London. "Edith Evans said, 'How do you like your tea?' to Rod. He said, 'I like vodka.' She looked at me and said, 'Robert, would you go upstairs and see if Jack Priestley is in and ask if he has vodka.'... I knocked at the door. Priestley was there. He gave me a bottle of vodka and I took it down and Rod had vodka. All the rest of us had tea...

"Afterwards, we went downstairs and stood by the road. Rod said, 'Can you imagine that old cunt? All she wanted to do was talk about the theatre and here she was talking with the most famous director in the world. When we get on set I'm going to cut her to pieces.' Ford just looked at him and said, 'She'll twist you around her little finger.' And they got along wonderfully."

The unit moved to Dublin, where shooting began on July 14, 1964. Rod was accompanied by Marco Lopez, with a by-now-heavily-pregnant Mary electing to stay back at home in Los Angeles. Sadly, production would take place without the screenwriter, John Whiting, who had died from cancer the year before; his death had come as a shock to everyone outside Whiting's family (including Whiting himself — he never realized how sick he was, his family elected not to tell him). However, Ford and the producers were confident they could make any necessary amendments to the script themselves.

By this stage, John Ford had just turned 70, drank too much, was wracked with health problems and had one of the foulest tempers in Hollywood. But he was one of the few directors Rod had worked under who could reasonably be called a genius and the actor found the experience inspirational. As he told Scott Eyman in the latter's biography on Ford, "His favorite phrase to me was, 'There are no problems, only opportunities.' He didn't give a fuck what happened, something good could come out of it. And if it was hard to get something good to come out of it, then goddam it, work until you do. And that's what he'd do with shots, scenes, actors who were failing or miscast. No problems, only opportunities. I've kept that slogan ever since I met him."

Not that life with the eccentric director was entirely smooth sailing. An early scene involved Rod having to cry by the grave of Cassidy's mother — watched by scores of Dublin children off-camera. With the cameras rolling, the actor knelt down, "And I had a little weep," he recalled. "And I wept... and I wept... shuddered..."

Rod expected Ford to yell "Cut!" But he heard nothing and did not know what to do next. So he stood up and walked out of range of the camera. He went up to Ford and said, "Jesus Christ, Jack — enough is enough!" Ford got up, kicked Rod in the shin and said, "You Australian son of a bitch, you made me cry! That's a wrap!"

Unfortunately, the director's health — never strong at this stage of his life — had started deteriorating almost from the beginning of the shoot. The strain eventually proved too much and after two weeks filming Ford came down with viral pneumonia. Production was shut down for several days while the director's personal physician flew out from Los Angeles. The prognosis was not positive and Ford was ordered home. It was not the first time he had failed to complete a film he started, *Mister Roberts* (1954) and *Pinky* (1949) being other examples. Ginna claims Ford did not want to leave and "cried all the way" to the airport. "He was going to make amends for the fuck-up of *Plough and the Stars*," says the producer.

A new director had to be found, or the whole project risked cancellation. Rod told Scott Eyman that the director gave him "some Irish bullshit about, 'Look, me darlin',' I'll give you my notes and you direct the fucker.'" Duly inspired, Rod alleges he went so far as to call Robert O'Brien and offer his services, but the studio president declined, asking, "You're going to go up against Flora Robson?"

The producers considered hiring Joseph Losey as a replacement, but he wanted to start the film from scratch, which they were not willing to do. Their attention then turned to Jack Cardiff, legendary cinematographer of *The Red Shoes* (1948), who had recently moved into directing, notably *Sons and Lovers* (1960). Cardiff received a call at his family home in Switzerland, flew to London, read the script, loved it, had a lunch discussion with the producers, flew on to Dublin and was shooting within 36 hours. Cardiff says the producers warned him he "might have creative troubles with Rod Taylor because like so many actors he was talking like a producer or a director... I think Rod was impervious to sarcasm and he did like to think that he was running the whole show. So when we started on *Young Cassidy*, I just made it clear that I was running things."

Filming on *Young Cassidy* resumed on August 8, only two weeks after production had stopped. The delay caused the loss of just one main cast member: Siobhan McKenna, who had to leave in order to begin rehearsals for a play. While waiting to fly to Dublin with Jack Cardiff, Ginna ran into Peter O'Toole and his wife Sian Phillips at London airport. Philips expressed sympathy for Ford's illness and said she wished she could help; Ginna said she could — and cast her on the spot.

Cardiff, who admitted he did not know a lot about Rod's work prior to coming on board the film, was delighted to find himself "with an intelligent actor of enormous potential who knew exactly what he was doing. If he weren't a star already this would make him one."

"Rod's fundamental gift is his extraordinary energy," added the director. "I think he is on his way to being a star in the true, old-fashioned sense of the word, like Gable, Cooper and Tracy."

Cardiff's appointment had the effect of resolving a disagreement between Ford and the producers that had festered during the first part of the shoot. It concerned the film's ending — the night of the *Plough and the Stars* riot, where Cassidy is condemned by Mick and loses Nora. Ford wanted to add a scene after this where Daisy (Julie Christie), now a prostitute, emerges from the dark to congratulate Cassidy on his play, then walks away in the rain. Ford told Peter Bogdanovich he liked the fact that "it took this poor little tart to appreciate what he'd done" and thought the scene "would have kicked the damn story up."

Rod says he wrote a scene himself along these lines to be used, but was overruled. After Cardiff took over, Ginna sent a letter to Ford telling him they decided against bringing Julie Christie back at the end of film, arguing that Maggie Smith was "so heartbreaking" in her final scene with Rod that "nothing could top or touch the bitter sweetness of that parting."

There was another interruption to filming — this time for a happier reason — when Rod returned to Los Angeles for the birth of his child. When Mary went into labor, she contacted her husband, who got on the next plane out of Dublin — only to run slap bang into an airline strike. In addition, Mary's elder sister was killed in a car accident the day before Mary went into the hospital; thanks to some garbled news reports, Rod was told it was his wife who had died. In the final event, the misunderstanding was cleared up, Mary spent three days in labor and Rod made it home in time for the birth.

Rod's daughter was born on August 28, 1964, at Cedars of Lebanon Hospital, in Los Angeles. Rod and Mary had been expecting a boy so they did not have a name ready; eventually they chose Felicia Rodrica Sturt Taylor. Redman Killanin, son of Lord Killanin, associate producer on *Young Cassidy*, agreed to act as godfather. Rod then headed back to Dublin, the unit having lost only three days of filming.

"There's no doubt the arrival of a baby solidifies things," reflected Rod. "I was selfish. Then suddenly, I had this little creature to think about. It certainly pulled me together."

Despite this, Rod later confessed he continued to harbor strong feelings toward Maggie Smith throughout the *Young Cassidy* shoot. So strong, in fact, Rod claims he even considered divorcing Mary to marry her — but Maggie would not have a bar of it, mostly on account of Rod's womanizing reputation. In years to come, Rod would often reminisce wistfully about Maggie Smith, declaring as late as 1983 that he still thought of her "with a lot of love."

The Rod–Maggie romance was just one of the many crises of *Young Cassidy*'s production — "Everything that could go wrong did go wrong," recalls Ginna. Cast and crew caught lice from a tenement house bought for filming; Julie Christie came down with appendicitis and had to have an operation; the company safe was stolen from the unit's headquarters at Marian College, with about $2,300 inside; Rod was almost hospitalized when a cartwheel collapsed near him; a fire broke out while the unit was at work, but was extinguished before any equipment was damaged. Finally, on September 18, 1964, Sean O'Casey passed away in a nursing home at 84 years of age. It was not a bad way to go, all things considered — the playwright had been full of life and spry to the very end and died knowing Hollywood was making a movie out of his life with a good-looking star to immortalise him on screen. Most writers should be so lucky. Shooting completed on September 24, only two weeks later than originally planned; Ginna claims it even came in $50,000 under budget.

There has been confusion over how much of *Young Cassidy* was actually directed by John Ford. Graff estimated this came to about 18 minutes of footage in the final film; Cardiff put it at four-and-a-half minutes. Based on a shooting schedule, dated June 9, 1964, the scenes Ford shot were as follows: Cassidy digging ditches, externals of Johnny with his mother and his family, Cassidy at a tenement room, the love scene between Cassidy and Daisy in Daisy's house and Cassidy and his mates at the Cat & Cage bar. Ford was scheduled to shoot the riot sequence just before he fell sick; after Cardiff came on board he re-shot the love scene between Rod and Julie Christie and the rest of the film is his. The final credits read: "MGM presents a John Ford film… directed by Jack Cardiff."

Young Cassidy had a dual world premiere in London and in Dublin on February 24, 1965. By and large the reviews were respectful rather than enthusiastic; nonetheless, they are worth quoting at length because it was the only time in Rod's career that his acting attracted much serious consideration from critics: "Notable principally for the top-rating performance of Rod Taylor in the title role… Taylor delivers a fine, strongly etched characterization, believable both in his romantic scenes and as the writer who comes up the hard way. Splendid support is afforded particularly by Maggie Smith." (*Variety*) "Rod Taylor, seems more muscular, well-fed and disposed in his whimsically amorous adventuring to try to keep up with Tom Jones that the image of the early O'Casey that the playwright and poet presented in his *Mirror in My House*." (*New York Times*) "Rod Taylor… is much too old for the boyishness he affects and who has an uncomfortable time with his Irish accent." (*The New Yorker*) "Rod Taylor, who plays the title role, is a resplendent animal, whom we in the audience will adore." (*Newsweek*) "Rod Taylor, though a capable and continually improving actor, suggests O'Casey about as much as he suggests Alfred de Musset." (*New Republic*) "Rod Taylor, ordinarily just one of Hollywood's muscle-bound leading men, is the surprise of the year as Cassidy — lifting a pickaxe, employing a perfect brogue, cursing the Irish poverty that is killing his family, drinking, wenching and brawling." (*Cosmo*) "Rod Taylor now joins the heavyweight class in the field of dramatic performances… take Taylor out of the playboy and pretty boy category and create an actor of power and authority." (*Citizen News*)

The New York drama critics, who knew O'Casey personally, weighed in with their opinions on the film and were generally more accepting of Rod's performance than their cinematic colleagues. *The New York Post's* Richard Watts said he doubted if O'Casey "was ever the muscular, handsome, pugilistic juvenile Rod Taylor has made of him," but that Rod still "attractively suggested the zestful, life-loving, yearning spirit of the great Irishman." Brooks Atkinson of the *New York Times* concurred: "Since O'Casey was a thin man with sharp features and a belligerent chin, Rod Taylor could hardly be more unlike him. Mr. Taylor is a broad-shouldered young man with a round, handsome face. But on stage and screen good actors and good directors can perform all the necessary miracles. Mr. Taylor's magnetism and spontaneity and the vivacity of his acting create a character that may not resemble O'Casey but somehow does idealize the O'Casey spirit."

In May 1965 *Variety* listed *Young Cassidy* as being the eleventh most popular film at the box office while in its fourth week of release. Unfortunately, that was about as good as things got commercially. After all, the film was about a playwright that not many people had heard of and it treated O'Casey/Cassidy seriously: despite the sexy Julie Christie scenes it was a long way from a *Tom Jones* romp and there were not many laughs. Movies like that were then (as now) a difficult sell, especially without an A-list star and/or consistently strong reviews. Rod was touted as a possible Oscar nominee, but critical reaction was not potent enough to push him to the forefront of voters' minds.

Nonetheless, John Cassidy stands as one of the greatest performances of Rod Taylor's career. The part was not an easy one to play, requiring an actor who can believably dig ditches, scrap with cops, seduce Julie Christie and hoon about with his friends, yet also tenderly watch over his family and Maggie Smith and worry about his art. Rod's performance does strike the odd bung note or two — for instance, he seems a little awkward in his first scene with Philip O'Flynn and his two big "crying moments" on the death of his mother are slightly over the top. But he is generally very good and when he has someone to play against he really excels: in particular, Rod creates wonderful sparks in his moments with Edith Evans and Michael Redgrave and the scene where he is seduced by Christie has genuine erotic charge. Most of all there are the love scenes with Maggie Smith, which have remarkable power — the rendezvous between Nora and Cassidy by the river is a sequence of raw emotional intensity unmatched in Rod's career, except perhaps for the climax of *Dark of the Sun*.

The film itself is more erratic. John Whiting's script is thoughtful, but falls down in a few places: it ambles along in a this-happened-then-that-happened way without really giving a sense of what is important and why; Cassidy's life and career is sort-of tied in with Irish politics at the time and sort-of tied in with "theatre for the people," but it never feels focused and Cassidy's climactic sacrifice seems to come in a rush. On the positive side, the support cast is excellent, as is the period flavor; considering Cardiff's minimal preparation, he did a remarkable job. *Young Cassidy* lacks the sparkle and inspiration of a great film, but it is an intelligent, well-made one and a reminder of what its star was capable of. Understandably, Rod loved the movie and would often refer to it as "the best film I was ever in."

Young Cassidy could have marked a real turning point in Rod Taylor's career, leading to widespread recognition of his abilities as an actor and opening up a whole new range of parts for him to play. Unfortunately, the film's lackluster reception seems to have scared him off from similar projects (and studios from casting in him them): over the next 15 years Rod mostly specialized in the action and adventure genre, leading to the underwhelming critical reputation that endures today. As pointed out by director Peter Werner, "He's a very good actor but I don't think he found the parts to push himself to make himself a really great actor."

AFTER FILMING COMPLETED ON *YOUNG CASSIDY*, JOHN FORD invited Rod and Mary to join him and his wife in Hawaii for a brief holiday on the director's yacht. The young star was now in great demand: on November 4, Rod's agents sent a telegram to Alfred Hitchcock Productions (as required under Hitchcock's contract with Rod) informing them that Seven Arts was exercising its option for Rod's services (under their contract with Rod) for a film called *Fifth Coin*, due to commence shooting on January 19. However, the following week, Rod was pre-empted by 20th Century-Fox (under their contract with Rod) for another film, a Doris Day vehicle called *Do Not Disturb*. (*Fifth Coin*, based on a script by an exciting young filmmaker, Francis Ford Coppola, was never made.)

Ever since *Pillow Talk* (1959), Doris Day had been one of the biggest (if not the biggest) stars in Hollywood, being ranked number one at the box office in 1960, 1962, 1963 and 1964. The films that kept her there were a series of glossy comedies with handsome co-stars, the best-known plots of which concerned Doris defending her virginity. The movies were often disparaged, but they were tremendously popular and to co-star in one was a major coup for Rod.

Doris was no virgin in *Do Not Disturb*; she plays the wife of an American wool executive based in London, who makes her husband jealous after she begins flirting with a French antique dealer. Although this was a rather weak concept for a film, Fox had just earned over $10 million in rentals on the Day vehicle *Move Over, Darling* (1963) and wanted a follow-up.

The male co-stars of Doris Day comedies were normally A-listers, such as Rock Hudson and Cary Grant, but with *Do Not Disturb* it seems Fox was trying to save its pennies in the casting. It originally announced the part of Doris' husband would be played by Mike Connors, a tough-guy actor who played a role once mooted for Rod in *Where Love Has Gone* (1964). When filming dates were pushed back, Connors dropped out and Fox settled on Rod. His fee was $75,000, plus co-star billing and the right to purchase the clothes he wore in the movie at half-price. By way of comparison, Doris Day received a $600,000 non-returnable advance against 10% of the gross.

Surprisingly, Rod only accepted his role with reluctance. "I thought, 'What is this Cary Grant-Rock Hudson thing they're expecting of me?' I can't go that route," he declared. "I was very insecure when we first started shooting."

This is astonishing when one considers the positive reception to Rod's work in *Ask Any Girl* and *Sunday in New York* — but by this stage the actor was clearly more comfortable in action/thriller-type roles. (He also may have been getting sick of movies where he had to support a bigger star than himself.)

Nonetheless, Rod ended up getting along tremendously with Doris Day, calling her "the most interesting, fun broad I've ever worked with." A good thing, too, because *Do Not Disturb* would make plenty of demands on the professionalism of both actors. The script was rewritten constantly throughout production, as various writers tried to pump life into the uninspiring story. At one stage director Ralph Levy came down with a virus and was hospitalized for several days, causing George Marshall to take over in his absence. Filming ended 14 days behind schedule, almost causing Rod to miss the start date for his next film.

The final cost of *Do Not Disturb* was estimated at $3,582,300; story and script rights cost $398,500. The end result was not worth the effort: the film is a silly, inconsequential trifle in which the two stars work well together but where the story is so slight and tired the audience's interest is barely engaged. (For example, the first 20 minutes are devoted to gags about Doris having arranged to live in the country instead of the city like Rod wanted — and that's it.) There is no real reason for *Do Not Disturb* to exist except for greed; Doris Day's popularity had turned everyone lazy and complacent.

The movie's mediocre quality was reflected in its comparatively weak box-office performance, earning estimated rentals of $3.5 million (indeed, it is a tribute to the pulling power of its star that takings were this strong). Rod would have better luck with Doris on their next outing together.

The biggest impact *Do Not Disturb* had on Rod's life was the friendship he formed during the shoot with Fred Hakim, a Lebanese-American working at Fox as a studio grip. The rugged, two-fisted type from Brooklyn really hit it off with Rod — so well, in fact, that on completion of the film he went to work for the actor full-time as a stunt-co-ordinator/ chauffeur/assistant/bodyguard. He and his wife Dolores even lived with Rod for a time, Hakim running Rod's personal affairs and Dolores supervising his household. Hakim also accompanied Rod to Europe for his next film, a big-budget adventure tale that looked as though it had the potential to launch its star to the highest level of fame.

THE LIQUIDATOR WAS BASED ON THE FIRST OF A SERIES OF comic adventure novels by John Gardner about the cowardly British secret agent Boysie Oakes. The story begins with Colonel Mostyn of British intelligence, who needs a special agent to do some assassination work; he decides the right man for the job is his old army friend Oakes, who Mostyn thinks, on entirely mistaken grounds, is a tough, fearless killer. Oakes enjoys the perks that come with his new occupation — women, money, gadgets — but dislikes the actual killing involved, so he hires someone else to do it for him. Eventually, circumstances arise where Oakes has to be genuinely brave.

In the '60s the success of the James Bond films had turned the world spy-mad and *The Liquidator* novel was a success, leading to seven more Boysie Oakes adventures. Film rights were bought by British producer Jon Penington, who set up the project at MGM, keen to jump on the secret agent bandwagon. Penington hired an Australian writer living in London, Peter Yeldham, whom Rod knew from their early days working in Sydney radio, to pen the script. "It began so well," says Yeldham. "Literally eight months after being asked to write it, we were in the South of France ready to start shooting. Nothing has ever been that quick before or since. Some things, as you know, take years. So I supposed I should have expected there'd be a pay off."

Several actors were discussed for the part of Boysie Oakes — among them allegedly Richard Harris — but from all accounts Rod's name came up early. "I think MGM regarded him very highly," says Yeldham. "He'd done a few films as a lead by then and I think he was sort of A2 category."

Although Rod was not perhaps the first person one thinks to play the part of a coward, he was keen to do a spy film, having missed his chance at Bond earlier. The studio sealed the deal by presenting Rod with a new Rolls-Royce.

The Liquidator was a big step forward for Rod: MGM was entrusting him with the star role in an expensive action movie without the protection of a name director or co-star — what's more, it was a film that could possibly go into a long-running series. It would be a strong-willed individual whose ego could resist all this attention — and by this stage Rod was a long way from being strong-willed: on *The Liquidator* he began flexing his star muscles like never before.

First up, Rod requested Jack Cardiff as director. "He liked working with me," Rod bragged. "And because of my good relationship at MGM, when I ask for something they usually co-operate."

Then he insisted on playing Boysie Oakes as an American. Although Boysie was British in the novels, Rod felt more comfortable using the accent of his adopted homeland and Yeldham had to rewrite the script accordingly. "We were all disappointed it was an Australian-American," says John Gardner. "Also disappointed that Rod wouldn't play it English, which he was perfectly capable of doing."

Filming started on the French Riviera. Since Yeldham knew Rod, the writer was sent to pick him up at Nice airport: "He came off the plane and I was up on the terrace — in those days you walked into the terminal. He looked up and saw me and yelled out: 'Hey, Pete, Jesus Christ it's a long way from Grace Gibson's fucking studio in Sydney!' Then he indicated two guys either side of him. 'Meet the Hoods,' he shouted."

The "Hoods" were Fred Hakim and Marco Lopez, now pretty much working for Rod full time. Not long after their arrival, a dinner was arranged for Rod and co-star Trevor Howard to meet and become acquainted; Cardiff, Penington and Yeldham also attended. Yeldham: "We were asked not to bring wives, because it wasn't a social occasion: it was important these two met and liked each other... But Rod arrived with his two hoods. It wasn't much of a start and they had to go and sit at another table, because Trevor objected to leaving his wife Helen Cherry at the hotel, while Rod arrived with this pair. (We all felt very pissed off about it.)

"The whole evening ended up a bit of a shit fight, with Rod annoyed by this and he and Trevor arguing a lot — dear old Trevor getting pissed and Jack and I having to take him home and deliver him to Helen, a charming British actress who had experienced him being delivered home like this before. I don't think he and Trevor really recovered from their first meeting."

Throughout the shoot, Rod would spend more time with Hakim and Lopez than with anyone else on the film. Their "job" seemed to mostly consist of doing daily workout sessions with the star to ensure French catering did not damage his figure and accompanying Rod while he went out drinking. Jon Penington's widow, Lisa, remembers one particular incident: "Rod and the minders went out to dinner and were hassled by a young, rich Frenchman who wanted to give the 'film star' a bad time. It ended rather badly with the Frenchman punched on the chin and Rod and the minders at the police station. It all ended OK — I think the parents of the rich guy didn't want any trouble, so Rod and his minders appeared back on set in the nick of time."

"Entourage life" was a charmed existence in many ways — filming in exotic locations, mucking around with friends, meeting beautiful people (Grace Kelly, who knew Rod from her MGM days, visited the set). There was a less pleasant side, however — regardless of the genuine affection there existed between the men (which seems to have been considerable), Lopez and Hakim were still employees and Rod was definitely the boss; for instance, according to an article Lopez wrote for Rod's own fan magazine, the actor would often bully Lopez on set, yelling out orders like, "Bring me some tea, oaf!"

Rod's entourage also served to make him appear somewhat silly at times — after all, he wasn't that big a star and didn't really require protection (Hakim and Lopez were for company as much as anything else). John Le Mesurier, who had a small role in *The Liquidator*, teased Rod in his memoirs for fancying "himself as a Hollywood great" by having bodyguards "to put himself somewhere in the league of Brando, with his round dozen, and Sinatra, who seemed to have a fully armed platoon."

Ray Barrett, a friend from the Sydney radio days, also wrote in his autobiography about Rod's big head at this time, calling him, "the complete Yank... with a broad accent and all the moves." Barrett met Rod at a London pub, where the actor took out "a wad of notes with a rubber band around it and plonked it on the bar," called Barrett "baby" and insisted on buying all the drinks. They then went up to Rod's hotel room, which Barrett described as containing an exercise bike, massage table and "all the paraphernalia of American stardom which he'd embraced so completely... it seemed so cardboard cut-out and phoney, not at all like the old Rod I had known."

Rod admitted when he walked on to the set of *The Liquidator* with his entourage he knew the crew was thinking he was "pulling the Sinatra bit." But he argued that after he did his own stunts "they came up and said, 'You're all right, Rod. Come on, we'll buy you a drink.'"

While Rod was running around the French Rivera with Lopez and Hakim, Mary was stuck back in Los Angeles with their baby and her nurse, which put further strain on the marriage. Rod had not been the most attentive of husbands since Felicia's arrival, frequently ducking out to socialize instead of staying at home. "These parties I attend without Mary are for business reasons and Mary understands," Rod explained. "Besides, somebody has to baby-sit with our daughter."

However, Mary was able to join Rod when *The Liquidator* unit shifted to London. On June 16, the two of them attended the re-opening of the Theatre Royal at Windsor Castle, where they were presented to the Queen and the royal family. (The theatre had been rebuilt following a fire and Rod had donated some money to the project.)

It should also be pointed out that for all of Rod's swollen-headed behavior on *The Liquidator*, the biggest behind-the-scenes crisis on the film ultimately turned out to be due to the producers. It went back to when Jon Penington originally acquired the rights to Gardner's novel; he did not have enough money to buy the option outright himself, so he brought in a partner, Leslie Elliott ("a wealthy young man who didn't want to be in his father's business anymore" — Lisa Penington), who contributed the necessary funds. Jon Penington told both Yeldham and Cardiff that Elliott was only just learning the film business and to take no notice of him.

However, the producer neglected to mention that his partnership with Elliott was weighted in the younger man's favor. Also significant was the fact Penington never actually signed a contract with MGM to make *The Liquidator*; all there had been was an informal memo containing a provision that when terms were agreed, they should be embodied in the "usual standard printed form" of MGM contracts. This became important when Penington and Elliott got into a fierce argument during filming. Lisa Penington recalls, "It was really quite a trivial dispute caused (to my belief) by an agent who was supposed to be working for Jon, but who gave Leslie the impression that things were being concealed from him. Not true, in fact, but there you go."

Elliot ended up firing Penington from the project, and brought in a line producer to complete the movie. After post-production was completed, MGM sought to release *The Liquidator*, but Elliott claimed ownership of the film and sued the studio for infringement of copyright. MGM responded by applying for an injunction to stop Elliot from interfering with their possession of the movie for distribution purposes.

"We all had to give evidence in the American Embassy, I recall," says Gardner. "It was long and involved."

The court ultimately ruled that the original memo between Penington/Elliott and MGM studios was an agreement to agree, which was not legally binding. So there was no contract and Elliott still owned the underlying rights; MGM was forced to renegotiate.

While all this was happening, *The Liquidator* sat on the shelf, unreleased. Yeldham says the delay started to cause bad word-of-mouth. "Anything held up a long time is always subject to rumor and the rumor mills of the film industry grind better than most. The delay was terrible. None of us really knew what was happening, except this bloody man was twisting MGM's tail and nobody knew if it would ever be released. Meanwhile, friends and others in the industry were asking what happened to it, was something wrong, etc., etc."

The Liquidator should have reached cinemas in March 1966, when the spy craze was at its height. *Thunderball* (with Sean Connery as James Bond) had come out in December 1965 and eventually earned $26 million in rentals; *Our Man Flint* (with James Coburn in the title role) premiered in January and brought in $6.5 million; *The Silencers* (with Dean Martin as Matt Helm) arrived in February and earned $7 million. "If it had come out when we finished the picture, I think it would have been a big success because it was just the right moment for it," declares Cardiff.

But *The Liquidator* was not released to cinemas until November, by which time the public had already been exposed to *The Spy Who Came in from the Cold*, *Arabesque*, *Modesty Blaise*, *Last of the Secret Agents?*, *Where the Spies Are*, *The Second Best Secret Agent*, *To Trap a Spy* and *The Spy With My Face* — not to mention Rod's other spy spoof, *The Glass Bottom Boat*. By the end of 1966, *Variety* anticipated *The Liquidator*'s rentals would be a disappointing $1.75 million.

Reviews were mixed. *Variety* thought the film had "plenty of action and some crisp wisecracking," with Rod giving his role "plenty of charm and guts," although "he hardly suggests a character with such fundamental failings and frailties as Boysie." *Newsday* thought that the film "might not have seemed quite so vapid in context a year ago. But yesterday's fashion is today's tired movie," adding that

Rod's "special talent as an actor is his comic ability to show sexual frustration" (an odd judgment). *Time* magazine thought Rod looks so much like Sean Connery in the film "that he even seems to be wearing the same Charles of the Ritz chest wig."

There are many enjoyable things about *The Liquidator*: the color and locations, Lalo Schifrin's dynamic score, the black humor, some beautiful women (Gabriella Licudi is a standout) and enjoyable villains. However, the film never really gels. It lacks excitement and Jill St. John is a weak female lead (Diana Rigg auditioned for the part, but MGM wanted St. John); in addition, the plot fails to build up narrative momentum by falling into two halves, one involving Boysie's sub-contracted liquidator, the other involving a plot to kill the Duke of Edinburgh.

Rod, looking eerily like his co-star Trevor Howard in some scenes, was perhaps the wrong actor to play Boysie Oakes; although he was an ideal action hero and proficient with comedy, the film probably needed someone more obviously cowardly to really work — a Peter O'Toole or a Peter Sellers. He is certainly not as well cast as James Coburn, Dean Martin or Sean Connery were in their spy films.

A proposed sequel, for which Yeldham had written a script, *Amber Nine*, was never made; unlike Matt Helm and Flint, there was only one Boysie Oakes adventure on the big screen. But as a glossy, colorful 1960s spy movie with stunning locations and beautiful women, it has had a long and happy life on television.

Yeldham says that a few years later Rod contacted him with a view of having the writer rework one of Rod's scripts. Yeldham turned the actor down. "I have the feeling it would not have been an easy collaboration," he says.

ROD'S LAST FILM OF 1965 SAW HIM REUNITE WITH DORIS DAY and proved to be a far happier experience than *Do Not Disturb*. In *The Glass Bottom Boat* he plays a top-level government scientist who hires Doris as his personal assistant; the two of them begin a romance, but things are complicated when someone overhears Doris making phone calls to her dog, Vladimir, and thinks she's a Russian spy; the secret service get involved and complications ensue.

Doris' character in *The Glass Bottom Boat* was considerably sexier than audiences had become used to: too old at 41 to keep realistically playing virgins, she was cast here as a widow and there is even one scene where she tries to lure Rod into bed before they are married (this happens after he starts thinking she's a spy, so he doesn't go through with it — but she's definitely up for it, no question). Things could have been even raunchier: Doris was to have been stripped down to a bikini and painted gold a la Shirley Eaton in *Goldfinger* (1964), but the make-up man refused because of the health risk; Doris appeared in a Mata Hari costume instead.

Shooting mostly took place on the MGM backlot, apart from a week's location work on Catalina Island off Los Angeles. At this time parts of Catalina were inhabited by wild boar, pigs, mountain goats and buffalo; one day, when not filming, Rod and Fred Hakim elected to go pig-hunting with one of the island rangers. They stumbled upon a boar which charged Hakim at close range; Rod fired off a shot with his rifle, hitting the pig and breaking its back. The boar was said to weigh 250 pounds, a record on the island for the previous several years.

Rod enjoyed working with Doris Day again ("The best pro I ever worked with. After two films I had her drinking, smoking and saying naughty words"). He also liked director Frank Tashlin, describing him as, "the most gentle, unselfish man, always considering other people's problems."

MGM was pleased with the results and booked *The Glass Bottom Boat* into Radio City Music Hall for its premiere. *Variety* declared Rod "lends his usual masculine presence effectively" and *The Hollywood Reporter* extolled the actor as "an excellent match for Miss Day" with "a flair for comedy." By way of contrast, the *New York Times* thought Rod was "unremarkably immobile during the hectic doings." The public liked it, though, and *The Glass Bottom Boat* became Rod's biggest hit since *The VIPs*, earning $4.32 million in rentals.

Glass Bottom Boat is a cheerful comedy, much preferable to *Do Not Disturb*. Rod and Doris work even better together this time, the title song is catchy and there are some first-rate performances from the support cast (including Paul Lynde, Arthur Godfrey and a young Dom DeLuise). Amazingly, this would be the last out-and-out comedy Rod made for almost 20 years — a ridiculous waste considering the skill he had for the genre and indicates, in my opinion, a massive misjudgement on his part. It is even more absurd when one considers other actors that Rod admired greatly, such as Clark Gable, Spencer Tracy and Marlon Brando, all consistently made comedies throughout their careers.

WITH A NUMBER OF POPULAR FILMS IN RELEASE AND THE prestigious *Young Cassidy* behind him, "heat" was well and truly gathering around Rod Taylor by this stage. Hedda Hopper wrote this career summary of him in 1965: "The metamorphosis of a wild young man from Australia into a star of global magnitude is something I've watched over the past years with delight and an occasional twinge of apprehension. Rod Taylor was destined to attract women — a rough-hewn, handsome he-man in an era when that breed is all too scarce. But he's a man's actor also: men love his salty personality, nimble wit, good sportsmanship and the solid talent which enables him to play comedy, drama or adventure equally well. He's box office all over the world because he can lift an audience out of the frustrations of everyday living and imbue them with a sense of devil-may-care assertiveness."

In the words of film historian David Shipman, Rod Taylor was now established in the public's mind as "an imaginative man of action, a romantic junior
executive, very self-confident." The characters he played were equally comfortable in white-collar surroundings such as a science lab or boardroom as they were
in the outdoors. They had little difficulty attracting women and dealt comfortably with them, either with skillful banter or tenderness. They were loyal friends
and smart thinkers. In times of action they were natural leaders and good with
their fists.

Shipman compared the Rod Taylor of this period to the Don Ameche or Ray
Milland of 20 years earlier. While Rod presented a far more rugged image than
either of those two actors, the comparison is useful: like Ameche and Milland
he lacked the uniqueness of the truly great stars; however, he still had considerable charisma and could play a wide variety of roles. In addition, both Ameche
and Milland flourished best under long-term contract to major studios; although
such arrangements were no longer common in the 1960s, Rod was doing the
next best thing by tying himself into multi-picture deals with companies such
as MGM and Universal.

Rod claimed his price per picture now ranged from $250,000 to $300,000,
but that he mostly made films under his various long-term deals, where his fees
were around $100,000 to $125,000.

"I'm the type that needs business managers; when it comes to money, I'm an
idiot," he admitted. "I have three hoods who won't let me spend anything. They're
nasty, tough and very good for me. Because of these men I have a long-range
security investment plan. I love what I do and I'd like to remain in this business
as an actor or director. It's a threat to every other love I have."

MGM was especially happy with Rod and keen for him to appear in future
projects at the studio. Hedda Hopper wrote that he had become the "fair-haired
boy of Robert O'Brien" and was signing a contract with MGM that would "make
him a millionaire."

Rod might have already become one had he been more amenable when the
studio asked him to talk to David Lean about playing the title role in *Dr Zhivago*
(1965). Rod said when he was told there was no script yet he refused — what
he later described as another of his "brilliant bleeping decisions" which he had
regretted "ever since."

Another project for which MGM had Rod in mind was *Caravans*, an adaptation of James Michener's bestselling novel about an American diplomat searching
for the missing daughter of a US senator in 1946 Afghanistan. This was intended
to be a big-budget epic, made on location in Afghanistan, with Rod and possibly Omar Sharif in the leads; while filming *The Liquidator* in France, Rod met
with Grace Kelly with a view to persuading her to play the female lead. However, MGM never found a script it was happy with and the project took its time

getting anywhere. (It was eventually made in 1977, with Michael Sarrazin in the role originally ear-marked for Rod.)

In addition, Rod continued to develop scripts through Rodlor and his name was mentioned in association with a number of projects outside MGM: a film version of Pierre Boulle's novel *Planet of the Apes* from Fox; two Seven Arts properties eventually made with other actors: *The Owl and the Pussycat* (supposedly opposite Elizabeth Taylor, which would have been interesting) and *The Man Who Would Be King* (co-starring with Richard Burton for John Huston — which would have been even more interesting); also England's Rank Organization wanted to star Rod in *Last Bus to Banjo Creek* and *William the Conqueror* (neither of which were made).

Last Bus to Banjo Creek came the closest of all these projects to being made with Rod. The script by British writer Ted Willis was based on a short story by West Australian author Helen Wilson. The plot revolves around a cool, laid-back English girl who decides to visit her Australian fiancé at his station along on the Birdsville Track. A mix-up in dates prevents the fiancé from meeting her, so she travels out to him on a truck driven by an ocker called Stu; the two of them quarrel at first, then fall in love: in other words, it would be *The African Queen* (1951) in a truck, in peacetime outback Australia.

Rank wanted Rod to play Stu and announced filming would take place on location in Australia in late 1966; Jack Cardiff and Maggie Smith were mooted as a possible director and co-star and both would have been perfect. Universal was interested in coming on board as a partner, but wanted more work done on the screenplay. According to Ted Willis, Bob Mitchum was also being considered for the lead around this stage, but Rod was the only actor mentioned in any announcements made to the press. Scripts were written and rewritten and eventually the project got bogged down in "development hell." Rod would spend the next decade trying to get the film made but was never successful.

Despite this hitch, by the beginning of 1966, Rod had every reason to be pleased with the progress of his career. He was earning lots of money and had the backing of a major studio behind him; his name was on the lips of casting directors and executives, his profile was high, the future seemed limitless. He did not realize that he had actually reached his peak.

CHAPTER 9

"You work in show business, you have stars."

THE HOLLYWOOD PEAK (1966–68)

ROD SPENT THE FIRST FEW MONTHS OF 1966 AWAY FROM THE camera, preparing his next slate of projects. The films he had planned seemed guaranteed to ensure his popularity would stay at a high level for the remainder of the decade: an adaptation of a bestselling novel with an all-star cast; a tough Western that would also mark Rod's debut as producer; an action-packed "guys on a mission" war saga in the vein of *Guns of Navarone* (1961); two detective stories, both from popular books, either of which had the potential of going into a long-running series; and the first American movie from one of the cinematic geniuses of the age. There were also two riskier projects, an adventure thriller and a mid-life crisis melodrama.

It was a mouth-watering line-up, on paper at least, albeit one with an over-concentration of action/adventure tales. Unfortunately, all the films failed to meet expectations in one form or another and Rod Taylor's status in Hollywood never recovered. However, most of them are worth watching, two became cult classics and one stands with the best work Rod ever did.

Firmly in the worth-watching category was *Hotel*, the all-star bestseller adaptation, based on Arthur Hailey's novel about the coming and goings at a fictitious hotel in New Orleans. The structure was similar to *The VIPs*, with several subplots being intertwined in and around the one location.

Hotel was financed by Warner Bros., one of the last productions personally overseen by founding vice-president Jack Warner. Originally, the intention was for all the main roles in the film to be played by well-known stars, but Warners wanted to keep the budget down; accordingly, producer Wendell Mayes remembers they had a "terrible time casting… It was one of those situations where the studio wants to make a picture because they need something to take care of their overhead. They had nothing shooting, so we had to move very quickly in the casting. We all recognized that it was an old-fashioned formula picture and perhaps if we had had bigger stars, it would have gone at the box office as well as *Airport* (1970) [also based on a Hailey novel]."

A2 category star Rod was selected to play the lead, hotel manager Pete McDermott. In the course of the film's running time he has to deal with robberies, collapsing elevators, racial tensions, union troubles and a takeover bid for the hotel.

"He's the kind of man a woman would trust and another man would rely upon," enthused director Richard Quine about Rod. "Besides that, he had a mischievous romantic air about him."

Rod did not have any long-term arrangement with Warners and, accordingly, could charge his market rate, $250,000. The support cast included Karl Malden (as a hotel thief), Kevin McCarthy (a tycoon), Catherine Spaak (the tycoon's mistress), Melvyn Douglas (hotel owner), Richard Conte (hotel detective) and Merle Oberon (a rich duchess) — familiar faces and talented actors, but a line-up which perhaps lacked the real star power of a *VIPs*.

Merle Oberon had enjoyed a brief fling with Rod during the early 1960s. (He later claimed she was under the impression that he was "the re-incarnation of a former lover.") Like Rod, Merle was known as an Australian, the official version being she was born in Tasmania before moving to England. However, she was actually from India and used Tasmania as a cover story.

Filming on *Hotel* started in May 1966, with a week's shooting in New Orleans and the rest on the Warner Bros. backlot in Hollywood. An immense hotel lobby set was built in the studio at an estimated cost of $325,000; Karl Malden remembers Warners would rent out portions of it to various TV shows for use at night after the film had wrapped for the day. "Not really a vote of confidence in the picture from the studio management," he quipped.

The final budget of *Hotel* was $3,651,700 and by the end of 1967 the film had earned $3 million in rentals. Rod never liked the finished product — or, rather, his performance in it. "I was so restricted I could not be my usual gregarious self," he grumbled. "I was so stiff, I hated myself in that."

Rod Taylor *is* a little stiff in *Hotel*, a movie whose main problem is the fact that its stories are not all brought together the way they would be in the far more successful *Airport*. Another problem is the hotel itself — admittedly beautiful, there is no escaping the fact it is owned by a man (played by Melvyn Douglas) who does not want black people as guests and contains an elevator so dilapidated it causes the death of one of its passengers. While Quine argued that "in *Hotel* we're simply saying that when you destroy the past you kill the future," on this evidence it's not really a tragedy that such a place be shut down. But, like *The Liquidator* and *The VIPs*, the film does have advantages: color photography, glossy production design and plenty of attractive movie stars in the cast (even if mostly second-rate ones).

ROD'S NEXT PROJECT, *CHUKA*, MARKED RODLOR'S FIRST SUCCESSFUL attempt at moving into production. The film was based on a novel by Richard Jessup about a group of stagecoach passengers who get holed up at a fort in the American west, circa 1876; the fort's troops consist of various army rejects — rebels, bullies, rapists, cowards, etc. — who have been dumped there by an embarrassed Washington. Personality clashes within the fort are brought to a head when the local Indians attack; "Chuka" is the nickname for the lead character, a taciturn gunfighter who joins in the fight.

Rod was first given a copy of Jessup's novel by producer Jack Jason while filming *The Liquidator* in London. The actor says when he read it he was "hooked immediately" as it was "a Western with no clichés... the characters were believable, there were no phoney heroics."

Rod was also attracted by the idea of playing the lead role, "a part that's the complete antithesis of the leading man types I've been doing." He thought the film could turn him into a "character star" and open up an entirely new range of parts for him to play.

Rodlor spent $25,000 acquiring the story and a script from Jessup. Paramount agreed to provide a budget of $1.7 million, of which Rod received $125,000 as salary to play the title role and Rodlor $75,000 as producer's fee (Rod would be credited as producer along with Jack Jason). Rodlor received 10% of the gross receipts of the film in excess of 2.75 times the negative cost and 25% of the net profits.

Like many an actor-turned-producer before him, Rod soon discovered that producing a movie was not as easy as it looked. He later admitted that he "never honestly knew what producers did before," but he "found out. Problems all day long and half the night."

In particular, it was difficult finalizing the script. Jessup wrote three drafts in succession, with Rod and Jason making suggestions along the way. Rod was still not satisfied, so Richard Fielder was brought in and he worked on it until early September 1966, after which he was replaced by Franklin Coen. Rod and Jason then wrote their own draft, Rod claiming he "had to rewrite big chunks... in order to get actors like John Mills and Ernest Borgnine to like it well enough to come in with me." Rod and Jason eventually tried to obtain a screenplay credit for themselves, but the Writers Guild determined Jessup receive sole billing.

Chuka's final script made a number of changes from the novel, most of them improvements. Several characters were dropped, including Chuka's two companions and a married couple who are passengers on the stagecoach. The Indians were given greater motivation for attacking the fort (namely, they are forced into it by starvation) and the 50-something Veronica Klietz had around 20 years lopped off her age and was turned into Chuka's ex-girlfriend. But the ending was made less clear: in the novel both Chuka and Veronica's young ward Helena escape (a very exciting sequence), but are happy to let everyone think they have been killed in order to start new lives. In the movie, the Indian chief lets Chuka and Helena live, but then there is a cut to an unmarked grave, implying that they died (or, alternatively, it could be Veronica's grave).

For a director, Rod hired Gordon Douglas, an old-school professional whose credits varied in quality, but who was capable of rising with a good script (e.g. *The Detective* [1968]); furthermore, he had prior experience making films for head-strong stars-turned-producers (Frank Sinatra, Alan Ladd, Jerry Lewis). Not that the collaboration with Rod would prove easy: Howard Gotbetter, an executive on *Chuka*, remembers one of the problems during production was "Rod Taylor was telling Gordon Douglas how to direct and I think both of them knew shit."

Rod ensured he was surrounded by some excellent supporting actors, including Ernest Borgnine, John Mills, Michael Cole, Louis Hayward and James Whitmore; Mills later enthused that Rod was "another actor's actor" and great to work with. Female interest was provided by Luciana Paluzzi (playing Veronica) and Angela Dorian (Helena). Rod did not forget his entourage, either: Fred Hakim was listed in the credits as "production associate" and Marco Lopez was given a significant role as the Indian chief; this performance seemed to kick-start Lopez's acting career and by the end of the decade he would be in constant demand for character parts, including a regular role on *Adam-12* (1968–75).

The quality of *Chuka*'s cast had one major downside: it was expensive and cut into the budget, necessitating the majority of filming to be done in the studio instead of on location as originally planned. Unfortunately, the artificial setting is all too apparent in the finished product.

Rod's mother and father were in town during the shoot and stayed with Rod, Mary and Felicia at the Beverly Hills house. Mona was uncomfortable with Hollywood life but Bill had a great time, living it up in bars and seeing the sights. Rod complained that his father "brought home every drunken bum I had been ducking in Hollywood for years." Meryl Wheeler remembers: "Bill really enjoyed that because he was able to drink with all these famous people that Rod had there — there was John Wayne and the big fellow that used to play Hoss in *Bonanza* [Dan Blocker], all these other names... [Mona] couldn't quite come to terms with the fact that they partied all night, whereas Mona would sleep all night and want to get up and do things in the day, but everyone was sleeping during the day because they'd been partying all night. She said it was a reverse type of living. She wasn't a lady that would have enjoyed a lot of people drinking... I can imagine, knowing her, she would have been horrified by all of that. And possibly now that when you think back, a lot of things, because I think she kept a lot of things quiet; Rod's father didn't handle drink very well."

Once shooting completed, Rod claimed he enjoyed the experience of producing and said he was keen to do it again. He also said that he was ready to "try his hand at directing, too," but that he would not try producing and directing at the same time. "I'm not an all-purpose genius," he declared.

However, Rod's dreams of launching his non-acting movie career with *Chuka* then struck an unexpected hurdle. During the film's production, Paramount was taken over by the industrial conglomerate Gulf and Western, who installed a new head of production, Robert Evans. *Chuka* was a non-Evans project and Gotbetter claims that Paramount's new management "didn't give a crap about what had been made earlier" at the studio and "abandoned" the film.

This is a common complaint in Hollywood by the makers of financially unsuccessful movies, but in *Chuka's* case it seems to be true: Evans did not mention the film at all when launching the studio's upcoming releases for 1967 and *Chuka's* eventual distribution was extremely erratic; for instance, after being trade-screened in April, the movie did not make it to New York until November, where it was thrown away on a double bill with the British adventure film *The Long Duel* (1967).

Ironically, when *Chuka* was shown, it received very good reviews on the whole. An example was *Variety*, who described the movie as "a well-paced period oater.... Taylor, of late confined to contemporary, sometimes reactive roles, gives an excellent title role performance as the bearded, rugged, totally virile saddle-tramp... with a bigger budget and somewhat more detailed elaboration of the principals' pasts, pic would have been a shoo-in for the big money and top playing time... as it is, there is enough going for it to turn out as a very pleasant surprise at the b.o."

Richard Schickel in *Life* magazine took some time out of his (positive) review of the film to sum up Rod's career: "Over a decade, since his first, brief appearance in *Giant*, he has slowly developed into one of our most dependable and dependably appealing leading men. He does not excite overheated publicity; he is a personality who is simply there, working carefully at his craft, content to serve his films rather than himself."

Unfortunately, *Chuka's* box-office performance did not match its crits: the picture failed to make *Variety's* list of top grossers of 1967. This cannot be blamed entirely on poor distribution; Westerns may have been a sure bet commercially in the '50s, but by the late '60s they generally had to either star John Wayne or be a really fresh take on the genre a la *Butch Cassidy and the Sundance Kid* (1969). And *Chuka* lacked freshness.

Watching the film today is an odd experience. In almost every scene you can feel the filmmakers trying to produce something memorable — but it never quite clicks. The unconvincing studio setting is a major flaw, as is the downbeat and slightly confusing ending. Although the central idea is terrific, with an inherently tense situation, there is a bewildering lack of suspense throughout.

The star's own performance is erratic. Rod was not well cast as a laconic, grizzled gunfighter; he is at his best when being gregarious and friendly, rather than as a hard-bitten loner. However, in other areas he is fine: Rod was a highly skilled on-screen fighter by this stage and he moves in the action sequences with lightning speed. He also romances Luciana Paluzzi with tenderness and engages in enjoyable macho by-play with Ernest Borgnine and James Whitmore. It's not an unenjoyable film by any means — just a frustrating one, because it could (and should) have been so much better.

When filming *Chuka*, Rod announced he would make his next films for Seven Arts and Universal; he also said there might be a reunion with Alfred Hitchcock. In actual fact, Rod's next picture was back at MGM and it turned out to be one of the best things he ever did.

DARK OF THE SUN WAS BASED ON *THE MERCENARIES,* THE SECOND novel by Wilbur Smith, a South African accountant who turned his passion for hunting and African history into highly readable, tremendously popular adventure tales. The hero of *The Mercenaries* is Captain Bruce Curry, a Rhodesian mercenary hired during the Congo troubles of the early 1960s to rescue residents of a distant mining outpost, where they (along with some diamonds) have been cut off. Accompanied by a number of fellow soldiers of fortune, Curry sets off to the outpost by train, fighting UN forces and savage native warriors as he goes.

The book offered an opportunity to make a tough, guys-on-a-mission film in the style of *The Bridge on the River Kwai* (1957) and *The Guns of Navarone* (1961). "It was a good movie book," confirms George Englund, who produced the film under a three-picture deal he had with MGM.

According to Englund, Wilbur Smith had little involvement in the making of the film. "His only involvement was a bizarre time in London. The title of the book was *The Mercenaries,* which MGM thought was too provocative. I had a meeting with Smith's agent and publisher and someone else at the Dorchester Hotel. No one knew anyone else and it was very stiff and tentative. Everyone was too shy about suggesting a new title. I thought, 'We've got to loosen this up,' so I called up the concierge and got them to bring up a bottle of whisky. So we started drinking that, then I called up and asked for a Bible. The concierge put two and two together — I've asked for a bottle of whisky and a Bible — and asked if I was OK. He thought I was going to kill myself."

Englund only wanted to find possible alternative names for the film. "We went through the Bible and got *Dark of the Sun*. That was the birthplace of that."

Filming was originally set to take place in Uganda in early 1965, but the deteriorating political situation there caused it to be postponed. Englund tried to find a suitable alternative African country, but they all proved either too dangerous or logistically unworkable. Someone then suggested Jamaica. The Caribbean island was not only an excellent visual substitute for Africa, the government offered support in terms of facilities and manpower. In particular, it would supply a train, something crucial to the script.

Rod's name came up fairly early in discussions over who would play the lead role of Bruce Curry. "The studio liked him a lot," says Englund. "And I agreed he was a good candidate to play that role."

Rod was delighted to come on board: not only would *Dark of the Sun* be a classy action film with excellent commercial prospects, the lead role was something he could really get his teeth into — Curry was a man who had led a very violent life, but still tried to hang on to his essential decency. In Smith's novel, Curry was a Rhodesian, but, as in *The Liquidator*, Rod elected to play the character as American. Unfortunately, this hurt the believability of the story, as there were few American mercenaries in the Congo during this time (Americans risked losing their citizenship if they served in foreign armies).

Jack Cardiff signed on to direct, making it his third film with Rod (a record for any director). American football player Jim Brown, who had recently impressed in *The Dirty Dozen* (1967), was cast as Curry's African sidekick, Ruffo. The other main roles were played by Kenneth More, as an alcoholic doctor who accompanies the mission, and Rod's old *Time Machine* co-star, Yvette Mimieux, as Claire, a woman they pick up along the way who becomes romantically involved with Curry.

According to Cardiff, when Englund broke the news of Mimieux's casting to Rod, the actor exclaimed, "My God, I wonder if I'm going to get a performance out of her?"

"Well, maybe the director will help a bit," replied Englund.

(When asked to confirm this, Englund could not recall Rod saying those exact words, but admits, "It's exactly the kind of thing that came out of him in those days. I think he's humbler now, but in that era he had a super and swaggering ego.")

Filming started in January 1967. Jamaica may have been an easier location to shoot in than Uganda, but everyone soon realized the country had problems of its own. "There was a lot of political unrest there at the time and there was an election, which was causing a lot of fighting," says Cardiff. Englund remembers driving up a mountain in his jeep one day, "To avoid some kind of political mob. They had blood in their eyes."

In his memoirs, Kenneth More recalls that production was plagued by organizational troubles. He alleges that Cardiff was "rather lax" about starting each day and the crew would have to wait until Rod or Jim Brown were ready — sometimes until as late as nine or ten o'clock. "This sort of casual indiscipline spread through the whole unit," wrote More, adding that "it was not a good atmosphere in which to work and encouraged tensions."

The chaos of the shoot was exemplified by the events of one night in particular. While filming a scene involving the train, one of the gas line generators used to supply the arc lights with power failed, plunging the set into darkness; cinematographer Ted Scaife eventually had to resort to using open flares to light the set. First assistant director Ted Sturgis then stumbled into a stack of metal railroad ties, gashing his leg and requiring five stitches. The axle on the trailer of the unit medic broke, causing the trailer to collapse. Photographer Laurie Turner fell into a pit of discarded diesel engine oil and the camera broke down. While the crew repaired the camera, the open flares used to light the set caused a pile of empty cardboard boxes to catch fire.

Kenneth More: "All the time the rain teemed down like something out of a Somerset Maugham short story. We were soaked all day on location and at night we only had each other's company in our hotel. Everyone's opinion was asked about different shots, except mine. And yet I had appeared in more films than the rest of the cast put together. If I had a good line in the script, it was cut down and then pruned and finally it would disappear altogether."

Dark of the Sun's script ended up being rewritten to such a degree that the original screenwriter, Ranald MacDougall, insisted his name be taken off the credits and replaced by a pseudonym, "Quentin Werty." Rod confessed to doing a lot of the rewriting himself, arguing he did it to make his part "more human." ("I rewrite everything now," he claimed at the time. "Not just to be a bloody nuisance, not to grab more lines, none of that crap, but to give depth to a part.")

Among Rod's contributions was helping devise a new ending. In an earlier draft of the script, Ruffo is killed by a vicious mercenary (played in the film by Peter Carsten), whom Curry then tortures and decapitates in revenge; Curry feels bad about this afterwards, but that doesn't stop him from going off into the sunset with Claire. In the final film, however, Curry decides to put himself under arrest for killing Carsten — the last shot has him sitting in the back of a truck, being held prisoner by his own men.

This is a highly unusual conclusion for an action film — the hero giving himself up voluntarily for the mayhem he has wrecked — and it indicates Rod (and Cardiff, Englund and company) were interested in making more than just a typical shoot-'em-up. *Dark of the Sun* tries to explore the violent nature of humans and the struggle involved in keeping this violence under control, especially in the name of civilization.

Another change was the shifting of the story's emotional focus. In contrast with the original novel, which centers around the romance between Curry and Claire, the film emphasizes the relationship between Curry and Ruffo. For all intents and purposes, *Dark of the Sun* is a platonic love story between these two men, with the female love interest pushed to the side (indeed, a love scene between Rod and Mimieux was cut from the final film).

Despite (or because) of this, George Englund remembers some interesting off-screen dynamics that took place between Rod and Jim Brown. "Rod Taylor was a very competitive guy and Jim Brown, God knows, was competitive. Rod Taylor kind of said to him, 'You're in the movie business now, this is what I know,' sort of thing. And sometimes he was very helpful to Jim and they worked well together. But there was a kind of jungle sniffing that went on between the two of them. Rod was more into it than Jim Brown, 'Who's the toughest guy?'... It was a kind of macho thing going on between them but it ebbed and flowed. Rod at the best of times would help Jim."

Kenneth More claims that Rod and Brown "appeared to hate each other" and would "threaten to settle disputes with their fists." Rod admitted that the cast and crew "were all at each other's throats" during the shoot.

Englund says Rod could be difficult, but was ultimately professional: "He's a rough, tough guy, Rod. It was friendly, but... You work in show business, you have stars. He wanted to make the picture well. He worked hard. He didn't always agree and we locked horns. He's very professional and that's a crucial thing. He knew his work, what goes into making a film — what sort of lenses go in the camera. We had some problems, some friction. But I was very happy with him. He had a good career, I thought. Drinking. That was an issue. You could see if he went on that his body would go."

"I never had any trouble with him and we never had any arguments," Jack Cardiff told Justin Bowyer. "He wasn't the sort of man to take anything lightly, though, and he would pick a fight with anybody. I remember one of the electricians had said something jokingly to him and Rod just quietly handed me his glass, which I knew meant that he was going to go for this chap. I had to calm him down; he was that sort."

There was no denying Rod's commitment to the role, though. One day he tore a tendon while jumping from a second-story balcony into a jeep; he was taken to hospital in Kingston and told by the orthopaedic surgeon to rest for at least six weeks. The star just bandaged his knee, took a bunch of painkillers and returned to work within three days, refusing to use a stunt double.

The lessons of John Saul had been taken to the extreme: Rod claimed he had to "live" the role of Bruce Curry "for many, many months" and that meant "every facet" of Curry's life. "If this means fighting his fights, then that's exactly what I intend doing. It would be an insincere performance if I allowed someone else to take over for me."

Rod's efforts were rewarded with a powerful performance, among the greatest of his career. One of his best moments comes during the scene where Curry goes mad with rage following the death of Ruffo. Englund: "What an acting challenge! He became very primitive. I'd read a book, *The Hunt for Kimathi*. The book had been written by a sergeant [Ian Henderson]. Kimathi was head of the Mau Mau, he lived like an animal, covered his body in dung. The sergeant said the only way to get Kimathi was to live like an animal and track him. He followed him for months. [The night before shooting that scene] I talked about it with Rod and we discussed what it was like to be an animal. He was creative and courageous. The best actors have courage, bravery and he had that."

Indeed, Rod became so tightly wound up in the part of Bruce Curry that he had trouble letting go of the role after filming. Sheilah Graham wrote of a meeting she had with the actor in London where he was "pounding tables, using four, seven and eight-letter words and assigning various people of the world to damnation." Rod said this behavior was due to the effect making *Dark of the Sun* had on him: "I played a dirty, stinking bum. You push and push and push… I don't care about me. I want people to understand this picture. I've made a movie about a piece of history to the utmost of my craft. I look at myself on screen and say, 'That's not me.'…

"The strangest things happened to me and the others. Some got ulcers, some had nervous breakdowns. We really went through hell to make a picture. It's an incredible piece of film. The publicity slogan should be, 'If you don't want violence, don't see this film.' In one scene instead of killing a man by ordinary means, I kill him like an animal. Then I wash the blood off my hands.

"My wife Mary saw the film in rough cut and she came out weeping hysterically and crying, 'Thank God you're here.' This is one picture where I will stand in the center of the ring and you can throw bottles at me and hate it, but this is what I believe in. I'm going to stand on everything I say because this is what can happen to a strong man. They've done this sort of thing before but it was fake. This is real. This has a rhythm, momentum. I thought I was going to be given another of those Errol Flynn parts, but suddenly it was something bigger than me… I flopped over the edge into an abyss."

When *Dark of the Sun* reached cinemas in July 1968, the critics were unanimously hostile — in fact, of the 20-odd contemporary reviews of the film I have perused, almost all of them were negative. A sample: "Often the violence is gratuitous and the pic also has to carry some glib philosophizing" (*Variety*); "exhausts inhumanity for its own sake and fails to illuminate a single character with believable motives or emotions" (*The Hollywood Reporter*); "an unconvincing melodrama that will backfire for all but the most indiscriminate of action fans" (*Los Angeles Times*); "I couldn't recommend any film less" (*Daily Express*).

In my opinion the critics were absolutely wrong — *Dark of the Sun* is a terrific, gripping action drama, full of numerous memorable scenes, that tries to deal with serious topics. The acting is top-notch: Rod's performance is one of the best things he ever did, as an intelligent man who nonetheless embraces his "animal" side with an intensity that later repulses him. Brown is extremely likeable as his idealistic friend, as is More as the alcoholic doctor who finds redemption and Mimieux as a shell-shocked citizen caught up in war. The action scenes are consistently thrilling; with the sequence of the mercenaries waiting to open a time-locked safe while the Simbas are on their way being particularly tense. It really looks and feels like it is taking place in Africa and Jacques Louissier's score is a haunting masterpiece. *Dark of the Sun* is one of the finest action movies of the 1960s and is among the greatest films that Rod ever made.

A factor that possibly affected critical reaction is that the story is set in an inherently depressing time and place: 1960s Africa. Unlike fighting the Nazis in World War II, there are no clear goodies or baddies in *Dark of the Sun* (compare it with *The Dirty Dozen* - no matter how nasty the dozen were, they were still only killing Nazis). There was no ultimate happy ending for the Congo, either — today the country remains a backwater of corruption, poverty and war.

This, in addition to the critical response, seems to have affected *Dark of the Sun*'s box-office performance: by the end of 1968 the film had earned estimated rentals in the US of only $2 million, although it performed better in Europe. "It didn't do as well as we thought it'd do," admitted Englund. "It was a little premature, a little ahead of its time."

Time has passed and the reputation of *Dark of the Sun* has improved significantly; indeed, a devoted cult has emerged around it. Martin Scorsese wrote about how much he enjoyed the film in his introduction to Cardiff's autobiography; Quentin Tarantino included it as part of a "Bunch of Guys on a Mission War Film" double-bill at the 2001 Quentin Tarantino Film Festival in Austin, Texas. In his introductory spiel to the film, Tarantino rhapsodized about Rod Taylor: "Most of you probably know Rod Taylor from *The Time Machine* or *The Birds* or the voice of Pongo from *101 Dalmatians*, he's the daddy dog in that. Actually one of my favorite voice performances in Disney history! Well, Rod Taylor was the Russell Crowe of his time. He was an Aussie and played the same sorts of roles as Crowe! You should really check out *36 Hours* with him and James Garner. Rod Taylor is one of the few guys on the planet that I could believe could whup Jim Brown.

"Now, I've heard a story. A tale I once heard from an old Playmate, not one of mine, but one of Hugh's. Now I'm not saying I believe this, but if I could believe it about anyone, I'd believe it about Rod Taylor. But this old Playmate told me about a party that Hugh Hefner had back in the day, might have even been while they were working on this film, where Jim Brown and Rod Taylor were both at the Mansion and got into it. Apparently they went out to the part of the Mansion where your car pulls up and went at it. Rod Taylor and Jim Brown actually fought. Now this sounds impossible, but as the story goes, Rod Taylor apparently beat Jim Brown."

Industry news website *Ain't It Cool News* reported on the screening: "There are very few times in the course of a year of filmgoing where a film can give you afterglow. Afterwards, this movie confirmed my entire belief in watching films that no one has heard of… *Dark of the Sun* is an immense film. This film was literally ripped straight from the headlines of the period. The civil wars and warring tribes of the Congo… The hacking deaths, the feeding of nuns to alligators… Death to all… Rod Taylor and Jim Brown are so fucking great in this movie…. Jack Cardiff's direction is absolutely the definition of perfection… The look of the film, the visceral horror of it all… the emotional hot poker to the eye of the flick… Just absolutely impeccable."

Hopefully time will see the fame of *Dark of the Sun* rank along with *The Time Machine* and *The Birds*; it deserves to be celebrated with them as Rod Taylor masterpieces.

CHAPTER 10

"I'm Tired of My Tough Image."

STAR DECLINE (1968–70)

IN 1968, ALAN HOROWITZ, A BUSINESSMAN WHO SERVED AS the executive vice-president (whatever that meant) of Rodlor, predicted that over the next few years, Rod Taylor would become the number one international male box-office movie star in the world. "Rod is a blinding talent," gushed Horowitz. "He's the most professional professional I've ever known in movies, both in front of and behind the camera. He can bloody well act and he has personality, charm and taste. He can play comedy, heavy drama or the action hero and he gives more than the usual one-dimensional performance that you get from the average matinee idol."

By this stage, however, it was clear Rod wasn't particularly interested in performing comedy or heavy drama anymore; all he wanted to play was the action hero: "I'd like to show what a real Aussie's like, you know. This is rough with men, gentle with women bit, the adventure type guy. That seems to be the way I'm being channelled. I love high comedy, but playing with Doris Day I always have this insecurity thing about Cary Grant. I feel people are saying, 'He's not Cary Grant — who the hell does he think he is.'"

In fact, Rod had become obsessed with his he-man "image" and was always bringing it up in conversations with the media. "I'm up to here with it," he whined. "They always want me to throw punches and make love in bed and I'm no good at either."

Unfortunately, playing all these tough-guy roles meant Rod was cutting himself off from the other parts he had enjoyed during his first decade and a half as an actor. Not only did this limit his range, it potentially hurt his career, as the public did not display an overwhelming desire to see him in action films. Indeed, his most successful pictures at the box office had been comedies, dramas and thrillers.

A case in point was Rod's next feature, *The Hell with Heroes* (1968). This was an action drama about two American pilots (Rod and Peter Deuel) running an air freight charter service in north Africa immediately after World War II. They are pressured into smuggling for a crime lord, whose mistress (Claudia Cardinale) ends up falling for Rod.

The Hell with Heroes was made at Universal, whom Rod still owed a picture under the contract he signed with them back in 1962. By this stage his market price for a film was (he claimed) $400,000 plus 10% of the gross, but Universal could hire him cheaply due to the earlier deal: $100,000, plus the use of a valet for seven-and-a-half weeks.

"He was a star at the time that people wanted to do films with, so the moment he came aboard Universal green-lighted the film rather quickly," recalls producer Stanley Chase.

Rod could have used his cheap rate at Universal to make himself more attractive to the producers of a really important studio film — one with, say, an A-list director, well-known source material or heavyweight co-star. After all, that was the technique Rod employed so successfully in the early 1960s. But *The Hell with Heroes* lacked any of these things. Despite Claudia Cardinale as love interest (she was paid more than Rod, $160,000), the film was dangerously close to being a B-picture: $1.6 million budget, first-time director and low-profile cast; *Variety* labeled it a "programmer… another of [Universal's] near-standard 101-minute features already pre-timed for TV." (*Chuka* had not been an A-picture either, but at least in that case Rod was the producer.) Contractual obligations aside, Rod and his advisers should have known even at script stage that *The Hell with Heroes* marked a step back for the actor.

Why the miscalculation? One can't help think Rod was chiefly attracted to *The Hell with Heroes* because of the character he got to play: a former war ace who is tough and cynical, but also humorous, loyal and secretly idealistic. This fit squarely within the persona Rod sought to convey at this stage in his career. He also may have enjoyed the power of being a big fish in a small pond — notably the ability to have his creative demands obeyed. It may also be significant that by this stage Wilt Melnick had stopped being Rod's agent (though the two men remained friendly until Melnick's death in 2001); his new representative was Hugh French.

Stanley Chase says that throughout the shoot, "Rod was motivated, always on time and he made suggestions about the script and his character which we used. He was pretty much into it all the way along the line."

When not required on set, Rod would retire to his trailer and work on future Rodlor projects. Among them were *Last Bus to Banjo Creek*, a version of the Charles Sturt expedition, and *That Woman*, a drama for director Edward Dmytryk.

(Incidentally, the trailer was one Rod had designed himself. It contained a desk, filing cabinet, telephone switchboard and all the other essentials for a business office. Rod would hire it out to studios for his various films.)

The Hell with Heroes ranks among Rod's flattest efforts of the '60s. The setting of post-war Africa is an exciting one and Claudia Cardinale is incredibly sexy (she and Rod have fantastic chemistry, the best any woman had with him apart from Maggie Smith), but the film never gels. Rod's on-screen relationship with Peter Deuel feels like a poor retread of the one he had had with Jim Brown in *Dark of the Sun*, right down to Rod's character thinking he is not as morally good as Deuel and Deuel meeting a tragic, violent death at the hands of the villain. Another problem is that Rod's character decides not to kill the villain when he has the chance 30 minutes before the end, making the last act feel like an anti-climax.

Rod should have been a natural in the lead, but while he has his moments his performance is, on the whole, patchy and over-the-top (for instance, following Deuel's death he becomes excessively weepy). Director Joseph Sergeant went on to have a distinguished career, with such credits as *The Taking of Pellham One Two Three* (1974), but on this occasion seems to have been unable to control the excesses of his star. By the end of 1968, *The Hell with Heroes* had grossed a mere $269,700 at the box office.

THIS WAS A DIFFICULT TIME FOR ROD PERSONALLY. HIS MARRIAGE to Mary continued to go from bad to worse — within the space of a few years they separated a half-dozen times or so — and in June 1968, Rod eventually sued for divorce on the grounds of extreme cruelty. Mary took Felicia and moved to Palm Springs, while Rod stayed in L.A.

During the divorce proceedings, Rod told the judge that Mary would get jealous of him because of his job. "If she saw a film in which I kissed my woman co-star, my wife went into a hysterical outburst which usually lasted all night," he complained. "Sex in films and passionate love scenes affect a man's marriage very badly."

Mary did not contest the suit and the court approved a settlement dividing community property believed to be worth more than $500,000. Rod agreed to pay Mary $4,500 a month for five years until 1974 and $1,500 a month thereafter until 1980, except if she remarried, in which case the payments would cease upon him transferring $20,000 to her outright. Mary agreed to support Felicia until she turned 16, after which Rod would pay his daughter $500 a month.

Rod never seemed too upset by the dissolution of his second marriage, but was very annoyed at the alimony it cost him. He started referring to Mary in interviews as "the Spider Lady" and depicting her as "a very poor model when I met and wed her, but a very rich model since our divorce."

Mary did not remarry until 1980, the year her alimony ran out, when she wed millionaire Arthur Rubloff, founder of the largest real-estate firm in Chicago. After he died in 1986, she married Lewis Schott, a wealthy lawyer;

they lived in Palm Beach, Florida, where Mary became an active socialite and charity fundraiser, particularly for victims of domestic violence. She died on March 7, 2009.

Felicia grew up with her mother and went on to enjoy considerable professional success in the media in her own right. She completed a degree in communications at Northwestern University and started a career in television, working as a news anchor and reporter in Chicago, London and New York. ("Dunno where she got this from," reflected Rod later.)

Now single again, Rod returned to a life of near-constant womanizing. As he himself once put it in the early '70s, he made "love to as many women who will let me. Basically I am a homebody. That is, I bring my bodies home."

ROD'S NEXT UNDERTAKING SEEMED CONSIDERABLY MORE promising than *The Hell with Heroes. The High Commissioner* was based on a best-seller by Jon Cleary, one of Australia's most internationally popular authors (*The Sundowners, You Can't See Round Corners*). The story revolved around Sydney detective Scobie Malone, who is sent to London to arrest the Australian High Commissioner for murdering his first wife. The Commissioner is chairing Vietnam War peace talks and refuses to return home until his mission is completed. When someone tries to assassinate the Commissioner, Scobie becomes reluctantly co-opted into the role of bodyguard.

Film rights were bought by America's Selmur Productions, an off-shoot of the ABC television network, who made the movie as a co-production with Britain's Rank Organization. Selmur's involvement seems to have been strictly financial; creatively the movie was almost entirely British, with the producer and director being Betty Box and Ralph Thomas respectively, a team best known for the Dirk Bogarde *Doctor* series. Although part of the story took place in Sydney and the Australian outback, all filming was done in London, either on location or at Pinewood Studios.

In the late 1960s, only two Australian actors had a high enough profile to be realistically considered candidates for Scobie: Peter Finch and Rod Taylor. Finch had worked with Box and Thomas previously, on the excellent *No Love for Johnnie* (1961), but of the two, Rod was easily the more physically appropriate to play a rough-around-the-edges cop. "I thought he [Rod] was as Scobie was at that stage, because he was unmarried and a bit callow," agrees Cleary.

Nonetheless, Rod was initially reluctant to accept the role. He had reservations about the screenplay ("The dialogue just didn't come alive") and was concerned about his ability to pull off an Australian accent. "I've been a phoney American so long that when I meet Aussies and start slipping back into the idiom it's funny," he admitted. Eventually, Rod agreed to play the part, but only on the proviso they let him "fiddle with the script."

"When I heard I'd got the part I invited some Aussie friends of mine over and said 'TALK,'" recalled Rod. "It took me a while to practice the lingo again — quite a long time — about an hour."

Among the script fiddling Rod did was rewriting the opening sequence. The original screenplay introduced Malone drinking beer in a Sydney pub; the Rod Taylor version starts with the detective arresting a cattle thief in the outback; Rod adds a line "explaining" Malone is on holidays. This change annoyed Jon Cleary. "The one thing about all the Malone books is that everything in it, even if sometimes I've got to ditch drama, is true to life," said the author. "I had people at homicide and in ballistics who were my advisers and that was the idea. The whole idea of the Malone books was that it's an ordinary man doing an extraordinary job, which is what it is with cops. You know, they never know when they're going to be knocked over... When I saw that bit I lost interest in the movie because no way in the world would a police commissioner send for a country sergeant in a country town to go to arrest the High Commissioner for murder."

The script went on to depart from Cleary's novel in other crucial ways: Scobie has sex with two women, one of whom (Daliah Lavi) is the villain and tries to kill him immediately afterwards, James Bond-style; any references to the Vietnam War are minimized, presumably so as not to offend American sensibilities; and the cultural differences between Australia and London, subtle in the book, were rammed down the audience's throat (for instance, while surveying the High Commissioner's residence, Malone blurts out, "Sure beats the old shearing shed").

At least the support cast was impressive: key roles were played by Christopher Plummer (the High Commissioner), Lilli Palmer, Daliah Lavi, Franchot Tone (in his final screen role) and Camilla Sparv. A number of Australian actors then living in London had small parts: Leo McKern played a New South Wales Premier loosely based on Sir Robert Askin (the best performance in the film); Ken Wayne was Plummer's chauffer and Charles Tingwell the cattle thief beaten up by Rod at the beginning. ("Rod asked me to do it under the Old Pal's Act," laughs Tingwell.)

But there was no doubt who the real star of *The High Commissioner* was — especially not in the mind of that star himself. An anecdote to illustrate: Sally Brass from the *LA Times* visited the set during filming and watched Rod finish up a scene. After Ralph Thomas called "cut," the actor walked off set, shouting to the director, "OK. Print three. Wrap it up! Lunch for everyone." He then hopped into his Rolls-Royce and had his chauffeur drive he and Brass to a sedate country pub for lunch ("I don't like to eat, I like to dine," explained Rod). Upon arriving, Rod banged his fist on the table and yelled, "Booze! Where's the booze!" A waiter asked if he could take their order and Rod responded by yelling, "Where the hell's the booze?" As wine was delivered to Rod, the actor admitted to Brass he liked to interfere with his films. "The cast hates me for it," he chuckled, adding that, "I've got a good thing with directors [though]. There's an immediate response when I tell them what to do."

By now Rod's ego was clearly out of control. Another example of his big-headed behavior came on the night of *The High Commissioner*'s London premiere, when Rod visited the Revolution Club in Mayfair with his occasional off-screen companion Zsa Zsa Gabor and co-stars Derren Nesbitt and Daliah Lavi. They were all on the dance floor together when Rod and Nesbitt ended up getting into a brawl with some other club patrons. Rod claimed he "saw some other guys fighting" and since he "had just seen my movie" he "dived in like the tough guy hero to break it up." Rod went back to dancing but said the men started fighting again, so he lunged back in and fell over on his backside. Rod tried to make light of the well-publicized incident, claiming he was "left sitting on the floor" afterwards and "didn't lay a glove on them." But he only came across as an idiot.

Reviews for *The High Commissioner* were encouraging: *Variety* described it as "a couple of smooth hours of undemanding entertainment" in which Rod "gives a thoroughly likeable and credible performance"; the *New York Times* thought Rod was "quite good" while *The Hollywood Reporter* praised him as "rough and likeable, in a manner that he has long perfected, no doubt because he gets little choice to act otherwise." The *Citizen News* gave him (and the film) a rave: "The suspense is terrific. Even if you can't understand half the genuine Australian dialect in it, you'll really understand the action and gape at all the beautiful people… Rod Taylor is as ruggedly excellent as always as the Aussie detective. He slips naturally back to his native dialect as if he hadn't been a Yank these many years ago. This is the season of Rod and that suits us to a T-aylor."

In my opinion, these critics were wrong and only served to encourage Rod to continue his increasingly boorish behavior. His performance in *The High Commissioner* is a prime example of true cinematic mediocrity: Scobie Malone comes across more like a sweaty, heavy-drinking, over-sexed film star than the decent, hard-working copper of the novel (for instance, on being invited to Lavi's apartment for sex he blurts, "Where's that beer you promised me?"). Despite Rod's professed desire to use the film to show the world "that we've got telephones in Australia as well as kangaroos" and that not "all Aussies live in the outback," everything in his portrayal here indicates the exact opposite. What should have been a perfect role for Rod was ruined by his own rampant ego, silly script changes and lazy acting.

Story-wise, the main problem with *The High Commissioner* is that the relationship between Scobie and the title character, the crux of the novel, comes across so blandly on screen. Rod was normally strong in films that explored platonic male friendship — *The Time Machine, The Dark of the Sun, Fate Is the Hunter* — but his chemistry here with Plummer is zero (according to Cleary, the two actors did not get on) and nearly wrecks the whole movie. Plummer's performance is another major debit; the actor sleepwalks through his role ("He was there only for the money" — Cleary) and is never remotely believable as an Australian — when he talks about how much he loves his country, it is laughable.

One market *The High Commissioner* was expected to do well in was, naturally, Australia. Local exhibitors remembered with fondness the impact of Rod's 1963 visit had on *The VIPs* at the box office and invited the actor home to promote the film's release. Rod agreed and flew back in September 1968 to attend premieres in Sydney and Melbourne.

Rod's arrival in Australia was still front-page news, with journalists keen to quiz the actor on his recent divorce and the fight in London. As before, Rod tried to paint himself as a regular bloke who hadn't changed since Lidcombe and much rather preferred bunging "a couple of steaks on a barbeque" to Hollywood parties. He called his present accent a "self-mockery" and claimed that after a few more drinks of alcohol, he'd be back talking Australian.

However, Rod ended up being far less disciplined in his dealings with the press than on his 1963 trip, reflecting the growing control alcohol (and ego) was having on him. He took a forthright, overly macho approach in interviews, hoeing into the beer, dropping cigarette ash on the floor, joking about being hung-over and sprinkling his conversation liberally with four-letter words. The *Daily Mirror* thought "the graffiti adjectives and insults" Rod threw around were embarrassing for everyone — "except the super star."

To drum up some extra publicity, Rod made a nostalgic visit to East Sydney Tech. A clerk in the registrar's office checked the old official records and found out that Rod still owed a term's worth of fees; during the visit, the clerk handed Rod a bill.

The Sydney premiere of *The High Commissioner* took place at the Sydney State Theatre on September 12. Crowds lined both sides of Market Street to watch Rod turn up in a police-escorted limousine accompanied by his glamorous date: Judy Lockey, Australia's Miss World representative in 1967. There was a police band, searchlights, a guard of honor composed of nurses and a guest list including various local TV and radio stars. According to Jon Cleary, however, audience reception to the film was far less enthusiastic than for *The VIPs*. "The place was packed. Jerry Wells, whom I'd known for... years, he was a lawyer and he handled all my stuff. And I believe when the picture finished he got up and announced in a loud voice: 'I'm advising Cleary to sue.'"

The High Commissioner was never destined to perform strongly at the box office, with rentals of only $605,000. After a negative cost of $1.055 million and allowing for interest, distribution fees, prints and advertising, the film lost approximately $1.185 million.

PLAYING SCOBIE MALONE SEEMS TO HAVE RE-ACTIVATED ROD'S
interest in his home country. Throughout his Australian trip, the actor talked constantly about his desire to play more Australian characters and make some films
locally. "Even with my phoney American accent I get so mad seeing Cockneys
playing Australians in films," he told one journalist. "I've often called myself a
phoney American but really I'm an Australian through and through. I have kept
my Aussie passport and I have always had the urge to see this unique person —
the Australian on screen. You find him all over the world, usually leaning against
a bar, I admit, but wherever you go he is there."

Specifically, Rod announced he intended to make two films locally, *Last Bus
to Banjo Creek* and *The Golden Jungle*. *Last Bus* would be part of a three-picture
deal between Rodlor and Reg Goldsworthy, a former radio colleague of Rod's
who had moved into film production; *The Golden Jungle* was an American story
set in Cuba and Miami that Rod wanted to make for CBS Films using Australian locations. There was also talk of an interest in a studio complex to be built
in Perth, plus two projects for an Australian-British company, Ajax Films: *The
Long Shadow* (from another Cleary novel) and *The Capital Man*.

On a wider level, Rod recognized that by this stage any Australian film industry would require government assistance to get off the ground. He was quite
prepared to do some of the necessary lobbying. "I think the government has got
to help Australia make movies themselves," he said. "We've got the topography,
the geography, the technicians and the rest of it, but we've also got a government
composed of a lot of lazy jerks."

"Of course anything I do here has to be a co-production," he added. "They can't
do pictures here on their own — they're too lazy and too tight with their money.
The government here should levy money on ticket sales as they do in Britain. The
levy provides a fund to make pictures with. I'm here partly to use what crummy
status I've achieved to make 'em sit up here and take notice...

"I'm going to go to Canberra, buy them a few drinks and say, 'Here's an Aussie
on the international screen. I had to leave Australia to do this. Why can't I come
back here and do the same thing?' If I can show them how to make money on
pictures those sons-of-bitches in Canberra will go, go, go!"

Rod did, in fact, go to Canberra on his visit, having dinner at the Lodge with
Prime Minister John Gorton; they watched *The High Commissioner* together and
afterwards discussed the state of the local film industry. Gorton was genuinely
interested in Australian filmmaking and was subsequently crucial to the establishment of the Australian Film Development Corporation and the Australian
Film and Television School, two events central to the revival of the industry in
the 1970s. What influence Rod had on this, if any, is impossible to determine, but
his efforts would not have hurt. Indeed, Rod's high-level lobbying on behalf of
the Australian film industry in the late 1960s is something he has never received

sufficient credit for; it is far more than many Australian expats of similar stature (e.g. Errol Flynn) ever did.

DURING HIS AUSTRALIAN VISIT, ROD ALSO MENTIONED HIS next Hollywood project: "They change the title every second day, but I think it's called *Zabrizi's Point* just at the moment. Yes, I suppose it's an arty film. I don't throw any punches and I don't end up in bed with the heroine, so it must be arty. It's about the 'generation gap' and it will be a complete change of image for me, which is about time…

"It's about a mod, wealthy lawyer. He thinks he's with it, he'd got a crush on this kid, his secretary, but she meets up with a hippie who really knows where it's at. The lawyer realizes he can't reach this girl. He thinks he's young, but he isn't."

The film was, of course, *Zabriskie Point*, the first (and only) American work from the legendary Italian director Michelangelo Antonioni. Throughout the 1960s, Antonioni was widely regarded as one of the greatest directors in the world, with a body of work that included such classics as *L'Avventura* (1960), *La Notte* (1961) and *Il Deserto Rosso* (1964). By the end of the decade, the director was riding high on the overwhelming critical and commercial success of his first English-language film, *Blow Up* (1966). The movie had been financed by a delighted MGM, who subsequently signed Antonioni to a three-picture deal, of which *Zabriskie Point* was to be the first.

Antonioni wanted to set his new movie in the US, so he traveled across the country for several weeks throughout 1967 to look for material. Early in his journey he passed through Zabriskie Point, an elevated outlook at the edge of the Funeral Mountains in the Californian desert, from which you could see a landscape of gullies and mud hills. The director was so struck by the view he reportedly told the MGM location manager accompanying him that he could envision "20,000 hippies out there making love, as far as you can see."

The location was integral to the final story. *Zabriskie Point* would center around a student activist who is on the run for shooting a police officer; he steals a light plane and meets up with a young girl, after which the two of them wind up at Zabriskie Point and make love in the desert — along with visions of hundreds of other hippies.

"It is a film about America — America is the true protagonist," explained Antonioni. "The characters… are only a pretext."

A number of writers worked on the script, including Sam Shepard (then an emerging playwright in New York); Antonioni's regular collaborator, Tonio Guerro; the director's girlfriend (and future director), Clare Peploe; and student activist Fred Gardner. Alarm bells may have been rung at MGM, however, when the director said the plot would be "much less strong" than *Blow Up*.

"In *Blow Up* there was a beginning and then something happens and then you go straight to the end," said Antonioni. "Not here." The beginning of the film would be "a mosaic of many things" from which the characters would emerge.

Antonioni cast two non-professionals, Mark Frechette and Daria Halprin, to play the young leads, believing they could provide greater naturalism and spontaneity than professional actors. Halprin was a student whom Antonioni had discovered dancing in an experimental film; Frechette was an apprentice carpenter who had been spotted by Antonioni's scouts at a Boston bus stop yelling "Motherfucker!" at a man who had thrown a flower pot at a quarreling couple; one of the scouts asked Frechette how old he was. "I'm 20," Frechette replied. The scout then shoved him into a limousine saying gleefully, "He's 20 and he hates!" It may have been the '60s and Antonioni, but the spirit of Lana Turner had not yet died out at MGM.

The other main role in *Zabriskie Point* was Lee Allen, an attorney for land developers who may or may not be having an affair with Halprin's character. According to the presbook, the actor who played Allen "had to be in his mid to late 30s, poised and articulate, independent and sufficiently attractive to persuade an almost-hippie Daria Halprin to work for him."

A number of actors were presented to Antonioni for this role, including Rod Taylor, but the director rejected them all. Then one day he was dining at a restaurant in Beverly Hills when his eye was caught by a man at an adjacent table. Antonioni observed the man right through lunch and knew he was the one he wanted. It was none other than Rod.

"He was right for that kind of man," confirms Harrison Starr, who was in charge of day-to-day production on the film. "The part was written for a man who was good-looking, powerful, with a little extra something; not just a businessman."

Antonioni had occasionally used well-known actors in the past, such as Steve Cochran, Alain Delon and Richard Harris. Nonetheless, *Variety* described Rod's casting as a "surprise," noting that the actor was not the sort normally associated with art house cinema, being "lately a staple of medium-budget adventure films."

This was mostly by design on Rod's part. The actor was not a big fan of the trendier sections of '60s cinema and had gone on record as saying "Fellini bores me to death," "bedroom scenes showing naked lovers are vulgar" and that he was "offended" by *Who's Afraid of Virginia Woolf?* (1966) — *Colossus and the Amazon Queen* was about as avant garde as he had ever gotten. Rod: "I think many of the so-called 'art films' are over-praised. There's no question but that some of them are vital — beautifully photographed, beautifully directed and acted. But these are the exceptions. By and large, their appeal is limited to audiences who consider themselves to be ultra-sophisticated. For simple, unadorned entertainment there is nothing anywhere in the world to come near the well-tried Hollywood formula. Give the audience something to laugh at, to cry over, to be thrilled and excited by and you've got it going for you. The moment the person who has paid for this ticket had to wonder what the movie is all about, you have lost him."

It is also unlikely Rod would have been overly sympathetic to the politics of a film like *Zabriskie Point*. During the social upheavals of this era, Rod painted himself as a social conservative, a man who as late as 1967 would say things like that "the basis of human society" was "the woman's place is in the home." In 1973 he even bracketed himself with the hawkish John Wayne, declaring, "It's high time we got back to taking pride in this great, big wonderful country of ours. I'm so sick of these loud-mouthed detractors. You bet I'm a flag-waver. Right in there with that great big, wonderful John Wayne. God, I love that man. He believes in his country and his government and stands right there to be counted. I was born in Australia but I couldn't love the USA more if I'd been born in the Alamo."

However, Rod still agreed to sign on to *Zabriskie Point*. After all, it was not every day you were offered a role in the new film by one of the most acclaimed (and fashionable) directors in the world. After *The High Commissioner* and *The Hell with Heroes* it would be nice to do something with some artistic aspirations.

According to Beverly Walker, who worked on the film as a publicist and subsequently wrote an article on its production, all the scenes in *Zabriskie Point* relating to Lee Allen were written by Sam Shepard. Antonioni said he wanted to use Rod's character to show how, "the levels of society are separated from each other, a situation which is so obviously true not only in America, but everywhere." Although Lee Allen was sympathetic on an individual level, he was clearly "cut off from everyone else" and interested in "solving idealized problems, not the real ones, the ones in the street below, the ones they cannot even see."

Antonioni wanted to preserve the freshness of the leads by refusing to allow them to be interviewed or to see rushes. Both Frechette and Halprin used their own names in the film, "because this story could have happened to them," said Antonioni. While shooting began their identities were kept under wraps and Rod Taylor was the only cast member listed to the press.

Zabriskie Point commenced its shoot on September 9, 1969, amidst great turmoil and controversy. All sorts of rumors had spread about what sort of film Antonioni had in mind: the hot gossip was there would be scenes involving desecration of the flag, an assassination, anti-American/pro-communist propaganda and hippie orgies (all of which, incidentally, was true). Filming permits were mysteriously withdrawn at the eleventh hour and the FBI and police monitored the production.

Not helping either was the fact that by this stage, *Zabriskie Point* was the only film shooting on the MGM lot in Hollywood. The late '60s were a time of crisis at the studio: Robert Weitman had resigned as head of production in 1967 and the power shifted to Robert O'Brien — who promptly began repeating the mistakes of the Vogel–Siegel regime, namely, spending too much money on too many pictures, most of which flopped (*Goodbye, Mr. Chips* [1969], *Ryan's Daughter* [1970], etc). This, in addition to the collapse of MGM's music division, caused the studio to haemorrhage money by the millions and halt production on all other movies. Accordingly, *Zabriskie Point* had to use more crew than Antonioni was used to, not to mention absorb all the studio's overheads. Throw in a long shooting schedule and some expensive sequences and the film's budget ballooned to $7 million.

Rod was only on the shoot a few weeks. Most of his scenes were with Daria Halprin, who recalls him as being "genuinely warm, generous and supportive." She found Rod "easy to be with and to work with for a novice and a totally untrained actor as I was."

Antonioni later praised Rod in an interview as "a good actor" whom it was easier to work than the inexperienced leads. "He did everything exactly, he was very humble, very co-operative and I would say I worked very well with him," said the director.

Nonetheless, Harrison Starr thought Rod was always a "little uncomfortable" on the set. "It was an eccentric company. Antonioni was not a director who related well to male stars of the American kind… Rod was having difficulty getting his make-up. He had a make-up man who was one of the Hollywood vipers… He told Rod that the assistant director had told something nasty about him and it was a lie. I confronted the make-up guy immediately and fired the guy. I was surprised Rod believed it. I think he was very insecure being on that set."

One part of the film Rod did not participate in, no doubt to his eternal regret, was the desert love-in scene, where approximately 200 people rolled naked in the sand all in the name of art. Teenagers from Salt Lake City and Las Vegas were bussed in to the desert for the sequence, along with Joseph Chaikin and members of his Open Theatre troupe; the latter had already been rehearsing their roles for two weeks in Las Vegas (!). When time came to film there were still not enough people to satisfy Antonioni's vision, so members of the crew were invited to join the fun; electricians, prop men, truck drivers and the unit auditor all ended up participating. (However, in the final film, Antonioni ended up using only a few couplings.)

Despite (or because) of moments like this, filming was often a difficult, unpleasant experience. Frechette turned out to have a ferocious temper and history of violence; he frequently clashed with Antonioni and even once quit the set and flew home, only returning on the condition that some of his dialogue be rewritten. (The charismatic but troubled actor would later be arrested for robbing a bank and die mysteriously in prison.) Antonioni also had troubles with his crew, who consisted of a mixture of Italians, young Americans keen to work with the legendary director and conservative MGM veterans. The latter were particularly taxing, doing things like laughing at the director's espresso machine and calling him a "wop" and "pinko dago pornographer" behind his back; Emilio Calori, an assistant cameraman on the film, slammed the Italians as "commies" and claimed it was a "shame MGM pours that much money into" the film.

Matters were not helped by the fact that none of the Italians spoke English except Clare Peploe and Antonioni's unconventional and spontaneous working methods caused unions to react harshly to variations in union rule.

"To a certain extent there was a clash between the Italians and MGM," says Starr. "I loved him and also hated him [Antonioni] because he made things difficult. He's an artist... It was the toughest shoot I've ever done and I've worked with Otto Preminger."

On May 23, 1969, a month after shooting finished, around 17 people connected with *Zabriskie Point* were subpoenaed to appear before a federal grand jury in Sacramento. It was rumored the subpoenas involved the Mann Act, a federal statute prohibiting the transport of persons across state lines for immoral purposes — specifically, the bussing of teenagers from interstate to take part in the desert love-in. The US Attorney's office denied this, saying they were only looking into the production of the film. They did not have to be any more specific: under the law, a grand jury proceeding was secret and juries were not required to make announcements or explanations. Hearings involved the secret testimony of more than 30 witnesses and were concluded without a recommendation from the Grand Jury. A transcript of the hearings was forwarded to the Justice Department in Washington, who decided to drop the case altogether and no charges were laid.

Further off-screen drama resulted through a change in management at MGM. The studio's major shareholder, Edgar M Bronfman, successfully moved for control of the whole company in alliance with Time Inc; O'Brien resigned and Bronfman appointed Louis Polk as president. Polk viewed footage of *Zabriskie Point* and demanded that cuts be made, including scenes involving fellatio, a riot, the orgy and some skywriting at the end that said "Fuck America." Polk's regime was only a couple of months old, however, when MGM suffered another take-over, this time by Las Vegas-based airline manufacturer Kirk Kerkorian. Kerkorian replaced Polk with Jim Aubrey, who demanded Antonioni recut the film the way the director wanted.

All these incidents received extensive coverage in the press, with *Zabriskie Point* typically described as a film "starring Rod Taylor." Rod, by this stage in London making *The Man Who Had Power Over Women*, hadn't received this much publicity in ages — all for a project he had relatively little to do with. No movie of his had ever been awaited with such anticipation, except for maybe *The Birds* and *The VIPs*. But when *Zabriskie Point* finally premiered, critical reception was harsh: "alternately brilliant, sometimes vague" (*Variety*); "a disaster, but, as one might guess, Antonioni does not make an ordinary sort of disaster... a huge, jerry-built, crumbling ruin of a movie" (*The New Yorker*); "incredibly simple-minded and obvious" (*Time*). Reviewers rarely mentioned Rod, except for Vincent Canby of the *New York Times* who wrote that, of the cast, "only Rod Taylor, a real actor, seems human."

MGM tried to run with the controversy, making up an ad with positive reviews on one side and negative ones on the other, a technique which had worked for *2001: A Space Odyssey* (1968). But *Zabriskie Point* never broke through to the general public the way *Blow Up* or *2001* did, lacking their (comparatively) clear stories, not to mention critical acclaim. The film also had to compete with a number of other movies that year dealing with campus unrest; by 1971 *Variety* estimated US box office rentals at only $1,072,518.

Over the years, *Zabriskie Point's* reputation has improved somewhat — from appearing in a 1978 book as one of *The 50 Worst Movies of All Time*, it featured in a 1998 article in *Premiere* magazine about "Noble Failures." The latter description is far closer to the mark: shorn of the hype, it is easier today to appreciate *Zabriskie Point* for what the film really is: a visually stunning, flawed, fascinating period piece. Full of striking images, it suffers from a lack of story and the two amateur leads, but is clearly the work of a director of awesome talent. Rod has little to do, but he is professional in his small part and it is lovely to see him playing a white-collar tycoon again. *Zabriskie Point* is indeed a noble failure; you can't help laugh at some of the scenes but it is worth seeking out and is certainly the most unique movie Rod ever made.

AROUND THE TIME OF *ZABRISKIE POINT,* ROD WAS GOING TO play the lead in *The Last Revolution* for George Pal; this was going to be a science-fiction drama about an inventor in the near future who creates a little "brain" that takes over countries and eventually rules the world. However, Pal's most recent film, *The Power* (1968) (the lead for which Rod says he turned down; it was played by George Hamilton), flopped and he was unable to raise finance. Rod's next movie was not science fiction, although the title sounds like it: *The Man Who Had Power Over Women*.

Based on a novel by Gordon Williams, *The Man Who Had Power Over Women* is a drama about a London music agent in mid-life crisis who, unhappy with his work and in his marriage, falls in love with his best friend's wife. Producer Judd Bernard says he originally tried to interest an English star to play the lead and had discussions with Nicol Williamson and David Hemmings; neither actor worked out, so Bernard went on a casting expedition to Hollywood, where he was impressed by Rod Taylor. "I thought he had qualities for the role," says Bernard. "He looked like an agent and wore clothes well."

Rod says he was attracted by the change of pace represented by the film, as it was a role where he "didn't shoot or punch up anyone… Let's face it, I've been hitting too many people lately! I've found to my surprise that some people are rather scared of me and I don't want that. I'd like to get away from that tough-guy image. Now this new film represents a good point of departure towards something a bit more subtle."

Although *The Man Who Had Power Over Women* was officially a Rodlor co-production, Bernard says Rod's creative involvement in the film was minimal, the Rodlor credit coming at the insistence of Rod's agent, Hugh French. Accordingly, he did not play a major role in the troubles that emerged during pre-production between Bernard and the original director, Silvio Narizzano (*Georgy Girl* [1966]).

The original script was written by Chris Bryant and Adam Scott, but then Narizzano started making changes to it with his own writer. Bernard thought these were making things "a little too cutesy"; he had a meeting with the director, "agreed to disagree" and Narizzano left the project. He was replaced by John Krish, a documentary filmmaker who had just made his feature debut with *Decline and Fall… of a Birdwatcher* (1968).

Krish and Bernard made several more changes to the screenplay, including the deletion of a number of fantasy sequences in which Rod's character imagines himself in a series of adventures with (often naked) women. (Bernard was worried about getting these past the censors.) The rewrites irritated Bryant and Scott, who took their names off the credits and replaced them with the pseudonym "Andrew Meredith."

Rod's role in *The Man Who Had Power Over Women* marked a major acting challenge for him. He was in nearly every scene and his character had to undertake a huge emotional journey incorporating divorce, love, regret, lust and grief. It was Rod's most serious straight dramatic part since *Young Cassidy* and required an actor willing to work hard, trust his director and behave conscientiously. Yet throughout filming, Rod continued his hard-drinking, womanizing, troublesome ways.

"He drank an awful lot at night, came in looking red-eyed," said Krish. "We couldn't shoot him in mornings because of the drinking. Also because he drank a lot he would sweat a lot, so we had to wash his shirts all the time… If you look at the film closely you'll see a blue shirt he wore get lighter and lighter."

According to Krish, the assistant directors were often afraid to call Rod on set because they feared the actor might be "in a mood… Every penny was going to his wife [in alimony] so he was reluctant to get on set at all. Co-operation was never the name of his game."

Rod clashed on set with Carol White, then a rising British star coming off the successful *Poor Cow* (1967), who played his love interest. Krish says this started from their first scene together. "Rod comes out from his caravan for a rehearsal and line-up and he stands there and there's no sign of Carol. So at the top of his voice he shouts, 'Where is this so-called fucking movie star?' It wasn't exactly uphill after that."

Judd Bernard recalls another fight between Rod and Carol while shooting a scene at Gatwick Airport that did not make the final film. "He looks at her and said, 'God, you've got a *great* big bum.' She started crying and left the set and it took four hours for her to get back to work. He only meant it as a joke, but she didn't see it that way."

Krish confirms the fight, although he remembers the details a little differently. "When it was time to do a take, Carol forgot her lines. In front of 500 people Rod said to her, 'Why don't you fuck off, we don't need you.' She burst into tears and left. I had to take her to the bar and sympathize, 'Yes, he's a bastard, but we have to film the scene.' All her make-up was wrecked through weeping. We eventually got a take. It was dreadful."

However, Rod did get along with James Booth, a similarly gregarious, tough-guy type of actor, who played his best friend. The two of them even discussed making another film together, an adaptation of Wilbur Smith's first novel, *Where the Lions Feed*; it was never made, but Rod later got his friend a small role in his next movie, *Darker Than Amber*.

It would not be a real Rod Taylor film without a brawl and *The Man Who Had Power Over Women* accordingly featured one: a punch up at a bachelor party. Filming this sequence went on for three days, during which Rod bruised his arm and had to change his shirt nine times.

"Rod Taylor is a man who more than anything else likes to get involved in a fight," said Krish. "The one scene I had where he was no trouble at all was the party scene, which ends in a brawl. He loved it; he knew how to cover a fight scene. He really helped me with it because I don't know much about fighting."

The Man Who Had Power Over Women was released in the US without trade screenings, never a sign of studio confidence. (Indeed, *Darker Than Amber* beat it to cinemas by several months.) When reviews did arrive they were not glowing, although Rod received some impressive personal notices: "A silly movie that wastes the talents of a generally good cast headed by the estimable Rod Taylor... no actor could survive this material, but Rod Taylor, whose face really looks like a fund of worldly trust, does pretty well. He is at his best in sexual comedy... and at his worst in sexual sentimentality with Miss White. But in this he follows the fortunes of the movie, which discovers a certain moral bankruptcy each time it pauses to take stock of itself." *(New York Times)* "The power Rod Taylor has over women in this pic is neither supernatural nor eerie. Just good old animal sex-appeal, which Taylor exploits athletically and successfully... Taylor's name should make this glossy pic a sound enough bet for most situations." *(Variety)*

"Rod Taylor... lifts his part from the near-doldrums... through sheer exuberance. But this picture of the op world is so hackneyed, so out-of-date, that credibility is sacrificed." *(Films and Filming)*

Variety over-estimated Rod's pull at the box office: by May 1971 *The Man Who Had Power Over Women* had grossed an estimated $11,400 in the US. According to Krish, the film's commercial reception was "non-existent" in the UK as well. "It had very poor distribution — it went out with a double feature, a horror film. It had a split poster, with *The Man Who Had Power Over Women* on the left and the horror film on the right. There was a crazed bloodstained face for the horror film but the way it was designed it looked like it was for *The Man Who Had Power Over Women*... I went to the first showing, at a cinema outside the West End — which was a bad omen — and I think there were four people in the cinemas, three of whom where usherettes."

The Man Who Had Power Over Women is an odd film, one of the most ambitious Rod ever made. There are many effective moments, such as the romantic scenes between Rod and Carol White and the by-play between Rod and James Booth, but its problems are all too exemplified in the scene between Rod and his father: initially a very touching moment, it is ruined by over-emphasis. And the climactic sequence where Booth is killed by a truck carrying toilet bowls, thereby conveniently enabling Rod to marry White without an excess of guilt, is too silly for words.

Reflecting on the film today and Rod's performance in it, Krish believes that Rod was not so much an actor as a "behavioralist...He brings a limited amount of acting ability to a role. He doesn't have an intelligent or intellectual grasp on a part. If you were to run three films of his one after the other you would see the same acting habits. One that represents charm, one that represents anger, one that represents doubt... He has a reservoir of three or four useful habits and that's his technique. He doesn't need a director because he doesn't relate to a director because he can't. He wants to get on and do it so he can go to the pub and screw someone.... I think he did it [*The Man Who Had Power Over Women*] for the money. You would have thought as an intelligent actor he would have leaped at the role, but that was not his attitude during filming."

Rod seems to have had a major problem with alcohol in the late 1960s and early 1970s. This, combined with a growing ego, filthy temper and an unstable home life, made him increasingly difficult to deal with on set. He never became totally unprofessional — even Krish admits Rod "never came down from his dressing room without knowing his lines" — but interviews with people who worked with him around this time leaves no doubt that he had become a major nuisance.

However, Krish's comments on Rod's acting ability are a little unfair. It is true that, like most actors, he had developed certain tricks and habits over the years;

a survey of any half-dozen Rod Taylor performances reveals that he used and re-used particular gestures: a tilt of the head to indicate he was listening, folding his arms or pointing a finger to emphasise a line, a raised eyebrow to show surprise, holding hands in front of his lap to denote formality. What is also equally clear, however, is that Rod was capable of emotional, complex work as an actor, even in *The Man Who Had Power Over Women*.

Indeed, his performance in the film is one of his best: flamboyant and full of gusto, humor and humanity. He does go a little over the top at times (Rod never quite mastered the art of crying believably on camera), but clearly understands the central character — a man stuck in an unhappy marriage, depressed with the direction of his career, fond of boozing and brawling with his male friends, having an exotic love life but looking for something more substantial. With a little more care and less turbulence during filming, *The Man Who Had Power Over Women* could have been something really special. As it was, the film sank without a trace — along with Rod's chance of establishing himself as a serious dramatic actor. For the rest of the 1970s he would almost entirely limit himself to action and adventure roles.

ROD'S NEXT PROJECT WAS MORE OBVIOUSLY COMMERCIAL: *Darker Than Amber* (1970) was based on the seventh in a popular series of mystery novels by author John D. MacDonald about a Florida-based sleuth, Travis McGee. McGee is a drop-out from conventional society who lives on a houseboat in Fort Lauderdale and earns his money looking for "salvage," taking half as proceeds. *Darker Than Amber* has McGee and his best friend Meyer rescue a girl, Vangie, after she is thrown off a bridge one night with a weight tied to her ankles; a second attempt to kill Vangie is successful and McGee goes after the killers, uncovering a blackmail racket in the process.

Series of novels featuring tough-guy heroes were all the rage in the '60s — James Bond, Harry Palmer, Tony Rome, etc. — and numerous producers were interested in the film rights to those starring Travis McGee. Jack Reeves was the successful candidate and he set up the project at Cinema Centre Films, a short-lived film production off-shoot of the CBS network. The director was newcomer Robert Clouse, later best known for *Enter the Dragon* (1973) and a number of other kung fu movies.

Casting Travis McGee would be tricky: the film needed a star, but not too big a star — the producers did not want their lead refusing to do any sequels down the track. Jack Lord expressed interest in the role and Robert Culp was a leading contender for a while; MacDonald pushed for Steve McQueen or Vic Morrow. Eventually, Reeves and his partner, Walter Seltzer, settled on Rod Taylor.

MacDonald initially thought this was a bad idea, arguing Rod did not have "enough of what our Latino cousins would call *fuerza*" and that he blended "too readily into the scenery — which would mean that you would have to keep him on camera to give him that necessary bite." The author then went to see *Dark of the Sun* and gradually came around; although he thought Rod was "maybe too squat and hairy and direct," he felt that if they did a lot of work on the script and gave "him some very deft and knowing direction, it could work out."

MacDonald later met Rod when he visited the set in Florida. The author admits to being apprehensive at first but was delighted to find he and Rod "hit what is called instant empathy... I like the guy. He has a face that looks lived-in and he projects a masculinity that can glaze the young female eye at 70 paces. But what matters to me is that he understands what McGee is all about — the anti-hero, tender and tough, with many chinks in the armor.

"The motion-picture McGee will be, I am confident, the McGee of the novels, altered to the extent to which Rod Taylor will add his own dimensional imagination. The final effect will be the amalgam of *my* McGee and *Rod Taylor's* McGee and I trust Rod's wit, irony and understanding to make the whole greater than the parts. We talked three times, totaling maybe an hour and I think we are friends, which is a valuable thing anywhere."

Rod described Travis McGee as someone "who gets knocked on his ass when he's trying to be the hero and doesn't always get to lay the broad." He loved playing the part, claiming it "probably gave me the least amount of trouble of all the roles I've played."

However, Walter Seltzer found working with Rod difficult. "He had very definite ideas of how he wanted to play the role. Clouse and I had divergent ideas. We eventually ironed it out, but... Rod is not an easy actor... It had to do with individual lines and interpretations taken. Nothing insurmountable. I mean, we did the picture on schedule...

"He was very difficult. I don't want to harp on it. He behaved very badly. We've seen each other since and I think he is rueful. I thought he was a splendid actor. I thought he had great potential. Unfulfilled potential. He fulfilled it in a couple of his early pictures. Unfulfilled as Travis McGee."

Theodore Bikel, who played Meyer, remembers Rod as being "an interesting character. I have worked with people like Rod before, Stanley Baker comes to mind, hard-living and real macho guys." Bikel says that filming in the Bahamas was interesting because Rod liked "roughing up with the boys in bars and doing the Australian thing" — namely, to drink beer and "use salty language."

A highlight of *Darker Than Amber* was the climactic fight between Rod and William Smith, who played the main villain. No stuntmen were used because the brawl took place in a small stateroom and doubles would have been obvious. According to Rod, Smith forgot the fight routine and accidentally belted Rod in the nose for real, causing his blood to "splat everywhere." Rod wiped his face and shouted, "Don't stop the camera. Keep rolling!" — and from then on, the rest of the clash was adlibbed. Rod ended up breaking three of Smith's ribs and

Smith broke Rod's nose. Smith, veteran of numerous punch-ups, called it "the best fight scene I ever worked on."

Darker Than Amber is another near-miss project from a time when Rod seemed to be making a habit out of them. The star should have been ideal as McGee, but neither his performance nor the film came together. Rod wears a series of ridiculous-looking tight shorts and outrageous '70s suits which make his character come across as unintentionally funny. A more serious problem is there is not enough story to sustain a feature, leading to a middle section where nothing much happens. On the positive side, Clouse's direction is visually attractive, Suzy Kendall is beautiful as Vangie and Smith makes a terrifying villain (the final fistfight is a masterpiece). But, ultimately, it fails to work.

Reviews were poor. The *Los Angeles Herald* agreed Rod was "suitably cast as McGee," but thought the film "all very cut-price Bond, too tacky to hold one's interest." *The Hollywood Reporter* claimed Rod played McGee "with a world-weary sophistication which probably came from years of television acting and reading MacDonald's book," adding that the actor "never pushes and the role is one of relaxed contentment that everything will unreel itself positively." Mac-Donald's own response to the film was mixed: convinced it would be "utterly rotten," he was "pleased to find it only semi-rotten."

Seltzer says the film performed very poorly at the box office: "I think possibly because it resembled too many other pictures that came out at the same time. There was nothing distinctive about it. We hoped the character would catch on, but he didn't." By the end of 1972, *Darker Than Amber* had grossed a total of $1,621,897; against that were negative costs of $2,607,328, plus prints, fees and interest, leading to an overall loss of $2,958,251.

Jack Reeves negotiated a deal to adapt another McGee novel, *The Deep Blue Goodbye*. Rod was still being discussed as a possible star at this stage, though not with enthusiasm — McDonald wrote to a friend that, "At $400,000 Jack thinks Rod Taylor too costly, and I gather that there is personal friction that would make it inadvisable" — but the film was never made.

Rod had now starred in five flops in a row and he had every right to feel a little nervous about the direction of his career. Perhaps it was time to return to television.

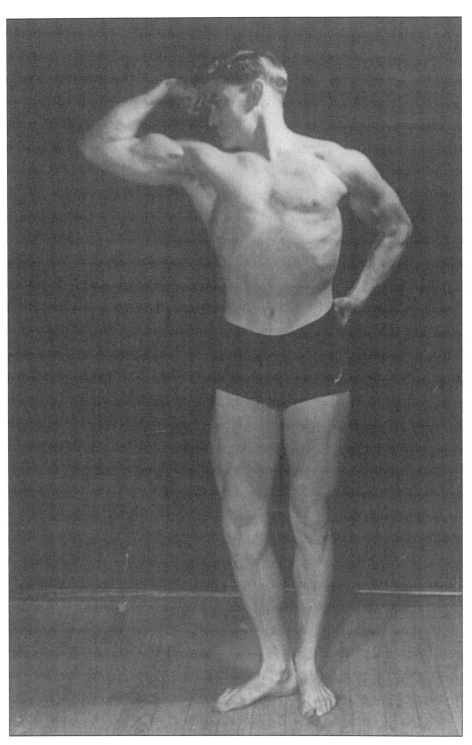

Facing page: *Young Rod Taylor hamming it up at the Lidcombe Gym.* Above: *Rod Taylor with his friend Bob Duff (on left).* COURTESY BOB DUFF

The young radio star, "Rodney Taylor." COURTESY NATIONAL FILM & SOUND ARCHIVES

The young Australia film star: Rod Taylor as Jake Janiero in King of the Coral Sea.

COURTESY PENN ROBINSON

Believe it or not, that's Rod Taylor as Israel Hands strangling Kit Taylor (as Jim Hawkins) in Long John Silver. COURTESY NATIONAL FILM & SOUND ARCHIVES

Rod Taylor as Douglas Bader (with John Ewart to his right) in a promotional photograph for Reach for the Sky. COURTESY NATIONAL FILM & SOUND ARCHIVES

The Hollywood star: Rod Taylor in Hollywood, most likely on the set of Fate is the Hunter.
COURTESY NATIONAL FILM & SOUND ARCHIVES

The Australian American: Rod Taylor as Palmer in The Picture Show Man. COURTESY
LIMELIGHT PRODUCTIONS

At last an Aussie role: Rod Taylor as Daddy-O in Welcome to Woop Woop. COURTESY
ANDREW URBAN

CHAPTER 11

"I need the bread, man."

STARDOM SUNSET (1971–73)

ON THE EVENING OF AUGUST 5, 1970, SHORTLY BEFORE THE premiere of *Darker Than Amber*, Rod was driving his Rolls-Royce northbound through Beverly Hills when he was momentarily blinded by lights from an oncoming vehicle. The glare caused Rod to drive off the road, smash his car and go through the windshield. He was rushed to UCLA Medical Center, where his injuries were fortunately revealed to be limited; he needed 27 stitches in the head and the Rolls-Royce suffered $5,000 worth of damage. In hindsight, the incident can be seen as a metaphor for the state of Rod's career at the time — somewhat out of control.

It was time for Rod to take stock. The Hollywood environment was changing rapidly around him — during 1969-71 the major studios reported combined losses of $600 million, plunging the industry into crisis. Most of them had been gobbled up by corporate multinationals and all the old moguls were either dead or retired; the American film-going audience had dropped from 4,060 million in 1946 to around 820 million by 1971. The new male stars were actors like Dustin Hoffman, Jack Nicholson and Elliot Gould, who had come to fame in unconventional films such as *The Graduate* (1967), *Easy Rider* (1969) and *M*A*S*H** (1970). In contrast, Rod was increasingly associated in the public's mind with an older Hollywood, the Hollywood of MGM, Hitchcock and Ford. To his credit, Rod had recognized this and made some trendier movies in an attempt to keep up with the times, notably *Zabriskie Point*, but none of them really struck a chord with the public.

Being old-fashioned was not the same as being unemployed and some old-time stars, such as Burt Lancaster and John Wayne, remained as popular as ever — it is often forgotten that for every unconventional hit during this era like *Easy Rider* there was a conventional one like *Airport* (1970). However, Rod was running low even on conventional hits, having not starred in a bona-fide commercial success since *The Glass Bottom Boat* in 1966. (Significantly, this was both the last time he appeared in a comedy and opposite an A-list co-star.)

Michael Caine once estimated that a star needed to appear in at least one hit film for every five they made "or else you're out." By that reckoning, Rod was "out." He could no longer pass himself off as an exciting up-and-comer or emerging name; he was a star who had not quite consolidated himself at the top.

Rod was not alone in his dilemma at this time: other actors who had come up through the dying days of the classical studio system were experiencing similar career anxieties, whether A2 category stars such as Stuart Whitman, George Peppard and James Garner, or bigger names like Yul Brynner, Tony Curtis, Natalie Wood and Glenn Ford; in fact, most of these actors never regained their previous position in the Hollywood firmament. This sort of generational change was not unique to this time; however, it was accentuated because the studios were making different types of movies (and in smaller numbers) than they had before.

A role that might have turned things around was that of police officer Eddie Egan, a.k.a. "Popeye Doyle" in *The French Connection* (1971). According to Gene Hackman, who eventually won an Oscar for the part, Rod was the real-life Eddie Egan's dream choice to play him in the film, but it appears no offer was ever made. It is fascinating to imagine what sort of Popeye Doyle Rod would have made — perhaps too handsome a one to go with the gritty vision that ultimately proved so successful.

Another one-that-got-away was *Harrow Alley*, a drama about the plague in 17th-century London. William Newman's script was a masterpiece, later earning a chapter in a book as one of the *Fifty Greatest Movies Never Made*; George C. Scott wanted to film it for his directorial debut, using Rod in the lead — but he could never get the funding.

Other possible projects floated for Rod at this time included a version of the Burke and Wills story, a pair of Westerns (*Slocum* and *Buffalo Man*) and the inevitable *Last Bus to Banjo Creek*. None eventuated.

Perhaps it was time to return to the small screen. Compared to Hollywood, television seemed wonderfully secure and stable, with growing audiences and a guaranteed market for product. Rod was not the only movie star thinking along these lines: 1971 saw the premiere of television series starring Tony Curtis, James Garner, Glenn Ford, Shirley MacLaine, Yul Brynner, James Stewart, Rock Hudson, Anthony Quinn, Gene Kelly and Henry Fonda.

Rod kicked around some ideas with Martin Ransohoff, head of the production company Filmways. The actor wanted to do a Jack London series, but Ransohoff sought to persuade him to star in something more commercial, like *Mannix* (1966–71). The impasse was resolved when Douglas Heyes, who had directed Rod's episode of *The Twilight Zone*, came along with the idea for *Bearcats!*

Bearcats! was about a pair of soldiers of fortune in the American Southwest, circa 1914. Rod played Hank Brackett, a former army captain who teams up with the younger Johnny Reach (Dennis Cole) after saving him from unjustly being lynched as a cattle rustler. They travel the countryside in a Stutz Bearcat helping people, setting their fee as a signed blank check; they would fill in the amount only after successfully completing their job — the amount being determined by the degree of difficulty encountered.

Sam Roeca, who co-wrote two episodes of the series, says the tone of the show was "playful action... It had a late Western kind of smell and feel to it, offbeat. A lot of tongue-in-cheek in it, good action and hopefully you could find a novel way of using the car. You know, action horseplay. Your tongue in your cheek and you try to amuse the audience."

Heyes had written the pilot back in the 1960s, but its 1914 setting was then a bit too unusual and scared off the networks. The success of *The Wild Bunch* (1969) and *Butch Cassidy and the Sundance Kid* (1969) changed that and Westerns set in the "Pancho Villa era" of the early 20th century became popular. Rod called it "an interesting and funny era, with old-fashioned melodrama and hissing the villain and all that." He thought *Bearcats!* should be played "partly for laughs, with the broad gesture and even maybe the girl tied to the railroad tracks — the Perils of Pauline bit" and that it "should have the feeling of looking at daguerreotypes or through a stereopticon viewer."

Assistant director Richard Glassman remembers working with Rod on the pilot as being a real challenge. "His reputation supersedes him. He carries a lot of baggage. When you get Rod, he was so volatile, you have to put up a lot with Rod and that's part of the deal with him. He's very much the star, he is the star. And he lets it be known he's the star. He's very outspoken and into everything that pertains to the show. He's not a laidback man at all...

"There were a lot of blow ups on that show. He was hard to deal with. If you don't do his close-ups he's very aware of himself and he feels if he's being put out in any way he doesn't roll with anything and he lets it be known...

"He's no dummy, though — when he makes a point his points are very astute and he's a bright guy. He's very good in the role; he's a good actor, no question."

Bearcats! was picked up by CBS for the 1971–72 season, with a reported budget of $190,000 an episode. It was scheduled to air against NBC's *The Flip Wilson Show* (1970-74), at the time the second most-watched program in the country. "If you've got to go up against someone, it might as well be the champ," sighed Rod resignedly.

In fact, he should have been more concerned about his other competition over on ABC: *Alias Smith and Jones* (1971-73), another semi-comic Western with two loveable buddy heroes. Nobody seemed to notice that this was far more likely to dig into the *Bearcats!* audience than *Flip Wilson*.

During filming Rod continued to be a handful; at one stage, CBS Program Practices even sent a memo around the network asking, "Glenn Ford is a pussycat. David Janssen is a pussycat. Why can't Rod Taylor be a pussycat?" This was compounded when *TV Guide* published a profile on Rod that described him in terms that were not exactly flattering: "Equating him with a docile tabby would be like expecting the ferocious Great Sandy Desert of his native Australia to become overnight a Down Under Disneyland… [He] is a man who does not speak; he roars. He does not walk; he lunges. He does not reason; he explodes with oaths and imprecations."

Bearcats! debuted in September 1971 to poor reviews. "Everything is a gimmick… somebody forgot to bring a script," snarled *Variety*, adding that the premiere episode showed "only enough dramatic heft or depth of character here to satisfy the most childish fantasizers. At best, this seduction is child molestation." The *New York Times* claimed "direction seemed nonexistent, the dialogue was inane and the acting embarrassing." However, the *Los Angeles Times* thought there was "good chemistry between series stars" and the show "displays enough potential to become a worthwhile series."

Ratings were poor from the outset and *Bearcats!* was soon running last in its time slot; within a few weeks people were already talking of the show's cancellation. Rod was light-hearted about it to the press. "I need the bread, man. I can't afford to have my show canceled. I have to pay my ex-wife, the Spider Lady, $5,000 a month. The next time you see Flip, would you ask him if he'll guest on my series. I certainly could use more viewers."

The axe fell in November. Rod had some consolation in the fact that he was not alone: out of all the movie stars who tried TV in 1971–72, only Rock Hudson returned for a second year.

Bearcats! was a fun, tongue-in-cheek show with great appeal for children that might, in a better time slot, have enjoyed the success of *The A-Team* (1983–87) some years later. The series concept was perhaps flawed, though: while the Stutz Bearcat was appealing to look at, there were not that many different ways it could be used; Brackett and Reach seemed to rescue hostages every other episode. In addition, visually, the series has a very "brown" look (desert, khakis) that became bland after a time. Although Rod and Cole bounced off each other nicely, Rod later complained that his co-star "should have been an older, fun-loving type"; the star looks as though he loved playing his part and his enjoyment is infectious, even if he was starting to get a bit heavy-ish for an action hero.

ROD NOW HAD A FLOP TELEVISION SERIES UNDER HIS BELT TO go with his recent run of dud films. It might have been perspicacious of him to take some time over selecting his next project. However, Rod never liked waiting for things to happen — and besides, there were extensive alimony and child support obligations to be met. He plunged into work, making three films in quick succession through 1972.

The first came out of an offer to support his friend John Wayne in *The Train Robbers*, a Western about some cowboys retrieving lost gold on behalf of a widow (Ann-Margret). Rod played one of Wayne's gang, who end up being chased by bandits and Pinkerton detectives.

Rod was billed above the title along with Wayne and Ann-Margret, but it was definitely a supporting part — not much better, in fact, than the one Rod had walked out on in *Circus World* nine years ago, but times had changed. To rub things in, his casting may have been only due to Wayne's insistence: writer-director Burt Kennedy later complained there were three actors in the cast that "I didn't want and it hurt the picture." (Kennedy did not specify who the three were.)

Wayne was still a commercial force to be reckoned with at this time, being ranked number one at the box office as late as 1971; however, his career was definitely on the slide, mostly because all the films he was making had a sameness about them. *The Train Robbers* was no exception — not only did it have a run-of-the-mill plot, it was shot in Durango, Mexico, site of most of Wayne's recent films and featured many cast and crew Wayne had used before.

Rod enjoyed the shoot, spending his spare time romancing local women, playing cards and drinking tequila with Wayne, Hakim and the boys. Rod's temper was still red-hot at this stage: one day Ann-Margret's husband, Roger Smith, made what was described as an "inappropriate comment" on the set and Rod threatened to punch him out. "It was a misunderstanding and me, like a big idiot, instead of taking things cool, I wanted to go to war," admitted Rod.

Steve Dunleavy, an Australian journalist who visited the set, wrote a colorful profile on Rod during filming: "Taking it easy around Rod Taylor is like having a siesta on a claymore mine. He has more movement than a Mexican jumping bean. His conversation is the color of the Mediterranean. His anecdotes (unprintable of course) are side-splitting. His dedication to his friends and colleagues is as fierce as that of a lioness to her cubs… He's the sort of guy who can get into more hot water than a boiled lobster. He's as likely to get himself punched as any man alive. But he wouldn't hesitate to go in swinging against King Kong."

Rod never denied his rages but claimed they were always short term. He argued that much of his "success came through guts and gall"; he took "no nonsense from anyone and I've got the talent to back it up." Rod admitted that he was "still somewhat an angry man, still brash," but that he had "no regrets over anything I've done."

Reviews for *The Train Robbers* were polite, the *New York Times* calling it "an interesting addition to the late history of the traditional unpretentious Western" with "fine restrained performances by… Rod Taylor." *The Hollywood Reporter* thought that "of the stars, Rod Taylor manages to squeeze the most from his lesser role, mugging his way as best he can through the film's cliché-ridden

'What'd you hit me for?' level of comedy." By July 1973 the movie had earned $2.6 million in rentals, among the lowest-performing Wayne vehicles of this period.

The Train Robbers is unpretentious and not un-entertaining, especially for Wayne fans, but lacks excitement and originality. Kennedy's fondness for scenes involving swirling clouds of dust and long rambling dialogues act as a kind of narcotic: enjoyable but cause one to watch with a sense of increasing detachment. Rod's role is only small and it would have been a better film had he been given something more to do. However, he and Wayne remained friendly until the end of the latter's life, Wayne taping a video message for Rod's *This Is Your Life* tribute some years later.

Rod then flew to Italy in May to begin pre-production on his next film. *The Heroes* was described by producer Alfred Bini as a "cross between *M*A*S*H** (1970) and an Italo Western." It was a light-hearted adventure tale about six people thrown together in North Africa during World War II who discover £2 million in an ambulance; Rod plays an American soldier.

The film was one of a number of international co-productions made in Europe around this time, with finance coming from Italy, Spain and France. To ensure the movie's global appeal, Bini wanted international names in the cast: Yul Brynner was supposed to star, but he pulled out; Rod Steiger took over his role and Rod stepped into the part originally meant for Steiger. Shooting took place mostly in Egypt, in and outside Cairo, with some additional filming in Spain; many of the cast came down with dysentery during the Egyptian leg of production, where Rod filled in his spare hours playing tennis in the desert.

In hindsight, *The Heroes* was another poor choice by Rod and what's more he was not even playing the lead. However, in his defence, there were some signs to indicate the film might not be a waste of time: the budget was a healthy $2,350,000; the screenwriters had written for Sergio Leone; and United Artists, who had enjoyed success with a number of jokey European action films, agreed to distribute in the US. Rod would also have been aware that several Hollywood actors, such as Charles Bronson and Clint Eastwood, had revived their careers in Europe.

Unfortunately, *The Heroes* turned out to be a highly mediocre movie that did little for anyone's career (as would be the case for all of Rod's subsequent European films). It is not terrible by any means — the story has several twists and turns, there is a fair bit of action and the acting is competent — but it all just sort of sits there. The characters are not engaging, the direction is pedestrian. With better handling, *The Heroes* might have amounted to something reasonable — but it does not.

The film reached Italian cinemas in early 1973, but was not released in London until the following year. *Films and Filming* panned it as "unwieldy and lacking in vitality"; the *Observer* said Rod "seethes like an amphetamined Edgar Kennedy." There appears never to have been a US theatrical release.

Keeping up the ferocious pace of work, Rod then went into a TV movie over at Universal: *Family Flight*, an adventure drama about a quarrelling family who crash their plane in the desert. In one sense a step down from features and TV series, it was actually one of the best projects Rod would be associated with this decade.

TV movies in the 1970s were a lot like the old B-pictures produced by Hollywood a generation earlier: made for a set fee under limited budgets and factory-like conditions, they were mostly of average quality, but some of the films were excellent; a few even became classics (*Duel* [1971] and *Brian's Song* [1971]). Universal was particularly skilled at turning out television movies, partly because by the 1970s it was the only studio that continued to operate under the classical Hollywood model, complete with long-term contract players and continuous mass production. It is significant that over the next decade Rod would work more for Universal than any other employer, making two television series and three telemovies for it; he seems to have thrived in a more settled filmmaking environment.

Rod's role in *Family Flight* was the paterfamilias, a tough former navy pilot who is hard on his brood (particularly his son), but whose skills help them survive after the crash. Producer Herve Bennett says when discussing casting, Rod's name came up right at the top of the list of actors considered. "The script developed qualities in this guy, tough, resourceful. If you were casting it today it would be Russell Crowe. Because in a way, Rod was the Russell Crowe of his time. We used to talk about his relationship with Errol Flynn and I think you could draw a line from Errol Flynn through Rod to Russell Crowe. You have the evolution of a kind of leading man that became popular in American film. In Rod's case it was this kind of 'don't-tread-on-me' Australian thing."

The director, Marvin Chomsky, remembers the shoot being a lot of fun, particularly working with Rod. "Rod is an Aussie; he's a great guy. He was always prepared, he knew his lines, he knew his character. If he had any questions you'd go off to the side and talk about them. There were no Freudian or sub-Freudian questions about what we were doing. We were doing entertainment, not trying to save the world.

"He was very craftsman-like to the core. An excellent craftsman. He was a movie star and everyone looked up to him. You can tell the ones who came up through the studio system. They were never late, they knew their lines, they were in make-up when they said they would be. The assistant director would go, 'Ready to go, Rod?' and he'd be there. The well-tempered ones."

Although Rod was the star of *Family Flight*, it is the character of his son who takes the biggest emotional journey in the story. This part was played by Kris

Tabori, who also loved working with Rod. "I thought he was one of the greatest guys — a great actor, pleasant and funny, created a great environment on set. I never understood why he wasn't a major major major star. There were still some negative feelings, I think, in the business then about TV films being a step down, but if he felt that way I never got any sense of it. He was there to make it as good as possible, to work his ass off, make it a good movie…

"He had this big mobile home that he'd rent to the company that was his that became his trailer. And that door was always open; there were always margaritas and food for everyone that came in. He was that kind of guy. For a young actor like myself it was very good to be around a guy like that, you see how to behave. Every night at end of shooting that door was open and all these other guys would show up, Rory Calhoun, all these old cowboy stars would come in and start drinking.

"He was a better actor than he's ever been given credit for. I think a lot of it is because he was so attractive and had the leading man musculature look he kept getting dismissed as a hunk. But he was a really good actor and funny. A great sense of humor. Always witty and charming."

In particular, Tabori mentions a scene where Rod's character is injured by a propeller. "I was watching him going, 'God, this is good acting. He's taking this material which isn't particularly engaging and giving it complexity and life — making the father complex and engaging.'"

Screenwriter Guerdon Trueblood remembers visiting the set one day and seeing Rod "paraphrasing things, rearranging lines. He was not reading the lines I wrote." However, Trueblood says Rod made amends later. "There is a scene where his son and girlfriend are asleep in the plane and the battery goes dead. The father (Rod) finds them and drags them out. He punches his son and he falls into the sand. And the father says, 'You're no damn good, you never were and you never will be.' And Kris, who was playing the son, says, 'I know, I know.' And you cut to Rod. He drops off the wing and he picks up his kid and scrapes the sand off him. Now I never could find the line the father would say then. I mean, you can't have the guy say, 'I'm sorry.' It needed a line."

Trueblood says Rod rose to the occasion when they filmed the scene. "Rod picks him up, gave him a little cuff on the side of the head and said, 'You're my buddy.' It was great. Rod Taylor's instinct was perfect. I forgave him all the bullshit with the earlier stuff. It was a fair trade. He found a line where I couldn't."

Family Flight is a well-done TV movie which, if not in the class of a *Duel*, is unpretentious and entertaining (it rated 21.4 with a 32 share, making it the 20th most watched show of the week). Rod had his best acting chance in a while and he took it, delivering a fine, layered performance which never plays for sympathy. Like so many Rod Taylor films, the emphasis is on his relationship with another man — in this case, his son. Interestingly, this was the first time Rod ever played a father on screen and he handles the challenge with skill and emotion, once more demonstrating what he was capable of when given the chance.

IN 1972, DAVID SHIPMAN PUBLISHED A STUDY OF MOVIE STARS from the post-World War II period, *The Great Movie Stars: The International Years.* There was an entry on Rod Taylor, in which Shipman summed up the actor's career at that point: "What Rod Taylor has in store for audiences presumably he alone knows. Handsome and brawny, he has nevertheless played comedy with some finesse and drama with considerable sensitivity; but he seems less to want to act than to blaze away as the beefy, breezy hero of what *Variety* called 'middle-budget action pictures.' While the fan magazines refer to him as a Tough Guy, critics call him 'underrated.' The public likes him. He says he waits for parts that interest him; then he adds that he has 'little patience with stars who sit around demanding the earth in exchange for their services. If I get the rate for the job I'm satisfied.' Perhaps that is what has kept him from that area where all the best parts are offered around."

The versatile days of the 1960s where Rod played a combination of scientists, businessmen and air force pilots were over. Since *Hotel*, his roles had been mostly rough-and-tough types: cowboys, soldiers, private eyes. This appears to have been a conscious decision on his part. Rod: "When I started out as a sort of beatnik, painting, I was surrounded by women. I've always been one for broads, booze and brawls. But then I also enjoy being with a bunch of real guys and when I've got a good crew working on a picture with me, I feel relaxed. We can play, drink and horse around and have a good sweat together. I've really roughed it and know now how to make the best of it. Guess I got so many rough and tough roles because producers saw me as what I really was — a muscular rowdy type."

Georgie Sterling made this observation: "As he started to grow and started to look more butch and these dirty great muscles, you know, it was a little bit difficult to put him into the airy fairy leading man lover roles, so he started into the action area. As he gets older, the parts he plays are fewer and fewer, not because his talent has left him, but because they don't write for those sorts of people anymore. Which is a shame, really, because he's not being offered the movies because they're not making those movies as you know now. The whole aspect of moviemaking has moved into another era. They're much more interested in what goes on in the mind than in the body. They're becoming very psychologically involved, an exploratory and psychiatric way.

"It's not that he's lazy or over-eating or anything of that nature, not at all, it's just that as he's getting older his aspect is one of strength, which, of course, they really don't want now. Because they're not writing that sort of thing. It happens to all of us."

The uninspiring direction of Rod's career seems to have prompted him to re-activate his ambitions as an independent producer. In October 1972, it was announced Rod would star in four films, one a year, to be produced in partnership between Rodlor and former MGM executive Maurice "Red" Silverstein. The first of these, *The Contact*, based on a book by Michael Stanley, would be shot in Australia the following year; Silverstein described it as "a gripping suspense story" set in Washington, New York and South East Asia, where the "emphasis would be deliberately Australian" (i.e. American director but Australian crew and support cast and Australian locations substituting for foreign ones).

By this stage the Australian film industry was well on its way to revival, helped by quotas for local drama on television and government funding through the Australian Film Development Commission (AFDC). Silverstein was always interested in Australia as a production center: his wife was an Australian, Betty Bryant, star of *40,000 Horsemen* (1940), and while head of production company CUC in the late 1960s, he invested in three Australian-made films produced by Rod's old radio colleague, Reg Goldsworthy.

Betty Bryant flew into Sydney in late 1972 to commence pre-production on *The Contact*, but plans hit a snag when the AFDC refused to finance the venture on the grounds it did not have enough information about the project. The movie was never made — and nor were any of the Silverstein-Rodlor projects (perhaps a blessing, when one considers the quality of the CUC-Goldsworthy films). Nonetheless, it was another indication of Rod's eagerness to do something back at home.

ROD'S NEXT PICTURE, *TRADER HORN*, MARKED HIS FIRST LEAD IN a studio feature since *Darker Than Amber*. Unfortunately, it would also be his last for the next 20 years (although he would continue to star in television series and non-Hollywood movies). It was also the final movie he made for MGM; a sad end to what had been a profitable association. In its way this was appropriate, though, as the studio had become a very different place under the reign of James Aubrey and Kirk Kerkorian.

Soon after Aubrey became president of MGM, he had introduced savage cost-cutting measures at the studio, capping film budgets at $2 million, canceling productions, firing staff and selling off part of the backlot, along with warehouses of props, costumes and other memorabilia; footage of this exists and it is heartbreaking — the old Hollywood literally being bulldozed before your eyes. MGM became more profitable, but its soul as a filmmaking entity had been mortally wounded.

Trader Horn was based on book by Ethelreda Lewis, previously filmed by the studio in 1931. Metro initially had some grandiose plans for the remake, discussing the possibility of a $3 million budget, Sean Connery in the lead and location shooting in Africa — but these dreams were unlikely to last long under James Aubrey. The new *Trader* ended up being filmed entirely on what remained of the MGM backlot in Hollywood, incorporating stock footage from *King Solomon's Mines* (1951) and starring the now-cheap Rod Taylor.

Nineteen Seventy-three was far too late to be making jungle movies in a studio, but ever the trouper, Rod put a positive spin on the project to the public: "This is an honest-to-god Hollywood movie in the old tradition shot right here in Hollywood and I'm telling you it looks as fine as though we'd all come down with malaria working in Africa. I've got the greatest respect for Jim Aubrey for filming this new *Trader* the way he did. We even got all the animals here, rhinos, cheetahs, monkeys and snakes — and I was every bit as scared working with them as if we'd been shooting on the veldt. This picture is going to be box-office."

Those on the set had few delusions about the sort of picture they were making, however. The widow of designer Maurice Vaccarino recalls her husband laughing all the way through production about what a lousy project it was; in particular, she remembers "they were spraying people black — there was no one black enough to play Africans."

Trader Horn was quickly shunted in and out of cinemas and by the end of 1973 had grossed only $180,934. The critics were not kind, *Variety* calling the film "laughably inane" and the *Los Angeles Times* panning it as "the most unintentionally hilarious movie to come out of a major Hollywood studio in recent memory." *Variety* added that Rod "has been in better films and he shows it."

In fact, while *Trader Horn* is no classic, it is not that bad, being cheery enough entertainment in an afternoon-matinee-serial kind of way that young children should enjoy. The main problem is that the cutting between the new, studio-based footage and the old, location-based *King Solomon's Mines* vision is awkward and obvious. Rod makes an ideal Trader Horn, brave, cocky and tough — although his stomach is a little large for a hardened African adventurer.

THE DEADLY TRACKERS WAS ORIGINALLY KNOWN AS *RIATA*, A treasured project of legendary writer-director Sam Fuller, who called it "probably one of the best scripts I ever wrote." The story concerned a Texas lawman, Riata, whose wife and son are killed by an outlaw, Brubeck. Riata chases Brubeck into Mexico, where he encounters a local lawman, Paco, on the same task, and Pompy, a French woman who is Brubeck's lover. Paco and Riata team up and have various adventures before capturing Brubeck; Paco is mortally wounded in the final shoot-out, but before he dies, he makes Riata promise that he will bring Brubeck back alive. Despite his lust for vengeance, Riata eventually does so.

"It hit on all the themes I loved telling stories about," enthused Fuller. "Father-son relationships. Outlaws and lawmen. Revenge and forgiveness. Fidelity and betrayal. Violence and peace. Love and rancour. Sacrifice and satisfaction."

Fuller had been working on the script since the mid-'60s — at one stage rock star Jim Morrison, lead singer of The Doors, expressed interest in playing Riata. When Richard Harris decided to come on board as star, Warner Bros. agreed to finance and filming began in Spain in October 1972. The production soon fell disastrously behind schedule: Fuller blamed this on the inability of his female lead to act, forcing him to cut down her role and shoot around her. Editor John Glenn paints a different story in his memoirs, claiming Fuller started behaving as though he had "lost the plot" and shot footage that did not cut together.

After five weeks of filming and a reported $1 million in costs, Warner Bros. shut down production. The studio gave no public reason for its actions other than "production difficulties," insisting the shoot would resume in the new year. Rumors spread like wildfire, most of it concerning Fuller's mental state: he was not to direct another Hollywood-financed film until *The Big Red One* (1980).

Warner Bros. was serious about reactivating the project, albeit with a different director and approached Fouad Said to co-finance. Said was a former camera-man who had gone into film production with the money he earned developing the Cinemobile, a single mobile location studio with modern lightweight equip-ment. He agreed to fund a new *Riata* on the condition they start from scratch. The script was rewritten by Lukas Heller and Said brought in Barry Shear (who had just made *Across 110th Street* [1972] for the producer) to direct. Of the original cast, only Richard Harris returned. Production manager Sam Manners suggested his friend Rod Taylor replace Bo Hopkins for the role of Brubeck (renamed Brand); it was Rod's first work as a villain since *Long John Silver*. Film-ing recommenced on May 7, 1973, in Durango, Mexico.

In the words of Manners, the cast of *The Deadly Trackers* featured "four of Hollywood's bad boys": Harris, Rod, Neville Brand (as one of Rod's gang) and Al Littieri (as the Mexican lawman who helps Harris), but they were generally well behaved. "They all promised to be good and they were until the last day," says Manners. "The last day they said 'to hell with it.'"

Rod got along very well with Richard Harris. The two actors had much in common: both were hard-living types, well known for hot tempers, roistering and womanizing; both had become stars in the '60s during the dying days of the studio system and enjoyed affairs with Merle Oberon; both had been offered the lead in *Young Cassidy* and co-starred in films with Chips Rafferty, Trevor Howard and Doris Day (a fact I mention simply because it is so random). Although Rod never enjoyed Harris' reputation as an actor, there was mutual respect between the two: Rod told Harris' biographer that when he first met Harris the Irishman "went on his knees" and complimented him on *Young Cassidy*. "He forgave this Aussie impostor doing O'Casey because I was great, he said."

Rod thought Heller's screenplay was "awful in parts," in particular lacking "a decent account of the villain's villainy." So he wrote some new scenes, with the support of Harris.

"He and Harris got along very well," says Michael Economou, one of the film's editors. "They tried to out-drink each other. But not on the set. You never saw Rod dead on the set. I would play piano and Rod would sing and Richard would gather all the little ones around and sing 'MacArthur Park.'

"One thing about Rod — later I edited and co-produced with Alan Alda, who is kind, precise, super professional. Rod reminded me of him. He was always on time, never late, always knew his lines, took direction well and had nice contributions."

Rod later professed to like *The Deadly Trackers*, but he would turn out to be one of the few people associated with the film to be happy with it. Fred Steiner, the composer, asked to have his name taken off the credits after the majority of his score was dropped, replaced by music from *The Wild Bunch* (1969). Lukas Heller also requested his name be removed, complaining that there was "not a single line in its entirety" that he recognized as his own in the end result — specifically, that Al Lettieri's character had been altered from "a cool, sardonic, intelligent fellow" to a "pathetic slob" and that the film's ending had totally been changed. Nor was Sam Fuller pleased, claiming his story had been "completely lobotomized."

To make matters worse, critical reaction to the movie was among the worst of Rod's career. "Even the Hollywood screening audience, usually respectful to a fault, greeted Warner Bros.' *The Deadly Trackers* with laughter, catcalls, moans, boos and hisses," reported *Variety*, which went on to slam the film for reaching "a new peak of oater violence." The *New York Times* called it a "distressingly chaotic adventure" in which Rod "is vague and bland." The *Los Angeles Times* claimed it "may just be the worst film released this year by a major company," accusing Rod of being "as broad" as he was "boring, chewing up [his] words to the point of intelligibility and every bit of scenery in sight."

The Deadly Trackers did minimal box office, not appearing on *Variety*'s list of top grossers for the year. It is hard to feel too sorry about that — it is a nasty film and not very enjoyable to watch. Rod is all right, but Harris hams it up and Neville Brand and William Smith make an unpleasant pair of psychos.

The one saving grace of the movie (even if it is under-developed) is the intriguing ending: Lettieri's character is so devoted to law and order that he shoots Harris dead after Harris has killed Rod — even though Rod has been portrayed throughout the story as a horrible villain who has killed Harris' family and, to be frank, deserves to die. This conclusion has an interesting parallel to the end of *Dark of the Sun*, where Rod's character puts himself under arrest for murdering a fellow mercenary, despite said mercenary being a horrible thug who slew Rod's best friend and assaulted his lover. Both endings were not in their original scripts, but added during filming with Rod's input.

Two other Rod Taylor films contain moments that are remarkably similar to the above, scenes in which Rod may have had a hand in the writing (I have been unable to confirm this): in *The Hell with Heroes*, his character beats to a pulp but ultimately refuses to finish off the crime lord who has murdered his best friend; in *Darker Than Amber*, his character ultimately refuses to kill the heavy who has executed his lover.

These were all films shot within a few years of each other and on which Rod had significant behind-the-scenes involvement. Even if it was simply a case of Rod re-using old ideas, his selection of those ideas is notable. While Rod never seems to have commented on this in any interviews with him that I have read, it seems he was fascinated by the topic of violence — not just as something to liven up an action film, but as a serious topic of study, in particular how it affects violent people and takes over their nature and the importance of the rule of law in controlling it. Even if *The Deadly Trackers* was garbage, Rod at least had the chance to make some sort of personal statement with it and not many actors can say that.

CHAPTER 12
"A Saleable Commodity."

INTERNATIONAL FILMS AND TV (1974–76)

ROD'S DAYS AS A STAR OF MAJOR FEATURE FILMS HAD PASSED, but he was still considered a "saleable commodity" within the entertainment world. Accordingly, in common with many fading Hollywood names, he remained in demand for projects shot in Europe.

Partisan was one of a number of internationally-financed movies made in Yugoslavia during the Tito regime, including *Battle of Sutjeska* (1973) and *Battle of the River Neretva* (1969). As the titles suggest, most of them centered around one topic: the partisan struggle against the German occupiers during World War II. "Partisan films were very much the only movies being made in Yugoslavia during that time," confirms Howard Berk, co-writer of *Partizan*. "All had close to the same theme."

The film's director was Stole Jankovic, a man with first-hand knowledge of the subject matter, having joined the partisans as a teenager in 1941. Jankovic later turned to politics and became a member of the Central Committee of the Communist Party in Serbia; his day job was directing films about partisans (e.g. *Partisan Stories* [1960]).

Jankovic originally intended to make *Partizan* solely for Yugoslavian television but then came into contact with Ika Panajotovic, a one-time Yugoslavian Davis Cup representative who had moved to the US and gone into law and film production. Panajotovic persuaded Jankovic that *Partizan* had the potential to attract US finance and become a feature film if internationally recognized actors were cast in the leads. "The US paid for the stars, the Yugoslavians paid for the below-the-line costs — each side paid its own costs," recalls Ika's widow, Eva. "We [the US] did our own editing."

Panajotovic played tennis with Rod socially and the actor agreed to come on board as a co-producer and star. He played an American-educated Yugoslav who returns to his home country to fight the Nazis alongside guerrillas; he becomes involved with a Jewish girl (Xenia Gratsos) and is pursued by a Nazi officer (Adam West). Although the guerrillas are communist, any Marxist propaganda in the final film was limited to Rod and his friends wearing red stars on their caps.

Principal photography commenced on November 15, 1973, and took place on location throughout Yugoslavia and at Kosutnjak Studios. The $2 million budget was larger than for a typical Yugoslav film, with the added advantage of government co-operation.

"We had the whole Yugoslavian army at our disposal," said Rod. "In some scenes we had 10,000 'extras,' natives of the towns and villages, all eager to work free! It was one hell of a location. Most of the time we were billeted in army barracks high in the mountains, sometimes in weather 30 below zero. We didn't go near the glamorous resort areas. Just little villages like Cabc, Tar and those snow-draped mountains. Our nightlife was being invited to dinner by the farmers who would roast us a pig in a brick oven and share their bread and booze with us."

Unfortunately, filming took a lot longer than originally scheduled, dragging on into 1974. "Stole took his time and everything was not above board," recalls Eva. "They didn't tell us what they had planned so it was not an entirely happy situation."

Inconvenience turned to tragedy when, on March 5, 1974, Fred Hakim, Rod's constant companion on film sets since *Do Not Disturb*, crashed his car while driving along a country road in hazardous conditions; the 49-year-old was killed instantly. Filming shut down while Hakim's body was transported back to Los Angeles.

For almost 10 years, Hakim had acted as Rod's bodyguard, assistant and minder. The two men were very close; a journalist once described Rod looking at Hakim at times "with something close to love." He was probably Rod's best friend in the world, the nearest thing the actor ever had to a brother.

"It was difficult and stopped things for a while," says Eva. "They had to fly the body back. It wasn't released right away. It was a very difficult time."

"Rod was very affected by Hakim's death," recalls Michael Economou. "He didn't stay home and cry every day but clearly it cost him."

Rod combated his grief by throwing himself into work. He decided to rescue the mess of *Partizan* and with Panajotovic's blessing, called in Michael Economou from *The Deadly Trackers*. Economou: "I got a call from Yugoslavia and I heard this [makes wind sounds] and, 'This is Rod.' 'Taylor?' 'Yes, cocksucker, who else would it be?' 'Where are you?' 'I'm in Yugoslavia a hundred thousand miles out of Belgrade. I haven't seen a frame of film, we have 10,000 soldiers and 10 tanks and the director is the number two man in the Communist Party. I want you to come here and see what is going on. What should I do? I'm concerned.' I said, 'Take all the negatives and everything that was shot and we'll do it here.'"

Rod set up Economou to supervise post-production on the film out of the actor's own house in Beverly Hills. Rod converted his garage into an editing room and used his own money to fund it. He also wrote an additional scene for the film between himself and Xenia which Economou shot on a ranch outside Los Ange-les. It is a romantic, wistful two-hander set in a barn where a post-coital Rod and Xenia talk about the war not going on forever and discuss taciturn fellow partisan Braka (played in the film by Bata Zivovinovic). "I love the son of a bitch, but I'll never let him know it," Rod's character says of Braka, even when holding a woman in his arms — another example of Rod's interest in platonic male love.

"He [Rod] thought more of the film than I did," says Economou. "However, an asterix should be added to this statement, that most actors think more of the film that they're in because they like their performance. This is how it is. They open the script, they see how many scenes they have, how many lines they have. Some of them, like Alan Alda, Clint Eastwood and Robert Redford, have the ability to see beyond their part and not let their participation on screen distort their appraisal on screen. I'm sure Rod was a bit distorted, or why else put his own money in it?"

Partizan is a passable war film whose main attraction is its production values: extras, explosions, tanks, locations, etc. The story is depressing and serious in the best brooding, Eastern European style: the Nazis hang citizens and die, most of the partisans die, most of the Nazis die, Rod's character dies. Rod's perfor-mance is professional, but he looks too old to play someone who supposedly graduated from college in 1940 and far too fat for a guerrilla leader living off the countryside.

A three-hour version of *Partizan* was shown on Yugoslavian TV in 1974; the feature-length US version debuted at the Pula Festival in August of the same year, after which it was picked up for release and had a short run in the US under the title *The Last Guerrilla*. In 1978 it surfaced in LA as *Hell River* for a week's run, supposedly to qualify for the Academy Awards ("Somebody must be pulling our legs," quipped *The Hollywood Reporter*). Nonetheless, Ika Panajotovic claimed that by this stage the movie was in the black.

Following *Partisan*'s completion, Rod announced he would make two more films for Panajotovic in association with a group of investors from Italy, Yugo-slavia and Switzerland: the first was to be *McDonald's Mission* from a script by Berk, with Rod playing a war correspondent; there was also an untitled love/adventure story by J.P. Miller, who had written *Days of Wine and Roses* (1963). Neither was made; in hindsight, Rod would have been better off concentrating his energies on getting cast in decent films made by others rather than trying to make his own.

ROD'S NEXT PROJECT WAS NEARLY BACK IN AUSTRALIA WHERE, after years of false starts, the local industry was finally up and running again: the success of films such as *Stork* (1971) and *Alvin Purple* (1972) and television series like *Number 96* (1972-76), among others, demonstrated that audiences would see home-grown stories in sizeable numbers. Australian actors and writers who had been forced overseas to find employment were delighted; many of them, such as Michael Pate, Charles Tingwell, Peter Yeldham and Ray Barrett, even returned home and found themselves with plenty of work. Could Rod, his Hollywood career in the doldrums, also be tempted?

In December 1974, it was announced Rod would star in the Australian film *Angel Gear*, about a truck driver and hitchhiker who get bogged on the Nullarbor Plain. ("Angel gear" is when truck drivers throw the gears into neutral and let the weight of their vehicle do the driving.) Rod was to play the truck driver and John Waters the hitchhiker, with Ebsen Storm to direct.

Unfortunately, the deluge of press coverage that followed this announcement seems to have scared Rod away from the movie. The producer, Lyn Bayonas, remembers: "I think they [the media] must have contacted Rod because one minute our negotiations were going well and then suddenly he withdrew. It was going to be his first movie back in his own country and I really think he got cold feet or was worried he was going back to work with a bunch of amateurs (I guess we were, really). Rod's manager was trying to talk me into Franco Nero (as an Australian truck driver!)."

Angel Gear ended up never being made. However, Australia was clearly on Rod's brain and he would be returning there soon.

ROD KEPT BUSY THROUGH 1975, MAKING THREE MOVIES IN ALL: two pilots for television series and a feature. *A Matter of Wife... and Death* was one of the pilots, based on *Shamus* (1973), a moderately successful Burt Reynolds film about a modern-day private eye. Both pilot and feature were produced by Robert Weitman, the former head of production at MGM, who had since forged a career as an independent producer. While two supporting actors from the original film, Joe Santos and Larry Block, were willing to reprise their big-screen roles, there was no way the increasingly popular Burt Reynolds was going to commit to a television series, requiring Weitman to look around for a new Shamus. The producer had kept friendly with Rod on a social level since he left MGM and asked the actor to come on board.

Don Ingalls, who wrote the pilot script, remembers Rod's casting altered the film slightly. "The concept was rewritten for Rod Taylor's type of personality," says the writer. "Rod was straighter — a straight-arrow type of guy. Burt Reynolds — now I'm not talking about him personally, I mean his screen persona — was more sly; funny, but a little underhand. Rod was a more straightforward kind of a guy. I would tend to trust 'Rod Taylor' and tend not to trust 'Burt Reynolds' any further than I could throw him."

After shooting completed, Rod claimed he was "not holding my breath about the possibility" of a series because "all it takes is one network executive to sigh in a screening room and there goes your show." One executive did sigh and NBC passed even before the pilot aired in late 1975, when it rated 16.2 with a 31 share.

A Matter of Wife... and Death is a well-written, professional TV movie whose main fault is that it feels too familiar. Rod is tough, confident and relaxed in the lead role — possibly too tough, confident and relaxed: Shamus never seems in much danger; he gets every woman going and solves the mystery quite easily. His character lacks the tension or humor of a Jim Rockford and the gimmicks of Shamus sleeping on a pool table, talking to his cat and having a phone in a basket that hangs from the ceiling feel just like that — gimmicks. There are shades of *Hong Kong* throughout the show — Shamus romances beautiful women and banters with a police officer and bartender — but it lacks *Hong Kong*'s spark.

More successful was Rod's second pilot of 1975, *The Oregon Trail*. He played an Illinois farmer who sets off to a new life in the Oregon Territory in 1842 along with his family, encountering Indians, disease and dissension in the ranks on the way.

Filming took place just outside Los Angeles. Cast member Linda Purl remembers Rod opted to stay out on set throughout the shoot and live in his motor home. "The caterers supplied him with food and Rod reported that he'd just light one of the set campfires and use prop pots and pans to cook in," she says. Rod was often accompanied by Terry Wilson, a former stuntman and actor who had become Rod's new minder in place of Fred Hakim (he is listed as "production associate" on the credits for *The Oregon Trail*).

Despite professional work from all concerned and a solid performance from the star in a rare family-man role, NBC decided to pass on *The Oregon Trail* as a series, too. The pilot aired as a stand-alone movie, which *Variety* described as a "standard, workmanlike example of Western pioneer family struggles" whose "strongest asset was an appealing cast headed by Rod Taylor." It rated 19.1 and a 31 share and was repeated later that year, rating 18.8 and a 34 share. Those were solid results and it was not the last that would be heard of the show.

While neither of Rod's 1975 pilots matched the quality of his '60s output, both were far superior to the feature film he made between them. In fact, *Blondy* (also known as *Germicide*) stands comfortably as the worst film Rod ever made. It was a French-German co-production from director Sergio Gobbi, who specialized in gangster movies, comedies and soft-core porn. Most of Gobbi's films were fairly obscure outside Europe but with *Blondy* he was keen to make a bid for the international market: the cast not only included Rod, but Ingmar Bergman favorite Bibi Andersson.

Rod played Christopher Tauling, the UN Secretary-General, who is married to a waif-like, red-haired younger woman called Patrice (Catherine Jourdan). While Tauling is away leading the fight against bacterial warfare, Patrice is lured into a sadomasochistic affair with a young man, who nicknames her "Blondy"; the affair turns out to be engineered by Patrice's friend, Mitta (Andersson), who is later exposed as a terrorist. Tauling is murdered and evidence points to Patrice committing the crime, but a detective (Hans Meyer) uncovers the truth.

Production took place in Paris during September 1975 and the film was released in France the following year. The local critics took to it with a vengeance: "Rod Taylor seems bored to death. Lamentable" (*L'Express*); "another dark rock in the Gobbi desert" (*Le Point*).

Rod once criticized European filmmakers for being "too artsy-crafty, pornographic, sexy, slutty for their own good" — yet had gone on to make a movie which ticked all those very boxes. Marked by lousy sound, poor acting and a confused storyline, *Blondy* is only enlivened by some gratuitous sex scenes. Rod, Andersson and Meyer do competent jobs, but it is sad to see such good actors in such a miserable film. It was an indication of just how undiscriminating Rod had become in the search for work. The actor claims he never saw the film, but said he heard it was a "dog." He was correct.

MORE PLEASANT NEWS THAT YEAR CAME WHEN ROD WAS informed he had been selected as the winner of the inaugural Chips Rafferty Award back in Australia.

Rafferty had died in 1971. In the last few years of his life, the actor-producer had expressed a desire to establish a trust fund with the purpose of sponsoring an annual award to a young writer and a young director, but never got around to it. A few years after his death, Lee Robinson and some other colleagues of Rafferty's came up with the idea of having a perpetual award in their friend's name and selected Rod as the first recipient.

After Rod completed shooting on *The Oregon Trail*, he flew out to Sydney for the ceremony. What he did not realize was that he was also being set up to star in an episode of *This Is Your Life* for Australian television. The show was produced by none other than Lee Robinson, who organized Rod's appearance secretly through the actor's manager, Murray Neidorf, and his then-agents Miles Kuhn and Phil Kellogg at the William Morris Agency.

Robinson went to meet Rod soon after the latter's arrival and was struck by how much his old friend had changed over the past few years. "He was an innocent, loveable, likeable fellow, but he'd lost his innocence," remembers Robinson. "Hollywood does that."

Nonetheless, the episode went off smoothly and was a high-rating success. Local guests included Rod's parents, Queenie Ashton, John Ewart, John Meillon, Charles Tingwell, Peter Yeldham and his old Lidcombe gym mates; in addition, several friends were flown in from the US, including Rod's daughter, Felicia (then 11 years old), Wilt Melnick, Murray Neidorf and the actor Stella Stevens (who knew Rod socially and whose son Andrew was in *The Oregon Trail*); John Wayne, Dinah Shore, Doris Day and Richard Harris appeared in taped segments. Although the tone was mostly congratulatory, there was an unexpected insight into Rod's domestic life when he revealed he had not seen Felicia at all in the past two years. (She was at that stage living with her mother in New York.) Robinson recalled that Rod "had no interest whatsoever" in his daughter around this time — but his relationship with Felicia improved in later years.

Rod turned out to be the first, last and only winner of the Chips Rafferty Award. (Robinson sold the prize's naming rights to the *TV Times*, which then went broke.) Nonetheless, it was pleasant that Rod had some sort of critical recognition for his career, however stage-managed — the actor had not received an honor of any note since the Rola Award in 1954.

Rod's Australian visit also sparked yet another revival of interest in *Last Bus to Banjo Creek*. By this stage the actor himself had done considerable work on the script himself: Rod claimed Ted Willis' original had been rewritten by some "hack" at the Universal Studios so he "added some dialogue and made it good and Aussie and, I thought, funny."

Based on a copy of the script I have read (undated, but from the mid-'70s), Rod's version of *Last Bus to Banjo Creek* has the English girl, Helen, now traveling along the Birdsville Track in order to visit her dying father; she still has a fiancé, but he is turned into a posh English television director who lives in London. Helen catches a ride with mailman Jim, who must make the run in quick time or he misses losing his mail contract. The two have a number of adventures and fall in love, with Helen electing to stay on in Australia.

Much of the new edition of the script feels very "Rod Taylor" — Jim likes to drink and brawl and has women constantly panting over him; the characterizations and dialogue feel as though they come came straight out of a 1950s pub (sample: "First Oaf: 'Hear that, Charlie? That good-looking limey Sheila's in 702, next door to us?' Second Oaf: 'Good-o, we'll have a few beers then burrow through the bloody wall.'") However, much of it is unexpectedly wonderful. There are a number of warm vignettes about life along the Track ("galah" sessions, tales of death and drought) and a surprising amount of romanticism and emotion. A real bond between Helen and Jim is formed and Helen is a strong character, sexy, classy and sympathetic — one cannot help but think Rod was channelling Maggie Smith when he was writing. This version of *Last Bus to Banjo Creek* was not perfect, but in the hands of the right director and co-star it would have made quite an entertaining film, much better than most of Rod's '70s output.

Reg Goldsworthy announced to the media that filming would proceed with a budget of AU$1.2 million and a cast including Rod, Olivia Newton-John, Peter Ustinov and John Mills. However, it turned out Goldsworthy did not even have the rights to the script, which still belonged to Rank. John McCallum then became involved, as did, later, producer Phil Avalon, but they could not raise the money either. This was the last burst of activity concerning *Last Bus to Banjo Creek* and the film was never made.

ROD HAD BEEN ACCOMPANIED ON HIS AUSTRALIAN TRIP BY Paul C. Ross, who was producing the actor's next film: *Jamaican Pie*, an adventure drama about modern-day treasure hunters in the Caribbean. Rod announced the movie would be shot on location in Jamaica, based on a script by Rod himself. He claimed he got the idea from a newspaper article about divers who found a sunken city with millions in bullion.

"I do a lot of rewriting, but this is the first one from scratch," he said. "There are not enough good scripts around and, God knows, I've read enough of them. I've gone through reams of junk. I don't rewrite to give myself more lines, hell no. I rewrite to give the characters more depth. It's not easy. It's really painful work, like giving birth."

Again, Rod's interest in masculine adventure tales comes to the fore: the heroes of *Jamaican Pie* are two old college football buddies (Rod and Stuart Whitman) who run into each other in Jamaica and get involved in looking for Sir Henry Morgan's treasure. There is some female love interest, but most of the action concerns the two brawling leads and the villains who try to stop them.

The film's crew included of several of Rod's friends, such as Sam Manners (line producer) and Terry Wilson (assistant director). Another pal, Keith Stafford, who had completed some post-production work on *Partisan*, edited. Ross was the executive producer for "Hall-Ross," in partnership with Frank Hall, a Miami businessman; the director was Hollywood veteran Henry Levin, whose credits included *Journey to the Center of the Earth* (1959), now at the tail end of his career.

Filming took place in Jamaica over a six-week period, in and around Kingston and Montego Bay. Rod had made *Dark of the Sun* in the country some years before and Keith Stafford remembers the actor delighted in showing him "the seedier side" of town. (Coincidentally, two other famous Australian stars, Errol Flynn and Peter Finch, also loved Jamaica, both buying property and living there for several years.)

Stafford recalls a fair amount of political intrigue behind the scenes on the film: "Somewhere along the line Rod seemed to be less involved from the financial end and power end, you know," he claims. "A lot of things went on that I was privy to that I don't feel was right."

"It was a bad piece of work for everyone concerned," confirms Sam Manners.

Neither Stafford nor Manners would go into much more detail than this, but it appears Rod, one of the initiating forces on the project, was "squeezed out" as production progressed. In addition, the script was rewritten by Walter Brough, an experienced television writer who later downplayed Rod's contribution to it. ("He shouldn't have had the credit," complained Brough. "We had a little battle with the Writers Guild about it.")

Stafford says that when the crew returned from Jamaica, they stopped off in Miami for a meeting with Frank Hall, who gave carte blanche to the editor to finish post-production at his own home. By that stage Stafford says there was no producer on the film. "If there was a producer I was it."

In early 1977, *Jamaican Pie* had been retitled *On a Dead Man's Chest* and Rod claimed it would probably be distributed by United Artists later that year. However, no theatrical release ever eventuated and the film disappeared from view until it turned up on video under the title *The Treasure Seekers*. By this stage, rights to the film were owned by Stuart Whitman who, in addition to being a good actor, was also an astute businessman, amassing a personal fortune into the millions.

Rod did not remember the experience with fondness. He later claimed that he was not paid for either writing or starring in the film, electing instead to take a percentage of the producer's profits; he said the producer subsequently told him the film had been impounded due to legal troubles, so there was no money. Years later, Rod was shooting *Marbella* in Spain when some English tourists presented Rod with videocassettes to autograph. To his surprise, it turned out to be the film, now titled *The Treasure Seekers*. "Those bastards changed the title and released it on tape — and I *still* haven't been paid," griped Rod.

The Treasure Seekers (to pick one title) is a lively film that could have been a lot better with more care. The main debits are a very evident low budget and Levin's comatose direction. On the plus side, Rod and Whitman have an enjoyable rapport — although they play nearly identical characters — and it is a respectable enough story.

IF THINGS WERE ON THE SLIDE FOR ROD PROFESSIONALLY, THEY were looking up on the personal front — specifically, his love life. It had taken a number of years, because Rod had been commitment-shy since his bitter and expensive second divorce. In the early 1970s he declared he did not want to get married again "because I don't like to cheat on a girl I like." He preferred casual romances on film sets: "You get together for a few weeks or months and when it breaks up there is no alimony to pay."

That all changed with Carol Kikumura. A San Francisco native of Japanese parents, Carol first met Rod when she worked as an extra on *Hong Kong*. They enjoyed a short romance, but eventually parted and Carol moved to Las Vegas. One night she saw Rod on *Bearcats!* and decided to give him a call; he was out but she left a message on his machine: "I just saw you on television and you're fat." Rod called her back, saying, "Come over here and say that!"

Carol flew out to Hollywood where they went out on a date. Rod said he "wined and dined her with all the charm that I could muster." The result was an "amazing" evening and "we started where we left off."

Despite this, Rod wasn't willing to settle down quite just yet, so they simply dated. Three years later, they were attending Alfred Hitchcock's 75th birthday party together when Rod realized he was in love. "There was something magical about that night and it made me see how much she really meant to me," he said. "She's highly educated, fun, very mature and self-sufficient."

Carol moved into Rod's house and the relationship went from strength to strength: both enjoyed gardening, painting and cooking, and Rod found for the first time in his adult life that he consistently preferred the company of a woman to carousing with his male friends. In October 1980 the two married at Caesar's Palace in Las Vegas. They are still together as of this writing.

From all accounts, Carol has been nothing but a positive influence on Rod's life. Over the course of writing this book, I have talked with a large number of people who have worked with Rod; when discussing the period from the mid-1960s to the early 1970s many of them were guarded and often very critical of his behavior, particularly with regards to his drinking, ego, temper and womanizing. Since the mid-1970s — the time Carol entered his life on a more permanent basis — almost all the comments have been positive. Although Rod still likes to drink and party, he seems to have toned down considerably from his wild days: less egotistical and fiery, more mellow and contemplative — yet without losing the energy and lust for life that has always been a part of the man. This is not coincidental. More than one person has said to me, "Carol turned him around."

CHAPTER 13

"An international wastrel with American wealth and American bodyguards."

TELEVISION (1976–1980)

EVER SINCE ROD LEFT AUSTRALIA FOR HOLLYWOOD, HE HAD tried to make a film back home, but never succeeded: *Lost Eden*, *Latitude 35*, *Last Bus to Banjo Creek*, *Burke and Wills*, the Charles Sturt story, *The Contact*, *The Golden Jungle*, *The Long Shadow*, *The Capital Man*, *Angel Gear*. His luck finally changed with *The Picture Show Man*.

The Picture Show Man was a comedy-drama about the adventures of a traveling film exhibitor in rural Australia during the 1920s; it was based on the memoirs of Lyle Penn, who grew up on the road with his picture-showing father. In the early 1970s, Penn sent a copy of his then-unpublished manuscript to Joan Long, a writer-producer he had seen on television being interviewed about a documentary she had made on the early Australian film industry, *The Passionate Industry* (1973). Long optioned the manuscript and succeeded in raising the AU$636,000 budget on the back of the success of *Caddie* (1976), which she had also made.

Two of Rod's old radio buddies were cast in the leads: John Meillon (as the title character) and John Ewart (as his piano-playing, womanizing offsider). An important, though not large, support role was that of Palmer, the cashed-up rival of the picture show man. After originally considering Chris Haywood, director John Power suggested to Long that Rod Taylor might be ideal for the part.

"We thought that Rod, first of all, was a good actor for the role, was going to be well cast for it and secondly, we thought it might give us an entrée for some overseas sales," says Power.

Long did not think they could afford someone of Rod's calibre, but nonetheless sent a cable off to his agent: "Realize money not in your class but wonderful thing for Australian films." Rod's agent wrote back: "Willing read screenplay but no acceptance implied." Long sent over a script and less than a week later Rod called back personally to accept.

The part of Palmer was not originally written as an American, but after hearing Rod's "Woolloomooloo Yank" drawl on the phone, Long became concerned with his ability to perform in an Australian accent. Accordingly, she altered the script so Palmer became an American. It was a realistic amendment because the story was set in a time when Australian film exhibition was coming under the domination of American companies. Yet, it was still odd that Rod Taylor was going to be playing an American character in his first Australian picture in over twenty years. Australian movies have often suffered the curse of an imported overseas star miscast in a local role (for example, Richard Chamberlain in *The Last Wave* [1977], William Holden in *The Earthling* [1980]); it is ironic that one of the few parts in an Australian film which could have justifiably been played by an imported American star went instead to a famous Australian one.

Rod signed on for a fee that he described as "significantly less" than he could obtain in Hollywood, even at that stage of his career. (He claimed in 1975 that this was $200,000 per picture, plus $1,000 a week for expenses and a chauffeur-driven car on call 24 hours a day.) Any financial sacrifice he was making, however, was eased when his agent signed him to film a series of TV ads while in Australia. He also received sole billing above the title, far out of proportion for the size of his role.

"John [Meillon] was wonderfully hospitable in allowing me to take top billing because that's necessary for my work overseas," Rod told the press. "I am basically doing a kind of guest shot, as I'm happy to help."

Others were less charitable about his motives. According to one industry observer, "In the Australian film industry, in those days at least, I think the general attitude was, 'He must be a bit hard up, because he's going to be third lead to John Meillon and Johnny Ewart.' I suppose I thought the same, because I knew he'd made a bit of a goose of himself a few times in Los Angeles."

"I got the sense that he wasn't getting much work when he agreed to do this," claims another. "He saw this as a chance to puff himself up as the returning star. I think he honestly believed this could lead to more leading roles in Australia, which he wanted to do."

Nonetheless, it was still news: Rod was the biggest Australian star to return home to make a film since Peter Finch in *The Shiralee* (1957). Accompanied by Terry Wilson, he flew into Sydney on October 12, 1976, greeted by a healthy amount of publicity. The prodigal son was returning home, full of wisdom and experience learnt from his two decades in Hollywood, ready to team up with his old mates and help a greenhorn industry get on its feet. However, in hindsight, it is apparent that *The Picture Show Man* started the decline of Rod's reputation in Australia.

The first four weeks of shooting were spent around Tamworth in northern New South Wales, followed by three weeks filming near Grafton. Jan Kenny, a clapper loader on the film, remembers the first time she saw Rod. "We were shooting with all these horses and buggies. At one stage one of these buggies got stuck in a creek when it was crossing, so we all attached a long rope to it, all the crew got on to this rope and everyone was pulling on it — and I turned around and Rod walked up and got on the rope and started hauling along with everyone else, which was very un-Hollywood. He just mucked in like a regular guy, which Australian actors would do, but not something I'd expect him to do.

"I was introduced to him later that day — he was just very affable. Remember he was also on a shoot that had his old drinking mates. The three of them was like getting the lads back together after all these years. They were very easy-going and relaxed and mixed in with the crew, which American actors don't usually — they don't usually like to be spoken to as a rule. I think that partly because his old mates were relaxed like that he fell into the pattern of behaving like they behaved — there was no star trip at all."

"It was a film of drinkers," recalls cinematographer Geoff Burton, who says John Meillon, John Ewart and Rod "were all drunk more often than not. But it never affected their performances. Except maybe Meillon; occasionally you could see it in his face."

"The boys could be pretty wild," remembers another crew member on the film. "They had all this baggage from the past. They were all hitting the booze like there was no tomorrow. If you just visited the set you would have thought everything was fine — but there was an undercurrent of tension."

In particular, there was ill feeling towards Rod from John Meillon. Meillon admitted that when he and Rod had worked together during the 1950s, Rod had been the golden boy, "the really good-looking guy, the one everyone else was jealous of because he had a kind of early Clark Gable look"; now, after years of struggle, Meillon had a lead role in a feature and here was Rod, flying back into town and receiving all the publicity.

"John was very possessive about being the star, that it was his film and Rod was the interloper," confirms Burton. "And, in a sense, Rod liked to perpetuate the image that was in the film. He was an interloper, better and brighter."

There was also some friction between Rod and Joan Long. "He got drunk the night he arrived and called Joan a rude four-letter word," recalls one of the crew. "It was actually meant to be flattering in a blokey way, about how well she'd done, but Joan didn't take it that way. They never got along after that, but they were polite to each other."

Rod did not spend all his down time in conflict with someone, however.

"He was obsessed with sex," remembers a crew member. "He'd get runners to find him women in different country towns... like a nurse from Tamworth Hospital, or something. It all became part of the mythology."

Rod made close friends with one woman on the shoot in particular. "She ended up sleeping with him but he got tired of her and moved on. The blokes in the production office got anguished about it."

Despite the amount of drinking and sex Rod took on board, he continued to be as professional as ever during work hours, knowing all his lines and turning up on time. John Power describes him as being "an angel to deal with" and "very sensitive to the feelings and moods of the other actors and their status." Power did admit, however, that Rod's casting may have unbalanced the film by making "the part of Palmer bigger than it was written."

"The thing I do remember about him that surprised me was that he was incredibly nervous before a take," remembers Kenny. "When he was actually working, his hands would shake.

"He wore these big lifts in his shoes, because he's actually quite short. He had the same shoemaker as the Duke [John Wayne]. He made a bit of a thing about his lifts in his shoes because the Duke told him to, he always wore them. I was interested that he felt he should tell us that. It's like people having a facelift and telling you they've had a facelift.

"He dropped names quite often. I got a sense that he was often acting. He walked with a real swagger — he probably learnt that from the Duke, too, I don't know. Very much aware of how he appeared to others. I sometimes wondered if this thing of going along and jumping on the rope was an icebreaker to say, 'Hey, I'm just one of you guys.' He saw an opportunity to just muck in with everybody which I thought was a good thing for him to do."

Neville Wran, premier of New South Wales at the time, had a high level of interest in the fate of *The Picture Show Man* (indeed, his personal intervention had helped Long raise the final necessary funds to make the film). Wran visited the set one day, whereupon Rod and horse wrangler Heath Harris decided to take him for a ride in one of the carriages.

"Rod had some experience using these things in America," recalls production manager Sue Milliken. "He thought he knew what he was doing. He said to Neville Wran, 'Hop on, I'll give you a lift.'"

Rod and Wran were crossing a river when the wooden bar joining the traces to the wagon snapped under the strain. One of the horses stumbled and it seemed as if the whole wagon was going to topple over, politician, film star and all.

"I thought, 'My God, we're going to kill the premier,'" laughs Milliken.

But the horse stayed on its feet and a national incident was averted.

"I can assure you it wasn't deliberate," said Rod. "I didn't try to kill Neville. After all, he's my friend."

The Picture Show Man had its world premiere on May 5, 1977, in Melbourne. Local box office was solid, not sensational; the movie's release, unfortunately, coincided with the introduction of color television in Australia. Nonetheless, it still ran for five months at one theatre in Sydney and picked up awards at the 1977 AFIs for art direction, costume design, music and best supporting actor (Ewart). By May 1978 *The Picture Show Man* had earned an estimated AU$650,000.

Reviews from local critics were remarkably snide, both about the film and Rod's performance: "One wonders what the point of it is" (*National Times*); "Rod Taylor pops in and out, never staying long enough to change anything but the level of Pym's blood pressure" (*Bulletin*); "Rod Taylor's bland, nervous interpretation of rival showman Palmer can only be described as a non-event" (*Cinema Papers*); "Rod Taylor... is out of place... Where the role calls for panache and impudence he gives to it no more than a kind of beefy brashness" (*The Australian*); "Rod Taylor was brought all the way from America to play this, but it doesn't do him, or us, much good" (*Daily Telegraph*).

Overseas, the film played the festival circuit, received a short cinema release in the US and aired on television in England. Foreign critics were far more accepting than Australian ones had been: "Cute without being cloying and episodic without being disjointed" (*Variety*); "charming, often very funny... Rod Taylor [is]... very likeable" (*Films in Review*); "so chipper it positively chirps... a pleasant movie trying hard to be a merry one" (*New York Times*). In addition, the movie was selected as one of the ten best of 1977 by the US National Board of Review of Motion Pictures.

The Picture Show Man is a hard film to dislike — it has a breezy, light air and it is inherently good-natured; John Meillon and particularly John Ewart are good value and there are some wonderful scenes, such as when Meillon screens *The Sentimental Bloke* (1919) to a small-town audience: the ability of film to bring together and delight a group of strangers in the dark has rarely been better illustrated. But there are flaws: the story proceeds in fits and starts and is short on cohesion and conflict; Rod's antagonist is fatally underdeveloped and lacks gravitas that would have made the drama stronger — the part of Palmer should have been bigger on the page. Most of all, the movie never seems to get its rhythm right — Long and Power clashed over interpretation of the script during filming and this strain is all too evident in the final result.

Rod's performance in *The Picture Show Man* is, admittedly, not excellent, but it is professional. He (and the film) did not deserve the caning they received from local critics, especially when one compares the response of their overseas colleagues. It was as if Rod was being punished for returning to Australia.

Australians have a reputation for living in the land of the tall poppy, where people are cut down to size if they are seen being too big for their boots. Aussies also have a reputation for suffering cultural cringe — a belief that anything happening in other cultures is superior to ours.

What happened to Rod here is evidence of both of these tendencies: while Rod was headed toward Hollywood, or making films there, he received, on the whole, enthusiastic support from Australians, from the 1954 Rola prize up until to the 1975 Chips Rafferty Award (apart from some criticism of his boorish behavior during the *High Commissioner* visit). But the moment he actually returned to make a film here, the critical daggers were drawn.

Another reason behind the media's hostility might have been the nationalistic atmosphere of 1970s Australia, a time when there was a backlash against the cultural cringe and passionate belief in the superiority of Australian culture. Perhaps "superiority" is putting it a little strongly when it comes to talking about Australian films, but there was a feeling — it persists today — that Australian filmmakers should never think they are never above doing something at home. Rod Taylor, with his pseudo-American accent and lack of iconic Australian performances on his resume, was out in the cultural cold in his homeland; *The Picture Show Man* appears to have done little to redeem him locally.

An example of the changing attitude toward Rod can be seen in the comments of screenwriter Bob Ellis in relation to the latter's film *Newsfront* (1978). This was an Australian film set in the immediate post-World War II period about the conflict between two brothers, Len, a newsreel cameraman who spends his life in Australia, and Frank, who elects to forge a career in America. In discussing the difference between the two brothers, Ellis invoked Rod's name, arguing that, "If Len had been like his brother, who is less of an Irishman, he would have had a Hollywood life like Rod Taylor or someone like that, a man who just became an international wastrel with American wealth and American bodyguards."

Was this a fair call? To slam Rod as "a man who just became an international wastrel"?

It is a little unreasonable to expect Rod to have stayed in Australia in the late '50s and '60s, when the local film, radio and television industries were practically non-existent. This was an extremely fallow time for Australian performers and almost all of Rod's actor friends — Ray Barrett, Ken Wayne, Charles Tingwell, Meillon, etc. — moved overseas to work for at least some period of time. Heath Ledger once contended that, "the beauty about being an Australian in Hollywood is we've got this sense of fearlessness that comes from knowing we can always go home" — but this was not an option forty years ago. Rather, Rod's main faults to cultural warriors such as Ellis seem to have been that: (a) he went "Hollywood" after he moved away and (b) he rarely returned to Australia, even after the local industry revived.

Both criticisms are valid, especially the one about Rod going Hollywood. With his bodyguards, big head and large entourage, Rod had become the sort of tall poppy who deserves to be cut down.

The second criticism also has a strong basis in fact. While it is understandable Rod could never earn the money in Australia that he could overseas, it is still exasperating he did not use the resources of the local film industry more effectively. It could have been a wonderful, mutually beneficial relationship: Rod obtaining top quality roles in decent movies at a time when his career badly needed both and local filmmakers acquiring the services of a talented, internationally famous actor. Instead, Rod preferred to make easy money in short-lived American television series and undistinguished "international" features.

Rod admittedly tried to get a number of projects going in Australia, but most of them were not actually set there, nor did they tell Australian stories; rather, they aimed to exploit the local scenery and cheap technicians a la *Long John Silver*: *The Golden Jungle* (set in Palm Beach and Cuba), *The Contact* (America and Asia), *The Castaway* (a tropical island) and two projects Rod said he wanted to make after *The Picture Show Man*: *The Sargasso Sea* (a thriller set in the Bermuda triangle) and *Lazarus* (a Western). *Last Bus to Banjo Creek* was the exception rather than the rule to Rod's strongly Hollywood-centric vision and the actor was not afraid to admit it.

"I've heard about some good movies made here lately but it doesn't matter how good they are if nobody's seeing them," he said in the late 1970s. "You can watch your own product in Australia and be proud of it but I want it to go and beat off the French and the English and the Americans... I honestly feel the only way is to bring in American dollars and Neville Wran is in favor of encouraging that with generous tax relief. Maybe you need to bring in a script, too, and an international star and, perhaps, a director. Then we can take advantage of the facilities here and the technicians — who are the best, I think — and we can make a damn good movie. That's the way it needs to be in the beginning. When we've opened the door and showed we can do it, then we can start sailing. If this thing [*The Picture Show Man*] gets off the ground, I'd like to come back here and live — for a while at least. I don't care whether I direct or produce or act. Any help I can give, I'm going to give."

Making things worse for Rod's cultural reputation were the series of television ads he made shortly after *The Picture Show Man*. The aim of these was to promote the 90% American-owned Utah Development Company, then the biggest exporter of Australian coal, having just announced an annual profit of $137 million. In fact, it was the size of these profits, being made by an overseas company out of an Australian natural resource, which prompted Utah to run the campaign. Rod's rumored fee was AU$160,000, almost one-third of *The Picture Show Man*'s budget.

Utah took Rod and a film crew to the town of Moranbah, Queensland, for six days of shooting. Rod flew up there in the company's Lear jet and stayed in the guesthouse reserved for Utah bigwigs. According to *The Australian*, he raised the ire of the locals during the shoot down at the local Black Nugget Hotel after he walked behind the bar and "goosed a barmaid."

A copy of one of the ads is held by the National Film and Sound Archive. It is embarrassing from the moment Rod first appears in flared blue pants and a cowboy hat, sitting on top of a horse. "I don't know why people call this the wide brown land," he says. "But I do know why they call it the lucky country." Rod gets off his horse and the camera wobbles. He talks about the developments Utah has made out of the largely undeveloped area: water, power, sealed roads; people can send their kids to church and school "the easy way"; they can come into town and see football games, swimming pools or a drive-in movie. "Utah: We're backing Australia."

The Australian government responded by taxing Rod $35,000 for the money he made on the ad. That did not quite kill the sour taste that came from an American company making money out of an Australian natural resource paying an American-based Australian star to tell Australian audiences how good the company was for Australia. The ads were not a triumph and were later pulled.

The Picture Show Man experience seems to have killed off any dreams Rod may have had about returning to live in Australia full-time. He was too well entrenched in Los Angeles and could earn too much money there, regardless of the quality of the projects he was making (important, since there were still alimony and child support bills to be met). Also, the small size of Australia's industry would have forced Rod to become a character actor if he wanted to work consistently and Rod remained a leading man until the late 1980s. He did not come back for another five years.

WHEN ROD ARRIVED BACK IN THE US, HE LEARNED THAT WESTERNS were the flavor of the month on American television and Universal had succeeded in selling *The Oregon Trail* as a series to NBC. There were some changes from the pilot, the most notable being the elimination of Rod's wife. "So we'll have a lot of beautiful guest stars, which is what I like," quipped Rod. "The only argument is with the network character who had to go and schedule us against *Charlie's Angels* (1976–81)." *Charlie's Angels* was then the number four show in the country; after his experiences with *Hong Kong* and *Bearcats!*, Rod was nervous about going up against a rating's juggernaut. The actor was heartened, however, when it was decided his new show would be filmed on location in Arizona at an estimated cost of $380,000 an episode.

"On expensive shows, they're inclined to search out a better time-slot for you if you don't make it in the first one," Rod argued. "Maybe that's a rule we all ought to follow in this business. Never get involved in a cheap show. Always go for the big-budget jobs."

In the mid-'70s, Hollywood was undergoing one of its periodic panics about the amount of violence shown on television and as a result *The Oregon Trail* had to tone down its action sequences considerably. Alan Levi, who directed a number of series episodes, describes *The Oregon Trail* as a "personal Western rather than a gunslinger Western. Stories were based on relationships between people, not necessarily gun fights." The director elaborated: "Rod's character was basically a guy who believed in family and morals — he had a rough exterior with a smooth interior. He was sensitive and helpful yet he tried to play rough and tough. When he was alone with someone he could come out and be a helping hand, a friend. And that's the way Rod really is — he had a rough exterior but was kind inside."

Rod, again showing his preference for stories about male relationships, said he was particularly interested in exploring the father-son dynamic on the series: "I believe this is the strongest element of the show that will help translate 1850 to 1977," he said. The actor even wrote a script of his own along these lines to be used; however, Rod is not credited as a writer on any of the episodes that were made.

A cast member who had not featured in the pilot but became a series regular was Charles Napier, playing a trail guide. Napier was then under contract to Universal Studios when he got a call to go on set at Tucson, Arizona. ("It was kind of like the military," remembers Napier. "I didn't know what it was for, I didn't bother to ask.") Napier checked into a hotel, "got a bar tab going" and waited for someone to call.

"Three days later someone calls and says, 'Are you Charles Napier?' I said, 'Yes, I am.' They said, 'Where have you been? We start filming tomorrow. Mr. Taylor is extremely upset.'

"I went down the hallway and I heard this racket. There were about 40 tables crashing and all this loud screaming. Rod Taylor opened the door, with wild eyes and hair standing up. He said, 'Who the f—k are you?' I said, 'I'm supposed to be in this series.' 'You Charles Napier? Come on in, mate.' I said, 'Sorry for the delay, I didn't know where to go.' He said, 'Don't worry about it. I'm the star of the show. What I say goes.' He was drinking with all these wranglers. It went on until the small hours and we got up and started filming the next day."

Rod and Charles Napier formed an instant bond on set, playing practical jokes on each other throughout filming.

"Rod always wanted the fastest horse and the biggest horse," says Napier. "A wrangler gave me a horse which Richard Boone used in *Have Gun — Will Travel* (1957–63). Richard Boone was drunk all the time and his horse could practically say the lines. But that was 20 years ago. I hated this horse. Rod told me, 'You're the co-star. Get a different horse.' He said, 'You've got to use your power, mate. I've been in this business longer than you and that's how you get things done.' So I went to them and said, 'I'd better get a horse tomorrow or I won't be in the show.' I got a horse, Bartender. Bartender was bigger than Rod's horse. Now that was a problem. So Rod got a bigger horse, Utah. Bartender was a side-kicker. He kicked out sideways and one of those kicks sent me into hospital. Rod thought that was extremely funny.

"One day we stuck cotton buds in his horse's ears so they stuck straight out. He said, 'I don't know what's wrong with my horse.' I said, 'That's a condition they go through. It's a listening phase, every now and then.' So they sent out a veterinarian which cost a couple of hundred dollars and the guy found cotton wool in the ears. It took him a while to get me back for that one."

The problem with this sort of behavior is it can easily slide into boorishness, which seems to be what happened on *The Oregon Trail*. Burt Brinckerhoff, director of a number of episodes, remembers Rod and Napier became involved "in some barroom escapades that didn't help either of them." One even involved them spending the night in jail. "The crew had to go and get them and bring them to the set the next day," confirms Alan Levi.

In addition, with filming on location from dawn until dusk it is not surprising there were some flare-ups, especially from the hot-tempered star.

"Rod was the star of the show and everyone understood that," says Napier. "He's ready to listen to a fair argument, but also ready to back up his own opinion with his fists."

Specifically, co-star Andrew Stevens claims there was "constant enmity" between Rod and Michael Gleason, the show runner. Producer Carl Vitale says that Rod got along with Gleason on the whole, but admits "on occasion things would happen where everyone was tired but nothing to detriment anyone's health." (Gleason did not wish to comment.)

Generally, though, Rod loved *The Oregon Trail* experience. "He was interested and questioning in all creative areas," remembers Brinckerhoff. "Because the show was a Western and a period piece, Rod always wanted everything to be as authentic as possible."

Alan Levi says Rod was fun to be around and a pleasure to direct. "He was a star long before the show and actually he was the star of the show, but he always said he wasn't — he said the star of the show was everybody, the family and Napier and the guest stars. He gave a lot of credit to a lot of other people.

"It sounds a bit like heaven on earth but it's not always the case — there are stars that are son of a bitches, there are relationships that don't work on set at all. Here everybody had a wonderful time, everybody was very supportive, especially Rod. He worked well with the family. He was very protective of everybody. If he saw something not right he'd call it — he called a spade a spade.

"He's a real man's man, a terrific character to sit down and have a yarn with, play cards with, he's a good old Aussie. It lent personality to the show. When he was young in the movies he was good looking. As he became older and crustier, he developed a hard exterior yet still had a soft interior and I think that's what gave the series personality. He really was the star of the show, how he handled himself and the scripts, it was marvelous."

When *The Oregon Trail* series debuted, it earned Rod some of his best-ever personal reviews:

"What *The Oregon Trail* really has going for it is Rod Taylor, the man himself... Taylor in real life is a free spirit with all the frontier-like independence that seems typically Australian as well as American... Taylor looks more at home along the Oregon Trail than Davy Crockett himself. The face is weathered and looks lived-in. He is comfortably masculine and he has the secure authority of a man who could have as good a time drinking alone as sharing a bottle with a lady or a roustabout." (*The Hollywood Reporter*)

"Many positive elements going for it, not the least of which is Rod Taylor.... A strong part for a strong actor. And Taylor does it exceedingly well." (*Variety*)

Unfortunately, during its first few weeks the show averaged a rating of only 14.3 — not enough to ensure its survival, especially with *Charlie's Angels* on 25.5. "People weren't watching Westerns, the Western era was over, except *Little House in the Prairie* and a couple of movies," argues Levi. "We were more into cop shows and PI shows and a lot of comedy."

Universal brought the unit back from location in Arizona and started filming around Los Angeles instead; scenes were rewritten so they could be shot indoors. "When you have to go back from location it's never a good sign," sighs producer Carl Vitale. "Once they lost interest in it they didn't want to spend money," recalls Napier. "They cut out the cattle and mountains and brought it interior; put it on a soundstage."

In November, NBC announced they had decided to axe the series, with a number of episodes remaining unaired. It was a shame, since the show had real heart and the potential for a long run, not to mention a relaxed performance from Rod in the lead. However, in hindsight, it is not surprising — Westerns never regained their prominence on the small screen; *The Oregon Trail* came along around ten years too late.

AT LEAST THE SHOW HELPED KEEP ROD'S NAME IN THE PUBLIC eye. He claimed he was still capable of earning $250,000 a film, but frequently accepted less in exchange for a share of the profits.

"I always disagreed with the stars that demand $1 million for a film," he declared. "I don't believe in holding up someone and preventing a film from being made."

A million dollars was the budget for Rod's next project, a television movie made in Ireland, *Cry of the Innocent*. This was based on an original story by Frederick Forsyth, bestselling author of *Day of the Jackal*.

Forsyth had recently settled in Ireland, attracted by the zero percent tax payable on literary income. One day he was interviewed on local radio by Morgan O'Sullivan, a broadcaster interested in getting into film production; O'Sullivan asked the writer if he was interested in doing something made in Ireland for the American television market, with an eye to a possible theatrical release elsewhere. Forsyth agreed and provided a 16-page treatment which sketched the basic outline for a story: Steve Donegan, a former US Green Beret living in Ireland, sees his wife and child killed when a plane crashes into his house; investigations reveal that the crash was not an accident and Donegan goes looking for revenge.

O'Sullivan says that although the character of Donegan was American, he did not want an American actor to play the part. "I wanted someone who at least looked European and felt European." O'Sullivan's wife was a fan of Rod Taylor and suggested him. O'Sullivan agreed ("I felt he had a European sensibility") and Rod accepted the role.

O'Sullivan recalls Rod being terrific to work with. "He is a lovely guy and can be a most charming man in a professional and social setting. We also had great fun making the movie. I always thought Rod was a great star but what made him special was that he had wonderful acting talent. I remember particularly a very touching scene from the movie after he lost his wife and family — his expression of grief. Without dialogue he managed to create a compelling moment. I always equate him with Richard Burton. To me they command equal respect as film actors."

The majority of the budget was provided by NBC, which was initially enthusiastic about *Cry of the Innocent*'s prospects, even commissioning a script for a sequel. (This was written by British writer Beverly Cross, who was married to Maggie Smith; interestingly, Cross got the job partly because of Rod — the actor had mentioned to O'Sullivan that he had worked with Smith on *The VIPs*.) However, somewhere along the line, the network lost interest in the film and dumped it on air over the summer where it rated 14.4 and a 26 share. The *New York Times* thought it was "several cuts above the average telemovie" in which Rod "gets to contribute some impressive emoting."

Cry of the Innocent is a pleasurable thriller with fine work from Rod and excellent support from Cyril Cusack (as a police officer) and Nigel Davenport (as the baddie), although the climactic fight is a little silly. Bizarrely, this was Rod's second film (after *Darker Than Amber*) where the leading woman played both a character that is killed and a lookalike of that character.

The movie was directly responsible for Rod's next job: his scenes with Cyril Cusack impressed the powers-that-be over at Anglia Television enough to reunite the two actors in an episode of *Tales of the Unexpected* (1979–82). This was a British TV anthology series based on the short stories of Roald Dahl; "The Hitchhiker" was about a driver (Rod) who picks up a hitchhiking pickpocket (Cusack).

Rod adored working with Cusack. "I loved every clever marvelous sneaky thing he did when we are acting together," he said. "I just watched him and laughed. We're like two very good boxers." "The Hitchhiker" is a clever, tightly structured piece with some strong performances; one cannot help think that if anthology drama had flourished through the '70s, enabling Rod to remind people what he was capable of, his career might not have declined the way it did.

BY THE LATE '70S, ROD'S ALIMONY OBLIGATIONS TO MARY WERE almost at an end, so he decided to splurge on a second home, a 160-acre ranch outside of Sacramento. "I wanted it to be like the farm I used to go to," explained Rod. "My treat every Christmas holidays was to go up to Uncle Charlie who was a real country bastard, who would work me from four in the morning till dark."

Since Rod had already made extensive improvements to his Beverly Hills house — carving his own furniture, designing and constructing the kitchen — he decided to make all the additions to his new property himself. He sunk wells, put up fences and even built a house. "I wish I had done this when I was 25 years old," he said. "But why not now?"

That was a long-range project, however, and Rod barely had time to start before flying over to Europe for another international movie, *A Time to Die*. This was based on an original screenplay by Mario Puzo about an American soldier, Rogan, who seeks revenge on the Nazis responsible for killing his wife and family in World War II. Rod played a CIA man who appears to be on Rogan's side, but actually is more interested in keeping alive certain ex-Nazis. John Goff, who worked on the script, describes Rod's character as being "kind of a villain, villainous in the sense the end justified the means and it didn't matter who the guy was in the overall picture."

Director Matt Cimber assembled an impressive support cast, including Raf Vallone and Rex Harrison (in his final film) and the shoot took place in such glamorous locations as Amsterdam, France and La Pologna. However, Rod did not enjoy the experience, later referring to Cimber as an "awful director" and the picture as "terrible."

Also unhappy was producer Charles Lee, a Korean theatre magnate who had raised the bulk of the budget. After the film was assembled into a rough cut, Lee arranged for additional sequences to be filmed by another director, most notably a new ending in which Rogan does not die.

"They thought they were going to make the picture commercial," complains Cimber. "They took something I thought was really powerful in its message and made it a mundane B movie action film."

Joe Tornatore is credited with directing additional scenes and as "action director"; William Russell is credited for writing extra scenes and Fred Chulack for doing further editing. Since Chulack had previously worked on some Rod Taylor films (*Darker Than Amber, Cry of the Innocent*) it is likely that Rod helped bring him on to the project.

"He [Rod] had his own ideas, I think, about the film," reflects Cimber. "I remember some of the stuff that he said and I think he wanted more in the picture than he got from me. Then when they did the rewrite he got more time on the screen."

The re-shoots, plus various legal wrangles between Lee and Puzo, meant that although *A Time to Die* was shot in mid-1979 it was not released theatrically until 1983. *Variety* called it "a tedious, unappealing exercise," but added that Rod was "pleasant to watch" even if "his role doesn't make much sense."

A Time to Die is an interesting movie that has clearly been chopped around a fair bit but is still quite watchable. Particularly intriguing is the fact that the hero (a tormented Edward Albert, Jr.) is not that sympathetic: he and his wife were spying on the Nazis, after all, so it was not that strange that they would try to kill him. Rod's CIA-man character, trying to ensure the stability of post-war Germany, comes across as understandable rather than villainous.

In the end, though, the project was all too typical of most of Rod's 1970s efforts: a promising-sounding assignment that ultimately self-destructed. The decade had done serious damage to his career — two flop television series, a pilot that failed to be picked up, several dud features made outside Hollywood, two uninspiring forays into independent production and a poorly received cameo back in Australia.

"They all thought I'd disappeared," recalled Rod. "If I had to do it over, I wouldn't have spent so much time away. Even today people say to me, 'Do you still live in Spain?' Hell, I never lived in Spain!"

Fortunately, the next decade was more satisfying.

CHAPTER 14

"I'm a little too old for all that macho bullshit."

THE '80S (1980–88)

THE 1980S SAW ROD RETURN TO BEING A MORE VERSATILE actor, concentrating less on the he-man roles that so dominated his resume throughout the previous decade. Admittedly, he could still be found throwing a punch with the boys, but he played other characters as well: an impotent serial killer, a secretary to the British royal family, a business tycoon. It was reminiscent of Rod's early acting days, when he performed in all sorts of parts.

This change was partly due to the fact that Rod no longer enjoyed the creative power in Hollywood he once had. He also may have finally realized, after years of flops, that the public did not particularly insist he only play macho characters. In addition, it could have reflected the influence of Carol Kikumura, whom Rod finally married in 1980; with a stable domestic environment for the first time in his adult life, Rod was finally mellowing on-and-off-screen.

Rod began the new decade with a small but striking part in *Hellinger's Law.* This was a first-rate pilot for a proposed TV series starring Telly Savalas as a crime lawyer; Rod played a Texas-based member of the Mafia (!) who employs one of Savalas' clients. The movie is full of top-notch acting, sparkling dialogue and a compelling story; Rod makes a very sympathetic crime lord, perhaps lacking a little in ruthlessness. The *Los Angeles Times* claimed he played his role "surprisingly well" — despite a 30-year career, critics still seemed to forget what Rod was capable of. Considering some of his '70s work, though, that is perhaps understandable.

He then had one of his best roles in a long time with *Jacqueline Bouvier Kennedy* (1981), a big-budget three-hour telemovie about America's most glamorous First Lady of the 20th century (played by Jaclyn Smith of *Charlie's Angels*). Although the subject herself did not co-operate with the project, it was an "affectionate portrait," i.e. there was no mention of JFK's extramarital affairs, Aristotle Onassis, the Bay of Pigs, Marilyn Monroe, the Mafia or assassination conspiracies.

Rod was cast as Jackie's roguish playboy father, John "Blackjack" Bouvier, a stockbroker whose marriage to Jackie's mother was destroyed by his womanizing and drinking. Bouvier adores his daughter (and she him), but that does not stop him from doing things like turning up drunk on her wedding day. It is the sort of flashy support role that invariably steals the show and Rod made ideal casting: all boozy buccaneering charm and responsible for his daughter having a distorted relationship with the opposite sex for the rest of her life.

The rest of the film is entertaining enough and not a total whitewash (for instance, it hints that JFK was not the most attentive husband). The main problem is that in this polite, glossy version of events, JBK does not seem worthy of a three-hour screen treatment: she was iconic and set fashion trends, but what did she do, really? Impressed the French, redecorated the White House... and ...? There is a fascinating story to be told about Jackie Kennedy, but it is not to be found in *Jacqueline Bouvier Kennedy*.

Nonetheless, the movie proved hugely popular — indeed, it was Rod's biggest hit in a long time — rating 27.4 and 42 share; a theatrical version was later released to some cinemas. Reviews were generally dismissive — but what critic was going to admit they enjoyed a film called *Jacqueline Bouvier Kennedy*? Rod took whatever positive comments were going: the *Globe and Mail* said he "nicely captures the increasingly decadent facade of dandy Daddy Bouvier," while the *New York Times* thought he acted "with rough but affecting compassion... the only character who brings a dash of life to the film's curiously bland proceedings."

Rod then received an offer to make a picture back in Australia. The local industry had altered markedly in the years since *The Picture Show Man* and Rod's new film would exemplify some of the less attractive aspects of the changes.

TOWARD THE END OF THE 1970S, THERE HAD BEEN INCREASING dissatisfaction within the Australian film industry over the way projects were financed, the most common of which had been direct funding through government bodies. As an alternative, the federal government introduced a tax incentive plan aimed at enhancing private investment; the scheme, known as Division 10BA of the Income Tax Assessment Act 1936, meant that provided a project complied with certain necessary requirements (such as obtaining a certification that it was "Australian"), investors in that project could write off up to 150% of their capital expenditure on it and be tax exempt for up to 50% of the net earnings from that investment.

The 10BA incentives worked like a treat: the number of features made in Australia shot up from 17 in 1979/80 to 30 in 1980/81. However, it soon became clear the system had serious flaws: films had to be finished by June 30 for tax reasons, causing production bottlenecks and leading to increased crew costs; tax experts, brokers, lawyers and accountants began to populate the industry, often charging considerable fees for their services (the average cost of an Australian film leapt from $1.53 million in 1980 to $3.32 million in 1981); rising expenses forced producers to seek overseas pre-sales and distribution guarantees, causing a boom in more seemingly commercial genres such as thrillers and action films; and it became apparent that a number of movies were being financed as a tax dodge rather than for artistic reasons. Even though much fine work was produced under 10BA, the expression "10BA film" became synonymous with needlessly expensive duds made to avoid tax. Unfortunately, Rod's fourth Australian movie was an example of a 10BA film par excellence.

On the Run was produced and directed by Mende Brown, an American film-maker who had emigrated to Sydney and worked in the local industry. Richard Hindley, *On the Run*'s editor, describes Brown as "a one-eyed New York Jewish hustler who moved out to Australia and exploited the scene and made a lot of money."

The movie's script was written by an American, Michael Fisher, and was originally set in America. Brown had Fisher relocate the story to Australia, and then attracted the interest of Bill Anderson, a wealthy property developer who was willing to put up most of the film's AU$1.6 million budget in exchange for the 10BA tax concessions.

Rod agreed to play the part of Mr. Payatta, a professional hit man who travels the world assassinating people, but who in his down time lives quietly on a property in rural Australia with a servant (Paul Winfield). Payatta's ten-year-old nephew (Beau Cox) sees his uncle kill two blackmailers and is about to be killed by him in turn — but Winfield's character turns against his boss and the two of them flee, with Rod in hot pursuit.

It was only the third time Rod played an Australian on screen and the first time he played one in an Australian film. There wasn't anything particularly Australian about the character, though; Payatta could just as easily have been an American. Indeed, Rod based his performance on a hit man he once met in Las Vegas. "One moment he's speaking politely to a local and the next he will think about killing someone," he said.

Filming started in February 1982 and took place in Sydney, Wiseman's Ferry, Katoomba and the Blue Mountains. Rod took Carol along with him and from all accounts production was considerably more easy-going than on *The Picture Show Man*. (Mende Brown was a hack, but a professional, well-organized one.) Among the cast was Ray Meagher, later to find cultural immortality as Alf Stewart on *Home and Away* (1988–), who describes Rod as a "really good bloke. He was very professional; he knew what he was doing. At that stage, he still liked a drink on a hot day and we enjoyed a few of those. There was definitely no 'side.' He was very down to earth. You'd have to get it out of him that he'd done all these other things."

According to Hindley, *On the Run* was never really intended to have a theatrical release ("Mende was very television"); the movie had one screening in Australia at a Bondi cinema on the last day of the financial year to qualify for the 10BA tax concession, before it was sold to television. *Variety* called the film an "old-fashioned, entertaining… action picture for which there seems to be no discernible audience" in which Rod was "not very convincing."

On the Run is not a terribly good movie and Rod is not very convincing as a hired killer. Apart from one bright moment when Payatta asks Paul Winfield to dig three graves and Winfield realizes this means he wants to kill Beau Cox, generally the movie feels too much like an episode of a television series and an average one at that. Many fine films were being made in Australia around this time and even at script stage Rod should have known that *On the Run* was not going to be one of them. Perhaps there were no other offers at the time. Perhaps he was still unable to resist a role that involved him playing a tough guy. Perhaps he simply had no taste.

Nonetheless, Rod remained upbeat about the prospect of working more in his home country. The local industry was booming and if he was less popular with Hollywood producers than in previous years, Australian producers were very interested in him. After all, since Peter Finch's death in 1976, Rod was the most internationally recognized male Australian film star (although Mel Gibson soon changed that).

Two projects in particular were discussed: another with Brown from a Fisher script, *Mates*, described as "*Captains Courageous* (1936) on land," about a boy who inherits an Aussie cattle ranch run by a tough but philosophical Rod Taylor; there was also *Go for Broke*, scheduled for filming in 1982 by director Joe Tornatore.

However, these plans received a setback in April 1982 when *On the Run* was refused a certificate as an Australian film by the Home Affairs Minister — which meant it could not qualify for the 10BA tax concession. The reason given was that *On the Run* had an American writer, director, producer and star; Rod was not considered Australian as he had recently become an American citizen.

For years, Rod Taylor had been a famous Australian actor, one of the best known in the world, and now, finally back in an Australian-financed movie — what's more, playing an Australian character — his citizenship meant that the film was considered un-Australian. It was part of a general crackdown on tax evasion at the time, which was then rife in Australia; the film industry, with its 10BA tax incentives and dodgy promoters, was a high-profile target.

Rod knew the ruling would make him less attractive to Australian film financiers: "Because I've just given up my Australian passport for a US one, I can quite sadly forget about being invited to do any more Aussie movies here because Australian Actors' Equity says I'm a Yank. How can they get so pompous when their film industry is so small? A few films like *Gallipoli* (1981) and they think

Australia is the biggest film producing country in the world. Crazy. Who could be more Aussie than me? For 29 years, I carried an Aussie passport but for tax reasons I switched. Now they're screaming that Rod Taylor's a Yank."

Mende Brown appealed the decision and eventually succeeded in getting the ruling overturned — Bill Anderson received his tax deduction. But it was the original verdict that had gotten all the publicity and the damage was done. *Go for Broke* was cancelled and *Mates* never happened. Rod did not make another film in Australia for 14 years.

AFTER *ON THE RUN* THERE WAS TALK ROD MIGHT MAKE A film with Tony Curtis, as well as an interesting-sounding movie to be shot in Texas called *Brother Otis*, starring Rod as a priest who seduces young girls. Neither project came to fruition; instead, Rod accepted a small role in another television film for the ABC network based on a true-life story: *Charles & Diana: A Royal Love Story*, about the wedding of Prince Charles and Diana Spencer.

Rod plays Edward Adeane, the long-time private secretary to Prince Charles. The actor was one of a number of well-known names who supported the film's unknown leads, including Christopher Lee, Mona Washbourne, Margaret Tyzack and Charles Grey; just as he had in *Separate Tables*, "Misalliance" and *Young Cassidy*, Rod's Australian background proved no barrier to slotting into a powerful English acting ensemble. Producer Clyde Phillips admits Rod was "not English but he has such a quiet elegance. We're the ugly Americans (laughs) so English, Australian…"

Phillips was full of praise for Rod. "He was the consummate professional and it was a difficult shoot," the producer says. "He was prepared, he was a leader on the set, he was appropriately proper if I can say. He was staid within himself the whole time. He's not in the movie a lot but what he is in he's memorable."

At the same time, another movie on the same topic was being made by rival network CBS, *The Royal Romance of Charles and Diana*. Whichever film got to air first was obviously going to have a big advantage: CBS originally announced *The Royal Romance* would air in December, then brought the date forward to September; ABC responded by bringing forward the screening of *Charles & Diana*, but not giving the exact date until four days out, ensuring CBS could not make a countermove. Eventually, *Charles & Diana* beat its rival to air by three days… but since ABC did not give out their air date until the last minute, the network's ability to promote the show was lessened. Accordingly, the ratings were a disappointing 40 million viewers; in contrast, *A Royal Romance* on CBS the next Monday was seen by 58 million.

Charles & Diana: A Royal Love Story holds up surprisingly well today: the scenery is pleasant, the acting satisfactory and the script does deal with some political matters around the wedding, such as the assassination of Lord Mountbatten and the need to produce a royal heir. Some moments even have unexpected resonance, such as the ceaseless pursuit of Diana by the paparazzi and a scene between Diana and her fiancé's best friends, Andrew and Camilla Parker-Bowles. Rod only has a few short scenes; his role is mainly of note in seeing him play an old-style "Rodney Taylor" part again.

ROD'S CAREER THEN TOOK AN UNEXPECTED UPSWING WHEN HE was cast in the lead of a new television series, *Masquerade*. This show centred around a fictitious government intelligence agency that recruits ordinary people with specialized skills to carry out particular missions. The head of the agency was a smooth-yet-tough middle-aged American, Lavendar, described by producer Renee Valente as: "He wasn't Dirty Harry but he was the lynchpin and one way or another he would get the bad guy." In other words, *Hong Kong*'s Glenn Evans, 20 years on. Rod's agent approached Valente to suggest his client for the part, but the producer says she was reluctant at first. "His reputation was a drinker that led to trouble. I passed! His agent kept calling, saying, 'You've got to meet with him.' I finally agreed and he was charming. He looked wonderful, said he was on the wagon, his drinking problem long gone. We did cast him and he was terrific. He was wonderful, conscientious; he worked so hard, he was very anxious for the series to be a big hit.

"No one else was considered once he said yes. We needed the networks and they approved Rod immediately. Everyone was a little concerned because they were warned he was tough. I found him to be a teddy bear. I think actors are tough because they are vulnerable; so much of it is a facade. Once the trust is established, so is the professionalism."

A pilot was shot in early 1983, with Greg Evigan and Kirstie Alley playing Lavendar's assistants. While waiting to hear whether the network would OK a series, Rod went home to Sydney for a quick visit. The occasion was a sad one: his father's funeral, Bill having died on May 3, 1983. Rod and Carol persuaded Mona to leave Lidcombe and live with them in Beverly Hills; the house at 18 Swete Street was eventually sold and knocked down.

ABC did not select *Masquerade* as one of its new shows for the 1983–84 season, but gave it the green light as a mid-season replacement show, i.e. one that would be put on air in case one of the new programs failed. It went into production at an estimated cost of $750,000 per episode.

Renee Valente found working with Rod an absolute joy. "Without Rod Taylor the pilot wouldn't have sold and the series wouldn't have sold," says the producer. "It would not have been credible, it would have been fantasy. The letters we got from viewers were amazing. Rod did it and loved what he was doing. The audience enjoyed him. Rod and Greg [Evigan] had a lot of fun with each other. You give him lines to say and you believe him when he says them.

"He became the character — that's what all good actors have to do, they become that person. He looked the part, too — tough guy! 'Be careful — don't fool around with me.' He had a great look. Very sexy. A middle-aged man, very sexy — he had it. Greg Evigan was the young sexpot; Rod Taylor was the older version.

"He did most of his stunts himself. I have such memories of trying to get him not to do everything. But it was like Burt Reynolds in another series I did, *Hawk* (1966). Machismo. It makes them feel good and you worry that they break a leg or something. They don't care (laughs). And they want everyone to know that they're doing it. 'Make sure the camera's on me so they know I'm doing it. Don't cut away so they think it's a stunt man...'

"Rod never lost his cool — he set the standard for the other actors on the set. Like most stars all he wanted was to be heard, a chance to give his creative input on his character. If you give an actor the respect of hearing what he has to say there will be a terrific camaraderie."

"Rod was wonderful, absolutely wonderful," confirms series director Phil Bondelli. "He had an unbelievable sense of humor. I got along with him beautifully. The man was a big star doing a TV series, but he never pressured anyone. He was a pro, there's no doubt about it, you couldn't fool him."

Rod's good humor would have been helped by the fact that several of *Masquerade*'s guest stars were old friends of his, including Lloyd Bochner, Joe Santos and William Smith (with whom Rod had yet another on-screen fistfight).

One of ABC's new shows, *Trauma Center* (1983), was rating poorly and the network decided to replace it with *Masquerade* on Thursday nights at 9 p.m. Again, Rod faced rough opposition, being up against *Simon & Simon* (1981–88) and *Cheers* (1982–93).

Most critics, on viewing the pilot, noted the program's lack of plausibility, but were cautiously optimistic about its chances. "Tighter scripting could give the series a chance... Taylor was well-cast" (*Variety*); "has a slick Paris setting, an amusing, well-paced story and reliable Rod Taylor" (*Women's Wear Daily*); "great fun... could turn out to be a winner" (*New York Daily News*). CIA spokesman Dale Peterson was asked to comment on *Masquerade*'s accuracy. He described the sort of missions in the show as "a little far-fetched, but in the field of intelligence, you never know"; he qualified this by pointing out the CIA would try to use foreign nationals on overseas assignments rather than American citizens.

Unfortunately, audience figures were poor from the beginning: the pilot rated 12.9 with a 21 share and by January episodes were consistently running last in their timeslot, averaging 14.1 with a 22 share. ABC tried the series for a few weeks in a different timeslot on Friday nights at 9 p.m., but the numbers did not improve sufficiently and it was cancelled by March.

Masquerade had an interesting concept that did lean to formulaic execution and far-fetched plotlines, but made for a generally entertaining show. The least successful episodes were those with a short-term ticking-clock plotline, where it did not make sense that new agents would be recruited to help out. Also, the series felt like *The Love Boat* (1977–86) at times, with agents pretending to be tourists and the regulars seeing off guest stars at the end of the episode as they return to their normal lives. However, some stories — particularly later ones in the series like "Winnings" and "The Spanish Gambit" — were genuinely clever and the show was clearly improving before it was axed.

Rod was perfect as Lavendar, handling the action scenes and complicated plots with conviction. Kirstie Alley and Greg Evigan offered strong support, having a nice bantering relationship with lots of unresolved sexual tension (presumably the main reason that Rod's character got to have romantic interludes with guest stars whereas they did not). But to no avail: Rod now had four unsuccessful TV series under his belt.

ROD THEN RECEIVED AN OFFER TO STAR IN A CAPER FILM shot in Spain, *Marbella* (1985). He plays a drunken ex-naval commander living on a yacht in the title city who seeks revenge on a gangster who rams his ship. Apart from Britt Ekland, who co-starred as Rod's accomplice, the rest of the cast was Spanish, as were the crew. Rod says the film's director and producer had a massive fight with each other during filming, so he worked for two weeks for free to help them out. "Even so, we missed winning an Academy Award by *that* much," he joked.

In fact, *Marbella* is surprisingly entertaining, despite an awful soundtrack and tendency to shove in as many shots of topless women as possible. The plot is pleasingly intricate and Rod gives an agreeable, laid-back performance. His character gets to go to bed with both Ekland and 18-year-old Emma Suarez, which is pretty good for someone who was in his fifties at the time. Naked co-stars, coastal Mediterranean locations… even if Rod was a faded movie star, life could still be very pleasant.

Rod was then among of a number of actors who made a cameo in the pilot for *Half Nelson* (1985), a short-lived TV series starring Joe Pesci as an ex-cop from New York who works as a private eye in Hollywood in between acting roles. Rod did it as a favor for executive producer Glenn A. Larson; Dean Martin, George Kennedy, Tony Curtis, Rory Calhoun and Doug McClure also put in appearances (*Houston Chronicle* claimed the pilot contained "more aging film faces… than Aaron Spelling frontloads in a season of *Love Boats*"). Director Bruce Bilson had troubles during production with Pesci, but recalls working with Rod and the other "pros" for a few hours as a highlight of "a very difficult shoot."

After that, it was then over to Scandinavia for another movie, *Mask of Murder*, a semi-horror/murder mystery, with Rod as a detective investigating a series of nasty killings. Although shot in Sweden with a local crew, the film was set in Canada and was officially a British-US co-production aimed at the US video and international theatrical markets. Rod was one of three non-Swedes who head-lined the cast, the others being Christopher Lee (as a police commissioner) and Valerie Perrine (as Rod's wife).

The picture's cinematographer, Tomislav Pinter, remembers night shootings in the woods in deep snow and temperature of -25 degrees. "The entire crew was well dressed and wore snow boots, but Rod Taylor had to act wearing just a thin shirt and light shoes. He worked professionally and without any comment. He never created any problems and always helped the crew resolve all possible problems with his spirit and great communication skills."

Mask of Murder is a solid mystery which keeps the audience guessing until the very end. Rod has one of his most challenging roles as a policeman driven to madness, possibly murder — although due to his and the filmmakers' skill, you are never really sure if his character is guilty until the final moments. Rod had never played anyone with so many sexual hang-ups before (he's impotent and a killer) and it is fantastic to see him broaden his range. The one big drawback of *Mask of Murder* is that its violence is genuinely nasty and mostly directed at young women; a censored version of the film would probably be more enjoyable. It made little impact on release, but is easily available on video.

By this stage, Carol's influence was clearly making for a gentler, mellower Rod off camera. "I still like a drink with my mates when I'm not working, but I use more discipline with booze now," he claimed. "Look what's happened to some of my contemporaries like Richard Harris, Peter O'Toole and Richard Burton. All hard-drinking tearaways, but it's caught up with them and they have things cut out of their insides. I'm proud God has given me a nudge to be sensitive and I'm enjoying life. My marriage is good and I feel better than I've felt in years."

Rod did recognize, though, that his career had suffered from making too many flops. "I don't get offered major studio films anymore," he admitted. "Nowa-days, they want Sylvester Stallone or Chuck Norris. Frankly, I don't blame them. I'm a little too old for all that macho bullshit. I would feel embarrassed doing a love scene with a much younger actress. If I went bare-chested on camera at my age, people would puke."

However, he wasn't quite on a trash pile just yet. While the studios may not have wanted Rod for features, they still considered him for small-screen work and that very year asked him to star in a new TV series. Would it be a case of fifth time lucky?

THE OUTLAWS WAS IN MANY WAYS A LAST HURRAH FOR ROD AS the star of rugged, macho entertainment that focused on male relationships. The series was about a group of cowboys who get transplanted from the 1899 American West to modern-day Houston and decide to set up a detective agency. Rod played the lead, a sheriff who is chasing a gang of outlaws when they are zapped into the future; the desperados consisted of William Lucking, Patrick Houser, Richard Roundtree and Rod's old friend Charles Napier, with Christine Belford as the modern-day police officer who helps them.

The show runner was Nick Corea, a hard-living former Vietnam veteran-turned-writer who had authored a number of *Oregon Trail* episodes. A friend of Corea's, Bruce Cervi, remembers: "I think when Rod was mentioned, Nick was very happy about that because of *The Oregon Trail* experience — I think he lobbied heavily for Rod. Rod was another one of those take-no-bullshit guys. He didn't take it from anybody, he had opinions about stuff, he didn't waffle or flip-flop (even if he was wrong). He was a strong guy and Nick admired him for that."

The series was produced by Universal who, despite (or because of) their long history with Rod, did not initially share Corea's enthusiasm for the actor. Charles Napier: "The people at Universal said, 'We don't want Rod.' They swore they'd never put he and I on the same show and same lot together. We were too much trouble. We did things like taking horses down to the commissary and they'd shit all over the place and stuff like that.

"Over two days they brought up different names. Johnny Cash, Stuart Whitman, Richard Widmark. Everyone but Rod. Everyone turned it down and they've gotta take Rod Taylor. They go to Nick Corea and say, 'You've gotta get Rod Taylor.' He said, 'He's sitting down in Palm Springs, knowing he's been treated this way and he's very angry. I'm going down there in a limo and you guys are coming with me. He's been in this business a long time and you guys have treated him with disrespect. But we've got to do it. We start shooting tomorrow and no one wants to do it.' They said, 'OK.'

"So we all went down to his home at Palm Springs. Nick and I went down. He says hello to me and Nick, but ignores these 8-10 execs. We have a drink for two hours while these guys are sitting there. Then he says, 'How come you guys aren't drinking?' They said, 'We don't drink.' 'You are today.'

"After I while I said, 'Have you punished them enough?' He said, 'A few more hours.' Eventually they called the agents and a deal was done. We started filming the next day. A lot of people ended up eating a lot of crow."

Bruce Cervi confirms that Universal was concerned about Rod's drinking, but that "Nick convinced them he could get him under control. And he did. Rod never blew a scene because of drinking or being up late at night."

The pilot for *The Outlaws* was directed by Peter Werner, who remembers Rod as being "great" to work with — though he could be challenging at times. "He was in the middle of a lot of people so he was fighting for space and wanted input into the show and he was the star of the show. But I don't remember any sort of star trip at all."

"A couple of cases were people Rod had brought in so they were facilitating to him, a couple of people Nick brought in so they were facilitating to him. In that situation it's kind of tough to bring an ensemble together, particularly a male ensemble in a very short time, but by the time we were finished we were a team. They were all guys at the point in their lives who had a lot to prove so there was a lot of testosterone to deal with but it was fun.

"I'm not sure I got a great performance out of him, though. There wasn't a hell of a lot of dramatic depth to it. I think if I were to direct him now I could get more out of him in that situation. He was… lazy isn't the right word because he wasn't lazy, but neither did he dig in and say, 'I'm the leader,' and really figure out how to play the part. And I think he had that in him. I don't know if at that particular moment he thought it was a just a TV show and it was beneath him, or it was partly his relationship with Nick and there was a bond there I couldn't penetrate.

"I'd love to work with him again because I think there was a gifted actor there which I couldn't access. He's a very good actor, but I don't think he found the parts to push himself to make himself a really great actor."

Even so, Rod loved making *The Outlaws*, telling *Starlog* magazine it was the most "delightful working situation" he had ever experienced. He even claimed he and the cast spent a lot of time together off-set, even rehearsing in their own time for the fun of it.

Napier says that Nick Corea allowed the cast a fair degree of creative input on the show. "Nick was a buddy so we were talking amongst friends. Nick would go, 'Here's the script. Try to stick to it as much as possible, but adapt it to yourselves.' Once we were shooting in Las Vegas. They didn't want us to take out horses. Rod said, 'We're taking our horses to Las Vegas.'They're not written in the script. Rod said, 'Write them into the script.' (It would mean the wranglers would come and they would get paid for the work.) We had the horses trucked to Vegas."

Inevitably, all this male bonding often had the effect of making the unit somewhat unruly. "Most of the conversations I had with Nick once the series started was about how difficult it was to handle the guys," says Bruce Cervi. "They all had opinions, they were all tough guys and you had to be careful you didn't start a fight. Rod and Charlie would drop a punch at the drop of a hat, followed by Bill Lucking not far behind. Richard Roundtree was a quiet one; he was a real pro… I met Rod once. He was real nice, but the kind of guy I didn't want to hang out with too much because I always got the feeling if I do or say something wrong he's going to hit me.

"If you ever see the show you'll notice there was not much night shooting. Once night fell the boys pulled out the liquor glasses and started going for it, so they weren't much use after dark. They couldn't afford take after take. So if you see the show there's a lot of sunshine."

Napier says his friend was always a tough guy. "He's totally Australian. He told me something once about hitting a guy. He said if you're having an argument with someone who's wearing a hat, say to them, 'That's a nice hat, can I see it?' Then when he takes it off, you hit him. He said, 'That's Australia, mate.' I think we worked it into the show...

"He was a great drinker, a great pal. He was a man's man. He had his share of women, but he was quiet about it. He never talked about his women or old movies. In the old days actors did their drinking hard, but always showed up for work. It's different now. Rod hit in the '50s and '60s, where there was a whole different climate of star, a whole different attitude. They'd work early in the morning and played hard at night. But they'd always show up for work, sick or sorry."

The time on the show increased Napier's appreciation for his friend's gifts as an actor. "He had the grand ability to look at something — dialogue — and remember it after a few minutes. He had great physical energy. A magnetism that can't be defined; his inner spirit or whatever came through. Certain people can just make it seem real. That can't be taught. Rod had never been to school, neither had I. He could just pull it off. Robert Mitchum had the same thing — a quick study, he could look at the scene and know what's wrong. He knew the high-tech end. Very stern with his producers. Never let them get over his head."

Like *Masquerade*, *The Outlaws* was given the green light as a possible mid-season replacement in case one of CBS's new shows failed. One of them, *Downtown* (1986), duly obliged and *The Outlaws* was scheduled to air on Saturday night at 8 p.m. (To give some idea of the ruthlessness of American television, the networks axed 48 shows in total by December that year!)

Initial critical reaction was generally consistent: poor about the show, positive about Rod. *TV Guide* slammed *The Outlaws* as "a stinker that traps a couple of our favorite actors in a premise that wears thin before the first commercial," but liked Rod, "who's always good." The *Seattle Times* panned the show as "one of the worst series I've ever suffered through," but added that "Rod Taylor, who is beginning to look wonderfully weather-beaten and full of character... [is] likable — or would be in more felicitous circumstances." The *San Francisco Chronicle* noted that "time has done interesting things to Rod Taylor... he's now round of belly, bulbous of nose, thin of hair and long of tooth. He's gone to seed," but added that, "he still has a masculine, relatable quality that's more fun to watch than anything else in the show."

Public response was initially encouraging, with both the pilot and the first episode winning their time slots. Even better was the news that *The Outlaws* would be up against two sets of sitcoms, *Sidekicks* (1986–87) and *Sledgehammer* (1986–88), on ABC and *The Facts of Life* (1979–88) and *227* (1985–90) on NBC. For the first time in his career, Rod was starring in a TV series which had not been scheduled up against a rating's powerhouse. From its second week onwards, however, *The Outlaws* regularly lost out to *The Facts of Life* and *227* and only narrowly beat *Sidekicks* and *Sledgehammer*. When ABC replaced the latter with *Starman* (1986–87), *Outlaws* started running last and CBS soon axed the show. It was the fifth Rod Taylor series that failed to survive its first season.

The Outlaws had its moments and the cast's sense of camaraderie and enjoyment in their roles comes across strongly on screen. The series did have its faults, though: the main characters were all a bit too similar and it felt like there was one too many of them. Although good in his part, Richard Roundtree, in particular, came across as the odd man out: not due to his skin color, but because he seemed so sensible and dignified whereas the others always looked as though they wanted to get up to mischief; one wonders how his character got along in the gang.

The scripts followed *The A-Team* (1983–87) template of our heroes helping stereotypical underdogs (battered wives, small shopkeepers, poor farmers) combating the forces of evil (property developers, unscrupulous businessmen and so on). There was not a great deal of imagination on display, though it was always watchable, particularly the episodes written by Corea. Yet, the audience did not take to it as they did *The A-Team*.

The Outlaws effectively brought an end to Rod's days as a Hollywood leading man — that is, someone who starred in films and television series made by major studios. This is not surprising when one considers that, despite working constantly, the actor had not really appeared in a hit for nearly two decades (*Jacqueline Bouvier Kennedy* was the exception). In fact, it is to the credit of Rod's talent and professionalism — not to mention the power of re-reruns of his old films — that he remained in demand for so long. This would also ensure he kept employed for the next decade as well.

CHAPTER 15

"I'm what's-his-name."

NOSTALGIA STAR (1988 ONWARDS)

THROUGH THE LATE '80S AND '90S, ROD KEPT ACTIVE AS A "nostalgia star" — that is, someone whose casting was primarily based on their work in the distant past. Most movie stars move into this phase sooner or later; while the change in status is sometimes traumatic, it can also provide the actor with a greater variety of roles once the pressures of maintaining a star image are removed. This was certainly the case with Rod Taylor.

Rod's period of nostalgia stardom began, appropriately enough, with a stint on *Falcon Crest* (1981–90), a television series that specialized in casting old Hollywood names. The show, set in the wine-growing region of California's Napa Valley, was one of a number of nighttime serials that flourished in the '80s (e.g. *Dallas* [1978–91], *Dynasty* [1981–89]) featuring attractive actors, gorgeous scenery and over-the-top storylines that had their rich characters suffer as much as possible.

Falcon Crest loved nostalgia stars, either as regulars or guests: Jane Wyman played the lead role and cast members over the years included Lana Turner, Kim Novak, Gina Lollobrigida, Cliff Robertson, Mel Ferrer and Cesar Romero. During Rod's first year on the series alone, guest appearances were made by Leslie Caron, Ursula Andress, Eddie Albert, Eve Arden, Theodore Bikel and Buck Henry.

Rod came on to *Falcon Crest* during its seventh season and stayed until its ninth and last. He was initially brought on board by show runner Jeff Freilich, who recalls, "I wanted a love interest for Jane Wyman. She played the matriarch who owns the vineyards and she's an evil woman. She's the villain of the show, at the same time the hero of the show. In the past, her relationships had been with stodgy people. What I wanted for her was a bigger person, somebody who could in a way mollify her, because if a good person got involved with her she would give her best dramatic material because she was playing a character who was always at odds with herself. It's always better to have that character joined with someone who's opposite.

"I talked it over with Jane. We can't take a guy off the Tylenol commercial and play him next to her; it has to be someone with stature. The first person I thought about was Robert Mitchum. He'd be difficult because he rarely played that sort of role. She said, 'Mitch is great, but you have to put toothpicks in his eyes to keep them open.' There were other possibles — James Garner was one. We wanted to find someone not necessarily her age but at least her age in business, someone with a track record who goes back a while.

"She went back to the dressing room and then called me. It was her idea. She'd never met Rod Taylor but always had a crush on him. But she could not remember his name. She said, 'Get me what's-his-name. He's so handsome. He's not as old as me, he's so handsome, he's rugged.' In 1987 there were probably 30 guys who had stature who were in their 60s who could fit the bill. I said, 'You're going to have to give me a clue.' She said, "You know the one from that Elizabeth Taylor movie." I started to list movies. '*The VIPs*?' 'That's the one.' 'Rod Taylor?' 'That's the one. Get me what's-his-name.'

"At the time I was not sure if I wanted Rod to do one episode or 40 episodes, it depended on what he was like to work with and how he worked with Jane. It was Jane's show and if she didn't like him it could make it difficult for me to work with him. The mood on the set, because of the amount of work we had to do, it was important to maintain at a congenial level.

"In this case Rod Taylor got on the phone himself to me and he was wonderful. I told him the story and he laughed — I thought, 'This is a good test' — I told him the what's-his-name story and he didn't get offended. He didn't hear negative things, but rather positive things: that she had this crush on him. He was touched and complimented and couldn't wait to meet her. So I arranged a meeting.

"Rod came up the stairs and into the room and Jane Wyman looked up at him. She looked like she was 12, her eyes batted; it was the first time I saw Jane Wyman intimidated. Rod gave her a big smile and said, 'Janey — I'm what's-his-name.' He called her 'Janey.' (Laughs.) She got up and gave him a big hug. She's a timid woman; he's a big guy — boom, that was it."

Rod's role on *Falcon Crest* was as Frank Agretti, the uncle of series regular Melissa (Ana Alicia). Agretti was similar to Les Mangrum in *The VIPs*: a businessman comfortable in the white-collar world, but still capable of using his hands; one of the show's writers, Lisa Seideman, summarized him as a "man's man. Rugged, with a sense of humor, doesn't take crap from anyone, who loved his niece Melissa but didn't wear his heart on his sleeve. Kind of an Australian Indiana Jones."

Freilich says Frank Agretti's function on *Falcon Crest* was to be "the one normal character in the whole show. The one guy people in the audience would look at and go, 'That's what I would do, he's doing the right thing.'" He claims

Rod's impact on the series was immediate. "The second year of mine [1987–88] the ratings shot up and lot of it was because of Rod Taylor. Not because he was a household name everyone in America had to watch. It was because of what he brought as an actor and character. Rod brought energy. He's not a stagy actor, doesn't take forever to say lines. When Rod came, the show got more ambitious and the more ambitious it was, the more he liked it. Rod is sort of guy who, you ask him to come over and paint a wall of a house, he'll want to paint the whole thing.

"I found Rod to be one of the most pleasant, prepared, professional, congenial people I've worked with in any capacity in the entertainment business. He was a joy on the set, he always knew what to do, he always took direction. He was accommodating; he was a cordial person as a man, someone that was kind and considerate. Because he loved acting so much he's one of those rare people who come to work every day in a great mood. I cannot remember a day I saw Rod in a bad mood.

"Rod Taylor was a guy who just loved to act. He had a very easy way of falling into character. He doesn't spend months researching his part; he has a very natural ability. His performances are different in everything I've seen him, but there are shades of him in everything. He finds a way to find the soul of a character.

"I was only aware of Rod's past credits and performances, I was not aware he was Australian. Now I have traveled the world I appreciate it. I'd never been to Australia. It seems to be people who got away from England and you can't say that for the US because a very few of them are left, this is going to sound clichéd and awful, but there is a pioneer spirit and dedication to hard work without feeling that hard work is punishment, hard work is a challenge.

"The other thing about Rod and a lot of Australians is he's a gregarious person. He enjoys good conversations and there's rarely a better place to have that than a movie set where actors spend 90% of their time sitting around. He spent 90% of his time out of his trailer, walking around the set."

Freilich says Rod and Jane Wyman "got on great" during production. "I can't speak for the last two years [of the show], but no way Rod would have lasted if Jane Wyman didn't like him. At the slightest mention of writing Rod out of the show Jane Wyman would have vetoed it. I think Jane Wyman felt the same way about Rod Taylor that her character felt for Frank Agretti."

In his best episodes, Rod's performance in *Falcon Crest* is professional and engaging. His scenes with Jane Wyman had genuine sparkle and he carries off the outlandish plots with assurance and sincerity. Rod survived for three years on the series, including two changes of show runner, making *Falcon Crest* his greatest popular success in 20 years. His small-screen jinx had been broken at last.

"The little old ladies are coming up to me in the markets again," Rod beamed at the time. "It's as if I hadn't left."

THE 1990S WERE A DECADE OF SLOWED ACTIVITY FOR ROD. Happily settled with Carol, he was content to play the occasional role as it came along, spending his spare time painting or building things in his workshop.

"Oils take up too much time and it's too messy but I do a lot of pen and wash and stuff like that," he said. "But when I'm not working if it's not writing, it's yearning to do something in the industry. But I also make furniture. I've got a workshop, with a lot of dangerous toys and I like to make tables and chairs."

Despite two divorces, 40 years of well-paid work and some competent financial advice meant that Rod was in reasonable financial shape. He bought another property at Carpentaria, a small town near Santa Barbara, "so I can get the hell out of Los Angeles and I've got my ocean and my surf and stuff like that."

He still had his Sacramento ranch, too, though that brought him mixed joy — "I built windmills like I remembered, I put up water tanks and I sank wells and got no friggin' water," he complained. "It was just a total folly. Total stupidity."

Years of drinking, smoking and heavy eating had taken its toll on Rod's appearance, but Carol was looking after his health now and he kept fit playing tennis and golf and practicing, of all things, yoga (Carol's influence). Rod had the benefit of a young soul and two parents with good genes: Mona, who had lived with him since Bill's death, passed away on July 22, 1991, aged 89.

Rod followed up his *Falcon Crest* success by being teamed with another nostalgia star, Eva Marie Saint, in the television movie *Palomino* (1991). This was one of a number of adaptations of Danielle Steel's popular romance novels made by NBC, who used them as counter-programming against sports events. They were the sort of movies where the lead couple make love on pink satin sheets and in a bathtub by candlelight and where the dialogue includes lines like, "You know how much I want you," and "You're wrong about me — about us." Rod was cast in a supporting role as a ranch worker whose relationship with a wealthier woman (Saint) mirrors the main romance; their scenes together are a delight and the whole movie is surprisingly enjoyable.

Less entertaining was the mini-series *Grass Roots* (1992), in which Rod had the small but flashy part of the head of a white supremacist organization who comes up against a Southern Senator's aide (Corbin Bernsen). Over *Grass Roots'* four-hour running time, Bernsen has to defend an alleged rapist in court, sleeps with the said rapist's nymphomaniac white-trash girlfriend, runs for the Senate, is accused of being a homosexual by a bitchy editor, cannot prove his heterosexuality because his girlfriend works for the CIA and wants to keep their relationship quiet and has to deal with an assassin working for Rod's organization.

The mini-series was a sequel to *Chiefs* (1983), also based on a novel by Stuart Woods. *Grass Roots* never enjoyed its forerunner's popularity though, despite being well acted and professionally made; the reason is clear from the above synopsis: unlike *Chiefs*, which centers around one event, *Grass Roots* involves a number of subplots which only loosely connect and lacks a cohesive story. Rod is only on screen for a short while, but is effective in a rare out-and-out villainous role.

He had better luck with *Open Season* (1996), a funny satire about the television industry from actor-writer-director Robert Wuhl. Rod plays an egomaniacal network planning executive who claims to draw his guidance directly from God. Wuhl says the character was based partly upon Tom Landry, the legendary coach of the Dallas Cowboys football team: "A legitimate wacko," says Wuhl. "But great at his job. Almost Patton-like in his absolute authority that HE IS RIGHT."

The role was originally meant to be played by Brian Dennehy, but when he dropped out Rod came on board at the eleventh hour. Wuhl: "He was great! Great! Great! Great to work with — great to hang out with — great to hear the stories. Always professional, always prepared. In fact, he wrote the cockney dialogue for the two 'programmers' who come up with the Impress Track. It was unfortunate that a few of his best scenes landed on the cutting room floor, but that was my fault in the structure of the narrative, not because of the quality of his work, which was magnificent."

Rod's performance in *Open Season* is an absolute cracker — broad, tough, hilarious — and might have marked something of a comeback, but the film took three years to find a theatrical release (it was shot in 1993) and never found the audience it deserved. Nonetheless, Rod received his best reviews since *Jacqueline Bouvier Kennedy*, the *New York Times* declaring the actor embodies his character "with just the right tone of ludicrous self-importance."

Another feature Rod made in the '90s, *Point of Betrayal* (1995), is also something of an unseen gem. Rod played the second husband of wealthy widow (Dina Merrill), whose son from her first marriage is so livid at the thought of a stepfather possibly causing him to miss out on his inheritance, he hires a nurse to drive mum insane, a la *Gaslight* (1944).

Director Richard Martini says that Rod's involvement in the film came as a result "of a fluke" after the original choice for the role fell out. Martini was not disappointed, though, as he loved working with Rod. "Rod is a force of nature. I think if he hears something he doesn't believe, or doesn't seem real to him, he'll speak up about it. Rod always gives 100% and I think even gave me a free day of second unit so I could help weave the film together. He's a consummate creative guy — he could write/direct/act if he wanted to. It's the old story of hiring people who know what they're doing and stay out of their way."

Two incidents in particular stood out for Martini. The first involved the death scene for Dina Merrill's character. "I had come up with a scene where Dina is losing her mind and she sees Rod when she thinks she's seeing her son. I was going to shoot both actors and then try to blend the images together, as if she was going in and out of consciousness... but it never would have worked. Rod came up to me while we were discussing it and told me about this incident that had happened when his mom was dying and how she'd mixed up Rod with his father. So I asked him if he could come up with something and the next morning he handed me the full scene, typed up — we shot it as he wrote it.

"The other was when we were pressed for time and trying to shoot the fight scene at the end [between Rod and Rick Johnson] — this is a film budgeted at a million US and we had only five weeks shooting time — we probably averaged five pages a day. So not a lot of time for retakes, or elaborate staging. The sun was going down out at this location and I was trying to manage a terrified production manager who thought the sky was falling and a cameraman who was telling me, 'I can't open it up any more,' as he took a look through his viewfinder. Rod had worked out all the details of the fight in advance, had rehearsed Rick Johnson on exactly what to do and when to do it... I shot it in two takes. Rod hit every mark and had trained Rick into hitting his. It's the scene I'm the most proud of in the film and it's all due to Rod's work."

Actor Ann Cusack, sister to John and Joan, who had a supporting role in the film, said she could "not say enough positive things" about working with Rod. "He came to work every day prepared. Lines memorized, with ideas about how to play the scenes. If there were problems with the scene, he had ideas about how to make adjustments or rewrite the scenes if need be. He was emotionally present as we worked. He and the other actors I worked with made the film better than the original script.

"He came on the set and the energy changed. He is just living his life, but his life has been and is larger than life, so he is and isn't aware of how he changes the energy in the room. It felt like something big was happening. He didn't dwell in the past at all. He was here and now."

Point of Betrayal was never released theatrically in the US so, as with *Open Season*, Rod's fine work failed to reach the audience it merited: even so, it is an entertaining film, worth seeking out by those interested in a solid thriller with off-beat touches, like the house built entirely underground. Rod is excellent, particularly during the scenes where Dina Merrill starts to lose her sanity — this is perhaps the finest (produced) example to date of Rod's screenwriting.

DURING THE LATE 1990S, ROD'S HIGHEST PROFILE ROLES WERE guest parts on recurring character television series (the type of roles he had avoided, incidentally, since 1955). In particular, Rod featured in episodes of *Murder, She Wrote* (1984-96) and *Walker, Texas Ranger* (1993-2001) — and proved so popular on both shows he was invited back for a return engagement.

Rod's initial *Murder, She Wrote* instalment was "Another Killing in Cork," where crime-solving writer Jessica Fletcher (Angela Lansbury) investigates a death at an Irish fishing lodge. Rod plays the lodge owner, an Irishman — a casting that partly came about due to Lansbury remembering Rod's performance in *Young Cassidy* (her husband had been an executive at MGM at the time). Rod's work was so well received he was asked back the following season to play another Irishman in a different Irish story, the excellent "Nan's Ghost." (Two other cast members from "Another Killing in Cork" also returned in different roles, giving the episode a bizarre déjà vu quality.)

"My memories of Rod are only good," enthuses Bruce Lansbury, who wrote scripts for both. "A real trooper. Grand sense of humor and a fine actor. What more could you want?"

Walker, Texas Ranger was a modern-day Western starring former karate champ-turned-'80s action hero Chuck Norris in the title role. Rod debuted in the show's fifth season as Gordon Cahill, the estranged, alcoholic father of series regular Alex Cahill (played by Sheree J. Wilson). His casting had been suggested by his former *Outlaws* boss, Nick Corea, then writing on the show. Director Tony Mordente recalls: "He came in with a good reputation; he's a very easy guy to get along with. Jovial and a great sense of humor. He knows his stuff and the crew really appreciates it when an actor knows his stuff. He has valid questions. When he left everybody was very unhappy. When a crew is happy with an actor you can tell because they want to get him again for other episodes — 'Why don't we get so-and-so back?'"

Indeed, Rod was bought back as Gordon Cahill for two more *Walker* episodes over the next few seasons, turning in polished work every time. It is not surprising when one considers the character he played: a hard-living, boozing man's man, estranged from his daughter, but capable of charm and bravery.

AN INTERESTING ASPECT TO ROD'S CAREER IS THAT DESPITE HIS success in *The Time Machine*, he played so few science-fiction roles. A notable exception was *The Osiris Chronicles*, a movie-length pilot for a TV series that never eventuated, which he made in the mid-'90s.

The project had been developed by military historian and bestselling novelist Caleb Carr in collaboration with film director Joe Dante. Dante says Carr's idea was basically try to do an "anti-*Star Trek* (1966-69)... a look at what might happen if The Federation collapsed and to see what the now-chaotic galaxy would be like."

The show is set in the year 2419, following the collapse of the Galactic Republic, an enlightened, paternal government of the future that had self-destructed, causing chaos in the universe. The lead character is Jonathan Thorne (John Corbett), a rogue adventurer whose sister is abducted by aliens; he teams up with a rag-tag group of adventurers and goes looking for her.

"We had to create a futuristic society that's fallen apart, so it had a lot in common with medieval movies," says Dante. "Caleb is a military historian so he imbued it with a certain medieval quality. He had such a long and complex bible for this show you can't tell from the pilot the direction it was going to go in. He had it very carefully worked out. It was really going to be a good show."

The Osiris Chronicles was picked up by Paramount TV, who succeeded in selling the pilot to CBS. A key role was General Sorensen, a former officer of the Galactic Republic who has his own agenda for helping Thorne. Dante: "On the *Dr Kildare* (1961–66) show there was always a Dr Gillespie, on *Ben Casey* (1961-66) there was an older guy. There's always a father-figure type, the paterfamilias to the younger cast members and also to appeal to a different demographic. And Rod fit that perfectly. He'd bring in the older movie-star demographic."

Dante was a major film buff and often cast nostalgia stars in his projects. His first choice for the role was Christopher Lee, who turned the part down for tax reasons. The director then thought of Rod and brought him on board as a replacement. "It was a different dynamic," Dante says. "Rod is younger, more of an action star and the character became less of a father figure and more of, I would say, a second lead."

Filming commenced at the end of 1995 on the Paramount backlot with a budget of around $10 million. Dante says working with Rod was one of the highlights of the shoot. "Rod is not only a good actor, but he also has a warmth that makes sitting through exposition a lot easier. He had so much stuff to tell John Corbett yet managed to modulate it and present it in a way that was not exactly Shakespeare but still very good. And he usually got it on the first take."

Producer Mike Finnell, too, had always been a fan of the actor. "The great thing about making movies is you can occasionally work with actors you grew up with. I mean we were 11-12 when *The Time Machine* came out… [Older actors are] so confident and they know exactly what to do and how to hit their lines. They're more seasoned. There's a discipline that's not always there with younger actors."

In fact, Dante and Finnell liked working with Rod so much they tried to cast him in two subsequent films, *The Second Civil War* (1997) and *Loony Tunes: Back in Action* (2003). Unfortunately, Rod was busy both times: throughout the former, he was in Australia making *Welcome to Woop Woop*; during the latter, he had to go in to hospital for an operation. "I also tried to get Henry Silva and George Kennedy, but those guys had operations, too," laughs Dante. "All these old actors and their operations!"

The Osiris Chronicles was not picked up for a series. The pilot was renamed *Warlord: Battle for the Galaxy* and run as a stand-alone TV movie on UPN, the Paramount network, three years later. It is an entertaining movie whose most absorbing feature is its intriguing "world" — a collapsing society under the threat of marauders, mercenaries and barbarians — that would have provided rich fodder for a series. The production design is impressive, but Corbett is wooden in the lead. Rod brings warmth and strength to his role, although his accent (which comes across as English at times) is a little odd.

Rod's most recent film is *Kaw* (2006), a straight-to-video thriller about a series of bird attacks on a small town. Rod plays the town's doctor, a casting in direct homage to *The Birds*. It is a taut, well-made movie that belies its low budget, with Rod as professional as ever.

In 2008, it was announced Rod would have a role in *Inglourious Basterds* (2009), Quentin Tarantino's eagerly-awaited World War II guys-on-a-mission movie. Tarantino is perhaps the most skilled nostalgia caster of them all, having given many sensational roles to actors thought to be past their prime: John Travolta, David Carradine, Robert Forster, Pam Grier, Michael Parks, etc. Rod was cast as Winston Churchill.

Tarantino offered Rod the part over the phone personally. A surprised Rod asked the writer-director why he did not use someone like Albert Finney instead; Tarantino replied, "If Rod Taylor turns me down, then I'll get Albert Finney." Rod, understandably flattered, signed on and went to Germany for ten enjoyable days of filming. His role ultimately turned out to be little more than a cameo overshone by others in the cast, but the film was a massive success at the box office (earning over $300 million on a budget of $70 million), winning a Screen Actors Guild Award for Best Ensemble Cast and giving Rod more publicity than he had in years. Perhaps this will lead to a new dawn for his career.

For all Rod's fine work over the past 15 years, though, there is no doubt that one performance in particular towers over them all. Indeed, it stands tall amongst his entire career: the first time he was given a great Aussie role in a real Aussie film.

WELCOME TO WOOP WOOP WAS BASED ON *THE DEAD HEART*, A novel by New York journalist Douglas Kennedy, about a man who gets stuck in a hellish Australian outback town cut off from civilization. Film rights were optioned in the early 1990s by the British production company Scala, who hired Australian expat Michael Thomas to write a screenplay. Thomas describes the story's central idea as "*Brigadoon* (1954) in the bush. I loved that idea because it gave me the opportunity to make an elegy about a lost Australia."

Thomas' script attracted the attention of Stephan Elliott, the Australian director then riding high on the massive (for an Australian film) box-office success of his second feature, *The Adventures of Priscilla, Queen of the Desert* (1994). Elliot was attracted by the idea of making a film that was "one last big kiss goodbye to the mass of old Australian culture which is disappearing."

During the 1990s the main sources of finance for Australian films were no longer tax shelter provisions like 10BA, but a new film financing body, the Australian Film Finance Corporation (FFC). Generally, the FFC would provide

50% of the budget for a feature, provided the filmmakers had a distribution deal and could come up with the rest of the money themselves. Officially, *Welcome to Woop Woop* was a British-Australian co-production, with finance provided by Scala and an American company, Goldwyn, together with the FFC and two state film bodies, the NSWFTO and SAFC. Creatively, the muscle behind the movie was Australian, with almost all key crew and cast being Aussies. Most of the filming would take place in Australia, with the majority of post-production in London. The budget was around AUS$10 million.

There were two lead roles: Teddy, the young American con man who winds up at Woop Woop, and Daddy-O, Woop Woop's patriarch and Collingwood-jersey-wearing symbol of old-style Australia. Patrick Swayze and Matthew Broderick were discussed as possible Teddys, but both fell through; the part eventually went to Jonathan Schaech, then an actor on the rise coming off *That Thing You Do!* (1996).

The part of Daddy-O was originally offered to Jack Thompson, who turned it down. ("He took one look at the script and never spoke to me again," laughs Thomas.) Elliott then came up with the idea of casting Rod Taylor. "An absolute bolt from the blue, a brilliant idea," enthuses Thomas.

The Time Machine had been one of Elliot's favorite films as a child and he had grown up watching Rod in such movies as *The Birds*, *The VIPs* and *Zabriskie Point*, not to mention "the big one," *The Picture Show Man*. Elliot remembered the latter in particular as it always "astounded" him that Rod played an American in an Australian film.

Rod was sent the script and "fell off the sofa laughing" while reading it. It was easy to understand why: *Woop Woop* was straight out of the Australia Rod had grown up in — a country of tariffs, White Australia policy, mateship and loyalty to the Queen; a place of binge drinking, women banned from pubs and doors not having to be locked at night; when restaurant dining consisted of (to quote Rod) "a meat pie and a fight," men sorted their disputes with their fists but nonetheless loved their Rodgers and Hammerstein, dialogue was laced with local slang and most people were related to someone who had died in a war. Rod knew men like Daddy-Os from Lidcombe, the Mona Vale Surf Club and the pubs of Sydney — sports-mad, ferocious creatures, who worked with their hands and loved their beer, but were not without soft spots. They were also men slightly out of time, uneasy at a changing world and desperate to keep things the way they were. There was a lot of Bill Taylor in the character — not to mention more than a little of Rod himself.

"Daddy-O's an utter dinosaur, but with nobility," explained Rod. "He believes whatever he's doing, beating someone up, he's doing it for the good of the town."

"You couldn't have found anyone more perfect," enthuses Dee Smart, who played one of Daddy-O's daughters. "Some Aussie actors have been around a long time and done a lot. You see your Bill Hunters a lot and this was something new."

"He was dying to play an Australian," says Thomas. "He was great, he really ate it up."

It was only Rod's fourth Australian role in a career of over 40 films and five television series. "He was himself amazed that he'd spent most of his life playing Americans," says Thomas.

The rest of the cast was filled with faces and names familiar to Australians, including Barry Humphries, Richard Moir, Dee Smart, Paul Mercurio, Rachel Griffiths and Shane and Bindi Paxton (the latter two non-actors enjoying 15 minutes of fame after being labeled archetypal dole bludgers on a current affairs show). Right-wing politician Pauline Hanson was approached to play Daddy-O's wife, but declined; that role eventually went to Maggie Kirkpatrick. "People were carefully picked for the madness their reputation would add to the film," says Antonia Barnard, who was recruited to handle the Australian end of the production.

Filming was scheduled to start in June 1996 and Rod flew in to Sydney for rehearsals. A week before the start date, however, disaster struck when Elliot fell ill. Doctors diagnosed jaundice and estimated it would take the director six to 16 weeks to recover. "It seemed everything was going to unravel," recalls Thomas. "That's when [producer] Finola Dwyer showed real balls and held the whole thing together."

Filming was pushed back eight weeks and Elliot recovered in time, but now principal photography, which mostly took place in the Australian desert (Mount Ooramina, 45 minutes out of Alice Springs), went into summer. Temperatures regularly reached 40 degrees or over; generators baked, camera parts melted and equipment broke down. Elliot wrote in his diary that, "This is *Apocalypse Now* (1979). I'm Martin Sheen."

"It was so hot it was not funny," remembers Dee Smart. "Every scene you could see flies crawling up people's noses. There was no sweat because it was so hot it'd dry up."

"We turned into a mini-Woop Woop," says Maggie Kirkpatrick. "We were as mad as cut snakes; we all went a bit troppo socially."

On the positive side, it also meant there was little on-set interference from executives and tremendous camaraderie was forged amongst the cast and crew. Kirkpatrick recalls Rod threw himself into it with abandon. "His status on the set was almost like his character in the film. He was the absolute ringleader, the absolute naughty boy. He's a big personality and loud personality. There's nothing of the Hollywood star garbage. There's something intrinsically Australian in spite of his time over there. I had one look at him on the set with those boots and shorts and he looked like he'd risen out of the dirt. He played it like to the manor born. I've seen him in all these romantic comedies, but put him out in the desert and it was as if he'd never been away."

Film journalist Andrew Urban interviewed the actor on set and was struck by his appearance. "Rod Taylor looks like something the cat's dragged in. His craggy face is dirty. His hair is tussled around a blue-and-white bandana, but the white gave up long ago. His torn footy shirt bears the scars of many mishandled snacks and a few beer stains as well. But his grin is as friendly as a bloke who's won the chook raffle."

"I thought Rod was absolutely wonderful," enthuses Thomas. "He really got into it, the whole Collingwood thing. He went around wearing all the sweaters and stuff. The guy did us a favor and worked his arse off. He wasn't up himself. Didn't give off any Hollywood vibes, didn't insist on any special treatment. He really entered into the spirit of the thing. He knew it was a low-budget movie."

"From our first meeting at the read-through he was heaven," says Dee Smart. "He sort of made a joke — 'I'm the dinosaur coming in to do this.' It really was amazing to work with someone who had so much experience. He was so accessible and down to earth on everybody's level. He made me think that it's the inexperienced actors who are the ones who are insecure. The experienced ones aren't, because they've got nothing to prove."

"I just loved him," raves Susie Porter, who played his other daughter. "I thought he was the nicest, most generous man I've worked with. He told great stories, lots of anecdotes about himself as a young stud in Hollywood. He loved a fag [cigarette], loved a drink. Having Rod there brought everyone together."

"A real hero of mine," says Schaech: "A man's man. When it was his turn for a take he really turned it on."

The part of Daddy-O required a daring, outlandish actor — someone who could believably wear a Collingwood jersey, tap dance on a bar, inquire whether Schaech had "poked" his daughter, kill a dog and command a town that made its money through pet food. Rod rose to the occasion, even wearing his outfit when not filming. By now Rod knew he did not need alcohol to be bold and brave, just confidence in his talent and the self-belief that comes from playing a role he totally understood for a director he trusted.

Elliot: "There's 40 years of Australian in him that's been building like Krakatoa. I'm usually one who likes big performances and I usually look at the actors and say, 'Bring it up.' This was the first time I've had to say, 'Pull it down, it's too big.' He was ferocious; it was like he was straining at the leash. He steals the movie as far as I'm concerned, walks away with it."

Rod got along very well with Elliott. "They're both larrikins, in the end," says Barnard. "He's very respectful of the director and Stephan was very respectful of Rod's status as an actor."

Or, as Thomas puts it, "Rod's a rager and Stephan's a rager, too."

Nonetheless, the shoot was not easy for Rod physically. During pre-production in Sydney, he had hurt his hip during tap-dancing lessons for a sequence

where Daddy-O dances on a bar. Rod already had a hip problem (he was pushing 70) and the stress caused it to degenerate, requiring a hip replacement. Since
the film could not afford to put back shooting any later, Rod decided to tough
it out and did the scene in the last week of filming. He could only do it once
and pulled it off in a single take. "He was in a lot of pain," says Thomas. "He was
hurting like hell, but he was an unbelievable soldier."

Shooting completed by the end of 1996, enabling Rod to get his new hip.

Elliott showed a rough cut of *Woop Woop* to Gilles Jacob, director of the
Cannes Film Festival, who asked if he could premiere the picture at Cannes.
Although it was still a work in progress, Elliott had fond memories of the festival from *Priscilla* and agreed. *Woop Woop* was given a midnight screening as an
official selection out of competition, the same position *Priscilla* held in 1994.

Rod flew to Cannes for the screening, which was eagerly attended by audiences and media keen to view Elliot's latest effort. However, it did not go well.

"Awful," says Barnard.

"The audience had no idea what to think about it," remembers Thomas. "The
Palais at Cannes has seats which flip up when you leave and go 'bang.' So all
through the film we could hear 'bang,' 'bang,' 'bang' as people left."

"I remember Rod putting his arm around me and going, 'It's OK,'" recalls
Susie Porter.

"After the screening we had a party, got pissed and said, 'Fuck me dead,' a lot
and tried to forget it," says Thomas.

Elliott re-cut the film, taking out over 20 minutes of footage, jettisoning the
original score and bringing in a new composer, Guy Gross. (Gross recalls that
when he saw the movie for the first time he thought, "Oh my God — Stephan's
finally done what he always wanted to do: offend everyone.")

Test screenings in the US were not encouraging. "One shot of a dead kangaroo and you should have seen those Americans," said Elliott. "They just flipped
out. I mean, freaked."

In particular, the Goldwyn company requested a change to the scene where
Daddy-O talks about the history of Woop Woop. Instead of him finishing with
the line, "It's Australia," Rod's lips were adjusted (expensively) via CGI so the
character says, "It's Woop Woop."

"It was Sam Goldwyn [Jr.] himself who asked for that," says Michael Thomas.
"He thought it was racist."

Post-production work on *Woop Woop* continued into 1998, pushing the Australian release date back from January to August. The film seemed cursed: planned
television advertisements for the movie were rejected by the Federation of Australian Commercial Television Stations as being offensive — particularly a clip
where Susie Porter says the line, "Part my beef curtains"; Adelaide City Council
banned one of the movie's posters containing an image of Porter's legs sticking

up in the air around Schaech's waist; Daryl Somers, host of the popular TV variety show *Hey Hey, It's Saturday* (1971-99), stormed out of a special preview VIP screening after only watching 15 minutes.

"All the girls in the media who reviewed the film told us to piss off and never come back," claims Thomas. "They saw it as everything they ever hated about Australia."

"I think it was unfairly treated by the critics here," says cinematographer Michael Molloy. "It was like they had a personal vendetta against Stephan."

Critical reception was not as universally bad as those comments indicate. David Stratton thought the film contained "some great moments of hilarity," Melbourne's *Herald Sun* described it as "a delightful, disgusting disgrace" and the *Sydney Morning Herald* called it "freshly funny, brash and a good laugh." Rod received some positive personal notices, Stratton praising him as "terrifically funny" and the *Sun Herald* calling him "enormous fun." (The *Sunday Age*'s reviewer did admit it took him a while to recognize the actor.)

The bad critics were, however, very nasty: "Very like *Priscilla*, apart from the fact it has 5% of the laughs" (*The Age*); "unbelievably bad" (*Adelaide Sunday Mail*); "the cast… do nothing for their reputations… entirely charmless, offensive and embarrassingly inept" (*Weekend Australian*); "one of the worst movies ever produced in this country" (*West Australian*). It was the most vicious critical assault any Rod Taylor film had received in Australia since — well, since *The Picture Show Man*, although in this case Rod was spared most of the brickbats.

Australian audiences did not take to *Woop Woop*, which ended up grossing around AU$400,000 at the local box office (in contrast, *Priscilla* had made over AU$15 million).

"I think Australians were offended at what Stephan suggested Australia might be," says Antonia Barnard. "Maybe it was a bit too cheeky for some people."

"It was the antithesis of something like *The Castle* (1997), which laughs at Australia in a gentle, affectionate way," argues Gross. "This one laughs at Australia in a horrendous, crass way."

The AFI awards could not turn things around; Antonia Barnard says the film was not entered in the competition "because Stephan doesn't like them" — a pity, especially when one considers Rod may have been a good chance for a Best Supporting Actor award.

Difficulties with the American release arose when the Goldwyn Company was overtaken by Orion, which was then bought by MGM. "Sales rights were passing from one person to another," says Thomas. "No one knew who had them. We got caught in that sort of executive meltdown which happens all the time." *Woop Woop* ended up earning a paltry $37,621 at the US box office. The *San Francisco Chronicle* noted that Rod had "aged considerably since his matinee-idol days of *The Time Machine* and *The Birds*," but said he "plays the hell out of Daddy-O, a salty, beer-guzzling despot who looks like 80 miles of pockmarked road."

As a film, *Woop Woop* has severe problems, starting with a very unsympathetic hero who runs over a kangaroo in the first ten minutes of the story — a common accident on Australian highways, but in this case it's because the driver has taken his eyes off the road. More crucially, the town of Woop Woop is not a nice place like Brigadoon or Shangri-La, but closer to the hellish communities found in *The Cars That Ate Paris* (1974) and *Wake in Fright* (1971) — it is not a particularly enjoyable place to spend time, even just as an audience member. While things like the chainsaw school and all the tins of pineapple are funny, sometimes the film is just plain off. It's a movie which has the courage of its convictions, though; the production and costumes are amazing and the actors give their all.

And in one respect at least, *Welcome to Woop Woop* was an absolute triumph: Rod Taylor. Daddy-O gives Rod the role of a lifetime and the actor embraces it with a gusto rarely matched in his career. After overplaying Australians in *The VIPs* and *The High Commissioner*, Rod finally gets the pitch right in this over-the-top extravaganza. Whether wearing his Collingwood clothes, tap dancing on bars, or cracking a beer, it is impossible to imagine anyone but him in the part and he is magnificent — hilarious, scary, even touching at times. Like *Point of Betrayal* and *Open Season*, Rod had delivered an excellent performance in what should have made an ideal comeback vehicle — only no one turned up to see it.

Nonetheless, *Welcome to Woop Woop* seems to have re-energized Rod creatively and he was keen on doing more work in Australia. Dee Smart introduced Rod to her agent, Piers Wilkinson, who agreed to represent him here. Wilkinson: "In the '70s and '80s he relied upon his name being what it was and I don't think that's sufficient because often with the Australian industry if you move away, it's not that the industry will forget you, but it will assume you are based in America and not very willing to come back. Australian productions don't generally have the kind of budget that will support flying someone in from the States."

Over the next few years, Rod's name was floated in connection with a number of local projects. Unfortunately, for a variety of reasons, they all fell through: Michael Thomas was keen to cast Rod as an old-time gangster in *The Night We Called It a Day* (2001), meant to be Thomas' directorial debut — but the film was eventually made by Paul Goldman with Tony Barry in the part instead; Lee Robinson wanted Rod to play a "Kerry Packer type" in *The Keeper of Dreams*, a project Robinson was trying to get financed shortly before his death in 2003; Sue Milliken sought him for the role of a politician in *Capital Man*, a mini-series that was never made; Rod was also attached to a project from director George Friend, *Kokoda*, that never went beyond script stage (and is not to be confused with the 2006 film of the same name). Rod himself tried to get up a script he had written, a ghost story called *Black Pearl*, but no film has resulted.

Wilkinson later retired from agenting, and as of this writing Rod is without representation in Australia. Today, his status is "semi-retired" — or, at least, as retired as any actor can be. (*The Inglourious Basterds* may see a revival of activity.) He keeps busy in America, appearing in the odd documentary or drama role, spending most of his time working on his art or with Carol. Wilkinson: "He's one of those people who doesn't seem to regret anything — the turn that his career happened to have taken at that point [in the late '60s] isn't really relevant in the greater picture... he's done such a huge amount of work and he's worked with such a variety of directors and producers — I think he feels privileged that he's been able to do that, in whatever medium, be it TV or film.

"He wants to keep working, it's the craft that he loves, what he lives for. He will go wherever the work takes him. He'd love to work here more, he just loves it — he enjoys the atmosphere, he enjoys Australian culture, he enjoys the food, the quality of the food here, he's got a lot of mates and there's less... of the Hollywood bullshit here. He's a great guy, a raconteur, a storyteller; he's full of life, full of laughter, a joy to be with."

"I want to go on and on until I'm 90. Acting is something I love. The fact that I'm going to be unsuccessful at times is pretty well balanced by the fact that I'm going to be successful at others. It doesn't frighten me. I'm not doing my work for constant success. I'm doing it because I love it."

ROD TAYLOR (1961)

CONCLUSION

ROD TAYLOR'S FIRST 15 YEARS IN ACTING COULD STAND AS A textbook example for young performers of how to develop a career. He started off a hard, enthusiastic worker, who took every job going to expand his skills. He backed his own talent, but also sought out advice from the best in the industry and learnt everything he could from them. He did not limit himself to a particular area of acting, but tried theatre and film as well as radio; he even dabbled with writing. He was pleasant company socially and learned to make connections that way.

When Rod arrived in Hollywood he used every contact he could find and continued to develop his craft by working as much as possible. He took advantage of the growth in anthology drama on TV to perform a wide variety of roles. As his profile rose, he became more discriminating, turning down large parts if they did not seem right, but accepting smaller ones if they were in high-quality projects. He did not panic into taking unsatisfactory offers: he only tied himself down to a long-term contract when the money offered was ideal (MGM) and only agreed to do a television series when given a percentage of the profits (*Hong Kong*). He kept himself in demand by keeping his price down, ensuring he worked with big stars and directors and signing multi-film deals with a variety of studios and production companies.

From the late '60s onwards, Rod's handling of his career became less sure. He appeared to become less interested in the quality of his assignments and more concerned with his "star image." He began concentrating on action and adventure films, betraying his versatility; he started to rewrite scripts and interfere with the direction on the movies he made, sometimes for the benefit of the project, mostly not. Alcohol, ego and temper gradually got the better of him, his judgement went from bad to worse and the box-office performances of his films went into decline.

By the time Rod put his personal life back together in the second half of the '70s, his professional standing in Hollywood had been severely damaged. Perhaps "damaged" is the wrong word — "ignored" may be closer to the mark, as to a large degree he simply dropped off the radar. This was unfair in many ways, because Rod continued to do first-rate work. He has remained steadily employed since then but has lacked that one, special breakthrough role — a high-rating television series, a support part in a hit film — to put him back into the mainstream. Nonetheless, it has been quite a ride.

ROD THE STAR

Rod was a star of considerable commercial value, but one who thrived under certain conditions. For instance, he prospered more as a sort of "permanent casual" employee of the studios, rather than a salaried one, or a freelancer. When Rod's fortunes were totally in the hands of one employer (for example, when he was under exclusive contract to MGM in the late 1950s), his career did not bloom; this leads one to surmise that the independent-minded actor would not have enjoyed the constraints of the classical Hollywood system at its height in the 1930s and 1940s. He did not flourish, either, in the "free market" that existed for actors in Hollywood from the 1970s onwards.

The economic environment within which Rod thrived best was the semi-regulated Hollywood of the 1950s and 1960s — a time when studios still used long-term contracts and/or multi-picture deals for actors, but when such arrangements were non-exclusive, enabling them to freelance as well. This meant Rod could enjoy simultaneous long-term relationships with several companies — MGM, Seven Arts, 20th Century-Fox, Alfred Hitchcock Productions and Universal — but still work for other employers, a combination which afforded him a degree of both artistic freedom and security.

Developing personal relationships was obviously key for Rod — for instance, he flourished at MGM when it was run by O'Brien–Weitman far more than he did under the studio's other managers; ditto in the case of Fox under Peter Levathes. He also thrived in the clubby, self-contained Sydney radio industry of the 1950s. However, Rod needed a corporate structure to underpin those dealings. The industry shakeups of 1969–71 effectively killed off the remnants of the old classical Hollywood system (except at Universal) and created an environment in which Rod did not blossom; from then on he essentially lived off the goodwill of a product, namely his star commodity, which had been created during the previous decade and a half.

Rod understood his stardom in economic terms. He would speak of himself as a "saleable commodity," talked about his "marquee value" and even formed a corporation whose main asset was the services of Rod Taylor. During Rod's early days of stardom in the 1960s he used a variety of tactics to ensure the commodity of "Rod Taylor" remained in demand: made certain he was supported by a name co-star; signed to long-term deals even when he could earn more money under one-off contracts; negotiated percentages of profits rather than large salaries; used a policy of "small parts in good films" rather than "big parts in bad films."

However, from the late 1960s onwards Rod started to forget these very tactics: most of his films were made without name co-stars; he demanded more money than he was worth at the box office and he only played big parts regardless of whether the films were good or bad. In commodity terms, it seems what he was trying to do was to upgrade himself from a class-A2 star to a class-A1 one. The transition was not successful and by the time Rod started to re-adjust his tactics (slash his price, change the types of movies he made), it was too late.

All movie star careers have their highs and lows; Rod's understanding of his value as a commodity contributed to his successes, but his later misestimating of it played a part in his failures. He was also hurt by elements outside of his control, notably the shifting Hollywood environment of the time. Nonetheless, Rod still earned millions of dollars over the course of his career and is reportedly very comfortable financially today; being a movie star, even if only a short-term A2 one, can be very lucrative — certainly more so than, say, a commercial artist, as his parents originally wanted.

ROD'S STAR PERSONA

Rod never had the uniqueness of the truly great screen stars like Clark Gable or Errol Flynn; nonetheless, he still developed a specific star persona throughout his career, one that was recognized by himself and the public. However, Rod did not always fully understand this persona and/or exploit it to the best of his ability.

Rod was most comfortably cast as an intellectual, virile man of action: a scientist who could fight (*The Time Machine*, *36 Hours*, the *Glass Bottom Boat*), a two-fisted journalist (*Hong Kong*, *Sunday in New York*), an air force pilot (*A Gathering of Eagles*, *The Hell with Heroes*, *Fate Is the Hunter*, *Family Flight*), a naval captain (*Seven Seas to Calais*, *Marbella*), a bird-combating lawyer (*The Birds*), a brawling playwright (*Young Cassidy*), a tycoon (*The VIPs*, *Zabriskie Point*, *Jacqueline Bouvier Kennedy*), a hard-living agent (*The Man Who Had Power Over Women*), an army officer (*Dark of the Sun*, *Bearcats!*, *Partizan*), and a hotel manager (*Hotel*).

Rod's own classification of his persona was a man who was "rough with men and gentle with women." This definition is a useful one, though incomplete: while Rod's characters did spend a lot of time beating up males and romancing the opposite sex, they were often gentle with men, too. In fact, they could be downright mushy — for instance, Rod's Nazi doctor in *36 Hours* tells his American enemy Pike (James Garner) he came to "really admire him" after studying Pike's life story for months and that Pike is "a hell of a guy"; the emotional climax of *Young Cassidy* is not between Rod and his love interest (Maggie Smith) but between Rod and his best male friend (played by Philip O'Flynn).

In fact, the platonic love a character played by Rod has for another man — what writer Cynthia Fuchs dubs "homosocial desire" — features not just in several projects Rod made throughout the '50s (*King of the Coral Sea*, *World Without End*, "The Long March," "The Great Gatsby," "The Raider," his unproduced treatment for Lee Robinson), but almost every single film he made in the '60s and '70s: *The Time Machine*, *Colossus and the Amazon Queen*, *Seven Seas to Calais*, *A Gathering of Eagles*, *Fate Is the Hunter*, *36 Hours*, *Young Cassidy*, *The Liquidator*, *Hotel*, *Chuka*, *The Mercenaries*, *The Hell with Heroes*, *The High Commissioner*, *The Man Who Had Power Over Women*, *Darker Than Amber*, *Powderkeg*, *Family Flight*, *The Train Robbers*, *Trader Horn*, *The Deadly Trackers*, *Partizan*, *A Matter of Wife... and Death*, *The Oregon Trail* and *The Treasure Seekers*. Four of Rod's television series — *Hong Kong*, *Bearcats!*, *The Oregon Trail*, *Outlaws* — center around Rod in a "buddy" relationship. Rod played characters who mourn their dead male friends in *Seven Seas to Calais*, *Chuka*, *Dark of the Sun*, *The Hell with Heroes*, *The Man Who Had Power Over Women* and *A Matter of Wife... and Death*; he was mourned in turn in *The Time Machine*, *36 Hours* and *Fate Is the Hunter*.

In contrast, Rod often played characters whose relationships with women were abortive or futile. He was united with Maggie Smith at the conclusion of *The VIPs* more out of gratitude than anything else; Tippi Hedren has a nervous breakdown by the end of *The Birds*; he lost the leading lady by dying in *Fate Is the Hunter*, *36 Hours* and *Partizan* and by putting himself under arrest at the end of *Dark of the Sun*; he was dumped by Maggie Smith in *Young Cassidy* and Daria Halprin in *Zabriskie Point*; he saw his girlfriend/wife die in *The Liquidator*, *Chuka*, *Darker Than Amber* and *Cry of the Innocent*; he left his girlfriend in "The Great Gatsby" and emotionally abused his daughter in *Jacqueline Bouvier Kennedy*. He did play characters who wound up happily with women at the end of *Hotel*, *The Hell with Heroes* and *The Man Who Had Power Over Women* — but in all those cases, the female characters were mistresses/wives of Rod's rival, putting a strong element of male competitiveness even in these relationships. He did enjoy happy endings in the bright comedies — "Capital Gains," *Colossus*, *Sunday in New York*, *Do Not Disturb* and *The Glass Bottom Boat* — and was to reunite with Jane Wyman at the end of *Falcon Crest*.

Although Rod's characters were usually depicted as loyal friends, he rarely played a father or a family man and never played a successful, content one (unless you count Pongo in *One Hundred and One Dalmatians*). Rod squabbled with his sons in *Family Flight* and *The Oregon Trail* and lost his child in *Cry of the Innocent*. He demonstrated great warmth toward his daughters in *Jacqueline Bouvier Kennedy*, *Welcome to Woop Woop*, *Walker, Texas Ranger* and *Osiris Chronicles*, but in all cases the relationships were dysfunctional.

Nonetheless, Rod's persona was generally of a man who was straight down the line. He usually played roles that reinforced establishment values: lawyers, businessmen, police officers and scientists; he portrayed several army officers, but never appeared as a soldier in the lower ranks. He rarely featured as a rebel or social outcast: in *Zabriskie Point*, the closest thing to a pro-revolutionary film that Rod made, the actor was cast as an establishment businessman. If Rod's characters had insubordinate moments, as in "The Long March" and *A Gathering of Eagles*, they eventually learned to toe the line. Even when he did play a rebel, as in *The Time Machine* or *Young Cassidy,* it was only against a tyrannical oppressor and the film's resolution normally involved his character becoming part of the system.

By and large, Rod played contemporary characters, only occasionally venturing into period movies. He was not often found in the future, either; despite *The Time Machine,* Rod made few science-fiction films.

Rod Taylor characters were rarely neurotic. For example, when Rod played the title role in *The Liquidator*, he seemed reluctant to play up the cowardly aspects required by the script. He was not believable as a loner, either, such as the grizzled gunfighter he played in *Chuka* — he specialized in people who were gregarious and friendly. Nor was he convincing as a passive person, as in *Hotel*; indeed, director Jack Cardiff pointed out that Rod's fundamental gift as an actor was his extraordinary energy.

Rod had trouble conveying viciousness and only played a villain a handful of times: *Long John Silver, Raintree County, The Deadly Trackers, On the Run, Mask of Murder, Grass Roots* and *Welcome to Woop Woop.* In all these cases, except for *Grass Roots,* the villainy was qualified somehow: for instance, Rod's characters in *The Deadly Truckers* and *Welcome to Woop Woop* may have been loathsome, but they loved their families; his politician in *Raintree County* was more opportunistic than evil, ditto his heavies in *Zabriskie Point* and *A Time to Die.* He was most effective as a loveable rogue, as in *Jacqueline Bouvier Kennedy.*

In summary, Rod Taylor was an actor who was versatile yet who created a recognizable star persona: a contemporary, gregarious, confident man of action, who was intelligent and attractive to women, but whose strongest emotional bonds were with other men. It was a persona that lent itself to a number of genres. As pointed out by Charles Napier, "Rod Taylor didn't necessarily play 'Rod Taylor,' he could step out and play someone else."

Rod himself was not particularly comfortable with this persona, however, and tried to adjust it, making it less intellectual, comic and romantic and more violent and tough. In doing so, he presumably gained satisfaction, but limited his range and appeal to the public.

During the heyday of the classical Hollywood system, stars could depend on studios to develop and protect their careers. In Rod's time, actors had to rely on themselves (and their advisers) for guidance. Rod can take credit for establishing his versatile, popular star persona — but must also take some of the blame for being unable to sustain it. Unlike most of the stars from the classical era, Rod at least had some control over his own destiny; he might not have made the right decisions all the time and sold his own talent short, but he had a say in those decisions. One cannot blame him for playing roles he wanted to when he had the chance — what actor would not? It is just a shame he limited himself to them for so long, thereby ensuring he failed to fulfil his potential as both an actor and a star.

ROD'S OFF-SCREEN PERSONA

Rod's off-screen persona was even more strongly distinguished than his on-screen one. His public image was of a two-fisted man's man, who enjoyed the outdoors, masculine pursuits such as hunting, drinking and brawling and messing around with his mates. He liked to play up his early struggles in Los Angeles, his battle against the odds to make it and his close relationship to the Hollywood A-list, as evidenced by his name-dropping of such figures as John Ford and John Wayne. Rod also embraced the star lifestyle, with all its attendant clichés: a large house in Beverly Hills, love affairs with other movie stars, marriage to a model, a large entourage and a swollen head.

Hollywood is famously able to accommodate stars with tempers, egos and drinking problems — but only if they are worth it. Patience for Rod eventually ran out within the film community and his career was damaged as a result. If Rod had been a more pleasant colleague in the late '60s and early '70s, for instance, he surely would have been considered for other, better roles than the ones he was offered.

Rod was a far more well-rounded, sensitive person than his off-screen persona allowed — for instance, the media rarely reported on his life-long love of art, or the fears that helped drive him to alcoholism. But since Rod was the one pushing that persona he could hardly complain. To put it another way: Rod's off-screen persona did not do him credit, but it did do him justice. In recent years, Rod's reputation has mellowed and his image has morphed into that of a lovable rogue who has done a lot of living, an old reprobate who has calmed down — far closer to the mark.

ROD AS AUTEUR

One of the most unexpected things I discovered writing this book was that Rod could be considered an auteur — that is, an actor whose films reflected his personal vision and preoccupations.

Since its emergence in the 1950s, auteur theory has traditionally concerned itself with the work of directors. However, in recent years, there has been a growing trend to recognize actors as auteurs. This school argues that the presence of a particular actor can reflect the "personal stamp" of that actor on a film as much, if not more so, than that of a director; for example, it would be more accurate to call Elvis Presley the auteur of *Blue Hawaii* (1961) than Norman Taurog. Noted film writer Patrick McGilligan argues that "Some actors are more influential than others; and there are certain rare few performers whose acting capabilities and screen personas are so powerful that they embody and define the very essence of their films. If an actor is responsible for only acting but is not involved in any of the artistic decisions of film-making, then it is accurate surely to refer to the actor as a semi-passive icon, a symbol that is manipulated by writers and directors. But actors who not only influence artistic decisions (casting, writing, directing, etc.) but demand certain limitations on the basis of their screen personas, may justly be regarded as 'auteurs.' When the performer becomes so important to a production that he or she changes lines, ad-libs, shifts meaning, influences the narrative and style of a film and altogether signifies something clear-cut to audiences despite the intent of writers and directors then the acting of that person assumes the force, style and integrity of an auteur."

While most screen actors are at the mercy of a director and/or studio in shaping their performances, I would agree with McGilligan that actors can influence a film as much as a director. Occasionally, this is done simply through the actor's presence — for instance, John Wayne's casting as Genghis Khan in *The Conqueror* (1956) totally throws that film off-balance. Rod's screen persona could similarly influence his films. His casting meant the hero of *The Birds* appeared less neurotic than was indicated in the script, gave his time-traveling scientist in *The Time Machine* "balls" and made his villain in *The Deadly Trackers* more sympathetic.

Sometimes acting auterism can go beyond the performer merely appearing on screen and involve them taking an extensive behind-the-scenes role. This can either be passive on their part (for example, construction of a specific vehicle for a star at the request of a studio or producer), or active (the actor turning producer, rewriting the script and so on).

Admittedly, Rod was not one of the great star auteurs — he was too versatile and an insufficiently big name to enjoy real clout in Hollywood. Nonetheless, he had a significant degree of control over his career for large periods of time and was enthusiastically involved in wielding as much power behind the scenes as he could: forming his own production company, turning producer, rewriting scenes, bossing around directors, choreographing fight scenes and so on. This, in addition to the consistency of the themes to which Rod returned again and again throughout his career, is a clear indication of some auteurism.

If one sought thematic consistencies in Rod's work, it is clear that the main "Rod Taylor" theme over the years has been male friendship. This goes back to *King of the Coral Sea* and that first unproduced treatment for Rafferty and

Robinson and features in almost every film Rod made as a star and every film (except *The VIPs* and *Point of Betrayal*) on which he had a hand in the screenplay: *Colossus and the Amazon Queen, Chuka, The High Commissioner, Dark of the Sun, The Hell with Heroes, The Deadly Trackers, Partizan* and *The Treasure Seekers.*

The other key theme of Rod's work is a little more surprising: fear of violence within. The ending of *Dark of the Sun* has its hero turn himself in for killing the villain. In *The Hell with Heroes* and *Darker Than Amber* the hero is tempted but refuses to kill the baddie. *The Deadly Trackers* ends with the hero being killed for refusing to obey the law. While Rod never seems to have commented on this in any interviews that I have read, it seems he was fascinated by the topic of violence — not just as an excuse for an action film, but how it affects violent people and the importance of keeping it under control.

Rod's creative demands mellowed somewhat by the 1980s, reflecting his reduced power in Hollywood. Renee Valente recalls that on *Masquerade,* like most stars, all he wanted was a chance to give his creative input on his character, but no more than that. None of the people associated with Rod's projects from the '80s onwards talk of the actor's behind-the-scenes contributions in stressful terms — on the contrary, they were invited and welcomed. For instance, Rod wrote additional scenes for both *Open Season* and *Point of Betrayal* and helped choreograph the climactic fights in *On the Run* and *Point of Betrayal,* all at the request of the directors of those projects.

It should be acknowledged that Rod's "auterism" was not necessarily a positive thing: *Chuka* (which he co-produced and rewrote) flopped; *The Treasure Seekers* and *Partizan* (co-producer, contributing writer) were barely seen; *The Hell with Heroes, The High Commissioner* and *The Deadly Trackers* (contributing writer) were received poorly; even a first-rate action film like *Dark of the Sun* (contributing writer) under-performed at the box office. Rod's preference for roles which emphasized what he considered his star persona probably hurt his career. He thought he was a star of whom the public expected certain things — when in fact he was not. Nonetheless, he has claim to being a genuine cinematic auteur, a status few actors ever achieve.

ROD'S REPUTATION IN AUSTRALIA

Rod only played actual Australian characters a handful of times in his career, performances which, unfortunately, all fell short of securing the actor's iconic status in his homeland. *The VIPs* was a massive hit, but Rod was overshadowed by the Elizabeth Taylor–Richard Burton road show; *The High Commissioner* was a mediocre film in which Rod gave one of his most over-the-top performances; *On the Run* was forgettable and *Welcome to Woop Woop* little seen. There is no really well-known movie or performance that cinematically links Rod to Australia in that way that, say, *A Town Like Alice* (1956) does for Peter Finch or the *Mad Max* series does for Mel Gibson. As a result, Rod remains widely unknown in his home country today; a great pity.

It was not always like this. Rod was generally positively received here during the first 25 years of his career; the relationship only started to sour when he returned home to make *The Picture Show Man* and it has never really recovered. This is a shame, since Rod did a fair bit for Australian filmmaking: he worked with Australian writers, such as Alec Coppell, Jon Cleary and Elizabeth Kata; pushed forward Australian stories, such as *Lost Eden, The Jungle* and *Last Bus to Banjo Creek,* for possible screen treatment; obtained work for Australian actors abroad, such as Charles Tingwell and Ken Wayne; lobbied the government to support local filmmaking; and promoted Australia as a possible location for Hollywood films.

Admittedly, Rod was not always successful with his Australian projects: his choice of material was often poor, he made those terrible ads for Utah Mining and most of the films he wanted to make in Australia intended to use the country simply as an exotic backdrop and source of cheap labor — he was not an ardent nationalist. But at least he tried and what's more, tried much harder than many Australian film stars in Hollywood, past or current. The Australian film community did not always pay Rod due respect in return, whether offering him inadequate roles, or providing obstacles to films he wanted to make here. In particular, the critical reception of *The Picture Show Man* and *Welcome to Woop Woop* and the tax office ruling at the time of *On the Run* seem unduly harsh.

ROD AND THE AUSTRALIAN ACTING STYLE

One of Rod's major contributions to Australia was that he helped blaze the trail for Australian actors abroad. In particular, he developed the sort of rugged screen persona that later Aussie talent, such as Mel Gibson and Russell Crowe, would trade on. Errol Flynn had already starred in many action movies, but he generally played the classical, romantic hero. Rod Taylor had a more no-nonsense and tough image, a persona that was less English and more American, more contemporary and recognizably "Australian." For instance, it is easier to imagine Rod than Flynn playing the parts of Gibson and Crowe.

Rod was also at the forefront of the development of the modern-day Australian acting "style." This was described by Chris Edmund, head of acting at the West Australian Performing Academy, as acting that featured "gumption, courage, attack, verve and an ability to take things as far as they can go." He later elaborated to Angela Bennie: "Australian actors take big risks. They are not interested in following a formula or dogma. There is an adventurousness and a certain courage. The consequence is a performance of openness and, to me, a strange kind of innocence… a certain kind of generosity at play in their work. This, to me, is at the core of the Australian character, I believe; this generosity of spirit… The English reserve and American introspection can cut things off; here, there is an outgoingness in the culture and this is reflected in our theatre practice and in our acting."

Anthony LaPaglia once argued that a key difference between American and Australian actors was the former tend to "over-think shit and it hurts them in the end," whereas the latter are more inclined to think: "What we do is not rocket science. Stop over-thinking it, just do it." John Clark of NIDA concurs: "There is a courage observable there in the kind of performances Australian actors give. This courage allows them to trust their instincts, trust their own physicalities, not to get caught up into traditional, 'correct' ways of acting. This quality allows them to simply launch in and give it a go."

Aubrey Mellor, head of acting at NIDA, claims Australian acting is a "hybrid" of American and British influences. "We have the British technique, which is about communication, physical, external things — these are part of our tradition. And we have the Method, the American heritage, introduced to us by Hayes Gordon, where we became more truthful and rebelled against the British method because it was so false. But the point is, we didn't throw either away, but incorporated them both into what we do on stage. I think that combo, those two poles and what we do with it, makes our actors the kind of actors they are."

When Rod began his career, Australian acting was thoroughly under the yoke of British cultural imperialism; Rod was part of a movement which broke away from this. Although he trained in traditional methods, such as voice and diction, at the Independent, he drew from elements of the Method, Stanislavski and the teachings of John Saul. He brought in aspects of his own life — a physicalness, boldness and brashness, a love of art and the great outdoors. He combined British elements with American ones, mixed them all up and came up with a very Australian technique. Admittedly, you could also say this about a number of Rod's contemporaries — Alan White, Guy Doleman, Charles Tingwell — but Rod was at the forefront of the pack.

When asked to explain the recent success of Australian actors in Hollywood, Geoffrey Rush offered this explanation: "There's a cultural, societal attitude here. We're a nice mixture of being a very laid-back culture, but we're also quite brazen; we get a bit feisty. I think that influences the work… There is a quality about Australians which is pretty similar to the average man, which is pretty no-nonsense, fighting, strong-willed and also an honesty. There is the expression of the little Aussie battler — the guy who no matter how many times he gets knocked down, he keeps on getting up to fight."

All these characteristics were displayed by Rod Taylor throughout his career. What is more, for around 20 years, he was the leading Australian displaying them. It is impossible to gauge how much of an influence Rod had, if any, on the actors who followed him, but he deserves some acknowledgement for being a pioneer of Australian acting.

ROD AND REPRESENTATIONS OF "AUSTRALIAN-NESS"

Rod's final contribution to Australia was the role he played in representations of "Australian-ness." This took place even though Rod spent most of his career playing Americans. For instance, Donald Horne argued in 1971 that the dominant ideologies of Australia were "egalitarianism, fraternalism and gregariousness" — there is not a better concise description of Rod Taylor's screen persona.

Even more specifically, Rod's characters generally had recognizable connections with the "typical Australian" described by Russell Ward in the 1950s: they were practical, great improvisers, willing to have a go; they looked as though they would swear hard and constantly, gamble, drink and womanize; they were loyal and independent and so on.

Perhaps the most Australian aspect to the Rod Taylor screen persona was that of mateship, a theme we have seen that he returned to time and time again. This was very much in line with Australian tradition: an attempt was once made to enshrine the word "mateship" in the Australian constitution and Brian McFarlane once went so far as to claim that "the sentimental ideal of mateship may well be Australia's chief contribution to the history of human relationship." With Rod Taylor as Australia's leading Hollywood star for over 20 years, he played a considerable part in this contribution. Indeed, an argument could be made that Rod propagated the myth of mateship on an international scale to a greater degree than any Australian before him.

It should be pointed out that Rod brought his own slant to representations of a typical Australian. In particular, his persona deviated from Ward's description in some key ways: his characters tended to be gregarious rather than taciturn; they were just as capable of flirting at the dinner table or running a company as they were of drinking a beer or punching someone out; they represented authority rather than rebelliousness. Rod also usually played contemporary, urban people, rather than the outback individuals glorified in Ward; not suburban, but urban and modern-day. Rod was conscious of this, describing his tycoon in 1963's *The VIPs* as the first authentic picture of an Australian he had seen on the international screen. "It's the first time an average Australian has been portrayed without slouch hat, broken-down horse and greasy merino."

There were a number of reasons for this. Firstly, it was a conscious decision on Rod's part — he expressed the desire several times that he wanted to "show audiences that we've got telephones in Australia as well as kangaroos." Secondly, there were Rod's qualities as an actor — he was comfortable in friendly roles, but less so as loners; he conveyed a contemporary quality rather than a historical one; and this in turn influenced the kind of roles in which he was cast. Thirdly, he had long-term contractual arrangements with film companies (MGM, 20th Century-Fox, Hitchcock) who specialized in more sophisticated genres of entertainment — glossy dramas, urban thrillers, romantic comedy — within which Ward's mythical Australian would fit awkwardly.

It is arguable, then, that his persona presented a more sophisticated portrayal of an Australian. Instead of a character based around the bushman, the pioneer, the Anzac and the ocker, Rod played the scientist, the cowboy, the businessman and the detective. He essentially took elements of Ward's myth and made it more urbane. In fact, when you think about it, there were some Hollywood stars whose screen personas actually came closer to Ward's Australian than Rod's (Robert Mitchum and Gary Cooper come to mind); however, since Rod actually was Australian, he had the greater influence in representing Australian-ness.

It is interesting that as Rod gained greater control over his career in the second half of the 1960s he actually moved closer to the typical Australian of myth. There were fewer urban dramas and comedies and more action films; there was less Baryshnikov, more Russell Crowe. For instance, the truck driver Rod was to play in *Last Bus to Banjo Creek* fairly steps out of the pages of Ward. This makes it all the more bewildering, then, that the actor did not find himself more at home in the revitalized Australian film industry of the 1970s and 1980s.

Writer Theodore F. Sheckls once listed 12 characteristics of the heroes found in Australian films of the '70s: love of freedom, anti-authoritarianism, anti-British sentiments, connection with the land, love of horses, love of mates, intensely competitive, love of drink, anti-intellectualism, sexism, underdog status and fatalism. This was all firmly in line with the Ward myth, which thrived that decade on Australian screens. The myth may have been something of a cliché by then, but it was at least an Australian cliché and thus highly attractive to an industry seeking to re-assert its cultural independence from Hollywood. Indeed, the Ward myth was still applying in Australian cinema well into the next decade; as pointed out by Brian McFarlane, among the most commonly recurring images projected by Australian films of the 1980s were those denoting mateship, anti-authoritarianism, the Aussie battler and the competitive instinct.

Rod's persona and acting skill meant that he could have slotted in perfectly with any number of excellent Australian films during that time: *The Money Movers* (1979), *Breaker Morant* (1980) and *The Man from Snowy River* (1982) are just some that spring to mind. However, when Rod did return to Australia, he was either cast as an American or very American-style characters, or tried to make films that were American stories using Australia as a backdrop. He seems to have identified himself as a phoney American so strongly by this stage that he was unable to make the leap back into satisfactory Australian roles. To me, this is the greatest tragedy of Rod Taylor's career.

Rod finally played an Australian role that suited his talents with *Welcome to Woop Woop* in the late 1990s. Rod Taylor's brawling, drinking "dinosaur" Daddy-O is very much the evil flipside of the mythical Australian and deserved to be recognized as an iconic cultural performance. Unfortunately, Rod's timing was out again: by that stage the Australian film industry had undergone what writer Philip Butterss described a "radical shift in its image of Australian masculinity" and enthusiasm for Ward-like mythical Australians had faded: shearers, diggers and ockers were out; ballroom dancers, drag queens and SNAGs were in. Rod's casting in *Woop Woop* as a relic from another era was all too appropriate.

Nonetheless, at a time when Australian movie stars were extremely thin on the ground, Rod represented aspects of the Australian character to the world. They may have been clichéd, restrictive aspects — but they were part of an oasis in a cultural desert at the time. For that he deserves some recognition.

THERE ARE THREE WAYS TO JUDGE AN ACTOR'S SUCCESS. FIRST is on the interpersonal level: the relations between the actor and his/her family and friends. This aspect of Rod Taylor's life has not been the focus of this book, so it would be inappropriate to discuss in great detail. I would point out that, from all accounts, his first two marriages were unfortunate, but his third marriage has been a long and happy one. He has also been blessed with a large number of friends throughout his life who talk about him with a great deal of affection and protection.

Secondly is the respect with which that actor is held by his peers. Apart from a dark period of the late '60s and early '70s, when Rod's ego and fondness for the bottle got the better of him, Rod has been highly respected by producers, directors, writers and fellow actors. He was recalled with warmth and praise; of all the people who worked with him that I interviewed for this book, very few had a bad word to say about him. Those that did worked with him during the "dark period."

Thirdly is the legacy that actor has left the general public. Rod Taylor has been acting in films, television, radio and the stage for over half a century. Like every performer, the quality of his work has varied, but like a true professional his overall career average is high. He performed in four films that have become classics — *Giant*, *The Time Machine*, *One Hundred and One Dalmatians* and *The Birds* — making major contributions to all except *Giant*. He appeared in a number of films that have emerging cults (*Zabriskie Point*, *Dark of the Sun*), as well as a large number who have proved extremely durable over the years (*The VIPs*, *Sunday in New York*, *36 Hours*, *The Liquidator*, *The Glass Bottom Boat*). He has done some excellent work on television, particularly on episodes of *Cheyenne* and *Playhouse 90*, as well as his own series like *Hong Kong* and in TV movies like *Jacqueline Bouvier Kennedy*. Like all actors, Rod made some poor choices, especially in the 1970s, and there are several films where his creative input seems to have hurt the final result (*Chuka*, *The High Commissioner*). However, it is a very strong, respectable legacy, one that has given hours of pleasure to many people.

Rod has one additional legacy — to Australia. Rod's great days as an actor came during the period of 1955–1970, when Australia's film industry was virtually non-existent, its radio drama dying out, its television drama slow to emerge and its theatre struggling. During that time he became famous around the world. He never hid his Australian nationality and played Australians in a number of films. At a time when Australians could rarely see or hear themselves on screen, stage and radio, Rod Taylor helped keep Australia in the public eye. While the actor often described himself as a "phoney American," he was a very Australian one. For all these things he deserves acknowledgement and that is why I wrote this book.

CREDITS

Title (Production Company, Year of release)

Feature Films

King of the Coral Sea (Southern International, 1954)
Long John Silver (Treasure Island Pictures, 1954)
The Virgin Queen (20th Century-Fox, 1955)
Hell on Frisco Bay (Warner Bros/Jaguar, 1955)
Giant (Warner Bros., 1956)
Top Gun (Fame/UA, 1955)
World Without End (Allied Artists, 1956)
The Catered Affair (MGM, 1956)
Raintree County (MGM, 1957)
Step Down to Terror (Universal, 1958)
Separate Tables (Hecht-Hill-Lancaster/Clifton, 1958)
Ask Any Girl (MGM/Euterpe, 1959)
The Time Machine (MGM/Galaxy, 1960)
Colossus and the Amazon Queen (Glomer/Galatea Film, 1960)
One Hundred and One Dalmatians (Disney, 1961) – voice only
Seven Seas to Calais (MGM/Titanus, 1962)
The Birds (Universal/Hitchcock, 1963)
A Gathering of Eagles (Universal, 1963)
The VIPs (MGM, 1963)
Fate Is the Hunter (20th Century-Fox/Arcola, 1964)
Sunday in New York (MGM/Seven Arts, 1964)
36 Hours (MGM/Perlberg-Seaton/Cherokee, 1965)
Young Cassidy (MGM/Sextant, 1965)
Do Not Disturb (20th Century-Fox/Melcher/Arcola, 1965)
The Liquidator (MGM/Leslie Elliot, 1966)
The Glass Bottom Boat (MGM/Arwin, 1966)
Hotel (Warner Bros, 1967)
Chuka (Paramount/Rodlor, 1967)
The Mercenaries (MGM, 1968)

The Hell with Heroes (Universal, 1968)
The High Commissioner (Rank/Selmur, 1968)
Zabriskie Point (MGM, 1970)
The Man Who Had Power Over Women (Avco Embassy/Kettledrum, 1970)
Darker Than Amber (Cinema Center/Major Films, 1970)
Powderkeg (Filmways/Rodphi, 1971) – TV movie
Family Flight (Universal, 1972) – TV movie
The Heroes (Finarco/Gerico Sound/Transister/Les Films Corona/Atlantida, 1972)
The Train Robbers (Warner Bros./Batjac, 1973)
Trader Horn (MGM, 1973)
The Deadly Trackers (Warner Bros./Cine Films, 1973)
Partizan (Avala/FRZ 41/Noble, 1974)
A Matter of Wife... and Death (Columbia/Robert Weitman, 1975) – TV movie
Blondy (Paris Cannes/TIT, 1976)
The Oregon Trail (Universal/NBC, 1976) – TV movie
The Treasure Seekers (Hall-Ross, 1979, filmed 1976)
The Picture Show Man (Limelight/AFC/NSWFC, 1977)
A Time to Die (CIP/Almi, 1983, filmed 1979)
Cry of the Innocent (Tara/NBC, 1980) – TV movie
Hellinger's Law (Universal, 1981) – TV movie
Jacqueline Bouvier Kennedy (ABC Circle, 1981) – TV movie
Charles & Diana: A Royal Love Story (Edward S. Feldman, 1982) – TV movie
On the Run (Pigelu, 1982)
Masquerade (20th Century-Fox, 1983) – TV movie
Half Nelson (Glenn Larson/20th Century-Fox, 1985) – TV movie
Marbella (Calepas/Jose Frade, 1985)
Mask of Murder (Power Line/Master, 1985)
The Outlaws (Universal/Mad Dog, 1986) – TV movie
Danielle Steel's "Palomino' (Cramer/NBC, 1991) – TV movie
Grass Roots (JBS/Spelling/Team Cherokee, 1992) – TV mini-series
Open Season (Legacy/Frozen Rope, 1996, filmed 1993)
Point of Betrayal (Trident, 1995)
Warlord: Battle for the Galaxy (1998, filmed 1996) – TV movie
Welcome to Woop Woop (Scala/Goldwyn/FFC, 1998)
Kaw (Sony, 2006)
Inglourious Basterds (Universal/Weinstein Company, 2009)

Documentaries

Inland with Sturt (Film Australia, 1951)
The Fantasy Film Worlds of George Pal (Arnold Leibovit, 1985)

Time Machine: The Journey Back (7th Voyage Productions, 1992)
All About "The Birds" (Universal, 2000)
The Making of "The Picture Show Man" (Umbrella Entertainment, 2005)
Not Quite Hollywood (City Films/FFC, 2008)

TV Series – As a Regular

Hong Kong (20th Century-Fox, 1960–61)
Bearcats! (Filmways/Rodphi, 1971)
The Oregon Trail (Universal/NBC, 1977)
Masquerade (20th Century-Fox, 1983–84)
The Outlaws (Universal/Mad Dog, 1986–87)
Falcon Crest (Lorimar, 1988–1990)

TV series – As a Guest star
(*Indicates an anthology series, i.e. one with no recurring characters other than the host)

The Lux Video Theatre – "The Browning Version" (CBS, 1955)*
Studio 57 – "The Black Sheep's Daughter" (DuMont/Revue, 1955)*
Studio 57 – "The Last Day on Earth" (DuMont/Revue, 1955)*
Studio 57 – "Killer Whale" (CBS, 1955)*
Lux Video Theatre – "Dark Tribute" (Lewman, 1955)*
Warner Bros. Presents/Cheyenne – "The Argonauts" (Warner Bros., 1955)
Suspicion – "The Story of Margery Reardon" (Revue, 1957)*
General Electric Theatre – "The Young Years" (Revue, 1957)*
Playhouse 90 – "Verdict of Three" (CBS/Screen Gems, 1958)*
Playhouse 90 – "The Great Gatsby" (CBS/Screen Gems, 1958)*
Schlitz Playhouse of the Stars – "A Thing to Fight For" (Revue, 1958)*
Studio One in Hollywood – "Image of Fear" (CBS, 1958)*
Lux Playhouse – "The Best House in the Valley" (Revue, 1958)*
Playhouse 90 – "The Long March" (CBS/Screen Gems, 1958)*
Playhouse 90 – "The Raider" (CBS/Screen Gems, 1959)*
Playhouse 90 – "Misalliance" (CBS/Screen Gems, 1959)*
The Twilight Zone – "And When the Sky Was Opened" (Cayuga/CBS, 1959)*
Zane Grey Theatre – "Picture of Sal" (Four Star/Pamric/Zane Grey, 1960)*
Goodyear Theatre – "Capital Gains" (Screen Gems, 1960)*
General Electric Theatre – "Early to Die" (Revue, 1960)*
Westinghouse Desilu Playhouse – "Thunder in the Night" (Desilu, 1960)*
Bus Stop – "Portrait of a Hero" (20th Century-Fox, 1961)*
DuPont Show of the Week – "The Ordeal of Dr Shannon" (NBC/Associated Rediffusion, 1962)*

Password (1964) – guest star on game show
This Is Your Life (Lifetime Associates, 1975) – guest star
Tales of the Unexpected – "The Hitchhiker" (Anglia Television, 1980)*
Murder, She Wrote – "Another Killing in Cork" (Corymore/Universal, 1995)
Murder, She Wrote – "Nan's Ghost – Parts 1 and 2" (Corymore/Universal, 1995)
Walker, Texas Ranger – "Redemption" (CBS/Amadea, 1996)
Walker, Texas Ranger – "Wedding Bells" (CBS/Amadea, 2000)

Radio (NB list not exhaustive)

Captain Singleton (1950), *Greyface* (1950), *Frenchman's Creek* (1950), *Morning Departure* (1950), *Nancy's Boy* (1950), *No Logic Before Breakfast* (1950), *And in Those Days* (1950), *Rocky Starr* (1951), *The Concert* (1951), *The Lady Asks for Help* (1951), *Children's Crusade* (1951), *The Innocent Sprite* (1951), *The Search for the Golden Boomerang* (1951), *A List of Names in Red* (1951), *Miss Bomb for 1951* (1951), *Point of Departure* (1951), *Thistledown* (1951), *Winterset* (1951), *Madame Bovary* (1951), *I'm a Dutchman* (1951), *Conscious Effort* (1951), *Two Loves Have I* (1951), *A Place Where You Whisper* (1951), *Call Me Cold* (1951), *Misfire* (1951), *The Strange Story of Deacon Brodie* (1951), *Famous Frauds* (1951), *Paula Lehman, New Australian* (1951), *I Hate Crime* (1952)*, *Kiss of Hate* (1952), *I Spy* (1952), *The Master of the House* (1952), *The Hands of Mary Clifford* (1952), *The Blue Lamp* (1952), *Joe the Magnificent* (1952), *Spaceways* (1952), *Black Lightning* (1952), *Richard II* (1952), *Star Chamber* (1952), *The Silent Inn* (1952), *The Informer* (1952), *Time Was My Enemy* (1952), *Trudy and the Quiet Life* (1952), *The Golden Ass* (1952), *I Am My Brother's Keeper* (1952), *The Second Threshold* (1952), *Like the Duke* (1952), *Out of This World* (1952), *Man Trap* (1952–53), *Night Beat* (1953), *Contraband* (1953), *Counterfeit* (1953), *Martin's Corner* (1953), *When a Girl Marries* (1953), *Three Roads to Destiny* (1953), *Johnny Raven* (1953), *Blue Hills* (1953), *To Live in Peace* (1953), *Because of the Lockwoods* (1953), *The Diamond Studded Noose* (1953), *You and Me Both* (1953), *The Devil's Plan* (1953), *It Never Rains* (1953), *Bonaventure* (1953), *For Art's Sake* (1953), *All My Sons* (1953), *The Ridge and the River* (1953), *Famous Trials – Lisbon Affair* (1953), *The Witness* (1953), *Abe Lincoln in Illinois* (1953), *Famous Fortunes – Edison* (1953), *With Cain Go Wander* (1953), *The Starlit Valley* (1953), *Trudy and the Quiet Life* (1953), *The Tragical History of Dr Faustus* (1953), *Deirdre of the Sorrows* (1953), *The Sundowners* (1953), *The Man Who Came to Dinner* (1953), *On the Way to Niagara* (1953), *The Laughing Woman* (1953), *The Amazing Mr. Malone* (1953), *The Right to Happiness* (1953), *This Happy Breed* (1954), *Three Secrets* (1954), *Crime and Punishment* (1954), *Cape Forlorn* (1954), *Gulliver's Cousin* (1954), *Walk East on Beacon* (1954), *We Were Children* (1954), *Gigi* (1954), *Be Your Age* (1954), *The Dance Dress* (1954),

The Mary Jane (1954), *Operation North Star* (1954), *Full Cry* (1954), *Ned Kelly* (1954), *The Animal Kingdom* (1954), *The Happy Time* (1954), *Remains to Be Seen* (1954), *Golden Boy* (1954), *The Musicians* (1954), *Oasis* (1954), *Something for Nothing* (1954), *The Burning Grass* (1954), *The Doomsday Men* (1954), *The Compelled People* (1954), *The Wages of Fear* (1954), *Such Men Are Dangerous* (1954), *The Hungry God* (1954), *Tarzan* (1954), *Crispin's Day* (1954), *Train for Thought* (1954), *Famous Trials – The Real McCoy* (1954), *Akhenaton* (1954), *One Green Bottle* (1954), *Sacrifice to the Wind* (1954), *Reach for the Sky* (1954), *O'Sullivan's Bay* (1954), *Wings off the Sea* (1954), *The Golden Fool* (1954).

Theatre

Julius Caesar (Independent, 1950)
Home of the Brave (Independent, 1950)
Misalliance (John Alden Company, 1951)
Twins (Mercury, 1952)
Comedy of Errors (Mercury, 1952)
The Witch (Mercury, 1952)
They Knew What They Wanted (Mercury, 1952)
The Happy Time (Mercury, 1953)

ACKNOWLEDGMENTS

FIRST OF ALL, I MUST THANK ROD TAYLOR. HE WAS ORIGINALLY interested in co-operating with this book and passed on some contact details and information for me, with the intention that we meet up for an interview when he was next in Sydney. Although he subsequently changed his mind, his original emails were most useful, as were his published interviews with various media outlets over the years.

Second, the book would not have been possible without the encouragement and support of Diane Tomasik, creator of the superb Rod Taylor website. Diane has been ceaselessly generous with tapes, articles and so on, and her enthusiasm has been extraordinary.

For tales of Rod's childhood I must thank Julie Bates, Meryl Wheeler, Vanja M. Neus, Marie James, Anthony Emerson, Les Wilson, Don Calnan, Doug Milner, Max Walker, Cliff Allen, Bob Duff, Paul Taylor and Fiona Campbell at Parramatta High School, Ken Mathers, the *Cumberland Argus* and Stuart Burley.

Information about East Sydney Tech and Rod's art career was provided by Ena Joyce, Susan Tooth, Chebbie Badham, Beryl Marchi (nee Eager), Guy Warren, Pamela Waugh (nee Cashel), Deborah Beck, Margaret Olley, Tom Bass, Lyndsay Churchland, Bert Flugelman, John Rigby, Tony Thompson, Earle Backen, Kevin Connor, Meran Essan, Therese Kenyon, Peter Rushforth, Kate Coolahan, Jill Chapman and Grace Cochrane at the Powerhouse Museum and Norma Flegg.

For information about Rod's work in radio and theatre, my thanks to Richard Lane, Neil Hutchinson, Frances Nightingale, John McCallum, June Dally-Watkins, Margaret "Peggy" Christensen, Nigel Lovell, June Salter, Gwen Plumb, Thelma Scott, Gwen Meredith (now Gwen Harrison), Betty Lucas, Dinah Shearing, David Nettheim, Georgie Sterling, Brian Wright, Owen Weingott, Barbara Reville (nee Brunton), Ben Gabriel, Babs Mayhew, Charles Tingwell, Jacqueline Kent and Warwick Hirst at the Mitchell library.

For information about his early Australian film work, my thanks to Graham Shirley, Tony Buckley, Judy Adamson of Film Australia, Roy Pugh, Pat Trost, Iain Macinnis, Michael Pate, Warren Moons, Lee Robinson, Penn Robinson, Ilma Adey, Don Connolly, John Adey, Margaret Ansara and Margot Holt and the staff at the National Film and Sound Archive.

For information about Rod's years in Hollywood I spoke with or corresponded with Russ Tamblyn, Edd Byrnes, Robert Wise, Viney Melnick, Murray Neidorf, Clint Walker, Booth Colman, Gore Vidal, Millard Kaufman, Martin Manulis, Shirley Knight, Loring Mandel, William Self, Sidney Ellis, Arthur Hiller, Donald S. Sanford, William Froug, Robert Blees, Keith Michell, Luther Davis, Jonathan Hughes, Lina Hsu, Tippi Hedren, Evan Hunter, Peter Nero, Robert Ginna, Dan Ford, Jennie Rathbun at Harvard University, Kevin Brownlow, Leo Askin, Peter Yeldham, Lisa Penington, John Gardner, Howard Gotbetter, George Englund, Stanley Chase, Leo McKern, Sidney Beckerman, Jon Cleary, Marcia Hatfield, Brian Chirlian, Daria Halprin, Harrison Starr, Marsha Kinder, John Krish, Judd Bernard, Theodore Bikel, Walter Seltzer, Martin Ransohoff, Bernard F. Pincus, Sam Roeca, John Boyle, Howard Williams, Caro Jones, Marvin J. Chomsky, Guerdon Trueblood, Harve Bennett, Kristoffer Tabori, Alfredo Bini, Sergio Donati, Dick Ziker, Carl Pingatore, Michael Economou, Howard Berk, Elena Panajotovic, Don Ingalls, Andrew Stevens, Linda Purl, Carl Vitale, Charles Napier, Stella Stevens, Julia McLaren, Alan Levi, Burt Brinckerhoff, Joe Morhaim, Walter Brough, Sam Manners, Tara Manners, Keith Stafford, Morgan O'Sullivan, William Link, Isidore Mankofsky, Clyde Phillips, John F. Goff, Matt Cimber, Jefferson Richard, Renee Valente, Harris Katleman, Phil Bondelli, Andrew Schneider, Bruce Bilson, Tomislav Pinter, Bruce Cervi, Karen Harris, David Chisholm, Jeff Freilich, Joanne Brough, Camille Marchetta, Cyrus Nowrasteh, Frederic L. Knudtson, Michael Hoey, Diana Kopald Marcus, Joseph Scanlan, George Kaczender, Lisa Seidman, Karol Ann Hoeffner, Stuart Woods, Robert Wuhl, Clyde Lucas, Rich Martini, Anne Cusack, Bruce Lansbury, Mark A. Burley, Laurence Heath, Tony Mordente, Glenn A. Bruce, Joe Dante, Michael Finnell, Tom Korman, Tura Satana, Richard Anderson, Justin Bowyer, Richard Glassman, Mrs Vaccarino, Peter Werner, and Robert Eisle.

For information about Rod's later work in Australia, I thank Mike Willessee, Phil Avalon, Lyn Bayonas, Jan Kenny, Sue Milliken, Peggy Carter, Grant Page, Tony Tegg, Geoff Burton, Harry Kirchner, Richard Hindley, Bill Anderson Jr., Graeme Dowsett, Ray Meagher, Antonia Barnard, Jonathon Schaech, Michael Thomas, Susie Porter, Maggie Kirkpatrick, Dee Smart, Andrew Urban, Michael Molloy, Guy Gross, George Friend, Mark Hartley, Tim Long and Piers Wilkinson.

I also thank various librarians at the Mitchell Library, Seaborn Foundation (NIDA), UCLA, USC, Harvard University, the British Film Institute, the Margaret Herrick Library, New York Performing Arts Library, the University of Wisconsin, the University of Iowa, Franklin and Marshall College, the University of Florida, the University of Reading, the National Film and Sound Archive and the Australian Film Institute.

Special thanks to all the librarians at AFTRS: Michele Burton, Debbie Sander, Elisabeth McDonald, Jillian Kelso, Margaret Gwynne and Anna Juniper.

And on the topic of AFTRS, thanks also to Peter Millyn, Annabelle Sheehan, Peter Duncan, Ron Blair, George Whaley, Jan Kenny, Pat Lovell, Jane Roscoe, Sean Maher, Yvonne Madon, Sam Meikle and that other guy who helped me with money. Special, special thanks go to Graham Shirley for his comments on an early draft, to Ben Goldsmith for ushering the MA (Hons) component of this project through its final stages, and Jocelyn Hungerford for her proofing.

Most of all I would like to thank my lovely partner, Louise, who has been supportive and tolerant of me all through this project. It is to her that I dedicate this book.

REFERENCES

Common Abbreviations

ABCW	*ABC Weekly*	LITV	*The Listener In-TV*
AHF	Alfred Hitchcock Files, MHL	MHL	Margaret Herrick Library
AMPAS	Academy of Motion Picture	PB	Pressbook
	Arts & Sciences	PH	*Photoplay*
BFIF	British Film Institute File on	R-L	*Rod-lore* (Rod's fan journal)
	Rod Taylor	NFSA	National Film & Sound Archive
CDT	*Chicago Daily Tribune*	NYT	*New York Times*
CT	*Chicago Tribune*	SMH	*Sydney Morning Herald*
DT	*Daily Telegraph* (Sydney)	TCM	Turner Classic Movies
DV	*Daily Variety*	TVG	*TV Guide*
F&F	*Films & Filming*	UCLA	University of California,
FW	*Film Weekly*		Los Angeles
HHC	Hedda Hopper Collection, MHL	USC	University of Southern California
HR	*The Hollywood Reporter*	Var	*Variety*
LAHE	*Los Angeles Herald Examiner*		
LAT	*Los Angeles Times*	n/p	Name of publication not available
LI	*The Listener In*	n/d	Date of publication not available

Interviews

If a person is quoted, it is from one of the following interviews with the author unless otherwise specified in the notes.

Judy Adamson (Film Australia) May 24, 2000
Ilma Adey Nov 16, 2000
Cliff Allen Jun 28, 2000
Bill Anderson Jnr Feb 24, 2003
Richard Anderson Jun 22, 2004
Chebby Badham Apr 29 2004
Antonia Barnard May 26, 2000
Tom Bass May 11, 2004
Lynn Bayonas Jun 23, 2004 (email)
Sidney Beckerman Mar 12, 2004
Harve Bennett Dec 9, 2003
Howard Berk Dec 9, 2003
Judd Bernard Nov 29, 2003
Theodore Bikel Jun 3, 2004

Bruce Bilson Nov 30, 200
Alfredo Bini Apr 1, 2003 (email)
Robert Blees May 12, 2004
Phil Bondelli Feb 28, 2004
Burt Brinckenhoff Aug 27, 2004 (email)
Joanna Brough Apr 14, 2004
Walter Brough Nov 24, 2003
Kevin Brownlow Jul 11, 2004 (letter)
Barbara Brunton Nov 6, 2000
Stuart Burley Jun 11, 2000
Geoff Burton Oct 30, 2000
Don Calnan Jul 3, 2000
Pam Cashel Jun 15, 2004
Bruce Cervi Mar 19, 2004

Stanley Chase Dec 12, 2003
Brian Chirlian Jan 24, 2004
Marvin Chomsky Nov 13, 2003
Margaret (Peg) Christensen Apr 8, 2004
Matt Cimber Jun 7, 2004
Jon Cleary Oct 2, 2004
Booth Colman Nov 19, 2003
Kate Coolahan Apr 30, 2004
Ann Cusack Apr 19, 2004 (email)
June Dally-Watkins May 1, 2001
Joe Dante Jun 23, 2004
Sergio Donati Jun 3, 2004
Graeme Dowsett Jun 16, 2004
Bob Duff Jun 28, 2000
Beryl Eager May 7, 2004 (letter)
Michael Economou Jan 24, 2004
Robert Eisele Apr 28, 2004
Anthony Emerson Jun 8, 2000
George Englund Dec 6, 2003 and
   May 30, 2004 (email)
Howard Epstein Jul 5, 2004
Mike Finnell Jun 23, 2004
Norma Flegg Jun 1, 2004
Jeff Freilich Feb 28, 2004
George Friend Feb 27, 2004 (email)
William Froug Jun 6, 2004 (email)
Ben Gabriel Nov 3, 2000
John Gardner Oct 7, 2003 (email)
Robert Ginna Apr 25, 2003
Richard Glassman Mar 12, 2004
John Goff Nov 23, 2003
Howard Gotbetter Dec 16, 2004
Guy Gross Nov 2, 2000
Dana Halprin May 12, 2003 (email)
Karen Harris Mar 19, 2004
Gwen Harrison Nov 8, 2000
Marcia Hatfield Jan 24, 2004
Tippi Hedren Apr 15, 2003
Arthur Hiller May 4, 2004 (email)
Richard Hindley May 25, 2000
Karol Ann Hoeffner Apr 28, 2004
Neil Hutchinson Apr 8, 2004
Don Ingalls Nov 27, 2003
Marie James Jun 4, 2000
Harris Katleman Jul 20, 2004
Millard Kaufman Dec 3, 2003
Jan Kenny May 25 & 26, 1999
Maggie Kirkpatrick Oct 1, 2003
Shirley Knight May 8, 2004 (email)

John Krish Jan 20, 2004
Richard Lane Jul 29, 1999
Bruce Lansbury Jun 20, 2004 (email)
Alan Levi Apr 8, 2004
William Link Jun 4, 2004 (email)
Nigel Lovell May 19, 2000
Betty Lucas Nov 3, 2000
Loring Mandel Jan 24, 2001
Isidore Mankofsky Nov 29, 2003
Sam Manners Dec 16, 2004
Richard Martini Mar 3 & 6, 2003 (email)
Ken Mathers Jul 4, 2000
Babs Mayhew Nov 16, 2000
John McCallum Nov 23, 2003
Ray Meagher Aug 11, 2000
Keith Michell Nov 20, 2003 (email)
Sue Milliken May 26, 2000
Doug Milner Jul 2000
Mike Molloy Nov 2, 2000
Warren Moons Oct 30, 2000
Tony Mordente Mar 3, 2004
Charles Napier Nov 28, 2003
Vanja Neus Aug 30, 2000
Peter Nero Apr 19, 2004 (email)
David Nettheim Apr 7 & 8, 2004
Frances Nightingale Nov 6, 2000
Margaret Olley Nov 3, 2000
Morgan O'Sullivan Mar 24, 2004
Elena Panajotovic Jan 26, 2004
Michael Pate May 25, 2000
Lisa Penington Jan 26, 2003 (email)
Clyde Phillips Mar 23, 2004
Antonio Pica Mar 25, 2003 (email)
Carl Pignatore Nov 20, 2003
Bernard Pincus Apr 8, 2004
Tomislav Pinter Jun 24, 2004 (email)
Liz Ploger Apr 14, 2004 (email)
Gwen Plumb Nov 7, 2000
Susie Porter Apr 4, 2000
Roy Pugh Nov 30, 2003
Linda Purl Mar 30, 2003
Martin Ransohoff Feb 2004
Sam Roeca Apr 8, 2004
Lee Robinson May 24, 2000
Sarah Rush Mar 16, 2005 (email)
June Salter Nov 3, 2000
Tura Satana Mar 28, 2003 (email)
Jonathan Schaech Jun 5, 2004 (email)
Andrew Schneider May 31, 2004 (email)

Thelma Scott Nov 7, 2000
Lisa Seidman Jun 27, 2004 (email)
William Self Nov 26, 2003
Walter Seltzer Nov 28, 2003
Dinah Shearing Nov 3, 2000
Dee Smart May 28, 2004
Keith Stafford Jun 22, 2004
Harrison Starr Dec 7, 2003
Georgie Sterling Jul 6, 2004
Andrew Stevens May 13, 2004 (email)
Stella Stevens May 16 & 17, 2004
Kris Tabori May 11, 2004
Russ Tamblyn May 5, 2004
Michael Thomas Aug 19, 2000
Tony Thompson May 2004 (letter)
Charles Tingwell Jun 27, 2000
Pat Trost Dec 3, 2003
Guerdon Trueblood Nov 30, 2003

Mrs. Vaccarino Mar 2004
Renee Valente Jan 31, 2004
Gore Vidal undated 2002 (letter)
Carl Vitale Mar 12, 2004
Clint Walker Sept 17, 2003 (email)
Max Walker Jun 28, 2000
Guy Warren Apr 29, 2004
Pamela Waugh Jun 15, 2004
Owen Weingott Nov 3, 2000
Peter Werner Mar 3, 2004
Meryl Wheeler Jun 19, 2000
Piers Wilkinson May 26, 1999
Les Wilson Jul 3, 2000
Robert Wise Jul 12, 2004 (letter)
Stuart Woods Apr 5, 2003 (email)
Brian Wright Nov 3, 2000
Robert Wuhl Jul 1, 2004 (email)
Peter Yeldham Jul 3, 1999

Introduction

"The most important thing to me…" – Jim Henaghan, 'Lock Up Your Daughters! Here Comes
   Rod!,' *Motion Picture* Nov (1961): 64.
Australians in Hollywood: Tony Clifton & John Horn, 'The Aussies Take Hollywood,' *Newsweek*
   Mar 25 (2002): 66, Michaela Boland & Michael Bodey, *Aussiewood: Australia's Leading Actors
   and Directors Tell How They Conquered Hollywood* (Sydney: Allen & Unwin, 2005). It should be
   acknowledged that many movie stars considered "Australian" were born overseas: Mel Gibson
   (USA), Russell Crowe (New Zealand), Nicole Kidman (USA), Naomi Watts (England), Guy
   Pearce (England).
Rod's 1963 visit: 'Star Back as VIP,' *Sun Herald* Sept 1 (1963): 1, 'Rod's Pot of Gold: £600,000
   Movie Offers,' *The Sun* Aug 31 (1963): 1, 'At a Gala Charity Premiere,' *SMH* Sept 5 (1963):
   10, 'VIPS Acclaimed at Gala Bow,' *The FW* Sept 5 (1963): 1, 'Phone Call Brightens Day for
   Rod Taylor,' *The Age* Sept 6 (1963): 3.
"After a reception…" – John Larkins, 'Rod Talks His Way Out of Trouble,' *Listener In TV* Sept 14-
   20 (1963): 7.
Ranking stars: The best-known method of this is the Quigley Publishing Top Ten Money
   Making Stars Poll which goes back to 1933 and is annually printed in the *International
   Motion Picture Almanac* (Groton, Mass: Quigley Publishing, 2005). See also *http://www.quig-
   leypublishing.com.*
"Phoney American" – 'Taylor: "I ain't no Gable,"' *PH* Oct (1969): 36.

Chapter 1: Early Life 1930 – 1948

Rod's birth date: Parramatta High School Register of Admission, Jim Fagan, 'My Son Rod
   Taylor,' *Australian Home Journal* Apr (1965): 11.
Charles Sturt: Edgar Beale, *Sturt, the Chipped Idol* (Sydney: Sydney University Press, 1979),
   Michael Langley, *Sturt of the Murray: Father of Australian Exploration* (London: Hale, 1969).
Rod's parents: Bill was the son of Frederick Taylor and Nellie McCracken; Frederick was the son
   of Joseph Taylor and Sarah Sturt Milton; Sarah Sturt Milton was the daughter of Eliza Sturt

(c1815-1880), who had married James Milton. Mona Thompson was born in Hull on Apr 8, 1902, the daughter of printer Frederick Thompson and his wife Trisenah. See *South Australian Births, Index of Registrations 1842 to 1906*, ed. Jan Thomas (Adelaide: South Australian Genealogy & Heraldry Society, 1997), William Sturt Taylor birth certificate, Births Deaths & Registration Office in South Australia, letter to author from Peter Court dated Apr 2004, New South Wales marriage certificate C255766 dated Aug 2, 1928, Rod's appearance on *This is Your Life*.

"My parents' relationship…" – Bill Davidson, 'Why Can't Rod Taylor Be a Pussycat?,' *TVG* Feb 23-29 (1971): 20.

"Tough son of a bitch…" – Yoram Kahana, 'Taylor-Made Comfort,' *TV Times* Oct 7 (1978): 22.

Lidcombe: Ted Stafford, *Living in Liddy*. (Ted Stafford: Ettalong, 1991).

"The great gateway…" – *Lidcombe Gala Week Jun 10 to 16, 1933: Official Souvenir and Programme* (Municipality of Lidcombe, 1933).

"First adventure in the world…" & "we were tolerant…" – 'Boy Who Became Big Star,' *TV Week* Mar 9 (1961): 12. For an example of one of her stories see: M Sturt Taylor, 'Flowers for Josie,' *Australian Women's Weekly* Mar 30 (1946): 4.

Parramatta High School: See also Ken Mathers, 'The Hollywood Hyphenate,' *People* Jan 25 (1967): 6, *Parramatta High School* website at *http://www.parramatta-h.schools.nsw.edu.au/*.

East Sydney Tech: *The Studio Tradition – The National Art School 1883 to 2001* (Sydney: Manly Art Gallery & Museum, 2001), *National Art School* website *http://www.nas.edu.au/*, John McDonald "Drawn from the ranks,' *SMH* Aug 2, 2008. Life drawing anecdote from letter Tony Thompson to author, May 2004.

Mona Vale Surf Club: Letter Rod Taylor to Mona Vale Club Mar 5, 1997.

"Learnt about life…" – 'How Rod Taylor Muscled in on Hollywood,' *TV Times* Aug 4 (1973): 11.

Rod's expulsion: There are no records of graduates between 1946 and 1947 and Rod is not listed as a graduate for 1948. *The Studio Tradition* ibid p76-79, Toni Holt, 'Rod Taylor: Especially Intrigues Him,' *Citizen News* Nov 7 (1970).

"I didn't wear…" – 'How Rod Taylor Muscled in on Hollywood,' ibid.

Guy Boyd Pottery: *A Guide to the Records of the Martin Boyd Pottery in the Powerhouse Museum* (2001).

"Could paint…" – 'The Hollywood Hyphenate,' *People* Jan 25 (1967): 6.

"Infested with rats…" – John Vader, *The Pottery and Ceramics of David and Hermia Boyd* (Sydney: Matthews/Hutchinson, 1977): 27.

"Ninety-nine percent…" – 'Four Young Artists Have Success with Ceramics,' *SMH* Aug 14 (1949): 9.

"Business quietly thrived…" – Vader, ibid p27.

"I got tired with…" – Denis Minogue, 'Mr Rod Taylor, frankly speaking', *Daily Mirror,* Sept 12 (1968): 3.

Chapter 2: Australian Actor 1949-1951

Laurence Olivier tour: Ann Leslie, 'Rod's Price is £120,000 a Film,' *Daily Express* Apr 30 (1965), Gary O'Connor, *Darlings of the Gods: One Year in the Lives of Laurence Olivier and Vivien Leigh* (London: Hodder & Staughton, 1984).

"I used to listen…" – Steve Swires, 'Rod Taylor – Time Travelling Hero,' *Starlog* Jul (1986): 25.

"Put up…" – Davidson, ibid.

Independent Theatre School: *The Independent Theatre 21st Birthday Souvenir* (The Independent Theatre, 1951), Rod's appearance on *This Is Your Life* (1975).

Australian radio: 'Equity Move on Imported Radio Shows,' *LI* Sept 8 (1951): 3, Richard Lane, *The Golden Age of Australian Radio Drama 1923-1960* (Melbourne: Melbourne University

Press, 1994), 'Our wage rises long overdue, actors declare,' *LI* Dec 15 (1951): 2, Phillip Lewis, "Meet Another 'Cover Girl' Plus Husband,' *LI* Dec 16 (1950): 9, Jacqueline Kent, *Out of the Bakelite Box: the Heyday of Australian Radio* (Sydney: Angus & Robertson, 1983). NB Mona Taylor described Rod's first acting job as consisting of one line in a serial – see 'Boy Who Became Big Star,' ibid.

Another version of how Rod got started: He was considering going to England to try his hand in the theatre there when he met Neil Hutchinson at a party, who encouraged him to audition. 'Studio News and Views,' *ABCW* Jun 17 (1950): 33.

"Discovered magic…" – *This Is Your Life.*

Shortage of male actors: 'Shortage of Radio Actors in Sydney,' *LI* May 20 (1950): 3. NB See also 'Sydney Shortage of Actors Denied,' *LI* May 27 (1950): 2.

"What impressed people…" – Richard Lane ibid p322.

"The profession gets…" – 'Studio News and Views,' *ABCW* Jun 17 (1950): 33.

"Another of those new young 'uns…" – 'Studio News and Views,' *ABCW* Jun 17 (1950): 33.

"Hopping from studio…" – Guy Austin, "The Hollywood Hyphenate', *People* Jan 25 (1967): 5.

"Rodney Taylor suggested well…" – 'This Week on the Air,' *LI* Dec 9 (1950): 4.

Example of Rod's accent: 'In the Footsteps of Sturt,' *Hindsight* ABC Radio National, Jan 2, 2000.

"The Australian accent…" – Alan Ashbolt 'Naturalism Ascendant' in "Acting," *Companion to Theatre in Australia* Eds Philip Parsons with Victoria Chance (Sydney: Currency, 1995): 19.

"When I started acting…" – John Bell, *The Time of My Life* (Sydney: Allen & Unwin, 2003): 52. Bell was talking about the 1960s but his comments were applicable a decade earlier.

"Very lonely…" – Vicky Roach, 'Back to Woop Woop,' *Sun Herald (Time Out)* Aug 9 (1998): 10.

"I think when you have a few drinks…" – Toni Holt, ibid.

"Truthful and untruthful…" – Charles Tingwell & Peter Wilmoth, *Bud: A Life* (Sydney: Pan MacMillan, 2004): 290.

Method acting: Shelly Frome, *The Actors Studio: A History* (Jefferson, N.C.: McFarland, 2001), Foster Hirsch, *A Method to Their Madness: A History of the Actors Studio* (New York: WW Norton & Co, 1984),

"The Method constructs…" – Richard Maltby, *Hollywood Cinema* (Malden: Blackwell, 2003): 161.

"Had to run across the desert" – Kent, ibid p262.

"When you start defending the acting…" – 'Rod Taylor' TV's 'Dark Horse'?,' *NY Herald Tribune*, Nov 27 (1960): 58.

"Disguise acting…" – Henry Fonda, 'Reflections on Forty Years of Make-Believe,' *Playing to the Camera: Film Actors Discuss Their Craft* Eds Bert Cardullo, et al (New Haven: Yale Uni Press, 1998): 210.

"When you put up…" – 'Rod Taylor Acquires or Loses Accents to Meet Exigencies of Various Roles,' *36 Hours PB* (MGM, 1964): 5.

"Cezanne said there is…" – Toni Holt, ibid.

"No right way or wrong…" – Angela Bennie, 'Enter, Stage Right, Ourselves,' *The Age* Oct 9 (2004): 3.

Chapter 3: Australian Films 1951-54

"That clever…" – 'Round the Sydney Studios,' *LI* Nov 4 (1950): 13.

"The greatest ever…" – 'In the footsteps of Sturt,' *Hindsight* ABC Radio National, Jan 2, 2000.

Charles Sturt expedition: *ABCW* Dec 16 (1950): 1, *LI* Dec 16 (1950): 13, Tony Birrell, 'Rod Got Corns on His Seat,' *People* (Australia) Jan 25 (1967): 7, 'Showbusiness,' *ABCW* Mar 17 (1951): 26, '300,000 Saw Trip of Sturt's Men,' *SMH* Feb 19 (1951): 8.

Inland with Sturt: 'Murray journey with Capt Sturt,' *Film Monthly* Aug (1951): 20.

"All the little…" – Sydney Tomholt, 'Inland with Sturt,' *ABCW* Aug 4 (1953): 14.

Rod's love life: Email from George Whaley to author dated Apr 7, 1999, June Salter, *A Pinch of Salt* (Pymble: Angus & Robertson, 1995).

Rod's marriage & wedding: New South Wales marriage certificate registration number 8262/1952 & 1955/021247.

"Marriage takes complete…" – Guy Austin ibid p5.

Independent Theatre: David Nettheim, 'Final Curtain for Doris,' *Equity* Jun (1985): 46-48, Doris Fitton, *Not Without Dust and Heat* (Sydney: Harper & Row, 1981). *Julius Caesar*: 'Independent's 'Caesar' Patchy Show,' *SMH* Oct 9 (1950): 4, *Home of the Brave*: 'Anti-Semitism As Seen From Moon,' *SMH* Oct 20 (1950): 10.

John Alden Company: Stanley Marks, 'Stratford-on-Sydney Harbour,' *LI* Nov 25 (1050): 6, the John Alden papers at the Mitchell Library in Sydney. *Misalliance*: 'Sparkle in Shaw Play,' *SMH* Sept 10 (1951): 2. Rod occasionally mentioned in interviews he acted in *Misalliance* for the Mercury Theatre. It is likely he was confused because the play was performed at St. James Hall, where Rod later acted in a number of Mercury productions. NB Immediately following *Misalliance*, Rod was credited in an advertisement as being in another production for Alden: *The Vigil*, a courtroom drama by Ladislas Fodor. However, Neil Hutchinson, who directed the play, did not remember him being in the cast and he is not listed in any of the reviews the author has seen, so it is possible that Rod pulled out.

Mercury Theatre: Sydney John Kay's scrapbooks at the Mitchell Library, Stephen Vagg 'Finch, Fry and Factories,' *Australasian Drama Studies* Vol 50 April (2007): 18. *Comedy of Errors/The Twins: ABCW* Apr 5 (1952): 15, 'Mercury's Plays Open Well,' *SMH* Feb 29 (1952): 4, *Daily Mirror* Feb 29 (1952). *The Witch*: *ABCW* Sept 20 (1952): 15. *They Knew What They Wanted*: *ABCW* Dec 13 (1952): 15, *SMH* Nov 15 (1952): 4. *The Happy Time: Bulletin* Jan 6 (1954), *ABCW* Jul 4 (1952).

History of Australian cinema: Graham Shirley & Brian Adams, *Australian Cinema: The First Eighty Years* (Sydney: Currency Press, 1989), Andrew Pike & Ross Cooper, *Australian Film 1900-1977: A Guide to Feature Film Production* (Melbourne: Oxford University Press, 1998).

King of the Coral Sea: Lee Robinson's papers at NFSA, Bob Larkins, *Chips: The Life and Times of Chips Rafferty* (South Melbourne/Crows Nest: Macmillan, 1986), Ilma Adey, 'How a King Became a Queen of the Silver Screen,' *Kino* Mar (1997): 28. Reviews: *Sunday Telegraph* Sept 12 (1954): 49, *FW* Sept 16 (1954): 11, *LI* Aug 21-27 (1954): 18.

"Oh, he was smart…" – Martha Ansara, 'Lee Robinson,' *Cinema Papers* Dec (1996): 20.

"We took about…" – Albert Moran, 'King of the Coral Sea,' *Continuum* Vol 1 No. 1 (1987): 107.

Image of Australians: Susan Dermody & Elizabeth Jacka, *The Screening of Australia vol 1* (Sydney: Currency Press, 1987).

"A practical man…" – Russell Ward, *The Australian Legend* (Melbourne: Oxford University Press, 1965, 2nd ed): 1.

Other Rafferty-Robinson projects: Southern International (Production & Distribution) Limited 1955 prospectus, D'Arcy Niland, 'The Ginger Giant,' *The Penguin Best Stories of D'Arcy Niland* (Ringwood: Penguin, 1987): 183.

Long John Silver: 'Louis Wolfson's Stake in "Long John Silver,"' *Var* Dec 8 (1954): 5, Joe Adamson, *Byron Haskin* (Metuchen & London: DGA & Scarecrow Press, 1984), Peter Woodruff, 'Joseph Kaufman's Plans,' *ABCW* Nov 21 (1953): 16, *Film Monthly* Dec 21 (1953): 1, 'Pirate Film in Colour,' *SMH* Jun 2 (1954): 2, Joseph Kaufman, 'Making Long John Silver,' *F&F* Jan (1955): 6, *Long John Silver PB* (DCA, 1954), Kylie Tennant, 'Lunch Hour Game for Pirates,' *SMH*, Sept 11 (1954) mag section, Hyatt Downing, 'A Long Way From Home,' *PH* Mar (1957): 57, 'Gala Film Premiere,' *SMH* Dec 17 (1954): 13. Reviews: *DT* Dec 17 (1954): 9, *FW* Dec 23 (1954), 'London Critics Severe on "Long John,"' *SMH* Dec 18 (1954): 3.

"It was a case…" – Graham Shirley, 'Byron Haskin,' *Cinema Papers*, Mar (1975): 21.

"Scrambling..." – 'Matinee Idol,' *60 Minutes* Channel Nine, Aug 30, 1998.

Berowra Waters bungalow: 'Radio Personalities: Rod Taylor,' *ABCW* Nov 28 (1953): 28.

"Still oddly nervous..." – Richard Lane, ibid p322.

Reviews of Rod's later radio performances: *LI* Jan 23-29 (1954): 4 *(This Happy Breed)*, *LI* Mar 20 (1954): 4 *(The Dance Dress)*, 'US Film star in espionage drama,' *LI* Apr 17 (1954): 4 *(Operation North Star)*, *LI* Jul 10 (1954): 4 (*Remains to Be Seen*), *LI* Aug 28 (1954): 4 *(Something for Nothing)*.

"The most spontaneous...." – 'Young Sydney actor wins ovation,' *LI* Sept 25-Oct 1 (1954): 4.

"Kids from Kogarah to Kununurra..." – Jacqueline Kent, ibid p111.

"The day we started Bader..." – Ewart quoted in Richard Lane ibid p322.

"For several minutes, he made..." – Jacqueline Kent, ibid p263.

"The event of the week..." – 'Top Rating Goes to Bader Serial,' *LI* Nov 13 (1954): 4.

Rola prize: 'Dual Role Wins Trip,' *LI* Sept 18 (1954): 2.

"I loved..." – Guy Austin, ibid p5.

"It was tougher for me..." – Dennis Minogue, ibid.

Chapter 4: America 1955-59

Hollywood in the 50s: Douglas Gomery, *The Hollywood Studio System* (London: Macmillan, 1986), Thomas Schatz, *The Genius of the System: Hollywood Filmmaking in the Studio Era* (New York: Metropolitan Books, 1996).

"Looked like a crock..." – Howard Thompson, 'Up the Ladder from Down Under,' *NYT* Jul 19 (1964): X5.

Early possible Rod projects: Edwin Schallert, 'Aldo Ray and Dick York Team Up,' *LAT* Jan 11 (1955): B7, 'Movieland Events,' *LAT* Feb 1 (1955): 19, *LI* Dec 11 (1954): 30, 'Chance for Aus star,' *DT* Nov 16 (1954): 10, Leo Sullivan, 'Even Flickerville Has Its Archives,' *Washington Post and Times Herald* Feb 24, (1955): 24. According to the *Rose Tattoo* casting files in the Hal Wallis papers, the lead roles had been cast by the time Rod arrived in Hollywood and Rod's name is not mentioned at all; the part he tested for may have been 'Rosario,' a small role eventually played by Larry Chance. See cast list dated Oct 21, 1954 in the Hall Wallis files at MHL, AMPAS.

"I got jobs in the end..." – Charles Higham, 'Rod Taylor just loathes seagulls,' *SMH* Sept 14 (1968): Weekend mag 18.

"Every time I had..." – Bill Tusher, 'He man from Down Under,' *Screenland* Mar (1961): 55.

"On the beach fishing..." – Hedda Hopper, 'He's Sick of People Who Want Only Stardom,' *LAT* Apr 15 (1962): M9.

"A dreary little room..." – Downing, ibid p98. The apartment was at 1318 N Crescent Heights, Hollywood –*World Without End* cast contact list dated Jul 21, 1955, MHL.

Search for new stars in the 1950s: 'Hollywood Fears New Faces Famine for Future Films,' *Var* Dec 30 (1953): 1, Thomas Pryor, 'Hollywood's Search for Stars,' *NYT* Jun 12 (1955): SM14, Clayton Cole, 'The Brando Boys,' *F&F* May (1955): 9, Clayton Cole, 'The Breeding Boys,' *F&F* Jun (1959): 26.

"Look, people walked..." Jim Murphy, 'No airs and graces, but... Rod's 'Bound For No. 1 Stardom," *LITV* Sept 21 (1968): 3.

Rod's first role: Rod later told a fan magazine that his first part in Hollywood was an off-stage voice on a TV show. Six weeks later, he starred on the same program. Jane Ardmore, 'Look Who's in the Mood for Love,' *PH* Dec (1961): 49. Rod later claimed *Lux Radio Theatre* gave him his first paid work in Hollywood but I have been unable to find confirmation of this. See Guy Austin, ibid p5.

The Virgin Queen: *The Virgin Queen* PB (20th Century Fox, 1955).

Giant: George Stevens papers at MHL, AMPAS. List of possible Karfeys dated Apr 4, 1955.

  Rod's casting: Memo Hoyt Bowers to George Stevens dated Apr 27, 1955.

"I landed in Hollywood…" – Howard Thompson, ibid.

"He warned me never to be…" – 'Vignette of Rod Taylor: A Spectacular Career From TV to Pictures,' *A Gathering of Eagles PB* (Universal, 1963): 6.

"Extraordinarily talented…" – Hyatt Downing, ibid.

World Without End: Tom Weaver, 'Edward Bernds,' *Interviews with B Science Fiction and Horror Movie Makers* (Jefferson: McFarland Classic, 1988): 47.

"I dove into it…" & "To know that I could work…" – Steve Swires, ibid p26.

Hell on Frisco Bay: Hyatt Downing, ibid.

"The standout performance" – *Var* Nov 3 (1955).

"Did not like television…" – 'He Came From "Down Under,"' *TVG* Apr 29 (1961): 19.

"As Australian Rodney…" – Pete Morrison, 'Film Tracks,' *FW* Sept 15 (1955): 3.

Somebody Up There Likes Me: Louella Parsons, 'Tony Martin Will Play Russ Columbo in Movie,' *Washington Post & Times Herald* Sept 7 (1955): 13, 'He Came From 'Down Under" ibid.

"As Australian Rod Taylor…" – Pete Morrison, 'Film Tracks,' *FW* Sept 15 (1955): 3.

History of MGM: Bosley Crowther, *Hollywood Rajah; the Life & Times of Louis B Mayer* (New York: Holt, 1960) & *The Lion's Share: The Story of an Entertainment Empire* (New York: Dutton, 1957), John Douglas Eames, *The MGM Story* (New York: Crown Publishers, 1975), British Film Institute, *MGM* (London: BFI Publishing, 1980), Thomas Schatz, *The Genius of the System: Hollywood Filmmaking in the Studio Era* (New York: Metropolitan Books, 1996), Dore Schary, *Heyday: an Autobiography* (Boston: Little, Brown, 1979), 'That Metro Gang Breaks Up,' *Var* Feb 8 (1956): 3.

MGM's star building programs: '78 Future Stars on Rolls,' *Var* Jan 25 (1956): 3, 'Metro to Build Stars – Again,' *Var* Dec 12 (1956): 5. 'M-G Resumes Star-Grooming,' *Var* Feb 27 (1957): 5. 'Metro Contract Players List 31, Down from 59,' *Var* Feb 6 (1957): 1.

Schary's attempt to change Rod's name: Steve Swires (1986) ibid.

The Catered Affair: Paddy Chayefsky papers at the University of Wisconsin. Nielsen's casting *HR* Nov 10 (1955): 2.

"Acts the way he is" – Hyatt Downing, ibid p99.

"Mild success" – *Var* Aug 22 (1956): 3.

"So genuinely touching…" – *Los Angeles Examiner* Jul 19 (1956).

Raintree County: Edward Dmytryk, *It's a Hell of a Life But Not a Bad Living* (New York: NYT Books, 1978), Larry Lockridge, *The Shade of the Raintree: The Life & Death of Ross Lockridge Jnr* (New York: Viking Penguin, 1994), 'MGM Prize Winner to Have All-Star Cast,' *LAT* Jul 17 (1947), '"Raintree County" A Budget Bust,' *Var* Sept 28 (1955): 3, Julie & Bill Fenden, *The Other Side of the Screen: The Story of Filming Raintree County* (Culver City: Kerr Printers, 1957), 'M-G Probably to Splash-Premiere "County" a la "Wind,"' *Var* May 1 (1957): 5; 'Vogel (with Reagan) Meets Press,' *Var* Jun 12 (1957): 24, 'Decides Hard Tickets the Hard Way,' *Var* Nov 13 (1957): 3.

"I was a little bit…" – Rod Taylor interview for TCM.

"Begins in tedium…" – *Time* Jan 6 (1958).

"A happy surprise…" – 'New York Soundtrack,' *Var* Jan 22 (1958): 4.

"A delight…" – Charles Tingwell & Peter Wilmoth, ibid p105.

"Get up there…" – Hyatt Downing, ibid at p99.

MPEAA "Youngsters with 'Star Potential": *Var* Jul 24 (1957): 13. The full list was Anthony Perkins, Joanne Woodward, Paul Newman, Vera Miles, Felicia Farr, John Saxon, Hope Lange, James Darren, Suzy Parker, Barbara Lang, Kerwin Matthews, Milko Taka, Kendall Scott,

Dennis Hopper, Rick Jason, Andrea Martin, Tania Elg, Patricia Owens, Rod, Inger Stevens, Anna Kashfi, Venetia Stevenson, Leslie Nielsen, & Anne Duringer.

"With some first rate…." – Hyatt Downing ibid at 99.

MGM's troubles: 'Ben Thau No. 1 at Studio in Schar's MG Move,' *Var* Nov 28 (1956): 1, 'Proxy Battle-Scarred Joe Vogel, Of Metro No-Fun Era, Is Dead,' *Var* Mar 5 (1969): 4.

Rod's late 50s efforts: Hedda Hopper, 'Tania Elg will star in Ballerina Role,' *LAT* Jul 11 (1957): C10, Thomas Pryor, '2 Added to Cast,' *NYT* Jul 24 (1957): 28, *Var* Jul 31 (1957): 21.

Maverick: 'He Came From 'Down Under,'' *TVG* Apr 29 (1961): 19.

"I was offered…" – Howard Thompson ibid pX5.

Separate Tables: '1959: Probable Domestic Take,' *Var* Jan 6 (1960): 34.

"Last great stand…" – Sheridan Morley, *David Niven: The Other Side of the Moon* (London: Weidenfeld & Nicolson, 1985): 280.

Step Down to Terror **review:** *HR* Sept 9 (1958): 3.

Rio Bravo: The role was Colorado, a hired gun who helps a sheriff (John Wayne) and his friends (Dean Martin, Walter Brennan) fight off a gang of outlaws. Hawks originally envisioned the role of Colorado as an older man, but by March 1958 had reconceived the role as much younger and was looking into young male actors such as Rod, Michael Landon, Stuart Whitman and football player Frank Gifford. He eventually picked Ricky Nelson. Todd McCarthy, *Howard Hawks: The Grey Fox of Hollywood* (New York: Grove Press, 1997): 555.

Psycho: Note dated Nov 2, 1959 in AHF. For this role, Hitchcock also asked to see film of Stuart Whitman, Cliff Robertson, Tom Tryon, Leslie Nielsen, Brian Keith, Richard Basehart, Peter Fleming, Kurt Fring and Jack Lord.

Ask Any Girl: '1959: Probable Domestic Take,' *Var* Jan 6 (1960): 34. 'Why Choice for Berlin Was Limited,' *Var* June 17 (1959): 17. **Reviews:** *HR* May 13 (1959): 3, *DV* May 13 (1959): 6, *LAT* Jun 20 (1959), *Los Angeles Examiner* Jun 20 (1959).

Chapter 5: Becoming a Star 1959 – 1961

The Time Machine: 'David Duncan,' in Tom Weaver, *Interviews with B Science Fiction and Horror Movie Makers* (Jefferson: McFarland & Company, Inc, 1988): 125, David Duncan interviewed by Don Coleman on May 29, 1999 in *http://www.colemanzone.com/Time_Machine_ Project/journey.htm* accessed April 27, 2005, 'George Pal to Leave Paramount,' *Var* Sept 21 (1955): 7, 'HG Wells' "Machine" Pal-Bogeaus Issue,' *Var* Oct 22 (1958): 4, Thomas M Pryor, 'Mexican Actress Signed By Brando,' *NYT* Oct 15 (1958): 46, 'Looking at Hollywood,' *CDT* Dec 6 (1958): 17, Gail Morgan Hickman, *The Films of George Pal* (South Brunswick & New York: AS Barnes & Company, 1977), Darin Scot, 'Filming *The Time Machine*' *American Cinematographer* 41, no. 8 (1960): 491, *Var* Jan 6 (1960): 28 (advertisement), 'Rental Potentials of 1960,' *Var* Jan 4 (1961): 47.

"We went to…" – Ed Naha, 'The Time Machine,' *Starlog* May (1978): 74.

"One of those men who are…" – David Duncan script at George Pal collection, UCLA.

"Science fiction picture…"&"There are areas…." – Bill Kelsay, 'Hong Kong,' *TV Radio Mirror*, Jan (1961): 65.

"Have been strong… I didn't attempt…" – Swires (1986), ibid p27.

"Felt god-damned silly…" – Charles Higham, 'Rod Taylor just loathes seagulls,' *SMH* Sept 14 (1968): Weekend mag 18.

The Time Machine **reviews:** *Var* Jul 20 (1960): 6, *HR* Jul 11 (1960): 3, *New York Journal American* Aug 18 (1960).

"Taylor is hardly…" – Bill Warren, *Keep Watching the Skies! Vol 2* (Jefferson, NC: McFarland&Co, 1986): 456.

The Time Machine sequel: 'If "Time" and its Sequel; George Pal's Wells Reprise,' *Var* Jun 22
     (1960): 2, 'Metro Starting 8 More Pix,' *Var* Aug 24 (1960), Philip K Scheuer, 'Bogarde to Star
     with Ava and Judy,' *LAT* Aug 9 (1960): 23.

"With doing sequels…" – 'Interviewing Rod,' *R–L* Apr (1964): 9. *The Journey Back*: see *http://
     www.colemanzone.com/Time_Machine_Project/journey.htm* accessed April 27, 2007.

"Devolves creatively…" – *Var* Mar 7 (2002).

Possible post-*Time Machine* roles: Hedda Hopper, 'Gleason Sought for Oliver Hardy,' *CDT*
     Aug 18 (1959): A4, *NYT* May 2 (1960): 34, Philip K Scheuer, 'Hunter Promoting Play from
     Movie,' *LAT* Aug 5 (1959): 27, Hedda Hopper, 'Karl Malden Will Portray Preacher,' *LAT*
     Jun 5 (1959): A7.

Misalliance: Var Nov 2 (1959).

"All behaved in the great…" – John Houseman, *Final Dress* (New York: Simon & Schuster, 1983):
     181.

"Intelligent, appealing…" – Marc Scott Zicree, *The Twilight Zone Companion* (Toronto, New York:
     Bantam Books, 1982): 62.

"Living next to a powder keg…" & "the chauffer, a little guy…" – n/p n/d BFIF.

"His surge to fame…" – Jim Henaghan, 'Lock Up Your Daughters! Here Comes Rod!,' *Motion
     Picture* Nov (1961): 64.

Hong Kong pilot: 'He Came From "Down Under,"' ibid, 'Rod Taylor' TV's "Dark Horse"?,' *New
     York Herald Tribune*, Nov 27 (1960): 58, 'Hong Kong TV Series Scheduled Next Fall,' *LAT*
     Mar 30 (1960): A10, 'Levathes Sells 'Paradise' to ATV,' *Var* Jun 15 (1960): 24.

"Not the usually muscular…" – 'Series Star Decries 'Hero' Type,' *LAT* Sept 28 (1960): A11.

"She is a real gem…" – 'Rod's Gone to Hong Kong,' *TV Week* Feb 2-8 (1961): 31.

"As big as Gardner.." – Hedda Hopper, 'Looking at Hollywood,' *CDT* Jun 9 (1960): C1

Colossus and the Amazon Queen: 'Half-Of-Italy's Stars Aliens,' *Var* Apr 26 (1961): 63.

"Colour and wide…" – Robert F Hawkins, 'Antiquity Cycle Rules Italy,' *Var* Jan 6 (1960): 167.

"The worst script…" – 'Taylor made,' *DT* Jun 9 (1960): 2.

"Hide that fiasco…" – Steve Swires (1986), ibid p25.

Rod's return to Australia: 'Actor son returns from USA,' *Daily Mirror* Jun 8 (1960): 37,

"It is gradually seeping…" – 'Local Boy Makes Good,' *SMH – Women's Section* Jun 9 (1960): 7.

"Probably in about 18 months…" – 'Taylor made,' *DT* Jun 9 (1960): 2.

Captain Cook project: Hedda Hopper, 'Looking at Hollywood,' *CDT* Jun 18 (1960): S10, 'George
     Pal Will Scout Locations for "Lost Eden" in Australia,' *Var* Jan 3 (1962): 62.

Hong Kong series: 'Interviewing Rod,' *R–L* Oct (1963): 5, 'ABC-TV's "Timeslot Roulette" Kicks
     Up a Madison Ave Fuss,' *Var* Jan 11 (1961): 17, Cecil Smith, 'Hong Kong Caper in Audience
     Bid,' *LAT* Jan 25 (1961): A8, 'Low On the Nielsen Poll,' *Var* Mar 15 (1961): 25, 'Kaiser Pours
     It All Back on ABC In 2-Show Buy,' *Var* Apr 19 (1961): 27, '20th-Fox in Timid Syndie Bid,'
     Var Dec 27 (1961): 22, George Rosen, "60-'61 TV Season – Ratings,' *Var* Nov 2 (1960): 1,
     Hedda Hopper, 'He's Sick of People Who Want Only Stardom,' *LAT* Apr 15 (1962): M9.

"Stars went out with…" – Vernon Scott, "'No Such Thing as TV Star,'" *New York Morning Telegraph*
     Dec 13 (1960).

"Big names aren't built…" – 'Rod Taylor' TV's "Dark Horse"?' ibid.

"Trifles with…" – *NYT* Sept 29 (1960): 71.

"In all his fourteen years…" – 'He Came From "Down Under"' ibid p18.

"Louse on the set…" – "Jim Henaghan, ibid p64.

"Lacks dramatic…" – *Var* follow up Nov 3, 1960.

"It's a true to life…" – 'Boy Who Became Big Star,' ibid p14.

"Learned to work…" – Cecil Smith, 'Rod Taylor Shanghaied by Hong Kong,' *LAT* (TV times) Jul
     23 (1961): 3.

"You have to give…" – 'Stardom and Marriage Finally Arrive For Australian Charmer, Rod Taylor,' *Fate Is the Hunter PB* (20th Century Fox, 1964).

"Cleared with one leap…" – 'He Came From "Down Under,"' ibid p18.

"For me, the whole jazz…" & "it was another…" – Cecil Smith, 'Rod Taylor Shanghaied,' ibid.

Market price $75,000: Interview with Hedda Hopper on Mar 24, 1965. HHC.

21 promising newcomers – Hedda Hopper, 'Tribune's Famed Commentator on Life in the Film Capital,' *CDT* Jan 1 (1961): B11. The others were Paul Anka, Paula Prentiss, Fabian, Carol Christensen, Vicki Trickett, Kendall Scott, Stella Stevens, Ingrid Thulin, David Ladd, Leticia Roman, Clu Gulager, Hayley Mills, James Shigeta, Ward Ramsey, Luana Patten, Yvette Mimieux, Mike Connors & Max Baer Jnr.

"A breath of spring…" – Jim Henaghan, ibid p65.

Hong Kong **Australian ratings**: Christopher Day, 'Drama,' *Australian Television: The First 25 Years*. Ed. Peter Beilby. (Melbourne: Nelson/Cinema Papers, 1981): 134. Also 'Top Rating Programmes' p 185.

One Hundred and One Dalmatians: Valeria Grove, 'Puppy Love,' *The Times Magazine* Mar 18 (1995): 18-21, *Screen International* Jan 17 (1992).

"The dog is supreme…." – 'Dog Voice Casting Proves Problem for Dalmatians,' *One Hundred and One Dalmatians press release* (Disney, 1961).

James Bond casting: Broccoli signed Sean Connery in Oct, 1961. I have been unable to find another source other than Rod to confirm that he was seriously considered for the role. Steve Jay Rubin. *The James Bond Films: A Behind the Scenes History* (London: Arlington House, 1981).

"One of the great mistakes…" – Steve Swires (1986), ibid p29.

Seven Seas to Calais: 'Metro's Worldwide Rights to "Seven Seas,"' *Var* Jul 17 (1961): 13, *Var* Dec 6 (1961): 15. **Reviews**: *Var* May 6 (1963), *Motion Picture Herald* Mar 20 (1963): 778.

"Didn't look quite…" & "I remembered…" – *Seven Seas to Calais PB* (MGM, 1963).

Errol Flynn: Errol Flynn, *My Wicked, Wicked Ways* (London: Heinemann, 1960).

"I can't help it…" – 'Vignette of Rod Taylor,' *A Gathering of Eagles PB* (Universal Studios, 1963): 6.

"I love what he presented…" – 'Matinee Idol,' *60 Minutes* television broadcast Aug 30, 1998.

Peter Finch: Trader Faulkner, *Peter Finch* (London: Angus & Robertson, 1979), Elaine Dundy, *Finch, Bloody, Finch* (London: Michael Joseph, 1980).

Rodlor & Coppel: *Var* Oct 18 (1961): 7, Philip K Scheuer, 'Shelley Produce in Unique Co-Deal,' *LAT* Oct 24 (1961): C9, Hedda Hopper interview Sept 20, 1962 – HHC, 'Letter from Liz,' *R-L* Apr (1963): 4.

Signing with Fox: Hedda Hopper, 'Rod Taylor signs deal with 20th,' *LAT* Dec 1 (1961): A13. While in Naples, Rod had also received a call from director Anatole Litvak asking him to co-star in *Five Miles to Midnight* (1962) with Sophia Loren. Hedda Hopper, 'Looking at Hollywood,' *CDT* Oct 26 (1961): D5. Anthony Perkins and Gig Young ended up supporting Loren.

"It's the old fashioned…" – Interview with Hedda Hopper on Feb 6, 1962 – HHC.

Unproduced Fox projects: *Rod Taylor Fan Club Journal*, Jan (1962): 1, 'Rod Taylor will star in the Jungle,' *LAT* Jun 26 (1961): 6 Part IV, Hedda Hopper, 'Looking at Hollywood,' *CDT* May 28 (1962): B7, Hedda Hopper, 'Doris Day Will Play "Unsinkable Molly,"' *LAT* Mar 2 (1962): C14.

Chapter 6: Consolidation of Stardom 1962-64

The Birds: 'Seabird Invasion Hits Coastal Homes,' *Santa Cruz Sentinel* Aug 18 (1961): 1, Steve Connor, 'Madness of *The Birds* explained,' *Independent* Jul 21 (1995): 2, Donald Spoto, *Alfred Hitchcock: The Dark Side of the Genius* (Boston: Little, Brown, 1983), AHF at MHL, Hitchcock Forum on Sept 23, 2003 'Joseph Stefano, Arthur Laurents and Evan Hunter Talk About Working with Alfred Hitchcock,' *http://www.edmcbain.com/Newsdesk.asp?id=229* accessed

May 13, 2005, 'Alf Hitchcock Gives Taylor 'The Birds," *DR* Feb 2, 1962, Memo to Norman Denning from Peggy Robertson Jul 3, 1962 – AHF, Kyle B Counts, 'The Making of *The Birds*' *Cinefantastique* vol 10 no 2 Fall (1980): 15, Harrison Carroll, 'It's for *The Birds*,' *LAHE* Apr 22 (1962): 1, 'Hitchcock Clipped $400 By Govt For Caging, Killing Too Many "Birds,"' *Var* Apr 2 (1964), Tony Lee Moral, *Hitchcock and the Making of "Marnie"* (Lanham: Scarecrow Press, 2002), Robert E Kapsis, 'Hollywood Filmmaking and Reputation Building: Hitchcock's The Birds,' *Journal of Popular Film & Television* v 15 n 1 Spring (1987): 4, '"The Birds" Caused Traffic Trouble,' *The Times* Aug 29 (1963). Reviews: *NYT* Apr 1 (1963): 54, *Esquire* Oct (1963): 23, *Village Voice* Apr 4 (1963): 15, *HR* Mar 28 (1963): 3, *Citizen News* Apr 12 (1963), 'The Birds is Given a Decade Top Audience for a Movie on TV,' *Wall Street Journal* Dec 28 (1970): 5.

"From now on..." – Evan Hunter, *Me and Hitch* (London: Faber & Faber, 1997): 19.

"Didn't want..." – Steve Swires (1986) ibid p28.

"In Hollywood that means..." – Barry Norman, 'Why Mr. Taylor (No Relation) Likes Working with Liz,' *Daily Mail* Feb 8 (1963).

"Mr. Taylor can't you see..." – Evan Hunter, ibid p58.

"Too much time..." – Steve Swires, ibid p28.

"Didn't get the kind of heat..." – 'Writing *The Birds*: A Talk with Evan Hunter,' *Scenario 5 No. 2 http://www.scenariomag.com/archives/v5n2/birds_talk.html* accessed on Aug 4, 2004.

"No depth..." – Peter Bogdanovich, *Who the Devil Made It?* (New York: Ballantine Books, 1997): 536.

"Perverse ode..." – Camille Paglia, *The Birds* (London: BFI, 1998): 7.

"Showing off..." – Paglia, ibid p39.

"The private interactions..." – Paglia, ibid p45.

"Any particular..." – Steve Swires, ibid p29.

"A magnificent piece..." – *All About the Birds*, d/w Laurent Bouzereau (Universal Studios, 2000).

"I couldn't keep up..." –Don Groves, 'The Many Facets of Rough Diamond Rod Taylor,' *TV Times* Dec 18 (1976): 10.

"I love Anita..." – Louella Parsons, 'Hollywood's Lonely Bachelor,' *LAHE* Dec 2 (1962): 1.

"Movies are more rewarding..." – 'Vignette of Rod Taylor,' *A Gathering of Eagles PB* (Universal Studios, 1963): 6.

Contract with Universal: *R-L* Apr (1963): 6. Telegram Rod Taylor to Alfred Hitchcock Productions May 22, 1962 AHF.

A Gathering of Eagles: Delbert Mann, *Looking Back... At Live Television & Other Matters* (Los Angeles: DGA, 1998), *A Gathering of Eagles PB* (Universal Studios, 1963), 'Top Rental Features of 1963,' *Var* Jan 8 (1964): 71.

"Two buddies in love..." – Mann ibid p293

"Such inspiring sights..." – 'Production Notes,' *A Gathering of Eagles PB* ibid p4.

A Gathering of Eagles reviews: *Newsweek* Jul 22 (1963), *Time* Jul 22 (1963): 80, *F&F* Aug (1963): 31, Le May in Mann ibid p295, *Var* Jun 5 (1963), *LAHE* Jul 4 (1963).

Post-*Gathering of Eagles* projects: Hedda Hopper, 'Shirley MacLaine Lauded for "Seesaw,"' *LAT* Sept 22 (1962): C7, John L Scott, 'Teaming of Schell, MacLaine Project,' *LAT* Jul 13 (1962): D13.

Ordeal of Dr Shannon: 'Cronin "Shannon's Way" To Be Made in London As NBC-Dupont Entry,' *Var* Oct 3 (1962): 29, *Var* Dec 19 (1962).

Chapter 7: At MGM 1963-65

MGM in the 60s: Gene Arneel, 'Hero Today, Gone Tomorrow: Joe Vogel Out as Metro Chief,' *Var* Jan 16 (1963): 3, 'Prez O'Brien Ads Vex Levin Corpn,' *Var* Jan 18 (1967): 4, Eddie Kalish, 'Weitman Details Metro Production,' *Var* Apr 1 (1964): 4.

"They're building me…" – Hedda Hopper interview with Rod Taylor Mar 24, 1965. Notes p 2. HHC.

The VIPs: *Var* Apr 24 (1963): 3, Sam Kashner, 'A First Class Affair,' *Vanity Fair* Jul (2003): 110.

"Oh my god…" & "every day I phone…" – Barry Norman, 'Why Mr. Taylor (No Relation) Likes Working with Liz,' *Daily Mail* Feb 8 (1963).

"Bar bells…" – Kashner, ibid p120 .

"If you stood…" – Kashner, ibid p122.

"Our modest Aussie…" – Charles Tingwell & Peter Wilmoth, ibid p155.

"Very fond…" – Peter Bogdanovich & Orson Welles, *This Is Orson Welles*, Ed Jonathan Rosenbaum (London; Harper Collins, 1993): 269.

"The first authentic…" – 'Home With £125,000 Contract,' *Daily Mirror* Aug 31 (1963): 2.

"With thick-lensed…" – Alexander Walker, 'It's Only a Movie, Ingrid,' (London: Headline, 1988): 91.

The VIPs **release & reception**: *Time* Oct 4 (1963): 122, *Var* Aug 14 (1963): 6, *LAT* Sept 13 (1963), *HR* Aug 13 (1963): 3, *F&F* Oct (1963): 22, 'Top Rental Films of 1963,' *Var* Jan 8 (1964): 37, *Var* Mar 11 (1964): 4.

The Yellow Rolls Royce: *Var* May 6 (1964): 26.

Sunday in New York: Hedda Hopper, 'Looking at Hollywood,' *CDT* Nov 14 (1961): B7, '7 Arts "Sunday" Play Buy,' *Var* Jan 31 (1962): 18, *Var* Mar 20 (1963): 26, '7 Arts Developing Muscle,' *Var* Jul 18 (1962): 3, Gavin Lambert, *Natalie Wood: A Life* (New York: Knopf, 2004): 191, 'Big Rental Pictures of 1964,' *Var* Jan 5 (1965): 39.

"I have nine films…" – Barry Norman, 'Why Mr. Taylor (No Relation) Likes Working with Liz,' *Daily Mail* Feb 8 (1963).

"Look, I've got…" – Terry Clifford, 'Rod Taylor, Too, Denis the Spy Spoof,' *CT* Oct 26 (1966): B7.

"Showing my affection…" – Mike Connolly, 'Rod Taylor – Conversation with a Puzzled Husband.,' *Modern Screen* Jul (1965): 87.

Sunday in New York **reviews**: *HR* Dec 18 (1963): 3, *Var* Dec 18 (1963): 6.

Mary Hilem marriage: Hedda Hopper, 'Romance Makes Star Forgetful,' *LAT* Dec 14 (1962): D15, Liz Ploger, 'Meet Mary Hilem Taylor,' *R-L* Apr (1964). 20, Liz Ploger, 'Jun Bride and Groom,' *R-L* Oct (1963): 9,

"Hottest bachelors…" – Sara Hamilton, 'Inside Stuff.' *PH* Feb (1962): 7.

"Seems to have inherited…" – Jacqueline Divine, 'Hollywood Diary.,' *LITV* May 18-24 (1963): 7.

"American women…" – Hedda Hopper, 'He's Sick of People Who Want Only Stardom,' *LAT* Apr 15 (1962): M9.

"The sweet smell…" – Rod Taylor, 'Success No Perfume for Women – Rod,' *CT* Mar 11 (1964): B3.

"If you go back to…" – Jane Ardmore, 'Look Who's in the Mood for Love,' *PH* Dec (1961): 50.

"When you go into…" – Louella Parsons & Harriet Parsons, 'Rod Knocks? Not Any More,' *LAHE* Oct 10 (1965): 1.

"Lord, what have I done…" – Rod Taylor & Jane Wilkie, 'Our Marriage Wasn't Made in Heaven,' *PH* Jun (1964): 79.

Circus World: *Var* May 8 (1963): 12, 'Rod Taylor Quits His New Film,' *SMH* Sept 26 (1963): 1. Pilar Wayne, *John Wayne: My Life with the Duke* (London: McGraw Hill, 1987): 246.

"Rod felt that…" & "We could have held him…" – 'Rod Taylor Quits Epic Star Role,' *Evening News* Sept 25 (1963).

"Everybody understands…" – Hedda Hopper, 'Looking at Hollywood,' *CHT* Oct 5 (1963): C4.

Post-*Circus* **projects**: 'Rod writes,' *R-L* Oct (1963): 1, 'Letter from Liz and Pat,' *R-L* Oct (1963): 4. *Fate Is the Hunter*: 20th Century-Fox files at UCLA, 'Says Dick Zanuck: "Formula Pictures Now Dead-End,"' *Var* May 31 (1961): 15, 'Zanuck Clears 9 Properties to Go,' *Var* Oct 17 (1962): 4, 'Widmark in Hunter Deal,' *HR* Dec 2 (1963), Stephen M Silverman, *The Fox That Got Away* (Secaucus: Lyle Stuart, 1988): 323.

"I just coast…" – Dorothy Masters, 'Rod Taylor, Man's Man and a Woman's Man, Too,' *New York Daily News* Aug 16 (1964).

36 Hours: 'Rod Taylor handed a new MGM contract,' *LAT* Mar 27 (1964), *Var* Mar 11 (1964), 'Top Grossers of 1965,' *Var* Jan 5 (1966): 36.

"Been mature enough…" – Louella Parsons & Harriet Parsons, ibid p1.

"The ideal of a…" – 'Happily Married Actor, Rod Taylor, Describes "Ideal Marriage" as Myth,' *Evening Star News Culver City* Sept 8 (1966): 667.

Chapter 8: Riding the Tiger 1965 – 1966

Sean O'Casey: David Krause, *Sean O'Casey: the Man and his Work* (London: MacGibbon & Kee, 1960), Saros Cowasjee, *O'Casey* (Edinburgh: Oliver & Boyd, 1966).

Young Cassidy: Robert Graff's papers at Harvard University, 'Germs Fell John Ford,' *Var* Aug 5 (1964): 4, Stephen Watts, 'O'Casey in a Movie "Mirror,"' *NYT* Sept 27 (1964): X11, Letter Ginna to Ford Sept 9, 1964, 'Add "Cassidy" Mishaps,' *Var* Sept 1 (1964): 18, Marco Lopez 'Ireland and Young Cassidy,' *R-L* Apr (1965): 15, 'Interviewing Rod,' *R-L* Oct (1964): 5, Hedda Hopper, 'Rod Taylor, Ford Friends in Europe,' *LAT* Aug 1 (1964): C6.

"Rod Taylor has finally found…" – Hedda Hopper, 'Looking at Hollywood,' *CT* Apr 16 (1964): B8.

"A good, Irish…" – Howard Thompson, 'Up the Ladder from Down Under,' *NYT* Jul 19 (1964): X5.

"More than just…" – William Goyen, 'Jottings from a Dublin Journal,' *Show* Jan (1965): 48.

"I got her in…" – Howard Thompson, ibid pX5.

"An Australian…" – Vicky Roach, 'Back to Woop Woop,' *Sun Herald (Time Out)* Aug 9 (1998): 10.

"His mind was clear…" Scott Eyman, *Print the Legend: The Life and times of John Ford* (New York: Simon & Schuster, 1999): 516.

Rod's Ford crying anecdote in Michael Tunison, 'Life with Pappy,' *Movie Maker Magazine Issue # 44 http://www.moviemaker.com/issues/44/ford.html* accessed on May 13, 2005.

"Some Irish bullshit…" – Eyman, ibid p516.

"Warned me that…" – Justin Bowyer, *Conversations with Jack Cardiff* (London: BT Batsford, 2003): 188.

"With an intelligent actor…" – Stephen Watts, 'O'Casey in a Movie 'Mirror,"' *NYT* Sept 27 (1964): X11.

"Rod's fundamental gift…" – Philip Bradford, 'Don't spare the Rod,' *Film Review* Apr (1965): 6.

"It took this poor…" – Peter Bogdanovich, *John Ford.* (London: Studio Vista, 1968): 106.

"So heartbreaking…" – letter Ginna to Ford Sept 9, 1964. For Rod's claim that he rewrote the ending, see Eyman ibid p517.

Birth of Felicia: 'Hi!!! I'm Felicia Rodrica Sturt Taylor,' *R-L* Oct (1964): 9.

"There's no doubt…" – Louella Parsons & Harriet Parsons, 'Rod Knocks? Not Any More,' *LAHE* Oct 10 (1965): 1.

"With a lot of love…" – Matt White, 'Taylor Tells of Love,' *Daily Mirror* May 24 (1983).

Ford vs Cardiff: 'Twenty Questions,' *Films and Filming* Jun (1965): 16, 'Critics Guessing Game,' *Var* Mar 24 (1965): 4, Jack Cardiff, *Magic Hour* (London: Faber & Faber, 1996): 236, shooting schedule dated Jun 9, 1964 in Graff's papers.

Young Cassidy **reviews**: *Var* Mar 3 (1965): 7, *NYT* Feb 23 (1965): 35, *New Yorker* Mar 27 (1965): 169-170, *Newsweek* Mar 22 (1965): 97A, *New Republic* Mar 27 (1965): 29-30, *Cosmo* May 1965, *Citizen News* Apr 14 (1965), Richard Watts Jnr, 'Two on the Aisle,' *New York Post* Apr 25 (1965) Ent 4, Brooks Atkinson, 'Critic at Large,' *NYT*, Apr 6 (1965): 36. In his autobiography Michael Redgrave described Rod as "an excellent actor if a trifle too robust for the part." Michael Redgrave, *In My Mind's Eye: An Autobiography* (London: Weidenfeld & Nicholson, 1983): 200. **Release**: *HR* Jan 29 (1965), *Var* May 19 (1965): 8.

"Best film…" – Ginna interview.

Fifth Coin: telegram Rodlor Inc to Alfred Hitchcock legal department on Nov 4 & 13, 1964, AHC.

Do Not Disturb: 20th Century Fox's files at UCLA, '20th's Doris Day Encore Set on BO Strength of "Move Over, Darling" Coin,' *Var* Jul 29 (1964): 4, *Var* Mar 23 (1965), *Var* Jan 4 (1967): 8. Stephen M Silverman, *The Fox That Got Away* (Secaucus: Lyle Stuart, 1988): 324. Mike O'Connor's casting see *HR* Dec 26 (1963).

"I thought, 'What…" & "most interesting, fun…" – Louella Parsons & Harriet Parsons, ibid.

Fred Hakim: *This Is Your Life* notes, Lee Robinson papers at NFSA.

The Liquidator: Harris' casting see Michael Feeney Callan, *Richard Harris: A Sporting Life* (London: Pan Books, 1992): 112.

"He liked working…" – Hedda Hopper interview with Rod Mar 24, 1965 p 6 of notes in HHC.

"Bring me some tea…" – Marco Lopez, 'Ireland and Young Cassidy,' *R–L* Apr (1965): 16.

"A Hollywood great…" – John Le Mesurier, *A Jobbing Actor* (London: Elm Tree Books, 1984): 100.

"Complete Yank…" – Ray Barrett & Peter Corris, *Ray Barrett: An Autobiography* (Sydney: Random House, 1995): 82.

"Pulling the…" – Clifford Terry, 'Rod Taylor, Too, Denis the Spy Spoof,' *CT* Oct 26 (1966): B7.

"These parties I attend…" – Mike Connolly, 'Rod Taylor – Conversation with a Puzzled Husband,' *Modern Screen* Jul (1965): 87.

Liquidator **legal troubles**: Justin Bowyer, *Conversations with Jack Cardiff* (London: BT Batsford, 2003): 190, 'MGM Sue Over "Liquidator" By 2 English Firms,' *DR* Dec 21 (1965), '"Liquidator" Suits Filed,' *HR* Dec 21 (1965), 'MGM Faces 3 Suits On Liquidator Rights,' *The Film Daily* Dec 21 (1965), Murphy, AD '"Liquidator" in Litigation, So Not in Release,' *DR* Feb 3 (1966), 'Metro Loses Case re "Liquidator,"' *Var* Feb 6 (1966): 29.

"If it had…" – Justin Bowyer, ibid p190.

Liquidator **release**: 'MGM's 27 Finished Features Gives it Exceptional Long Market Slotting,' *Var* Jun (16): 1965: 5, 'End Litigation Over "Liquidator"; MG Global Distrib,' *DR* Jul 31 (1966)'Big Rental Pictures of 1966,' *Var* Jan 4 (1967): 8. **Reviews**: *Newsday* Oct 31 (1966), *Var* Aug 31 (1966): 6, *Time* Oct 21 (1966): 121.

The Glass Bottom Boat: Army Archerd, 'Just for Variety,' *Var* Sept 3 (1965), 'Rod Bags Wild Boar Charging at Friend,' *Los Angeles Herald* Sept 16 (1965): C6, Marco Lopez, 'A Happy Island Called Catalina,' *R–L* Oct (1965): 21.

"The best pro…" – Clifford Terry, 'Rod Taylor, Too, Denis the Spy Spoof,' *CT* Oct 26 (1966): B7

"The most gentle, unselfish…" – Louella & Harriet Parsons, ibid.

The Glass Bottom Boat **reviews**: *Var* Apr 20 (1966), *NYT* Jun 10 (1966): 54, *HR* Apr 20 (1966): 3.

"The metamorphosis…" – Hedda Hopper, 'Rod Taylor Ex-Maverick, Learns a New Kind of Life,' *LAT* May 23 (1965): 010.

"An imaginative man of action…" – David Shipman, *The Great Movie Stars: The International Years* (London: Angus & Robertson, 1972): 505.

"I'm the type…" – Hedda Hopper, 'Hedda Hopper's Hollywood,' *CT-NY* May 23 (1965): 1

"Fair haired boy…" – Hedda Hopper, 'Looking at Hollywood,' *CT* Oct 4 (1965): B8.

"Brilliant beeping…" – Don Groves, 'The many facets of Rough Diamond Rod Taylor,' *TV Times* Dec 18 (1976): 10.

Possible roles: *Dr Zhivago*: According to Lean's biographer, Kevin Brownlow, the idea of Rod as Zhivago "sounds like an idea of MGM's rather than of Lean's" and he never came across Rod's name in researching the making of the film (letter to author Jul 11, 2004). However, Julie Christie was cast in the film partly on the basis of a plug from John Ford following her work in *Young Cassidy*. Kevin Brownlow, *David Lean* (London: Richard Cohen Books, 1996). *Caravans*: 'Anatole de Grunwald sets a Range of Pix Following "Caravans,"' *Var* Mar 17

(1965): 17, 'Courageous Rod Taylor..,' *Newark Evening News* Mar 21 (1965), 'Liz Writes,' *R-L* Apr (1965): 4, Hedda Hopper 'Hedda Hopper,' *LAT* Nov 22 (1965): D22, 'Yank-Iran Co-Prod "Caravans," a \$12 Million Test of Country's Effort to Build a Film Industry,' *Var* Dec 28 (1977). *Planet of the Apes:* Brian Pendleigh, *Legend of the Planet of the Apes* (London: Boxtree, 2001): 32. *Owl and the Pussycat:* Hedda Hopper, 'Hedda Hopper,' *LAT* Apr 5 (1965): D14. *The Man Who Would Be King:* 'Earthy Gals Send Rod Reeling,' *New York World-Telegraph & Sun* Jul 10 (1965). *William the Conqueror:* Letter Page Buckey to HH dated Dec 18, 1964. HHC, Hedda Hopper, 'Wayne Likely to Star in "Unvanquished,"' *LAT* Dec 23 (1964): C6. *Last Bus to Banjo Creek:* 'Interviewing Rod,' *R-L* Apr (1965): 8, HH Wilson, 'The Skedule' in *Australian Signpost: An Anthology* Ed TAG Hungerford (Melbourne: FW Cheshire, 1956): 251, Ted Willis, *Evening All* (London: Macmillan, 1991): 198, Letter Page Buckey to HH dated Dec 18, 1964. HHC, 'Film of Story to be Made In SA,' Nov 16, 1965 – n/d n/pd Helen Wilson papers at National Library of Australia, 'Sydney Box's \$10 mill Prod Program,' *Var* Jan 26 (1966).

Chapter 9: The Hollywood Peak 1966–68

Hotel: Warner Bros archives at USC, 'Big Rental Films of 1967,' *Var* Jan 3 (1968): 25, 'US Film's Share-of-Market Profile,' *Var* May 12 (1971): 205.

"It was one of those…" Rui Nogueira, 'Wendell Mayes.' *Backstory 3: Interviews with Screenwriters of the 60s.* Ed Patrick McGilligan. (Berkeley: University of California, 1997): 266.

"He's the kind of man…" – 'Actor Taylor Advises on Sparing the Rod,' *Hotel* PB (Warner Brothers, 1967): 3.

"The re-incarnation…" – Don Groves, ibid p11. For Oberon's "Australian" ancestry see Charles Higham & Roy Moseley, *Princess Merle: The Romantic Life of Merle Oberon* (New York: Coward-McCann, 1983) & the documentary *The Trouble With Merle* (ABC, 2002).

"Not really a vote…" – Karl Malden with Carla Malden *When Do I Start?* (New York: Proscenium Publishers Inc, 1997): 300.

"I was so restricted…" – Don Groves, ibid p10.

"In *Hotel* we're…" – Rex Reed, "'I Am – How You Say? – A Smart Kid,'" *NYT* Jun 12 (1966): D13

Chuka: Richard Jessup, *Chuka* (Greenwich: Fawcett Publications, 1961), production files for the film in Paramount collection MHL including deal memo between Rodlor and Paramount dated Apr 1, 1966.

"Hooked…" – 'Producer-Star Rod Taylor Shuns Clichés,' *Chuka PB* (Paramount, 1967).

"A part that's…" – 'A New Phase in Rod Taylor's Career Begins with Chuka,' *Chuka PB* (Paramount, 1967): 3.

"Never honestly knew…" & "rewrite big chunks…" – Dorothy Manners, 'Success Unspoils Rod Taylor,' *New York World Journal Tribune* Jan 22 (1967): 7.

Attempt to get credit: Paramount inter office memos in *Chuka* Paramount files at MHL including memo Elene Whitman to Mary Dorfman of WGA West dated Dec 14, 1966.

"Another actor's…" – Philip K Scheuer, 'Mills: Patriarch of Acting Family,' *LAT* Dec 6 (1966): D22.

"Brought home…" – Bill Davidson, ibid p20.

"Try his hand…" – 'A New Phase in Rod Taylor's Career Begins with Chuka,' *Chuka PB* (Paramount, 1967): 3.

Chuka **release**: 'Evans "Sleeping Giant Now Awake": Par's Hollywood Product'n Pep Rally,' *Var* Jan 25 (1967): 3. **Reviews**: Richard Shickel, 'Deftly Taylored Epic of Cavalry and Indians,' *Life* Sept 29 (1967), *Var* April 19 (1967).

Dark of the Sun: 'Ranald MacDougall Sez: Better Scout Locations Before Making Decisions,' *Var* Nov 4 (1964): 15, 'George Englund on Art of Negotiation,' *Var* May 26 (1965), *Dark of the Sun PB* (MGM, 1968), Jack Cardiff, *Magic Hour* (London: Faber & Faber, 1997).

"My God I wonder…" & "there was a lot…" – Justin Bowyer, ibid p188.

"Was rather lax…" & "All the time…" – Kenneth More, *More or Less* (London: Hodder & Stoughton, 1978): 207-208.

"We were all at each…" - Sally K Brass, 'Rod Adds Authenticity to Aussie Film' *LAT* Sept 15 (1968): 58.

"I rewrite everything…" – Charles Higham, 'Rod Taylor just loathes seagulls,' *SMH* Sept 14 (1968): Weekend mag 18.

"Appeared to hate each other…" – More ibid p208.

"I never had…" – Justin Bowyer, ibid p190.

"Pounding tables…," "if this means…" & "I played…" – Sheilah Graham, 'Rod Taylor Refuses to Shake Off Movie,' *Newark Evening News* Jun 17 (1967): 8.

Dark of the Sun reviews: *Var* Feb 14 (1968): 16, *Spectator* Feb 16 (1968), *Time* Jul 26 (1968), *Daily Express* Feb 9 (1968), *The Times* Feb 8 (1968), *Sun* Feb 7 (1968), *LAT* Aug 21 (1968), *Commonweal* Aug 23 (1968), *NYT* Jul 4 (1968): 13. **Box office:** 'Big Rental Films of 1968,' *Var* Jan 8 (1969): 15, 'Computer Tally of 729 Films, 1968,' *Var* May 7 (1969): 34. **Tarantino screening:** Harry Knowles, 'QT5: Guys on a Mission War Films,' *http://www.aint-it-cool-news.com/display.cgi?id=9985* Aug 24, 2001.

Chapter 10: Star Decline II 1968-70

"Rod is a blinding…" – Jim Murphy, 'No airs and graces, but… Rod's "Bound For No. 1 Stardom,"' *LITV* Sept 21-27 (1968): 3.

"I'd like to show…" – Sally K Brass, 'Rod Adds Authenticity to Aussie Film,' *LAT* Sept 15 (1968): 25.

"I'm up to here with it…" Charles Higham, 'Rod Taylor just loathes seagulls,' *SMH* Sept 14 (1968) Weekend magazine 18.

The Hell with Heroes: Stanley Chase papers at UCLA, Hedda Hopper, 'Looking at Hollywood,' *CT* Nov 15 (1965): C6, 'Rod Taylor, Star of *The Hell with Heroes*, Keeps Portable Room-Office on Set,' *The Hell with Heroes publicity sheet* (Universal, 1968), 'Computer Tally of 729 Films, 1968,' *Var* May 7 (1969): 34. In Rod's defence, apparently he was reluctant to do the film – Sheilah Graham ibid.

"Programmer…" – *Var* Aug 14 (1968).

Other films: 'Family Act for Rod,' *Citizen News* Aug 5 (1967), Betty Martin, 'Movie Call Sheet,' *LAT* Nov 22 (1967): C7.

Marriage break-up: Mike Connolly, 'Rod Taylor – Conversation with a Puzzled Husband,' *Modern Screen* Jul (1965): 49, 'Our Marriage Wasn't Made in Heaven,' *PH* Jun (1964): 43, Louella Parsons, 'Rod Taylor's Having Problems,' *LAHE* Dec 3 (1964): F10, 'Rod Taylor Sues Wife for Divorce,' *LAHE* Jun 28 (1968), 'Divorce for Rod Taylor, Cause – Movie Kissing,' *LAHE* Sept 17 (1969).

"If she saw a film…" – 'Rod Taylor Sheds His Wife,' *New York Post* Sept 18 (1969).

"Spider Lady…" – *New York Daily News* Nov 28 (1971): 51.

"A very poor model…" James Bradford, 'How Rod Taylor Muscled in on Hollywood,' *TV Times* Aug 4 (1973): 11.

Mary Hilem obituary – see Jason Schultz, 'International model helped support victims of domestic violence', *Palm Beach Post,* Mar 10 (2009).

"Dunno where..." – Andrew L Urban, 'Not Like a Phoney,' *Urban Cinefile* (1998), *http://www.ur-bancinefile.com.au/scripts/cinefile/Interviews.idc?Article_ID=1419* accessed May 17, 2005.

"Love to as many..." – Steve Dunleavy, 'Rod Taylor Takes Over Where Errol Left Off,' *Melbourne Herald* Jun 24 (1972): 5.

"The dialogue...," "I've been a..." & "when I heard..." – Sally Brass, 'Rod Adds Authenticity to Aussie Film,' *LAT* Sept 15 (1968): 25.

"Saw some other guys..." – 'That Night with Zsa Zsa,' *Daily Mirror* Sept 10 (1968): 1. See also 'Party Punch,' *Var* Aug 28 (1968): 2.

The High Commissioner **reviews:** *NYT* Dec 12 (1986): 62, *Citizen News* Sept 27 (1968), *HR* Sept 25 (1968): 14, *Var* Aug 28 (1968): 6. **Box office:** Lee Beaupre, 'ABC Films Results: 30 of 36 In Red; Total Loss $47 Mil,' *DR* May 31 (1973): 3.

"That we've got..." – Brass, ibid p25.

"Charged..." & "the graffiti adjectives..." – Dennis Minogue, ibid.

Australian visit: Marguerite Davies, 'Rod Taylor flies in with ideas for our film industry,' *The Australian* Sept 11 (1968): 3, 'Rod Taylor enjoyed his gala film show,' *SMH* Sept 13 (1968): 15.

Australian projects: John Messer, 'Rod Taylor,' How about dinkum Aussie film?,' *The Age* Sept 14 (1968): 3, 'Rod Taylor weights offers for 5 Pix in Native Land,' *Var* Nov 20 (1968).

"The graffiti..." & "even with my..." – 'That Night with Zsa Zsa,' *Daily Mirror*, Sept 10 (1968): 2.

"I think the government..." – Ron Saw, 'Rod Taylor? Worth a dollar any day,' *DT* Sept 11 (1968): 6

"Of course anything I do here..." & "I'm going to go to Canberra..." – Charles Higham, ibid.

"They change the title..." – Jim Murphy, ibid.

"It's about a mod, wealthy..." – Charles Higham, ibid.

Zabriskie Point: Beverly Walker, 'Michelangelo and the Leviathan: The Making of *Zabriskie Point*,' *Film Comment* Vol 28 No 5 Sept (1992): 36, *Zabriskie Point PB* (MGM, 1970).

"20,000..." – Lawrence M Benskey, 'Antonioni Comes to the Point,' *NYT* Dec 15 (1968): D23.

"It is a film about..." – 'Ponti, Antonioni in NY,' *Var* May 1, 1968.

"The characters are only..." – Louise Sweeney, "Zabriskie Lives!" *Show* Feb (1970): 42.

"In Blow Up..." – Marsha Kinder, 'Zabriskie Point,' *Sight & Sound* Winter (1968-69): 20.

"Had to be in..." – 'Rod Taylor 'discovered,' *Zabriskie Point publicity release* (MGM, 1969).

"Surprise casting development..." – 'Antonioni's Pick of Rod Taylor as Lead,' *Var* Sept 11 (1968): 4.

"Fellini bores me..." Clifford Terry, 'Rod Taylor, Too, Denis the Spy Spoof,' *CT* Oct 26 (1966): B7.

"I think many of the so-called..." – 'Rod Taylor and Jim Brown Tear at Each Other in "Dark of the Sun,"' *Dark of the Sun PB* (MGM, 1968): 3.

"The basis of human..." – Guy Austin, ibid p5.

"It's high time we got back..." – Dorothy Manners, 'No Nude Centrefolds for Rod Taylor,' *LAHE* May 13 (1973).

"Cut off..." – Guy Flatley, 'Antonioni defends "Zabriskie Point,"' *NY Times* Feb 22 (1970): D15.

"Because this story could..." – Marsha Kinder, ibid p30.

MGM troubles: Peter Bart, *Fade Out: The Calamitous Final Days of MGM* (New York: Doubleday, 1990), 'When fiscal telescopes train on old Hollywood glamour, they seem to pick up only one – MGM,' *Var* Jul 30 (1969): 4.

"A good actor..." – n/p Mar (1970): 13 see *Zabriskie Point* clippings file at the New York Public Library.

"Commies..." – Louise Sweeney, ibid p81.

Zabriskie Point **Mann Act Issue:** 'Mann Act Charge on MGM Pic,' *HR* May 26 (1969): 1, Ray Loynd, 'Grand Jury Probes Movie Orgy Scene,' *LAT* Jun 23 (1969) Part IV 18, James Powers, 'Sacramento Jury Hears "Zabriskie" Witnesses,' *HR* Jun 2 (1969): 1, 'MGM Sees "2001" Kinship for "Zabriskie,"' *Var* Feb 18 (1970): 7, 'US Films Share-of-Market Profile,' *Var* May 12 (1971): 182, 'MGM Write Downs & Burn Ups,' *Var* Apr 22 (1970): 5. **Reviews:** *NYT*

Feb 10 (1970): 47, *Var* Feb 11 (1970): 16, *The New Yorker* Feb (1970), *Time* Feb 23 (1970).
Reception: 'Festival Focus on Taste Gaps, *Var* May 6 (1970): 2. 'Noble Failures,' *Premiere* Aug
(1998): 81. Harry & Michael Medved, *The 50 Worst Films of All Time* (New York: Warner
Books, 1978). **Mark Frechette:** Dave O'Brian, 'Mark Frechette: A Manipulated Life,' *The
Boston Phoenix* Oct 7 (1975): 9 at *http://www.trussel.com/lyman/frech4.htm* accessed Oct 8,
2003. 'Jailed Actor Directs a Play,' *Var* Feb 19 (1975): 2.

The Last Revolution: 'Revolution,' *NYT* Sept 22 (1968): D35.

The Man Who Had Power Over Women: *The Man Who Had Power Over Women PB* (Avco Embassy,
1970), 'US Film's Share-of-Market Profile,' *Var* May 12 (1972): 122, **Reviews:** *F&F* Feb
(1971): 53, *Var* Oct 28 (1970): 26, *NYT* Mar 4 (1971): 28.

"Don't shoot or punch up...." & "let's face it..." – 'Taylor: 'I ain't no Gable,'" *PH* Oct (1969): 36.

Darker Than Amber: John D MacDonald Papers (JDMP), Dept of Special & Area Studies
Collections, George A Smathers Libraries, University of Florida, *Darker Than Amber PB*
(National General, 1970).

"Not enough..." – Letter JDM to Jack Reeves Jun 28, 1967 JDMP.

"Maybe too squat...." Letter JDM to Dan Rowan Oct 8, 1968 in *A Friendship: The Letters of Dan
Rowan and John D MacDonald 1967-1974* (New York: Fawcett Gold Medal 1986): 106

"I like the guy..." – Letter to Harry Mines Nov 1, 1969. JDMP.

"Who gets knocked...." – Charles Higham, ibid.

"Probably gave me..." – Lana Wells, 'The New Flynn,' *Melbourne Herald* Sept 26 (1970): 6.

"The best..." – Louis Paul 'William Smith: Tougher Than Leather,' *http://www.trashvideo.com.
au/Trash%20Confidential/William%20Smith.htm* accessed Sept 7, 2004. *Darker Than Amber*
Reviews: *Los Angeles Herald* Aug 26 (1970), *HR* Aug 12 (1970).

"utterly rotten..." – JDM, *A Friendship*, ibid p201.

"Personal friction" – Letter JDM to Donald Farber Apr 21, 1971. JDMP.

Chapter 11: Stardom Sunset 1971-73

Rod's accident: *Var* Aug 5 (1970), *LAT* Aug 30 (1970).

Hollywood: Jim Hillier, *The New Hollywood* (London: Studio Vista, 1993): 6. Thomas Schatz, 'The
New Hollywood,' in *Film Theory Goes to the Movies*, ed. Jim Collins, Hilary Radner & Ava
Preacher Collins (New York, London: Routledge, 1993): 15. **Michael Caine's theory:** *What's
It All About?* (London: Century, 1992): 242. **French Connection:** Judy Klemesrud, 'A Cops and
Crooks Movie That Doesn't Cop Out... And the Actor It Makes a Star,' *NYT* Nov 21 (1971):
D15. **Harrow Alley:** 'Let George Do It,' *NYT* Jan 2 (1972): 41. Chris Gore, *50 Greatest Movies
Never Made* (New York: St. Marks, 1999): 101. **Slocum, Burke and Wills:** Lana Wells, 'The new
Flynn,' *Melbourne Herald* Sept 26 (1970): 6. **Buffalo Man:** *Var* Nov 25 (1970): 25, *Var* Jan 6
(1971): 27.

Bearcats!: Bill Davidson, 'Why Can't Rod Taylor Be a Pussycat?,' *TVG* Feb 23-29 (1971): 16,
'1971-72 Network Primetime Season at a Glance,' *Var* Sept 15 (1971): 37, 'TV Still Counting
on Stars,' *Var* Apr 26 (1972): 1. **Reviews:** *NYT* Sept 17 (1971): L85, *Var* Sept 22 (1971), *LAT*
Sept 16 (1971): H22.

"An interesting and funny..." – Davidson, ibid p16.

"If you've got to..." – Kay Gardella, 'He-Man Aussie Rod Taylor to Star in New TV Series,' *New
York Daily News* Sept 1 (1971).

"Equating him... "- Bill Davidson ibid p16.

"I need the bread..." – *New York Daily News* Nov 28 (1971): 51.

"An older..." – Don Groves, ibid p11.

"Didn't want…" – Ronald L Davis, *Duke: the Life & Image of John Wayne* (Norman: Uni of Oklahoma, 1998): 301.

"It was a misunderstanding…" – Steve Dunleavy, 'Rod Taylor: Last of the Hollywood Hellrasiers,' *Coronet* Sept (1972): 8.

"Taking it easy…" – Steve Dunleavy, "Rod Taylor Takes Over Where Errol Left Off" *Melbourne Herald* Jun 24 (1972): 5.

"Success came through…" – James Bradford, 'How Rod Taylor Muscled in on Hollywood,' *TV Times* Aug 4 (1973): 11.

The Train Robbers reviews: *NYT* Feb 8 (1973): 36, *HR* Jan 30 (1973): 3. **Box office**: 'Top Films For 1st Half of '73,' *Var* Jul 25 (1973): 14.

The Heroes: *Var* Apr 26 (1972): 26, *Var* Jul 6 (1972): 28.

"Cross between…" – 'Bini Chooses UA Deal on 'Heroes'; 2d Pact Pending,' *Var* Sept 13 (1972): 3.

The Heroes reviews: *London Observer* Feb 17 (1974): 31, *F&F* Apr (1974): 47.

Family Flight: *Var* Oct 24 (1973): 42, 'Made-For-TV Movie Rankings For 1972-73,' *Var* Oct 24 (1973): 42.

"What Rod Taylor has…" – David Shipman, *The Great Movie Stars: The International Years* (London: Angus & Robertson, 1972): 504.

"When I started…" – Bradford, ibid at p11.

The Contact: 'Rod Taylor joins Maurice Silverstein in production deal,' *HR* Oct 26 (1972), '4 Rod Taylor Pix with Silverstein,' *Var* Oct 25 (1972), 'Silverstein to Shoot Pic in Aussie,' *Var* Dec 6 (1972): 27, Jack Percival, 'Rod Taylor in $1m Film,' *Sun Herald* Nov 19 (1972): 3. 'Financing Delay Shifts Silverstein's' Proposed Aussie Pic Elsewhere,' *Var* Dec 20 (1972): 6

Trader Horn: Peter Bart, *Fade Out: The Calamitous Final Days of MGM* (New York: Doubleday, 1990), *Trader Horn* PB (MGM, 1973), 'Var chart summary for 1973,' *Var* May 8 (1974): 244. **Reviews**: *LAT* Jun 13 (1973): G24, *Var* Jun 13 (1973): 16.

"An honest…" – Dorothy Manners, 'No Nude Centrefolds for Rod Taylor,' *LAHE* May 13 (1973).

"Probably one of…" & "it hit on all the themes…" – Samuel Fuller, *A Third Face: My Tale of Writing, Fighting & Filmmaking* (New York: Alfred A Knopf, 2002): 456.

"Lost the plot" – John Glenn, *For My Eyes Only* (Virginia: Brasseys, 2001): 75.

"Production difficulties…" – Molly Johnson, 'Warner Bros Drops 'Riata,'' *LAT* Dec 30 (1972).

The Deadly Trackers: 'Musicians Asking 25G from WB for "Trackers" Score,' *Var* Feb 13 (1974), Lee Beaupre, 'Fred Steiner Wins Divorce From "Trackers" Music Credit,' *HR* Nov 23 (1973)

All Rod's quotes on film from Michael Feeney Callan, *Richard Harris: A Sporting Life* (London: Pan Books, 1992): 175. Michael Economou says that Rod wrote the scene where his character visits his daughter and breaks down and cries, as well as the scene where Neville Brand has rail road on his arm and where Rod's character talks about his father.

"Not a single line…" – Lee Beaupre, 'WB Refuses Pleas of Heller to Take Name Off "Deadly,"' *HR* Nov 20 (1973): 1.

"Completely lobotomized…" – Fuller, ibid, 461.

The Deadly Trackers reviews: *LAT* Nov 22 (1973), *Var* Nov 28 (1973): 14, *NYT* Dec 22 (1973): 11.

Chapter 12 – Small Screen Star II 1974 – 76

"saleable commodity…" – Nan Musgrove, 'Rod Taylor: from hell-raiser to quiet dignity,' *The Australian Women's Weekly* Nov 12 (1975): 5.

Partizan: 'Rod Taylor's Yugo Pic,' *Var* Dec 5 (1973): 6, 'Rod Taylor's Pair,' *Var* Oct 2 (1974): 3,

"We had…" – Dorothy Manners, 'Rod Taylor Back from Yugoslavian Filming,' *LAHE* Sept 8 (1974).

"Something close to love…" – Steve Dunleavy, "Rod Taylor Takes Over Where Errol Left Off" *Melbourne Herald* Jun 24 (1972): 5.

"Somebody must be..." – *HR* Dec 11 (1978): 17.

A Matter of Wife and Death: 'Made-For-TV Movie Rankings For 1974-75,' *Var* Oct 8 (1975): 54.

"Not holding my breath..." – Bob Williams, 'On the Air,' *New York Post* Mar 27 (1975): 47

The Oregon Trail pilot: 'Made-For-TV Movie Rankings For 1975-76,' *Var* Oct 6 (1976): 54. Review: *Var* Jan 14 (1976).

Blondy reviews: *L'Express* Jan 19-25 (1976): 8, *Le Point* Jan 19 (1976): 55.

"Too artsy..." – Dorothy Manners, ibid.

"Dog..." – Don Groves, 'The many facets of Rough Diamond Rod Taylor,' *TV Times* Dec 18 (1976): 11.

Last Bus to Banjo Creek 70s version: 'Rod Taylor in $1m Aust Film,' *The Sun* Jun 16 (1975). Lee Robinson papers at NFSA.

"Rewritten by some hack..." – 'Rod Taylor,' *Cinema Papers* Jan (1977): 247.

Treasure Seekers: *HR* Apr 8 (1975), *Var* Mar 3 (1976): 41, 'Rod Taylor,' *Cinema Papers* ibid.

"I do a lot..." – Julie Kusko, 'Wild Man Rod's a Stay-at-Home These Days!,' *TV Week* Nov 1 (1975): 7.

"Those bastards..." – Steve Swires, 'Rod Taylor – Outlaw Time Traveller,' *Starlog* May (1987): 25.

Walter Brough gets sole screenplay credit in the 1979 video release of the film, with credit for original story going to Paul C Ross. However this credit is clearly a late insert, being different in style from the rest of the credits.

"Because I don't..." & "you get together..." – Charles Champlin item dated Feb 27, 1973. From Charles Champlin collection, MHL.

"I just saw you..." – 'Matinee Idol,' *60 Minutes* Aug 30, 1998.

"Wined and dined..." & "there was something magical..." – Hal Jacques, 'Rod Taylor: It Took Me 3 Years of Going Steady to Find Out I Was Deeply in Love,' *National Enquirer* Nov 12 (1974): 41.

Chapter 13: Television 1976-1980

The Picture Show Man: Harry Robinson, 'Long day's journey into success,' *The Bulletin* Jan 17 (1978): 48, David Stratton *The Last New Wave* (London, Sydney: Angus & Robertson, 1980), 'Australian Film Budgets & Grosses,' *Var* May 10 (1978), Lyle Penn & Martin Long, *The Picture Show Man* (West Melbourne: Thomas Nelson, 1977).

"We thought that Rod..." – John Power interviewed by Mike Carlton, *AFTRS Open Program Resources Unit* (AFTRS, 1978).

"Significantly less..." – Walter Sullivan, 'Bid to Boost Local Films,' *DT* Oct 21 (1976): 17.

"John was wonderfully..." – Don Groves, 'The many facets of Rough Diamond Rod Taylor,' *TV Times* Dec 18 (1976): 10.

"The really good looking" – Don Groves, ibid p11.

"An angel to deal with..." – Don Groves, ibid p10.

"The part of Palmer..." – 'John Power,' *Cinema Papers* Jul (1976): 24.

"I can assure you..." – James Cunningham, 'Wran hitches wagon to a star...,' *SMH* Nov 8 (1976).

The Picture Show Man reviews: *Bulletin* May 14 (1977): 63, *National Times* May 16-21 (1977): 23, *Australian* Apr 30 (1977), *DT* May 13 (1977), *NYT* Oct 26 (1980): D26, *Var* Apr 13 (1977): 20, *Films in Review* quote u/d from files on *The Picture Show Man* at the Australian Film Institute.

Cultural cringe: N T Feather, 'Attitudes Towards the High Achiever: The Fall of the Tall Poppy,' *Australian Journal of Psychology* (Vol 41, 1989): 239, A A Phillips, *The Australian Tradition* (Melbourne: Cheshire, 1958). The notion of the cultural cringe has come under criticism – see LJ Hume, 'Another Look at the Cultural Cringe,' reprinted in *The Rathouse* Winter 2003 at *http://www.the-rathouse.com/Another_look_at_the_Cultural_Cringe.htm* accessed on Sept 1, 2006. Kenneth Minogue, 'Cultural Cringe – Cultural Inferiority Complex and Republicanism in Australia,' *National Review,* Dec 31, 1995.

"If Len had been like…" – Phillip Noyce & Frans Vandenburg, 'The scriptwriter: an Interview with Bob Ellis,' in Raffaele Caputo & Geoff Burton ed. *Third Take: Australian Filmmakers Talk* (Sydney: Allen & Unwin, 2002): 125.

"The beauty about being…" – Michaela Boland & Michael Bodey, *Aussiewood: Australia's Leading Actors and Directors Tell How they Conquered Hollywood* (Sydney: Allen & Unwin, 2005): 267.

Unfilmed Australian projects: Anthony Ginnane, 'Rod Taylor,' *Cinema Papers* Jan (1977): 244.

"I've heard about some…" – Walter Sullivan, 'Bid to Boost Local Films,' *DT* Oct 21 (1976): 17.

Utah ad: Barry Newman, 'Deluge Down Under,' *Wall Street Journal* Oct 2 (1980): 1, Leigh Bottrell, 'Rod's running all the way to the bank,' *DT* Nov 22 (1978): 6.

"Goosed…" – Phillip Cornford, 'Rod rips on roaring,' *The Australian* Dec 17 (1976).

The Oregon Trail **series:** '1977-78 Network Primetime Season at a Glance,' *Var* Sept 14 (1977): 73, '1977-78 Regular Series Ratings,' *Var* May 3 (1978), Bob Knight, 'NBC & CBS Pack Up Prime Time,' *Var* Nov 16 (1977): 55

"So we'll…" & "on expensive shows…" – Bob Williams, 'TV reads its way back for its new Westerns,' *New York Post* May 25 (1977): 51

"I believe this…"- *HR's TV Preview* Sept (1977): 55

The Oregon Trail **reviews:** *The HR's TV Preview* Sept (1977): 55, *Var* Sept 28 (1977)

"I always disagreed…" – Kay Gardella, 'Tough-talking Taylor hits the 'Oregon Trail,'' *New York Daily News* Sept 21 (1977): 85.

Cry of the Innocent: 'Made-For-TV Movie Rankings For 1979-80,' *Var* Sept 17 (1980): 64. **Review:** *NYT* Jun 19 (1980): C23

Tales of the Unexpected: Michael Billington, 'The Man Behind the 'Unexpected Tales,'' *NYT* Sept 30 (1979): D35.

"Every clever…" – Rosalie Horner, 'What's This About Men in Rod's life?,' *Daily Express* Mar 22 (1980).

"I wanted it to be…" – Andrew L Urban, 'Not Like a Phoney,' ibid.

A Time to Die: 'Almi Sued Over Release of '82 "Time To Die,"' *DR* Feb 26 (1985) 'Almi Pictures Hit with Breach of Contract Suit,' *Var* Mar 6 (1985). **Review:** *Var* Oct 19 (1983): 24.

"Awful director…" – Rob Lowing, 'Back to Woop Woop,' *Sun Herald (Time Out)* Aug 9 (1998): 9.

"They all thought…" – Roderick Barrand, 'A Star Is Born: How "Falcon Crest's" Jane Wyman Helped Rod Taylor,' n/p n/d p 33.

Chapter 14: The '80s: 1980-88

Hellinger's Law: *LAT* Mar 10 (1981): 8 part 6.

Jacqueline Bouvier Kennedy: – C Gerald Fraser, 'Portrait of a First Lady,' *NYT* Oct 11 (1981): Sec 2A p 3, *Var* Sept 29 (1982): 54, '"Jackie Kennedy" For Theatres,' *Var* Mar 24 (1982): 74. **Reviews:** *NYT* Oct 14 (1981): C31, *The Globe and Mail* Oct 12 (1981): 15.

Background to 10BA era: David Stratton, *The Avocado Plantation: boom and bust in the Australian film industry* (South Melbourne: MacMillan, 1990), 'Feature Film Production: Australian Features Since 1970,' *AFC http://www.afc.gov.au/gtp/mpfeatures1970.html* accessed June 1, 2006.

On the Run: Ray Loynd, 'Aussie connection turns Fisher Film to frugal reality,' *HR* Mar 9 (1982): 1, 'Brown returns to film production with "On the Run" and other prod'ns,' *HR* Mar 9 (1982), 'Rod is now a true blue Yank,' *DT* Jun 21 (1982): 18, 'Rod Taylor Escapes Death… Just,' *TV Week* Apr 17 (1982): 9. **Review:** *Var* Dec 19 (1983): 15.

"One moment…" – Robert Thomson, 'Hit-man makes a hit with Rod,' *The Herald* (Melb) Mar 3 (1982).

"Because I've just given up…" – Matt White, 'Taylor-made Hellraiser,' DT, May 24 (1983): 69.

Tax issue: *HR* (Aust) Apr 20 (1982), CJ McKenzie, '"Aussie" law hits new film,' *Sunday Telegraph* Apr 11 (1983): 13.

Charles and Di: Val Adams 'CBS' ratings carry the Di,' *New York Daily News* Sept 23 (1982): 117.

Masquerade: 'Network "Second Season" New Shows as a Glance,' *Var* Jan 4 (1984): 158, Tim Boxer, 'Rod Taylor: Back in the saddle,' *New York Post* Mar 30 (1984): 94, Leslie Bennetts, 'ABC Plans 8 New TV Series for Fall,' *NYT* May 1 (1984): C18. **Reviews:** *Women's Wear Daily* Dec 14 (1983), *Var* Dec 21 (1983), *New York Daily News* Dec 15 (1983): 138.

"A little…" – Ed Schiffer, Spies Like Us: Civilian Spooks,' *Wall St. Journal* Feb 6 (1984).

Marbella: 'Spanish Film Production,' *Var* May 7 (1986): 384.

"Even so…" – Steve Swires, 'Rod Taylor – Outlaw Time Traveller,' *Starlog* May (1987): 25.

Half Nelson: *Houston Chronicle* Mar 28 (1985): 6.

Mask of Murder: 'Swede Mattson Helming British-US Co production,' *Var* Mar 13 (1985): 40.

"I still…" – Matt White, ibid.

"I don't get offered…" – Steve Swires (1986) ibid p29.

The Outlaws: Dave Kaufman, '3 Webs Order 21 New Series,' *Var* Oct 22 (1986): 452.

"Delightful working situation-…" Steve Swires, ibid p23.

The Outlaws **reviews**: *Seattle Times* Dec 28 (1986): 2, *San Francisco Chronicle* Dec 28 (1986): 3, *TV Guide* Mar 21 (1987): 40.

Chapter 15: Nostalgia Star 1988 onwards

Falcon Crest: Robert Rorke, 'Falcon Crest: At the Crossroads,' TVG Nov 3 (1987): 31, 'Falcon Crest: Thumbs Down!,' *Soap Opera Digest*, Dec 27 (1989), Matt Roush, '"Falcon Crest" will try a new recipe for scandal,' *USA Today* Jul 18 (1989).

"The little old ladies   " – Roderick Barrand ibid.

"Oils take up…" & "so I can get…" – Andrew L Urban, 'Not Like a Phoney,' ibid.

Life with Carol: Elaine Lipworth, 'Rod Taylor,' *Hello* (1998).

Palomino: John J O'Connor, 'Sports to Defeat?,' *NYT* Oct 21 (1991): C16.

Open Season review: New York Times May 10 (1996): C18

The Osiris Chronicles: Bill Warren, 'The Osiris Chronicles,' *Starlog* Apr (1996).

"If Rod Taylor…" – Scott Eyman, 'Tarantino's latest find: Rod Taylor as Churchill in "Inglourious Basterds", *Palm Beach Post,* August 21 (2009).

Welcome to Woop Woop – *Welcome to Woop Woop* PB (Goldwyn, 1998), Douglas Kennedy, 'Writer Blocked,' *London Times* (Metro) Sept 12-18 (1998): 16, 'Hanson Vetoed,' *Herald Sun (Melbourne)* Aug 15 (1998): 126, Andrew L Urban, 'Subversion in the Outback,' *Urban Cinefile http: //www.urbancinefile.com.au/scripts/cinefile/Features.idc?Article_ID=1432* accessed May 17, 2005, *SMH* Aug 26 (1996): 14, Brett Thomas Susan Owens 'Cannes the Aussies,' *Sun-Herald* May 11 (1997): 11, Mark Naglazas, 'Making Woopee,' *West Australian* Aug 12 (1998): 5, Ben Hart, 'Hey hey it's not his day,' *Herald Sun* Aug 7 (1998), Ben Holgate, 'Director cut from larrikin cloth,' *The Australian* Aug 4 (1998): 3.

"One last big kiss…" – Andrew L Urban, 'Urban Subversion,' ibid.

"Fell off…", "Meat pie and a fight…" and "Daddy-O's…" – Rob Lowing, 'Back To Woop Woop,' *Sun Herald (Time Out)* Aug 9 (1998): 9.

"The big one…" – Jan Epstein, 'Cannes' Favourite Son,' *Cinema Papers* Nov (1997): 15.

"This is Apocalypse Now…" – Stephan Elliott, 'Big Woop,' *Who Weekly* Aug 31 (1998): 52.

"Rod Taylor looks like…" – Andrew L Urban, 'Not Like a Phoney,' ibid.

"There's forty years…" – 'Looking at Woop Woop,' *Movie Trader* Sept (1998): 16.

"One shot…" – Claudia Sammut, 'The nonconformist,' *Sunday Telegraph (Sydney) Sunday Mag* June 9 (2000): 16.

Welcome to Woop Woop reviews: *SBS Movie Show* Aug (1996), *Sunday Age* Aug 16 (1999): 4, *SMH* Aug 13 (1998): 10, *Weekend Australian* Aug 15 (1998): 21, *Sunday Herald* Aug 16 (1998): 11, *The Age* Aug 14 (1998): 7, *West Australian* Aug 15 (1998): 94, *Herald Sun* Aug 13 (1998): 38, *San Francisco Chronicle* Nov 13 (1998).

Conclusion

"I want to go on…" – Bill Tusher, 'He man from Down Under,,' *Screenland* Mar (1961): 55.

"Rough with men…" – James Bacon, '"Shamus" Moves to Small Screen,' *LAHE* Apr 9 (1975).

"Homosocial…" – Cynthia J Fiuchs 'The Buddy Politic,' *Screening the Male: Exploring Masculinities in Hollywood Cinema* Eds Steven Cohan and Ina Rae Hark (London: Routledge, 1993): 195.

Auteur Theory: Andrew Sarris, 'Notes on the Auteur Theory in 1962,' in *Film Theory and Criticism* Eds Gerald Mast, Marshall Cohen & Leo Baudy (New York: Oxford University Press, 1992): 585-605, Dudley Andrews, *Concepts in Film Theory* (Oxford: Oxford Uni Press, 1984): 107-132.

"Some actors are…" – Patrick McGilligan, *Cagney: The Actor as Auteur* (South Brunswick: AS Barnes, 1975): 199.

"Gumption, courage…" – Angela Bennie, 'Enter, Stage Right, Ourselves,' *The Age* Oct 9 (2004): 3

"Over think…" – Michaela Boland & Michael Bodey, ibid.

"There is a courage…" – Angela Bennie, ibid.

"We have…" – Angela Bennie, ibid.

"There's a cultural…" – Steve Chagollan, 'Wonders from Down Under,' *Var* Jan 4 (2000).

"Egalitarianism…" – Donald Horne, *The Lucky Country* (Sydney: Angus & Robertson, 1971): 47.

  "The sentimental ideal…" – Brian McFarlane, *Australian Cinema* (New York: Columbia University Press, 1988): 54.

"The first…" – 'Home With £125,000 Contract,' *Daily Mirror* Aug 31 (1963): 2.

Australian film: Theodore F Sheckls, *Celluloid Heroes Down Under Australian Film, 1970-2000* (Westport: Praeger, 2002): 11, Brian McFarlane, ibid p47.

"Show audiences…" – Sally K Brass, 'Rod Adds Authenticity to Aussie Film,' *LAT* Sept 15 (1968): 25.

"A radical shift…" – Philip Butterss, 'Becoming a Man in Australian Film in the Early 1990s,' *Australian Cinema in the 1990s* Ed Ian Craven (London: F Cass, 2001): 79.

"Phoney American…" – 'Taylor: "I ain't no Gable,"' *PH* Oct (1969): 36.

INDEX

A Gathering of Eagles 89, 90, 91, 104, 239, 240, 241, 253

A Matter of Wife... and Death 184-185, 240, 254

A Patch of Blue 101

A Place Where You Whisper 31, 256

A Time to Die 203-04, 241, 254

A Town Like Alice 80, 245

ABC *(American Broadcasting Company)*, 70, 75, 138, 169, 209-11, 216-217, 254

ABC *(Australian Broadcasting Corporation)*, 20-22, 29, 31, 34

Abe Lincoln in Illinois 31

Academy Awards 88, 112, 212, 183

Actors Studio 26, 47-48

Adam-12 126

Adey, Ilma 35-36, 259

Adler, Buddy 71

Adventures in Paradise 70-71

Airport 124, 167

Ajax Films 142

Albert, Eddie 219

Albert, Edward *(Jr.)* 204

Alda, Alan 179, 183

Alfred Hitchcock Presents 83

Alfred Hitchcock Productions 238

Alicia, Ana 220

Alien Seed 91

All About the Birds (documentary) 88

Allen, Cliff 14, 259

Alley, Kirstie 168, 210, 212

Allied Artists 49-50, 253

Alvin Purple 183

Amber Nine 119

Ameche, Don 121

Anderson, Bill 106, 207, 209

Anderson, Judith 5

Anderson, Richard 89, 260

Andersson, Bibi 186

Andress, Ursula 219

Angel Gear 184, 191

Angeli, Pier 52

Anglia Television 202, 256

Ann-Margret, 171

Ansara, Margaret 36, 259

Antonioni, Michelangelo 8, 143-48

Arden, Eve 219

Ashley, Edward 43, 49

Ashton, Queenie 21, 186

Ask Any Girl 6, 60-61, 70, 97, 114, 253

Asquith, Anthony "Puffin" 94-95, 97

Astaire Fred 52

Aubrey, Jim 147, 176, 177

Australian acting in the 1950's 27

Australian Actors' Equity 208

Australian Film and Television School 142

Australian Film Development Corporation 142, 176

Australian tall poppy syndrome 6, 195, 197

Auteur theory 242-244

Aylmer, Felix 58

Baker, Diane 60

Baker, Snowy 6, 81

Baker, Stanley 153

Barnard, Antonia 229-232, 260

Barrett, Ray 20, 24, 41, 43, 117, 184, 196

Barwick, Sir Garfield 7

Baryshnikov, Mikhail 5, 8, 16, 248

Bass, Tom 15, 259

Bautzer, Greg 100

Bayonas, Lyn 184, 260

Bearcats! 168-70, 189, 198, 239-40, 255

Beatty, Warren 98

Belford, Christine 214

Bells with Drums 101

Ben-Hur 68

Bennett, Herve 173

Bennie, Angela 245

Bergen, Polly 59
Berk, Howard 181, 183
Bernard, Judd 33, 148-50
Bernds, Edward 50
Bernsen, Corbin 222
Berrell, Lloyd 20, 41
Berwick, Ray 86
Bibi Andersson 185
Big Man, Big River 81
Bikel, Theodore 153, 219
Bilson, Bruce 212
Bini, Alfred 172
Black Pearl 233
Blackman, Joan 60
Blanchett, Cate 7
Blees, Robert 81
Block, Larry 184
Blocker, Dan 126
Blondy 185-86, 254
Bloom, Claire 68
Blow Up 143-44, 148
Blue Hawaii 243
Blue Hills 24, 31, 256
Bochner, Lloyd 74, 211
Bogart, Humphrey 8
Bogdanovich, Peter 95, 110
Bogeaus, Benedict 65
Boleslavsky, Richard 26
Bondelli, Phil 211
Booth, James 150-51
Borgnine, Ernest 53, 125-26, 128
Boulle, Pierre 122
Bowyer, Justin 131
Box, Betty 138
Boyd, David 15-18
Boyd, Martin 17
Brand, Neville 178-79
Brando, Marlon 25-28, 46-77, 57, 116, 120
Breaker Morant 248
Brinckerhoff, Burt 200
Broccoli, "Cubby" 77
Bronfman, Edgar M. 147
Bronson, Charles 56, 172
Bronston, Samuel L. 100-01
Brooks, Richard 53-4
Brother Otis 209
Brough, Walter 188-89
Brown, Bryan 80-81
Brown, Jim 129-34, 137, 280

Brown, Mende 207-209
Browne, Coral 43
Brunton, Barbara 23, 32, 34
Bryant, Betty 176
Bryant, Chris 149
Brynner, Yul 168, 172
Buckner, Bob 79
Buffalo Man 168
Burke and Wills 168, 191
Burton, Geoff 193
Burton, Richard 5-6, 8, 94-95, 97, 106, 122, 202, 213, 244
Bus Stop 82, 255
Butch Cassidy and the Sundance Kid 127, 169
Butterss, Philip 249
Byrnes, Edd 51
Calhoun, Rory 174, 212
Calori, Emilio 147
Canby, Vincent 148
Cannes Film Festival 231, 254
Capital Man 233
Capra, Frank 101
Captain Henry Morgan 46
Captain Singleton 22, 256
Caravans 121
Cardiff, Jack 79, 109-12, 115-18, 122, 129, 130-31, 133-34, 241
Cardinale, Claudia 101, 136-37
Carey, Macdonald 58
Caron, Leslie, 52, 219
Carr, Caleb 225
Carson, Jack 59
Carsten, Peter 130
Casablanca 75
Cassavetes, John 52
CBS 70, 142, 152, 169, 209, 216-17, 226, 255-56
CBS Films 142
Cecil, Amber Mae 41
Cervi, Burce 214-15
Chamberlain, Richard 192
Chang, Wah 66
Charisse, Cyd 52
Charles & Diana: A Royal Love Story 209, 254
Charlie's Angels 198, 201, 205
Chayefsky, Paddy 53
Cherry, Helen 116
Cheyenne 50-51, 70, 250, 255
Chiefs 222

Chips: Story of Outback 35
Christian, Linda 94, 96
Christie, Julie 8, 107, 110-12
Chuka 8, 125-28, 136, 240-41, 244, 250, 253
Chulack, Fred 204
Churchland, Lindsay 15
Cimber, Matt 203-04
Cinema Centre Films 152
Circus World 100-01, 103, 171
Clark, John 28, 246
Cleary, Jon 138-42, 245
Cleopatra 5, 78, 82, 94-95, 97, 102
Clift, Montgomery 6, 8, 25-26, 47, 49, 54-57
Climpson, Roger 34
Clouse, Robert 152-54
Clurman, Harold 26
Coburn, James 118-19
Coe, Fred 59
Coen, Franklin 125
Cole, Dennis 168
Cole, Michael 126
Colossus and the Amazon Queen 71-72, 144, 240, 244, 253
Columbia 47, 254
Come Away Pearler 46
Comedy of Errors 33, 257
Connery, Sean 77, 106, 118-19, 177
Conte, Richard 124
Contraband 31, 256
Coolahan, Kate 16, 239
Cooper, Gary 109, 248, 271
Cooper, Gladys 58
Coppel, Alec 81, 245
Corbett, John 225-26
Corea, Nick 214-15, 217, 225
Cotten, Joseph 65
Country of the Blind 68
Courtney, Tom 107
Cover, John 21
Cox, Beau 207-08
Cracknell, Ruth 20, 43
Crime and Punishment 41, 256
Crispin's Day 41, 257
Cross, Beverly 202
Crowe, Russell 5, 8, 9, 80, 133, 173, 245, 248
Cry of the Innocent 202, 204, 240, 254
Culp, Robert 99, 152
Cummings, Robert 100
Curtis, Tony 168, 209, 212

Cusack, Ann, 224, 266
Cusack, Cyril 202-03
Dadswell, Lyndon 15-16
Dahl, Roald 203
Dalton, Audrey 58
Dante, Joe 225, 226
Dark of the Sun (The Mercenaries) 79, 93, 112, 128-30, 132-34, 137, 140, 153, 180, 188, 239-40, 244, 249, 253
Darker Than Amber 8, 150, 152, 153, 154, 167, 176, 180, 202, 204, 240, 244, 254
Darren, James 47
Dateline San Francisco 81-82
Davenport, Nigel 202
Davion, Alex 74
Davis, Bette 48, 53-54
Day, Doris 8, 99, 113-14, 119, 120, 135, 178, 187
de Grunwald, Anatole 94, 97, 283
de Teliga, Stan 15
Dean, James 26, 47, 49, 52
Delon, Alain 144
DeLuise, Dom 120
Dennehy, Brian 223
Derek, John 47
Dern, Bruce 88
Desperate Journey 96
Destination Moon 63
Duel, Peter 135, 137
Disney 39, 77, 133, 253
Disney, Walt 8, 77
Distributors Corporation of America 39
Dmytryk, Edward 136
Do Not Disturb 113, 114, 119, 120, 182, 240, 253
Doleman, Guy 20, 32, 39, 246
Don Quixote 95
Donahue, Troy 60
Dorian, Angela 126
Douglas, Gordon 126
Douglas, Kirk 100
Douglas, Melvyn 124
Douglas, Paul 59-60
Dr Zhivago 93, 121
Dr. Strangelove 89, 91
Drake, Sir Francis 78-79
Dressler, Marie 52
du Maurier, Daphne 22, 83
Duel 173-74

Duncan, David 63-64
Dundas, Douglas 15
Dunleavy, Steve 171
Dwyer, Fiona 229
Eager, Beryl 8, 16, 18
Eastwood, Clint 172, 183
Economou, Michael 179, 182-83
Edmund, Chris 245
Ekberg, Anita 6, 69, 71, 78, 88, 94-95, 99
Ekland, Britt 212
El Cid 100
Elg, Taina 52
Elliot, Sumner Locke 20, 33
Elliott, Leslie 117-18
Elliott, Stephan 227-28, 230-32
Ellis, Bob 196, 260
Emerson, Anthony 13, 14, 259
Englund, George 128-31, 133
Ensemble Theatre 27
Errol, Leon 43
Evans, Edith 107, 112
Evans, Robert 60, 127
Evigan, Greg 210-12
Ewart, John 42, 161, 186,
    191-93, 195
Fail-Safe 89
Falcon Crest 219-22, 240, 255
Family Flight 173-74, 239-40, 254
Fate Is the Hunter 90, 102-04, 140, 162, 239-
    40, 253
Father of the Bride 53-54
Ferber, Edna 48
FFC 227-28, 254-55
Fielder, Richard 125
Fifth Coin 113
Filmways 168, 254-55
Finch, Peter 5, 7, 20-21, 27, 33, 43, 80, 105,
    138, 188, 192, 208, 245
Finnell, Mike 226
Finney, Albert 227
Fisher, Michael 207
Fitzgerald, Barry 53
Fleming, Rhonda 99
Flight to Mars 49
Flynn, Errol 5, 7-9, 15, 43, 48, 79-81, 88, 96,
    99, 112, 132, 143, 173, 188, 239, 245
Fonda, Henry 25, 28, 168
Fonda, Jane 6, 8, 98-101
Fong, Harold 74

Ford, John 8, 52, 60, 102-03, 106-13, 167, 242
Ford, Glenn 52, 102-03, 168-69
Forsyth, Fredrick 202
Frechette, Mark 144-46
Freilich, Jeff 219-21
French, Hugh 136, 149
Frenchman's Creek 22, 256
Friend, George 233
Fuchs, Cynthia 240
Fuller, Sam 177-79
Fury, Ed 71
Gable, Clark 52, 73, 109, 120, 193, 239
Gabor, Zsa Zsa 140
Gallipoli 208
Gann, Ernest K. 102
Garbo, Greta 52
Garcia, Russell 66
Gardner, Ava 52
Gardner, Fred 143
Gardner, John 71, 114-18
Garland, Judy 52
Garner, James 51, 93, 103-04, 133, 168, 220,
    239
Garson, Greer 52
Gaslight 223
Gavin, John 60
Giant 6, 48-51, 127, 249, 253
Gibson, Mel 5, 9, 80-81, 208, 245
Ginna, Robert 106, 107, 109-11
Glassman, Richard 169
Gleason, Michael 200
Glenn, John 178
Go for Broke 208
Gobbi, Sergio 185-86
Godfrey, Arthur 120
Goff, John 203
Golden Boy 41, 257
Golden Globe Award 75
Goldfinger 106, 119
Goldsworthy, Reg 142, 176, 187
Goldwyn 228, 231-32, 254
Goldwyn, Sam (Jr.) 231
Gone with the Wind 54-56
Goodyear Theatre 69, 255
Gordon, Hayes 27, 246
Gotbetter, Howard 126-27
Gould, Elliot 167
Graff, Bob 106, 111, 282
Graham, Sheilah 132

Grand Hotel 93
Granger, Stewart 48, 52
Grant, Cary 84-85, 87, 113-14, 135
Grass Roots 222, 241, 254
Green, Guy 106
Grey, Charles 209, 255
Griffiths, Rachel 229
Grimsdale, Gordon 27, 31
Gross, Guy 231-32
Group Theatre 26
Guerro, Tonio 143
Gulf and Western 127
Guns of Navarone 123, 128
Hackman, Gene 168
Hailey, Arthur 123-24
Hakim, Dolores 114
Hakim, Fred 114, 116-17, 120, 126, 171, 182, 185
Half Nelson 212, 254
Hall, Frank 33, 120, 188-89, 254
Halprin, Daria 144-46, 240
Hamilton, George 64, 68, 148
Harlow, Jean 73
Harris, Heath 194
Harris, Richard 107, 115, 144, 178, 187, 213
Harrison, Rex 144, 146, 203, 259
Harrow Alley 168
Haskin, Byron 39-40, 46
Hathaway, Henry 101
Hawaiian Eye 70
Hawks, Howard 60, 276
Hayden, Sterling 50, 59
Hayward, Louis 126
Haywood, Chris 191
Hayworth, Rita 58
Hedren, Tippi 84-88, 240
Hell on Frisco Bay 46, 50-51, 81, 253
Hell River 183
Heller, Lukas 178-79
Hellinger's Law 205, 254
Hemmings, David 148
Henderson, Ian 131
Henry, Buck 219
Hercules 71
Heyes, Douglas 168-69
High Noon 50
Hilem, Mary *(second wife)* 6-7, 12, 90, 99-100, 103-04, 108, 110, 113, 117, 126, 132, 137-38
Hiller, Arthur 79

Hiller, Wendy 58
Hindley, Richard 207-08
His Majesty O'Keefe 39
Hitchcock, Alfred 6, 8, 58, 60, 82-88, 98, 105, 113, 128, 167, 190, 248, 253
Hoffman, Dustin 167
Holt, Tim 51
Home from the Hill 68
Hong Kong 6, 70-81, 84, 88, 185, 189, 198, 210, 237, 239, 240, 250, 255
Hopkins, Bo 178
Hopper, Dennis 57, 276
Hopper, Hedda 76, 100, 107, 120-21
Horne, Donald 247
Horowitz, Alan 135
Horton, Robert 74
Hotel 123-24, 175, 239-41, 253
Houseman, John 68
Houser, Patrick 214
Houston, Walter, 51
Howard, Sidney 34
Howard, Trevor 116, 119, 178
Howarth, Jocelyn 6
Hudson, Rock 7, 46-49, 89-91, 99, 103, 113-14, 168, 170
Huggins, Roy 51, 74
Humphries, Barry 229
Hunter, Evan 47, 83-88
Hunter, Jeffrey 47
Hunter, Kim 59, 68
Hunter, Tab 47
Huston, John 51, 122
Hutchinson, Neil 21, 31-32, 259
I Hate Crime 31, 256
Imaginary Invalid 33
Ingalls, Don 184
Inglourious Basterds 227, 234, 254
Inland with Sturt 31, 254
Jacob, Gilles 231
Jacqueline Bouvier Kennedy 205-06, 217, 223, 239-41, 250, 254
Jamaican Pie 188-89
'James Bond' 115, 118, 139, 152
James, Mervyn 17
Jankovic, Stole 181-82
Jann, Gerald 74
Janssen, David 169
Jason, Jack 125
Jessup, Richard 125

Johns, Eric 31
Johnson, Rick 224
Johnson, Van 91
Jones, Carolyn 60, 68
Jones, Dean 52
Jourdan, Catherine 185
Jourdan, Louis 5, 94, 95
Journey to the Center of the Earth 64, 188
Julius Caesar 33, 257
Kaiser, Henry J. 71, 75
Kangaroo 29
Kata, Elizabeth 101, 245
Kaufman, Joseph 39-40, 46
Kaufman, Millard 55
Kaw 227, 254
Kay, Sydney John 33
Keel, Howard 52
Kellaway, Cecil 5, 43, 96
Kellogg, Phil 186
Kelly, Gene 52, 168
Kelly, Grace 52, 84, 116, 121
Kendall, Suzy 154, 274, 278
Kennedy, Burt 171-72
Kennedy, Douglas 227
Kennedy, George 212, 226
Kenny, Jan 193-94
Kent, Jacqueline 27, 41-42
Kerkorian, Kirk 147, 176
Kerr, Bill 43
Kerr, Deborah 58
Kikumura, Carol *(third wife)* 76, 99, 189-90, 205, 207, 210, 213, 222, 234
Killanin, Redman 110
King of the Coral Sea 32, 35, 36, 37, 38, 44, 52, 80, 159, 240, 243, 253
King Solomon's Mines 177
Kirkpatrick, Maggie 229
Kokoda 233
Koster, Henry 48
Krasna, Norman 98
Krish, John 149-51
Kruschen, Jack 74
Kuhn, Miles 186
La Dolce Vita 69
Ladd, Alan 51, 81, 126
Lancaster, Burt 58, 81, 167
Landry, Tom 223
Lane, Richard 21, 41-42
Langan, Glenn 41

Lansbury, Angela 59, 224-25
Lansbury, Bruce 225
Lanza, Mario 52
LaPaglia, Anthony 246
Larson, Glen A. 212, 254
Last Bus to Banjo Creek 122, 136, 142, 168, 187-88, 191, 197, 245, 248
Latitude 35 81, 91, 191
Laura 102
Lavi, Daliah 139-40
Lazarus 197
Lazenby, George 7
Le May, General Curtis 90
Le Mesurier, John 116
Ledger, Heath, 9, 80, 196
Lee, Charles 203-04
Lee, Christopher 209, 213, 226
Lee, Margot 32
Lehrer, Tom 89
Leigh, Vivien 19, 33
Lemmon, Jack 47
Leone, Sergio 172
Levathes, Peter 81-82, 238
Levi, Alan 199-201
Levin, Henry, 188-89
Levine, Joe E. 8
Levy, Ralph 114
Lewis, Jerry 126
Licudi, Gabriella 119
Lidcombe 6, 12, 14, 141, 157, 186, 210, 228
Littieri, Al 178
Lloyd-Davies, Hermia 17-18
Lockey, Judy 141
Lockridge Jr., Ross 54
Lollobrigida, Gina 219
Long John Silver 39-40, 43, 46, 160, 178, 197, 241, 253
Long, Joan 191-95, 253, 255
Lopez, Marco 76, 84, 108, 116, 117, 126
Losey, Joseph 109
Lost Eden 73, 191, 245
Louis Shurr Agency 46
Louissier, Jacques 133
Lovejoy, Frank 59-60
Lovell, Nigel 40, 259
Lovely, Louise 5, 81
Lucas, Clyde 68
Lucking, William 214-15
Luhrmann, Baz 5

Lupino, Ida 70
Lux Video Playhouse 48
Lynde, Paul 120
Lynley, Carol 60
MacCallum, John 21
MacDonald, John D. 152-54
MacDougall, Ranald 79, 130
MacLaine, Shirley 60-61, 168
Macnee, Patrick 68
Mad Max 245
Madame Bovary 31, 256
Malden, Karl 124
Maltby, Richard 26
Man Trap 31, 256
Mandel, Loring 59-60
Mann Act 147
Mann, Delbert 58, 89-90
Manners, Sam 178, 188
Marbella 189, 212, 239, 254
Marlowe, Hugh 50, 65
Marnie 85
Marshall, Alan 43
Marshall, George 114
Martin, Dean 118-19, 212
Martinelli, Elsa 94, 97
Martini, Richard 223
Marty 39, 46, 53
Marvin, Lee 55
Masefield, John 34
Mask of Murder 212-13, 241, 254
Mason, James 48, 64
Masquerade 210-12, 216, 244, 254, 255
Mates 208-09
Mathers, Ken 14-15, 17, 259
Maugham, Somerset 130
Maverick 51, 58, 71, 74,
Mayer, Louis B. 52
Mayes, Wendell 123
Mayhew, Babs 22, 259
MCA 46
McCallum, John 20, 43, 187, 259
McCarthy, Kevin 124
McClure, Doug 212
McDonald's Mission 183
McFarlane, Brian 247-48
McGilligan, Patrick 243
McKenna, Siobhan, 68, 107, 109
McKern, Leo 139
McQueen, Steve 152

Meagher, Ray 207
Medak, Peter 95
Medworth, Frank 15
Meillon, John 20, 24, 40, 43, 186, 191-93, 195, 196
Mellor, Aubrey 246
Melnick, Wilt 44, 46-47, 57, 70, 100, 136, 186
Mercurio, Paul 229
Merrill, Dina 60, 223, 224
Method acting 24-28, 48, 246
Meyer, Hans 186
MGM 5, 51-57, 60-61, 64, 65-68, 70, 78, 81, 84, 93-94, 97-99, 103, 106-07, 111, 115-22, 128, 143-48, 167, 176-77, 184, 225, 232, 237-38, 248, 253-54
Michaels, Nicola 99
Michell, Keith 78
Michener, James 121
Milland, Ray 121
Miller, J.P. 183
Milliken, Sue 194, 233
Million Dollar Mermaid 96
Mills, John 125-26, 187
Mimieux, Yvette 8, 66-67, 129, 130, 132
Minnelli, Vincente 100
Mirisch, Walter 50
Mirror in my House 105
Misalliance 33-34, 59, 68, 209, 255, 257
Mister Roberts 109
Mistral 81
Mitchum, Robert 37, 96, 122, 216, 220, 248
Modesty Blaise 118
Moir, Richard 229
Molloy, Mike 232
Moment to Moment 81
Mona Vale Surf Club 228
Montana 96
Mordente, Tony 225
More, Kenneth 129-32
Morley, Robert 68
Morley, Sheridan 58
Morning Departure 22
Morrison, Jim 178
Morrow, Jo 99
Morrow, Vic 152
Move Over, Darling 113
Mr. Buddwing 104
Murder, She Wrote 224, 256
Mutiny on the Bounty 68, 93

Nancy's Boy 22, 256
Napier, Charles 199-201, 214-16, 241
Narizzano, Silvio 149
National Film and Sound Archive 38, 41, 198, 259
NBC 75, 86, 169, 185, 198, 201-02, 216, 222, 254-55
Neidorf, Murray 186
Nelson, Ricky 60
Nesbitt, Cathleen 58
Nesbitt, Derren 140
Nettheim, David 22, 94, 259
Newman, Paul 7, 47, 52, 57, 87
Newman, William 168
Newsfront 196
Newton, Robert 39
Newton-John, Olivia 187
Nicholson, Jack 167
NIDA 28, 246
Nielsen, Leslie 52-53, 57
Night Beat 31, 256
Nightingale, Frances 32, 259
Niland, D'Arcy 31, 38
Niven, David 58, 60, 64
No Love for Johnnie 138
Norris, Chuck 213, 225
North by Northwest 87
Northwest Passage 57
Novak, Kim 219
NSWFTO 228
Number 96 183
Nuyen, Frances 6, 76, 78-99
O'Casey, Shivaun 107
O'Brien, Margaret 59
O'Brien, Robert 93, 106-07, 109, 121, 146-47, 238
O'Casey, Sean 80, 105-07, 110-12, 179
O'Flynn, Philip 239
O'Sullivan, Michael 42, 202, 257
O'Sullivan's Bay 42, 257
O'Toole, Peter 106, 109, 119, 213
Oberon, Merle 99, 124, 178
Objective, Burma! 79
Olivier, Sir Laurence 19, 33, 78
Olley, Margaret 15, 17, 259
On a Dead Man's Chest 189
On the Beach 96
On the Run 207-08, 241, 244-45, 254
On the Waterfront, 27

One Hundred and One Dalmatians 8, 33, 77, 240, 249, 253
Open Season 223-24, 233, 244, 254
Operation North Star 41, 257
Orion 232
Osiris Chronicles 240
Outlaws 178, 217, 225, 240
Paglia, Camille 87
Pal, George 63, 64-67, 73, 139, 148, 254
Palmer, Lili 139
Palomino 222, 254
Paluzzi, Luciana 126, 128
Panajotovic, Eva 103-04, 181-82
Panajotovic, Ika 181-83
Papas, Irene 52
Paramount 63-64, 125, 127, 226, 253
Parker, Eleanor 52
Parsons, Louella 100
Partizan, 181-83, 188, 239, 240, 244, 254
Pasternak, Joe 61
Pate, Michael 20, 39, 43, 46, 49, 81, 96, 184, 259
Patten, Luana 60
Patton 60, 223
Paxton, Shane and Bindi 229
Peach, Mary 89-90
Peckinpah, Sam 50
Penington, Jon 115-18
Penington, Lisa 117
Penn, Lyle 191, 259
Peploe, Clare 143, 147
Peppard, George 68, 168
Perkins, Anthony 57, 87
Perlberg, Bill 103
Perrine, Valerie 213
Pesci, Joe 212
Peterson, Dale 211
Phillips, Clyde 209
Phillips, Sian 109
Pidgeon, Walter 52
Pillow Talk 113
Pinter, Tomislav 213
Planet of the Apes 122, 284
Plautus 33
Playhouse 90 59, 68, 250, 255
Ploger, Liz 76, 266, 281
Plough and the Stars (play), 109
Plummer, Christopher 139-41
Point of Betrayal 223-24, 233, 244, 254

Point of Departure 31, 256
Polk, Louis 147
Porter, Susie 7, 230-31
Powderkeg 240, 254
Power, John 191, 194-95, 254
Preminger, Otto 147
Presley, Elvis 243
Project Unlimited 66
Psycho 60, 83-87
Pugh, Roy 30, 259
Purl, Linda 185
Puzo, Mario 203-04
Queen Elizabeth II 117
Quine, Richard 124
Quinn, Anthony 168
Rackin, Marty 39, 46, 51
Rafferty, Chips 20, 35-38, 43, 52, 72, 80-81, 96, 178, 186-87, 196, 243
Chips Rafferty Award 186
Raintree County 6, 54-57, 241, 253
Randell, Ron 5, 20-21, 43, 48
Rank Organization 122, 138
Ransohoff, Martin 168
Rattigan, Terence 8, 58, 94, 96-97
Ray, Johnnie 36
Ray, Nick 101
Reach for the Sky 42, 161, 257
Redford, Robert 82, 98, 183
Redgrave, Michael 107, 112, 282
Reed, Carol 106
Reeves, Jack 152, 154
Reeves, Steve 71
Rene, Roy 20
Rennie, Michael 64
Return of the Time Machine 67
Revue 70, 255
Reynolds, Burt 53, 184, 211
Reynolds, Debbie 52-54
Richards, Ann 48
Richards, Jeff 56
Richards, Shirley Ann 6, 43
Rigg, Diana 119
Rio Bravo 60
Robbins, Harold 101
Robertson, Cliff 60, 99, 219
Robinson, Edward G. 51
Robinson, Lee 35-36, 38, 44, 72, 186, 233, 240, 244, 259
Robson, Flora 107, 109

Roche, Jean 17-18
Rocketship X-M 63
Roeca, Sam 169
Romero, Cesar 219
Rosenberg, Aaron 102
Ross, Paul C. 188
Roundtree, Richard 214-15, 217
Rowlands, Gena 52
Rubloff, Arthur 137
Rush, Geoffrey 246
Rutherford, Margaret 5, 94, 97
SAFC 228
Said, Fouad 178
Saint, Eva Marie 103-04, 222
Salter, June 20, 32, 259
Santos, Joe 184, 211
Satana, Tura 99
Saul, John 24-26, 28, 31, 48, 56, 57, 131, 246
Savalas, Telly 205
Saxon, John 57
Scaife, Ted 130
Scala 227-28, 254
Schaech, Jonathan 7, 228, 230, 232
Schaffner, Frank 60
Schary, Dore 52-56
Schenck, Nicholas 57
Schenck, Nikki 57, 99
Schickel, Richard 127
Schifrin, Lalo 119
Schlesinger, John 106
Schott, Lewis 137
Scofield, Paul 64
Scorsese, Martin 133
Scott, Adam 149
Scott, George C. 168
Scott, Thelma 43, 259
Screen Actors Guild Award 227
Seaton, George 103
Seideman, Lisa 220
Self, William 70, 74
Sellers, Peter 119
Selmur Productions 138
Seltzer, Walter 152-54
Separate Tables 6, 58, 81, 107, 209, 253
Sergeant, Joseph 137
Serling, Rod 69, 98
Seven Arts 98, 113, 122, 128, 238, 253
Seven Seas to Calais 77-79, 81, 97, 239, 240, 253

Shadow of a Doubt 58
Shakespeare, William 21, 25, 27, 33, 226
Shamus 184-85
Shane 48, 229
Sharif, Omar 121
Shark Bait 68
Shaw, George Bernard 27, 33, 68
Shear, Barry 178, 259
Shearing, Dinah 22-24, 27, 32, 42-43
Sheckls, Theodore F. 248
Shepard, Sam 8, 143, 145
Shipman, David 121, 175
Shore, Dinah 187
Siegel, Sol 64, 93, 146
Silva, Henry 226
Silverstein, Maurice 'Red' 107, 176
Sinatra, Frank 126
Sing, Mai Tai 74, 76
Sister Kenny 96
Slocum 168
Smart, Dee 228-30, 233
Smith, Jaclyn 205
Smith, John 101
Smith, Maggie 8, 94-97, 107, 110-112, 122, 137, 187, 239-40
Smith, Roger 171
Smith, Wilbur 128-29, 150
Smith, William 153-54, 179, 211
Soldier of Fortune 75
Somebody Up There Likes Me 51
Someone Will Conquer Them 101
Somers, Daryl 232
Sons and Lovers 109
Sousa, John Philip 99
Spaak, Catherine 124
Sparv, Camilla 139
Spelling, Aaron 212, 254
St. John, Jill 60, 119
Stafford, Frederick 88
Stafford, Keith 188-89
Stallone, Sylvester 213
Stanislavski, Konstantin 26-28, 246
Stanley, Michael 136, 153, 176
Stapley, Richard 49
Stark, Ray 8, 100
Starr, Harrison 144, 146
Steel, Danielle 222, 254
Steiger, Rod 25, 90, 98, 172
Steinbeck, Muriel 20, 39

Steiner, Fred 179, 288
Stella Stevens 186
Step Down to Terror 58, 253, 276
Sterling, Georgie 19, 21, 24-25, 27-28, 43, 56, 59, 67, 175, 259
Stevens, Andrew 49, 200
Stevens, George 48-49
Stevens, Inger 76, 99
Stevenson, Robert Louis 39
Stewart, James 87, 168
Stewart, Warren 15
Stork 183
Storm, Ebsen 184
Strasberg, Lee 26
Stratton, David 232
Stuart, Gil 49
Studio 57 48, 50, 57, 255
Sturgis, Ted 130
Sturt, Sir Charles 11, 29, 136, 191
Suarez, Emma 212
Summer of the Seventeenth Doll 48, 96
Sunday in New York 93, 97-100, 101, 114, 239-40, 249, 253
Tabori, Kris 173-74
Tales of the Unexpected 203, 256
Tamblyn, Russ 56
Tandy, Jessica 85, 87
Tarantino, Quentin 133, 227
Tarzan 41-42, 257
Tashlin, Frank 120
Taurog, Norman 243
Taylor, Bill "Squizzy" Sturt *(father)* 7, 11, 12, 13, 19, 23, 32, 126, 186, 210, 222, 228, 239
Taylor, Elizabeth, 5, 6, 8, 48-49, 52-56, 94, 95, 97, 122, 220, 244
Taylor, Felicia Rodrica Sturt *(daughter)* 110, 117, 126, 137-38, 186-87
Taylor, Grant 24, 29-31, 39, 43
Taylor, Kit 39, 160
Taylor, Robert 52-53
Taylor, Rod
  "Rodlor" own production company 81, 116, 122, 125, 135-36, 142, 149, 176, 238, 243, 253
  1960 visit to Australia, 73
  1963 visit to Australia, 5-7
  1968 visit to Australia, 141
  1975 visit to Australia, 186
  1976 visit to Australia, 186

1982 visit to Australia, 207
1983 visit to Australia, 210
1996 visit to Australia, 229, 230-31
Acting style, 26-28, 40, 42-43, 48, 50, 54, 74-76, 78, 108-09, 112, 131-32, 152-53, 174, 216, 245
Alcohol, 23-24, 76, 80, 108, 116-17, 120, 131, 139, 141, 142, 149, 151, 153, 171, 174-75, 179, 182, 190, 193, 199, 200, 207, 210, 213-16, 222, 230, 237, 242, 249
Arriving in Hollywood, 46-47
as "Rodney", 22, 23, 48, 52, 210
as Australian, 9, 153, 201, 216, 220, 221, 245, 248
as Australian actor, 48, 57, 81, 135, 142, 173, 192, 208, 221, 228, 229, 246, 249
as Auteur, 242, 243, 244
as Father, 104, 110, 117, 137-38, 187
as Nostalgia Star, 219, 221
as Producer, 8, 123, 125-26, 136, 176, 181, 243-44
as Singer, 90
as Writer, 38, 72, 96, 119, 125, 130, 174, 179-80, 182, 187-89, 199, 222-24, 233, 237, 240, 243-44
Australian identity, 37-38, 96
Australian Theatre, 32-34, 43
Bad reputation, 151, 169, 170, 210, 214
Born, 11
Career decisions, 43, 51, 55, 58, 65, 70, 71, 76-77, 81, 88, 101, 107, 114-15, 120-21, 135-36, 138, 148-49, 170, 175, 186, 201, 237-39, 242
Career summary, 8, 120, 123, 127, 167, 175, 237, 240, 241, 249, 250
East Sydney Technical College (art school), 15, 16, 17, 18, 23, 141, 259
Independent Theatre School of Dramatic Art, 20, 26, 28, 246
Leaving Australia, 43-44
Mona Vale Surf Club, 16-17, 23, 228
Off-screen Persona, 74, 95, 131, 199, 242
Olivier visit to Australia, 19
Parramatta High School, 14-15, 259
Pottery career, 17-18
Radio, 19-25, 27, 29, 31, 41-43, 250
Reputation in Australia, 77, 193, 196, 244-45
Rod-lore (fan magazine), 76
Rola Award (Rola Prize), 42, 105, 187

Sport, 15, 17, 56, 120
Star Behaviour, 74, 76, 95, 115-17, 129, 139-41, 169, 194, 197, 200, 237
Star Persona, 9, 37-38, 43, 74, 76, 120-21, 124, 130, 135, 140, 175, 184, 199, 206, 239-48
Sturt re-enactment, 29-31
Unfilmed projects, 38, 46, 67, 68, 73, 81, 91, 101, 113, 119, 121-22, 148, 150, 154, 168, 176, 183-84, 187-88, 191, 197, 202, 208-09, 233
with 20th Century-Fox, 71, 81, 84, 102, 113, 238, 248
with MGM, 52-57, 60-61, 64-68, 70, 78, 81, 84, 93-98, 107, 111, 115-17, 119-21, 128-29, 143-44, 145, 147, 176, 237-38, 248
with Paramount, 127
with Sterling & Saul, 24-27, 28, 31, 57, 67, 131, 246
with Universal, 89, 90, 173, 238
with Warner Bros., 124
Taylor, Sam 34
Television Episodes:
 "Another Killing in Cork" 224-25
 "Nan's Ghost" 225, 256
 "The Argonauts" 51, 255
 "And When the Skies Were Open" 69
 "Capital Gains" 69, 240, 255
 "Early to Die" 59, 68, 255
 "Killer Whale" 50, 255
 "Love, Honor and Perish" 76
 "Portrait of Sal" 68
 "The Best House in the Valley" 58-59, 255
 "The Black Sheep's Daughter" 48-49, 255
 "The Browning Version" 48, 255
 "The Great Gatsby" 58-60, 240, 255
 "The Hitchhiker" 203, 256
 "The Long March" 58, 59, 240, 241, 255
 "The Ordeal of Dr Shannon" 91, 100, 255
 "The Raider" 59, 60, 240, 255
 "The Spanish Gambit" 212
 "The Story of Margery Reardon" 59, 255
 "The Young Years" 59, 255
 "Thunder in the Night" 69, 255
 "Verdict of Three" 59, 255
 "Winnings" 212
That Woman 136
The Adventures Of Priscilla: Queen of the Desert 227, 231-32

The AFI awards 195, 232
The African Queen 122
The Australian Legend 37
The Birds 6-8, 83, 84-89, 93, 97, 105, 133, 134,
    147, 227-28, 232, 239-40, 243, 249, 253, 255
The Birds II: Land's End 88
The Boxer 35
The Capital Man 191
The Capital Man (novel) 142
The Cars That Ate Paris 233
The Castaway 197
The Castle 232
The Catered Affair 53-55, 253
The Contact 176, 191, 197
The Country Girl 103
The Dance Dress 41
The Dead Heart 227
The Deadly Trackers 8, 177-78, 179, 180, 182,
    240, 241, 243, 244, 254, 288
The Deep Blue Goodbye 154
The Desert Rats 43, 96
The Dirty Dozen 93, 129, 133
The DuPont Show of the Week 91
The Earthling 192
The Enemy Within 81
The First Wife 91
The Flavor of a Kiss 72
The French Connection 168
The Gang's All Here 68
The Gazebo 66
The Ginger Giant 38
The Glass Bottom Boat 93, 118-20, 167, 239-40,
    249, 253
The Golden Jungle 142, 191, 197
The Great Escape 96
The Happy Time 34, 41, 257
The Hell with Heroes 8, 135-38, 145, 180, 239-
    40, 244, 254
The Heroes 172, 254
The High and the Mighty 102
The High Commissioner 96, 138-42, 145, 233,
    240, 244, 250, 254
The Home of the Brave 33
The Hunt for Kimathi 131
The Informer 106, 256
The Jungle 81, 245
The Keeper of Dreams 233
The Last Guerrilla 183
The Last Wave 192

The Liquidator 8, 93, 115-19, 121, 124-25, 129,
    240-41, 249, 253
The Long Duel 127
The Long Shadow 142, 191
The Lost World 64
The Man from Snowy River 248
The Man Who Had Power Over Women 147-52,
    239-40, 254
The Man Who Would Be King 122
The Money Movers 248
The Oregon Trail 185-87, 198-99, 200, 201, 214,
    240, 254-55
The Osiris Chronicles 225, 226
The Outlaws 213-17, 254, 255
The Overlanders 35
The Owl and the Pussycat 122
The Phantom Stockman 35
The Picture Show Man 163, 191-98, 206-07,
    228, 232, 245, 254-55
The Pleasure of His Company 68
The Plough and the Stars 105-06
The Quiet Man 106
The Ridge and the River 31, 256
The Rola Show 42
The Rose Tattoo 46
The Sargasso Sea 197
The Shiralee 38, 80, 192
The Short Happy Life of Francis Macomber 81
The Song of Bernadette 103
The Spy Who Came in from the Cold 118
The Spy With My Face 118
The Sundowners 31, 37, 96, 256
The Third Day 104
The Time Machine 6-8, 50, 63-68, 70, 73, 76, 78,
    84, 87, 133-34, 140, 225-26, 228, 232, 239-
    41, 243, 249, 253
The Train Robbers 171-72, 240, 254
The Treasure of the Sierra Madre 51
The Treasure Seekers 189, 240, 244, 254
The Twilight Zone 69, 168, 255, 277
The VIPs 5-7, 93-97, 100, 107, 120, 123-24,
    141, 147, 202, 220, 228, 233, 239-40, 244,
    247, 249, 253
The Virgin Queen 48, 253
The Wild Bunch 169, 179
The Witch 34, 257, 271
The Yellow Rolls-Royce 97
They Knew What They Wanted 34, 257
This Happy Breed 41, 256

This Is Your Life 14, 172, 186, 187, 256

Thomas, Michael 227-31, 233

Thomas, Ralph 138-39

Thompson, Jack 228, 259

Thompson, Mona *(mother)* 11-14, 19, 23, 32, 75, 126, 186, 210, 222, 239

Thornhill, Dorothy 16

Thunderball 118

Tierney, Gene 102

Time Machine: The Journey Back (Documentary) 68, 255

Time Was My Enemy 31, 256

Tingwell, Audrey 44, 57

Tingwell, Charles 20, 24, 26, 29, 33-38, 42- 44, 51, 57, 95-96, 139, 184, 186, 196, 245, 246, 259

Todd, Mike 55

Todd, Richard 48

Tom Jones 106-07, 111

tom thumb 64, 66

Tone, Franchot 139

Top Gun 50, 253

Torn Curtain 84, 87

Tornatore, Joe 204, 208

Tracy, Spencer 52, 54, 73, 109, 120

Trader Horn 176-77, 240, 254

Travers, Bill 52

Treasure Island 39, 253

Trost, Pat 30, 259

Trueblood, Guerdon 174

Tuckson, Tony 15

Turner, Lana 54, 144, 219

Turner, Laurie 130

Tuttle, William 66

Twelve O'Clock High 89

Twins 33, 257

Tyzack, Margaret 209

United Artists 172, 189

Universal 84, 88-90, 93, 121-22, 128, 136, 173, 187, 198-99, 201, 214, 238, 253-56

Urban, Andrew 230

Ustinov, Peter 187

Utah Development Company 197-98, 245

Vaccarino, Maurice 177

Vader, John 18

Valente, Renee 210, 244

Vallone, Raf 203

Van Nutter, Rik 94

Vargas, Alberto 50

Vertigo 81, 85

Vessel, Hedy 79

Vidal, Gore 8, 53-54

Vitale, Carl 200-01

Vogel, Joseph 55, 93, 146

Vogel, Paul 65

Wagner, Robert 47

Wake in Fright 233

Walker, Clint 51

Walker, Max 12, 14

Walker, Robert 54, 56-57

Walker, Texas Ranger 224-25, 240, 256

War and Peace 69

War of the Worlds 63

Ward, Russell 37-38, 96, 107, 247-49

Warlord: Battle for the Galaxy 226, 254

Warner Bros. 47, 51, 52, 123, 124, 178, 179, 253, 254, 255, 284, 288

Warner, Jack 123

Warren, Bill 67, 276

Warren, Gene *(Sr.)* 66

Warren, Guy 15, 259

Washbourne, Mona 209

Waters, John 184

Waugh, Pam 16

Wayne, John 6, 8, 100-01, 126, 127, 145, 167, 171-72, 187, 194, 242-43

Wayne, Ken, 26, 35, 43, 139, 196, 245

Weingott, Owen 34, 259

Weitman, Robert 93, 146, 184, 254

Welcome to Woop Woop 7, 164, 226-29, 231, 232-33, 240-41, 244-45, 249, 254

Welles, Orson 5, 94-95, 97

Wells, Herbert George "HG", 11, 50, 63-65

Werner, Peter 113, 214

West, Adam 181

West, Morris 20, 42

Westinghouse Desilu Playhouse 69, 255

Wheeler, Meryl 6, 13, 126, 259, 267

When Worlds Collide 63

Where Love Has Gone 101, 113

Where the Lions Feed (novel) 150

White, Alan 246

White, Carol 149-51

Whiting, John 106, 108, 112

Whitman, Stuart 60, 168, 189

Whitmore, James 126, 128

Who's Afraid of Virginia Woolf? 144

Widmark, Richard 90, 214

Wild Women of Wongo 71
Wilde, Oscar 27, 80
Wilding, Michael 48, 55
Wilkinson, Piers 233-34
William Morris 46, 186
William the Conqueror 122
Williams, Esther 52
Williams, Gordon 148
Williams, Sybil 97
Williamson, Nicol 148
Willians, Marie "Peggy" *(first wife)* 32, 35, 44, 259
Willis, Ted 122, 187
Wilson, Dick 14
Wilson, Helen 122
Wilson, Les 12, 14, 259
Wilson, Sheree J. 225
Wilson, Terry 185, 188, 192
Winfield, Paul 207-08
Winterset 31
Wise, Robert 51
Wives and Lovers 91
Wolfson, Louis 39-40
Wood, Natalie 47, 98, 168
Woods, Stuart 222
Woodward, Joanne 57

World Without End 48-50, 65, 240, 253
Worth, Irene 79
Wran, Neville 194, 197
Wright, Brian 20, 23-24, 40-41, 43, 259
Wuhl, Robert 223
Wyman, Jane 219-21, 240
Yeldham, Peter 7, 20, 115-19, 184, 186
Young Cassidy, 8, 80, 90, 93, 97, 105-13, 120, 149, 178-79, 209, 225, 239-41, 253
Young, Alan 8, 66-68
Zabriskie Point 143-48, 167, 228, 239-41, 249, 254
Zanuck, Darryl F. 102
Zanuck, Richard 102
Zicree, Marc Scott 69, 277
Zimbalist, Sam 53
Zivovinovic, Bata 183
10BA 206-08, 227, 290
2001: A Space Odyssey 93, 148
20th Century-Fox 39, 47-48, 70-72, 74, 76, 81-82, 84, 93, 98, 102, 113-114, 122, 238, 248, 253-255
36 Hours 93, 103-04, 133, 239, 240, 249, 253
40,000 Horsemen 29, 35, 176
77 Sunset Strip 51

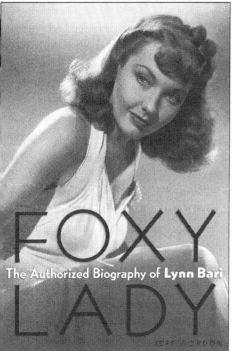

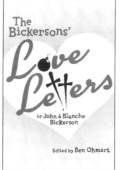

Printed in Great Britain
by Amazon